SMALL CHRISTIAN COMMUNITIES TODAY

SMALL CHRISTIAN COMMUNITIES TODAY

Capturing the New Moment

Joseph G. Healey
and Jeanne Hinton

editors

ORBIS BOOKS

Maryknoll, New York 10545

Second Printing, January 2006

Founded in 1970, Orbis Books endeavors to publish works that enlighten the mind, nourish the spirit, and challenge the conscience. The publishing arm of the Maryknoll Fathers and Brothers, Orbis seeks to explore the global dimensions of the Christian faith and mission, to invite dialogue with diverse cultures and religious traditions, and to serve the cause of reconciliation and peace. The books published reflect the views of their authors and do not represent the official position of the Maryknoll Society. To learn more about Maryknoll and Orbis Books, please visit our Web site at www.maryknoll.org.

Manufactured in the United States of America

Library of Congress Cataloging-in-Publication Data

Small Christian communities today : capturing the new moment / edited by Joseph G. Healey and Jeanne Hinton.
    p. cm.
  Includes bibliographical references and index.
  ISBN-13: 978-1-57075-618-4 (pbk.)
  1. Church renewal. 2. Basic Christian communities. I. Healey, Joseph G. II. Hinton, Jeanne.
BV600.3.S63 2005
262'.26 – dc22

                                       2005009191

*To Christian leaders around the world
who have committed themselves for many years
to Small Christian Communities as a prophetic new way
of being church, especially*

*José Marins, Carolee Chanona, and Teo Trevisan
in Latin America,*

Bob Pelton in North America,

Ian Fraser, Jim O'Halloran, and Peter Price in Europe,

Christopher Mwoleka (deceased) in Africa,

and Jim Cranswick in Oceania.

Contents

Part Three
EUROPE

Part Four
AFRICA

Part Five
ASIA AND OCEANIA

Part Six
INTERNATIONAL

Foreword

The French Dominican priest Yves Congar, who made a huge impression on me as a young priest in the late 1950s, was right then about the need for Basic Christian Communities. And he is even more right now.

Small Christian Communities (SCCs), he wrote in *Lay People in the Church*, are "little church cells wherein the mystery is lived directly and with great simplicity." They enable people to experience the church directly — the hierarchically structured people of God "to whose life all its members contribute and which is patterned by a give and take and a pooling of resources." For many of his contemporaries, he explained, "the church's machinery, sometimes the very institution, is a barrier obscuring her deep and living mystery, which they can find, or find again, only from below."

Congar hit on an important truth: that renewal in the church has come about, time and time again in its history, in and through the inspiration of small communities — monastic, evangelical, missionary, lay communities, communities of women — fired by the Holy Spirit. They have been enormously diverse, but they are all well described in the Acts of the Apostles, where the earliest church members are described as "devoting themselves to the apostles' teaching, and to fellowship, to the breaking of bread and to the prayers" (Acts 2:42).

For the first nine years of my priestly ministry (1957–66), I was the curate in two parishes in the south of England. I felt frustrated because there was no quick way to bring people to greater commitment to the love of Christ and the mission of the church. But this frustration was itself tempered by the discovery that the renewal and flourishing of faith in the parish for which I hankered was not going to come about by any words or initiatives of mine, but by the manner in which the Spirit of God became fruitful in people's lives. Towards the end of my period in the first parish, a group of people invited me to join their monthly meetings. They met together in different houses to pray, to read a passage of the Gospel, and to reflect on the circumstances of their daily lives. It was my first lesson in the value of a Basic Christian Community.

In my next parish I helped to form ten of these basic communities and, before long, out of a parish of a thousand or so practicing Catholics, about two hundred people were meeting regularly. It was in these faith clusters, or communities, that a whole mix of people — married, unmarried, young, and old — discovered a new and deeper experience of faith through prayer, scripture, community, and service to others. Through these small communities the parish came alive.

The Catholic Synod of Bishops held in Rome in 1987 noted "with great satisfaction that the parish is becoming a dynamic community of communities, a center where movements, basic ecclesial communities and other apostolic groups energize it and are in turn nourished." Pope John Paul II, in his apostolic letter on the new millennium, *At the Beginning of the New Millennium*, emphasizes the theme of communion and the promotion of "forms of association, whether of the more traditional kind or the newer ecclesial movements which continue to give the [Catholic] Church a vitality that is God's gift and a true springtime of the Spirit."

There will be some people who look beyond the parish for spiritual nourishment, and there is no reason at all to discourage this. Small communities are not only an integral part of the communion which is the church. They are also an important spur to renewing the mission of the church. Perhaps today we are coming to understand with greater clarity that all baptized Christians are called to this responsibility of evangelization. Evangelization begins with each person accepting the Word of God. In accepting that Word more fully, individually, and as a community, we become more committed to Christ and to his will for us in our lives.

These are the reasons that basic parish communities are at the heart of the program for parish renewal — discussed in chapter 13 by Stuart Wilson on the "At Your Word, Lord" Renewal Program — which I have initiated in the Diocese of Westminster. There are many aspects to this process, but at its core is the formation of Small Christian Communities, enabling parishioners to reflect in a personal way on the Word of God, on their faith, and on their call to holiness and discipleship of Jesus in their daily life. This will not come about easily; it demands commitment and courage. But I have great hope. If we are generous in response to the Lord's invitation to "launch out into the deep" (Luke 5:4), then he will provide a "catch" beyond our wildest imaginings. The evidence is already present here in our diocese.

But this "new moment" of SCCs is a global moment, one that is true of the church at all points of its compass. That is why Joe Healey and

Jeanne Hinton have done us all a favor in bringing together the varied, prophetic experiences of Small Christian Communities around the world, and allowed them to speak to each other. Taken together, they offer a glimpse of a church endlessly refired by the Holy Spirit, just as it was at the beginning in Jerusalem.

Cardinal Cormac Murphy-O'Connor
Archbishop of Westminster, England

Introduction

A Second Wind

A new moment. The words became a hope, a refrain, and a certainty. This was in 2001, following visits to Chile, Argentina, and Brazil. It was the time of the Sixth Latin American Meeting of Basic Ecclesial Communities (BECs) · in La Rioja, Argentina. Jeanne had been at the gathering in La Rioja together with colleagues from England.

Joe and Jeanne first met in 1991 at the first international gathering of Small Christian Communities (SCCs) at the University of Notre Dame in the United States. Participants came from Africa, Asia, Europe, Latin America, and North America. Joe came as one of the African delegation, Jeanne as part of the European. Christopher Mwoleka, a Catholic bishop from the Diocese of Rulenge in western Tanzania, was a member of the African delegation. "I am Christopher Mwoleka, a member of the Small Christian Community in Bushangaro parish." The way Christopher introduced himself immediately won the hearts of the European delegation. For Mwoleka that gathering was highly significant. "I always had a dream that people from Small Christian Communities would come together from across the world. And here we are. I did not think it would come so soon." He saw ahead of his time how important are the international links. The African and European delegations became very close in those days. Such friendships are a part of this book. The contributions gathered here are more a result of friendship links than anything else.

Ten years later when Jeanne left in the fall of 2001 to visit Latin America, and in the following spring to visit SCCs in Africa, the comment of friends at home and abroad was, "Why are you going? Base communities are a thing of the past." "No one is interested in reading about Small Christian Communities," publishers told her. She went nevertheless, and what she saw belied these comments. That SCCs were struggling with fewer numbers and with opposition from the church hierarchy was true, but something new was being born in this moment.

1

Thinking this over, Jeanne approached Joe and asked if he would be interested in working on a book that captures the life of Small Christian Communities today. It meant that both would need to draw in many others to communicate across six continents — Latin America, North America, Europe, Africa, and Asia/Oceania. Joe too felt the time was ripe for such a book: a multiauthored book that would be a voice for all.

In September 2003 Joe and Jeanne met with Cardinal Cormac Murphy-O'Connor, the cardinal archbishop of Westminster, England, and shared their ideas with him. He too said he recognized the need and the timing for such a book and the value of knowing more of what is happening today worldwide. He agreed then to write the foreword. Others who were approached responded positively, sensing the new moment to be true. They are the contributors to this book that is a sharing of the praxis and pastoral strategies of SCCs in different places around the globe — an update of what is happening now as well as a resource to draw on for the ongoing journey. So this book is not a history nor an overview of SCCs, but a portrait of new moments in the last five years.

A Church and World in Crisis

On September 11, 2001 (popularly known as 9/11), participants at the gathering at La Rioja were meeting in small groups. The word went around that something extraordinary was happening right at that moment — unbelievable news. The gathering broke up. We didn't know any of the details, but eventually a large screen was set up and the pictures from the terrorist attacks on the World Trade Center in New York City were live before us. All further meetings were suspended that day, but later we gathered to pray — a solemn moment.

Much of the reflection before that had been about the negative effect of globalization on the countries represented. Again and again concern was expressed about the effect on jobs and on the environment and of spiraling disparities between rich and poor both within and between countries. Democratization and an opening up of the global economy had benefited the few, not the many. It was agreed: "We can no longer deal with these matters on a local level only; we have to tackle them globally." The bombings in New York coming as they did underlined the seriousness of the issues being discussed. A world divided. "It is important that a very careful analysis be made of the reasons behind all this" was a frequent comment during the days that followed.

Seeds of Hope

It is in response to the challenge of the Gospel that small communities world-wide respond creatively to needs as they present themselves day to day. What is striking is how many concerns are shared across six continents. People at risk from social, political, economic, and environmental causes are at the heart of these concerns, and indeed it is primarily these people who form and make up many of these communities. Small Christian Communities are still the church of the poor and for the poor, helping to create an alternative from the base. Seeking to live this alternative way is where it's at, whether in the shantytowns of Kisumu in East Africa or in the "rich" cities of Rome, London, or New York. How to be alongside and form community with those dying of AIDS, with the asylum seeker, the refugee, and the migrant worker, with those without homes or jobs, with at-risk youth and with street children — these are priorities that tie these communities together, as is the commitment to find ways to bring about change through nonviolent protest, to seek alternatives to war and conflict, to create "zones of peace," to broker reconciliation in places of conflict.

In Brazil the base communities have given birth to "energetic" movements for social justice such as the Movement of Landless Rural Workers and the Workers Party, which has now formed the backbone of the new government of Luis de Silva. Likewise the communities have helped to pioneer the World Social Forum that seeks to promote change around social values that are not purely economic. "Another world is possible," the theme of 2004 Forum proclaimed. Having made their contribution the communities stand back. They are used to working more at a micro than a macro level, creating alternatives at the base. They do not seek out publicity. The work of the communities is mostly hidden and perhaps all the more potent for that.

Seeds of Renewal

With the sexual abuse crisis, drastic closing and merging of parishes, and decline in priestly and religious vocations, we need hope and renewal in our beleaguered churches in the West. SCCs are one important means of renewal and transformation in our institutional church. SCCs are a significant new way of being church in these discouraging times and serve as a vehicle of parish and spiritual renewal. The SCC model of church is a way to build up the parish community from within. More lay participation through SCCs brings a spirit of hopefulness.

Rich Diversity in SCCs

Small Christian Communities do not all think and act the same. We are using "Small Christian Communities" as the common name/umbrella term
throughout in this book, but they go by many names — Basic Ecclesial Communities, Basic Christian Communities, New Way of Being Church, and
many others. The names themselves indicate differences (see the "Explanation of Terms"). It is sometimes said that this new way of being church is
a movement. It is not a movement as such, but is better described as "the
church on the move." It can also be described as a mass phenomenon being
fired by the Holy Spirit.

While many issues faced are shared across the continents, SCCs also differ
from one another in significant ways. They seek to develop contextually
and to respond first to local needs. The largest number of communities is in
Catholic countries in the Southern Hemisphere, where to date churchgoing
is still strong. This has helped the growth of especially parish-based small
communities. Churchgoing remains strong too in North America where
communities are numerous, but in Europe, Australia, and New Zealand —
countries included in this book — it is the opposite; church membership
has fallen and continues to do so. In these more secularized societies the
communities are growing more "on the edge" of the church than within
the mainstream. The ecumenical dimension is strong here too; there is less
uniformity.

How then have the connections been made between these communities?
Perhaps rather like in the New Testament church there have been those who
have traveled, visited, and discovered others with a similar root and orientation. Relationships have been formed, invitations made, participation taken
place at each other's gatherings — a strong rope twined. This has not been
organized; there is no one manual. Christopher Mwoleka said, "There is no
blueprint for building Small Christian Communities." Ian Fraser in his book
Wind and Fire gives an apt description of the worldwide growth of SCCs:
"The spontaneous combustion of the Spirit." The sense of being caught up
in the Spirit's spontaneity continues to be profound. As we read the contemporary signs of the times, the chapter on SCCs in Dar es Salaam, Tanzania,
reminds us to continue to "listen to what the Spirit is saying to the churches"
(Rev. 2:7).

While SCCs are not in themselves a movement in the Christian churches,
they join hands with many others who walk the same path, who share the
same dream. This is true whether it is a social or political movement or

within the churches. We have therefore included in this book examples that are not strictly SCCs but from wider movements. One valid SCC model is a small community or small group within a movement, such as appears in the chapter on the Sant'Egidio Community.

The Same Resources

Participants at Notre Dame in 1991 shook with laugher. Those from Asia were making their presentation using visual aids. "But that's the same material we use," said the Africans; the only difference was the Asian faces on the screen. "We also," came the chorus from other participants. The educational materials being presented came from the Lumko Institute, named after a place in South Africa. Small Christian Communities from all continents draw on the same resources that come from a liberation/contextual theology: the use of the pastoral cycle — see, judge, and act and its many adaptations; new ways of reading the Bible such as the Seven Step Method and the Bible/Community/Reality. In England in 2003 Joe visits a small group in a Devon village and finds they are using the Seven Step Method and is able to tell them it is the same where he lives in Dar es Salaam.

The New Moment

There is little triumphalism in the new moment we seek to capture in this book. In recent years the communities have had much to discourage them, not least in Latin America where it all began. As we point out at the beginning of this introduction much has been said and written in recent years about the falling off of the BECs, both in numbers and impact. "The communities are in crisis, with declining participation and less impact in the neighborhood and village around," write Barbara Fraser and Paul Jeffrey in *National Catholic Reporter* in November 2004. One reason they give for the crisis is the loss of many key leaders, some killed by the military, and others absorbed by political parties; their energy has been pulled away from the BECs. Another is the democratization of many of the Latin American countries and the enticements of consumerism, felt more in cities than in rural areas. Fraser and Jeffrey see these more as the reasons for a falling off than the appointments of conservative bishops whose lack of support has been felt. There is another reason not mentioned which has adversely affected the communities: the growth of pentecostal or evangelical movements to which members of BECs have been attracted. Nevertheless there is still energy and commitment thirty years on. "Despite what many are thinking, this way of being church is not over yet and any talk of its impending demise is premature," says Gerry Proctor in his report on the Latin American meeting gathering of BEC advisors in November 2004.

It is not only in Latin America that the strains of thirty years on have been felt. Basic Christian Communities in Europe have also been struggling with fewer members and less energy — "a tired moment." Here too, as Peter Macdonald writes, there is "a moment of revitalization." In other places seeds have been sown that are only just beginning to grow. "Reformulation" is the word used in Chile to describe coming out of these years of discouragement. Whether diminished or not, the truth is that the growth of BECs fanned the wind that blew worldwide, and that has brought into being a truly new way of being church. The wind carried seeds that in some places are only now beginning to ferment and grow. And now "a second wind."

Building for the Future

The new moment is a prophetic moment, challenging the Christian churches to new ways of being and living church and new ways of ministry and service. SCCs can be on the cutting edge and challenge the status quo. This includes helping in the reform of the struggling hierarchical church in the United States.

The new moment is a mission moment. Mission and outreach are an essential dimension of SCCs. Part of this is sharing the SCC story with others. A Ugandan proverb says: "One who sees something good must narrate it." The new moment is a networking moment for SCCs internationally: sharing and learning from each other's rich and diverse SCC experience. We are called to promote the relationships between communities. We are challenged to develop broader and deeper networking, including twinning (see below p. 157). "This is an opportunity we must not lose. We must now build on it," says Bob Pelton.

In fact the writing and editing of this book has been an experience of international networking on six continents. We are grateful for the rich diversity of the contributors: men and women; ordained, religious, lay; representing a variety of religious denominations. To each contributor a heartfelt thanks.

Explanation
of Terms

"Small Christian Communities" (SCCs) is an umbrella term used in the title and throughout this book. Across the world, however, many different terms are used for this new way of being church. Often a subtle difference is indicated in the words used. Below we give a brief explanation of the main terms that occur in this book.

Small Christian Community (SCC). Used throughout Africa and also in Asia and North America, where large Catholic parishes form a network of parish-based SCCs — a community of communities. Small enough to create real community and personal relationships. Chosen in many other countries too as the preferred term for a wide variety of SCCs.

Comunidades Eclesiales de Base **(CEBs).** Used throughout Latin America. Also known by the English translation "Basic Ecclesial Communities (BECs)." The word "base" indicates from the grassroots or base of society and also the preferential option for the poor that so characterizes these communities. The word "ecclesial" emphasizes that these communities are in themselves "church" — church at the most local level. BEC is also a term used often in Asia, notably in the Philippines.

Basic Christian Community, or Base Christian Community (BCC). BCC is the expression that is most used within the European context and often of communities that are more on the edge of mainstream church, whether Catholic or Protestant. The word "basic" is again important, indicating from the grassroots or base of society and also the everyday realities of life and the basics of Christian living.

New Way of Being Church. A phrase first coined in Latin America and often used in the West — United Kingdom, Australia, New Zealand — to cover numerous ways whereby Christians of many different denominations seek to find meaningful ways to be church in more secularized societies.

A background paper for the "International Consultation on Rediscovering Community" at Notre Dame, Indiana, in 1991 compiled over three thousand different names, titles, terms, and expressions for SCCs/BCCs. Whatever the name, it is a handle only. It is the lived reality that is important! In the titles and the explanations of the chapters in this book we have tried to be faithful to the names used in local situations. So the reader will find Base Community, Base Community Group, Basic Parish Community, Christian Base Community, Faith Cluster, Faith Sharing Group, Gospel-Based Community, House Church (different meanings in different parts of the world), Neighborhood Gospel Group, Small Church Community, Small Community, and Small Faith Community.

Part One

Latin America

Our journey begins in Latin America. Appropriately so, since this is where it all began. Or perhaps not. What of the small house churches of the New Testament and the many forms — monastic, lay, cell — taken by the Christian Churches down the ages, particularly in the hard times of persecution and unrest? In every age the Small Christian Community (SCC) has taken new forms, true to its roots. Today SCCs have perhaps an even greater significance. "The future shape of the church" is a phrase often used. In many places that shape has arrived.

What took place in Latin America in the 1950s, 1960s, and 1970s was a new moment: possibilities opened up by Vatican II and in response to the harsh realities of life brought about by economic injustice and the rule of the oligarchies. Out of this context, which we do well to remember, the inspiration spread worldwide — the breath of the Spirit.

What is the new moment in Latin America? The chapters in this section point to the great ability of SCCs to surmount struggle and opposition and tell how SCCs are forging new relationships to support and strengthen one another. And how, true to their own pastoral practice, they continually stop to reflect and analyze the present moment, seek to respond faithfully, and make whatever changes are indicated.

Some things have not changed. "The base communities are a humble experience because they represent the reality of the poor and marginalized. They have not emerged out of great theoretical speeches but rather from the faith and love of a poor and simple people," writes Alicia Butkiewicz. That remains true.

9

I

Pastoral Commitment to BCCs
in Bolivia

Alicia Butkiewicz

Base Christian Communities (BCCs) have been recognized in Bolivia, as in other Latin American countries, as a source of joy and hope, and as a humble and fragile ecclesial experience. The BCCs are a humble experience because they represent the reality of the poor and marginalized. They have not emerged out of great theoretical speeches but rather from the faith and love of a poor and simple people. In communion with church leaders the people have searched for ways to live out their faith on a continent experiencing extreme poverty, pain, exploitation, violence, and desires for liberation.

The people from these communities want to follow in the steps of Jesus in a radical way. They want to be a church that responds to our Father's call to us, to commit themselves deeply to the construction of the reign of God here on earth and to create a society that is more just and in solidarity with the poor, where living conditions improve — not just in a spiritual sense but also in tangible ways — where, as Jesus taught us, we are fully alive.

The BCCs, by their very nature, have been intimately tied to life and the concrete realities of their members. Their dynamics are the result of the connection with the world and the commitment to bring the church closer to the people, inculturated and missionary. Those who have assumed the pastoral work of spreading the word about the BCCs and the "Pastoral Theological Reflection" of this way of being church have not tired of reminding us that BCCs are not a "movement in the church" but are a "church on the move."

The Catholic Church in the Context of the Bolivian Reality

The church leaders in Bolivia have known how to respond to the challenges of the political, economic, cultural, and ecclesial realities of the people. They

11

have offered pastoral theological orientations that allow for the organizational programs of the church and proposed ways to deepen and energize the faith of the people. They made options and commitments with the new evangelization, and with this they opened up the church to the problems of the country and played an important role in the dialogue between the government and the groups in conflict. In the same way, they supported the process of self-determination by the indigenous populations.

One of the regrets of church leaders through the years has been their inability to infuse the hearts of the people and the decision-making structures with the proclamation of the good news — even though Catholic Christians are the majority in Bolivia. What has been lacking is coherence between the faith we profess and the life that we live. Church leaders also recognize that the evangelization in Bolivia was not very effective. The leaders recognize that Bolivian Catholics have not assumed the form or the manner of being church as proposed by Vatican II — the church as the people of God, as community.

Today, Bolivia presents challenges that will require radical answers. The leaders of the church in Bolivia are aware that they must respond to the call for renewed evangelization and that the good news of life and hope is for everyone. The church cannot fail the people in the way that the government and politicians have in the past.

Base Christian Communities in the Evangelistic Context of the Catholic Church in Bolivia

Faithful to their mission, the Catholic bishops of Bolivia responded clearly and courageously to the reality that touches their lives. Their options and pastoral orientation have allowed them to not only organize and program all evangelization in general, but they also add value and give qualitative direction to the BCCs that have been one of the main foci and priorities of the "Pastoral Directions" of the Bolivian Episcopal Conference. In 1973 the bishops emphasized the goal: "To assume, accompany and provide BCCs as the living cell and privileged expression of the evangelizing church, prophetic, acculturated and missionary."

Now in 2005 BCCs are still considered an ongoing priority of the Bolivian church. The church leadership recognized the urgency of renovating the church in order to effectively evangelize. They acknowledged the scope and potential of these communities not only through baptism, but also as a means of renewing these same parishes and making them "communities of communities." Their new pastoral document established these guidelines:

- Prioritize the basic formation, integration, and permanence of the BCCs' animators.

- Encourage the coordination of the communities from inside the parish through ordinary gatherings within the parish.

- Animate the BCCs' members so they become involved in popular organizations, syndicates, and political parties offering testimony of the Christian faith that is orientated by the social teachings of the church.

- Provide formation for religious, priests, and seminarians within this concept of a church as community — participative and missionary.[1]

With this push Bolivian BCCs came to be a significant ecclesiastical component from a theological point of view — pastoral and institutional. Theologically they began to shine new light on basic biblical and traditional aspects of the church's doctrine, making it meaningful and valued. In a pastoral way they created and enlivened the evangelization process and the development of Christian faith and life in a manner that responds to the needs of the majority of the people. Institutionally they represent an ecclesial organizational paradigm quite different from previous models.

The Evangelization Potential of Base Christian Communities

Evangelization, in this model of church whose center is the laity, the community, the Word of God, and the salvation and liberation of human beings both individually and socially, has produced significant conversions. Simple people are discovering their value and capacities and are developing into leaders who today play a significant role in different parts of Bolivian society.

Life Testimonies

Abdias, an Ayamara farmer, forty-two years old, married with three children, had to migrate from a rural area to the city. For many years he lived as a small vendor. Later, as a result of his experience in the Community of Villa Pagador, he became a leader of the BCC as well

1. *Pastoral Focus and Guidelines of the Bolivian Episcopal Conference 2001–2005, Third Millennium, Challenges for Everyone.*

as of the town. Today he coordinates a trash collection and recycling microenterprise.

Amalia, fifty-four years old, married with seven children, wife of a construction worker. She says that her experience and formation within the BCC has opened her eyes and given her an opportunity to serve people like herself. Today, she is the coordinator of "Habitad" in Cochabamba. She coordinates, along with others, home construction projects for poor families.

Ambrosio, nineteen years old, an orphan responsible for two younger brothers. The invitation he received to participate in the Community of Our Lady of Guadalupe was the beginning of a new life. Now he animates and accompanies youth who are struggling with alcoholism.

Juana and **Nicolas**, a Quechua couple, members of the Community of Peregrinos en la Fe (Pilgrims of Faith), understood that God wanted his Word to extend beyond their small village. Because of this belief they themselves became pilgrims and visit towns to form communities.

These and many other testimonies help us comprehend that BCCs have become a phenomenon in spreading the Gospel message and are an expression of the mission of the church. The BCCs are spaces that look for the rejuvenation of the church in every dimension. They are making an effort to identify, recognize, announce, and develop the values of the reign of God in concrete everyday reality. This option for the poor is very clear, and the poor also prefer such a church because they need community.

Along their paths of observation, decision making, action, evaluation, and celebration, people like Abdias, Amalia, Ambrosio, Juana, and Nicolas are also active subjects of their own evangelization — agents of their own conversion.

Through reading the Word of God, reflection, and prayer — as an integral part of a member's life — comes a profound and deep relationship with God. A personal relationship with God and recognition of their full human dignity mark the lives of these people. This brings them to conversion and a maturity of faith, and most important of all, allows them to forget themselves to encounter and serve the other.

This encounter or meeting with the God of life and the deepening of the spiritual life of the members, strengthened by prayer, listening to the Word, meditation, and reception of the sacraments help them to move ahead in spite of the discouragement their cruel realities provoke and the changes outside of and within the church. There is no doubt that the internal dynamism that grows from this experience is a transforming energy for the people.

Today's Challenges in Times of Change

As in all vital processes, many tensions have arisen both inside and outside of the Basic Christian Communities. Today, at junctures both socially and ecclesiastically, there is neither euphoria nor renewal; there is simply indifference. With the exception of some official documents from the Bolivia Episcopal Conference, few people are animating BCCs or speaking about them. In recent years they have not grown well. Those that remain are like islands in an immense sea, and many have been integrated into the parochial system. Today there is a less receptive environment for the process of theological pastoral decentralization that the BCCs offer. What is clear is the tension that exists between the church model that BCCs propose and the church structures today of this same church. On the other hand, the options of the Bolivian church for "movements" and "traditional parishes" have accentuated these difficulties. These options are accompanied by an active backing of the parishes and have made the movements grow. They have multiplied and are established in many parishes. They are the most lively sector and energy in the church. The movements say that they include all sectors of the population; however, it appears that they embrace only the privileged classes.

These challenges invite us to look inside the BCCs and acknowledge that we have not known how to conduct a meaningful evaluation of the experience from inside these communities. We have not evaluated how the persistence of the community aspect might affect the personal aspects or how the social aspects can function to the detriment of ecclesial and the immediate loss of the eschatological. We have not stopped to review if these elements end up opposing each other.

The experiences of the BCCs are abundant and profound and impact the lives of members. We did much with little. But many times these experiences were isolated, and we did not know how to connect, to network, and to prepare for the global changes. The experiences of BCCs left us angry in the initial stages, and more recently we have let go of the larger analysis, the global project. One was not looking for utopia! You might say that we did not see the forest for the basic needs of the trees in front of us!

It is certain that there is still a great energy inside the BCCs. The actual historical process of ecclesial and political evolution in Latin America, and in particular in Bolivia, exists as part of a consciousness and ongoing discernment of the BCCs. We have to ask ourselves, in moments like these in which we live, where we need to focus and to lead the formation of the animators and their components as well as the base projects on the local level such as cooperatives. There are risks and dangers in being prophetic and challenging the church structures — even more so if we are not protected, encouraged, and inspired by some prophetic church leaders. We have to know that there are risks in the middle of a globalized, secular, consumer world where the poor are exposed to, and even absorbed by, the system.

A New Space for Hope

We live in drastic times, in a world threatened by misery and desperation. Utopian dreams and hopes of the past have died. In periods like these, there is no time for passivity or for simple hope, much less for confusion or desperation. "It is better to light a candle than to curse the darkness." Times such as these are not times of great numbers, of successes or triumphs. It is a time for reflection, for going deeper, for discernment, and for challenges of creativity.

From the actual evolution of BCCs, some say that they've had their time and that they are being replaced by other pastoral forms. Many in Bolivia believe that BCCs do not respond to new situations and are therefore disappearing. For those convinced and committed to the proposition of BCCs, they do not think they have stopped evolving or have been replaced, but that as with all church institutions they have to pass through a period of "reformation." As José Comblin said, they should try to return to their origins and roots.

Comblin affirms that all real reformation comes from new people who come from these same structures and have liberated themselves from them in order to return to their origins. They question the institution in order to be more faithful to her. This is what is happening now with the BCCs. They are a people who left themselves and asked that the BCCs return to their origins. This is why the BCCs are far from being overcome and are more real than ever, because in the ambition of the church this is a privileged period to multiply the power of the Holy Spirit, the Word, and the theology of service on the part of all and to make real in a radical way the Christian message through Jesus. God came to this world in order to be in the world of the poor and hopeless and to provide an option for them.

Today, the Base Christian Communities are necessary. They are a hopeful space for the poor. We need more BCCs, but they have to be born and be faithful to their origins and to their program and formed by the poor of this time. The same historical evolution exists in the church as a model of the church as people of God and communion of communities and movements. It is time to listen in a new way to the voice of the Holy Spirit and to read the signs of the times in a new way.

2

Fruits of El Salvador–Chile SCC Twinning from Within

Irma Chávez

"Irma, Irma, what's happening in Chile? Did you see the television report? I only saw the newspaper, and I don't know if it is affecting our friends or not? Do you know? Can you find out? We're all so worried!"

This was just the first of many frantic calls I received that day from the three Small Christian Communities (SCCs) of El Salvador (Oasis — my own, Agua Zarca, and Nueva Jerusalén), which had twinned with three counterparts in Chile. It was also the day when I realized that in fact we had really been twinned — that is, we felt as though we were all born from the same womb of Christian faith sharing.

Before Barb Darling contacted me about this twinning project in 2002, I don't think any of us in El Salvador would have done more than glance at the headlines of flooding in Chile. To us it was like China or Antarctica, even though unlike those faraway places El Salvador and Chile share a common language and faith tradition. Yet after months of conversing via electronic mail about our faith and our families, our struggles and our successes, our joys and our journeys, we felt that we knew each other even though we had never met. I suppose all of us would have agreed intellectually that we were part of the body of Christ worldwide, but we had never before emotionally experienced that unity. Now, however, when the body in Chile hurt, the pain throbbed in El Salvador.

Actually it had all started with humming telephone lines, but those bursting with electronic mail rather than human voices. Michael Brough, executive director of RENEW International, asked me to work with Barb on an international project called "The 2002 Global Small Community Research Project." I was delighted later to also receive communications from the two other project directors, Anne Reissner and Father Bob Pelton. But it was Barb who introduced me to my Chilean counterpart, Jaime Carmona, who would coordinate the three SCCs (Luz y Esperanza, Paz y Amor, and Carlos Camus) as I would do with the three communities in El Salvador. Although most of the communication that we national coordinators established between and among the small communities in our countries was through electronic mail, the exchange was very personal.

The first personal effect was the surprising and striking similarity in the way that the various groups gathered, prayed, and reflected on God's Word. Despite the fact that various different processes and individuals had founded, inspired, or guided each group, we were all amazed that we had so much in common. This may again be a manifestation of the body of Christ around the world that, although many parts, shares one spirit.

As a matter of fact, most of the small community members were surprised to know that other countries even had such communities! Each had been fairly isolated or at best knew only of local attempts to do something similar among the faithful. But almost no one suspected that SCCs were indeed gathering around tables in Latin America, under trees in Africa, on mats in Asia, in offices in the United States, and all in such similar scenarios. Having worked with the International Office of RENEW for two decades, I had more experience than most, but even I was touched to tears by this very personal and vibrant encounter between ordinary Christians retrieving what is now considered an extraordinary way to be church. And I gloried in being able to share this novel and global experience with my brothers and sisters!

To bishops or theologians or others who regularly gather in national and international conferences, read global Christian magazines of prestige and influence, or otherwise have regular contact with the worldwide church, this may seem naïve. But I assure you that for the average Catholic the extent of our experience of church is our parish or the neighboring one. If you don't believe me, just ask any local parish organization: "What do you know about other Catholics around the world who speak your language? Where do they live? How are they different from you? What are their major concerns at the moment?" Unfortunately the average, well-intentioned, practicing Catholic could not answer the first two questions very adequately. Although globalization has been a part of our church since the time of St. Paul, the felt effects of globalization are much more apparent and readily articulated in our work than in our church.

People may also be surprised that Salvadoran and Chilean small communities could connect on such a profoundly personal level without ever meeting face-to-face or even hearing one another's voices. But it is true. A young man from the Salvadoran community Nueva Jerusalén, after reading the introduction from his corresponding Chilean group, exclaimed: "I always thought that Chile was a rich country! But they're struggling just as much as we are. We're united not only in our humility, but in the dignity that comes from acting on our faith!"

Perhaps such apparently impersonal communication as e-mail worked well for the following reasons. First, the small community members were already committed and experienced in sharing their faith. That zeal and practice lent itself to overcoming any barriers. I recall a widow in my own group exclaiming: "We chose to be called Oasis because here together we drink from the water of the Spirit and then take that water to refresh our family and communities. But now we get to taste the waters of faith in Chile and bring our bit of oasis to them as well!"

Second, most of us are used to sharing the faith through the written word. By that I mean not only sacred scripture, but a wide variety of formal and informal scriptural reflections, questions, etc., published in everything from slick books to newsprint broadsheets. So we were comfortable with a literate expression of the Word of God in a variety of formats. In fact, sometimes I was surprised with how influenced we really were by God's Word even in our daily lives. For instance, some of the letters between the different small communities sounded like St. Paul's Epistles: "The Christian Base Community Paz y Amor greets the faithful in Christ of the Salvadoran community Agua Zarca."

Electronic mail just happened to be our newest style of written reflections, but was very effective. Now what about Web sites, Web cams, chat rooms, and all the other marvelous ways we can now spread and share the Word of God around the world? The church was global long before McDonald's, but I am told that children around the world recognize Ronald McDonald long before they can speak the name of Christ. Perhaps it is time to start using today's technology for more than fattening our children for the global marketplace! Why can't we make sharing the Word of God as pervasive as Spiderman?

The formal twinning project to which we had all committed lasted about six months. But since we found it hard to stop the zeal of sharing the greatness of God among ourselves, the communication has continued longer. For Christians, distance is like time: in the end all of us will be one in Christ forever. People reading this brief report on what it felt like to participate "from within" the SCC twinning between El Salvador and Chile may understand what I mean. For any of us who consider ourselves "within" Christ, we can never consider anyone no matter how different or distant to be "on the outside." Long before the Internet, Christ's love interconnected the world, and we are all twinned.

3

Learning from the Cuban House Churches

Robert Pelton

"I am the only Bible that most people will ever read," a laywoman said recently, while leading scripture study at a *casa culto* (Spanish for "worship house" or "house of worship") or *casa de oración* (Spanish for "house of prayer" or "prayer house"), that is, a house church[1] located near Cuba's National Shrine of Our Lady of Charity. Her statement may seem overblown and self-aggrandizing to those of us who weigh it from a North American or European perspective, but it accurately reflects the prevailing reality in Cuba and many other Third World nations whose populations are impoverished not only in economic terms but also by limited access to churches, by shortages of clergy, by restrictions on the distribution of religious publications and by a lack of community. For millions of Cuban Christians whose faith is systematically frustrated, if not overtly persecuted, these house churches or houses of prayer offer a new way of being church and, in many instances, the "only" feasible way of being church.

This fact is confirmed by Archbishop Juan Rodríguez, who views the 120 house churches active within the Archdiocese of Camagüey as "one of the greatest treasures in the Cuban Church.... They have especially encouraged a marvelous growth in lay ministries" (*Verdad Esperanza*, Catholic Press Union of Cuba, 2003). Discreetly left unsaid, but clearly visible between the lines, is the strong possibility that the prayer houses are also fostering movements toward greater grassroots freedoms and responsibilities throughout both the religious and secular spheres.

---

1. "House church" is used in the specific context of Christians gathering to pray in their homes in Cuba. This article is about Catholic house churches that are extensions of the parish. There are also many Protestant house churches in Cuba. "House church" has different meanings in different parts of the world.

The Vatican agrees. The *Instrumentum Laboris* of the Synod of America recognizes Small Christian Communities (SCCs) as "the primary cells of the Church structure" and it praises them as "responsible for the richness of faith and its expansion as well as for the promotion of the person and development." In his Post-Synodal Exhortation, *Ecclesia in America*, Pope John Paul II twice recognizes the Small Christian Communities: once in the context of renewing parishes so that each might become a community of communities (No. 41) and again when discussing the challenges of the sects (small, independent Pentecostal and evangelical movements that are not mainstream Protestant groups), in which context SCCs are seen as being especially capable of promoting interpersonal bonds of mutual respect within the Catholic Church (No. 73).

Like many others who firmly believe that the SCC movement is a manifestation of the Holy Spirit, I am convinced that the small communities will not only fulfill the mandate the Holy Father has offered them but will go on to countless additional contributions to the kingdom of God.

Until recently, such predictions could have been based only upon anecdotal observations and faith in the Holy Spirit. During the earliest years of the SCC movement, there were few opportunities to conduct comprehensive studies of the many thousands of grassroots communities. That situation changed dramatically with a watershed study conducted by the Institute for Ministry of Loyola University. Directed by Bernard J. Lee, S.M., in collaboration with the Research Center at the University of Maryland and with William V. D'Antonio of Catholic University, the study serves as a complete census of Small Christian Communities in the United States, focusing on their memberships, attitudes, goals, practices, and problematic areas. Major effort went into identifying the latter to help SCCs overcome their areas of vulnerability. Although some weaknesses are significant, they can be overcome. To that end, we must continue fostering communion on every level of church life by expanding both the quantity and the quality of opportunities for lay participation; by encouraging more and better evangelization initiatives; and by expanding the role of small communities in ecumenism, in social justice campaigns, and in building solidarity within the church by promoting interpersonal bonds of mutual support.

It is essential that we maintain a spirit of reasoned and mutually respectful dialogue, unity, and trust with those bishops, priests, and laypersons who, for whatever reason, may choose to ignore or even oppose further development of SCCs. All viewpoints need to be heard and to hear each other, so we can move forward together in our shared commitment to our church and her works. Specifically, we must interpret how official church teaching looks at small communities within the larger sense of communion, and we must determine whether communion is to be understood in a structural sense or whether we need to encourage broader theological paradigms.

The Theology of Communion

To understand communion in a more horizontal way, we need to study the rich potential for deeper experience of communion within the local church. As Hermann Pottmeyer writes, the communio concept has become the central interpretation of the ecclesiology of Vatican II:

> Without doubt, the postconciliar ecclesiology has enriched our theo-
> logical thinking about the church. Especially since the Extraordinary
> Bishops' Synod of 1985, communio has become the *leitidée* of ecclesi-
> ology. Together with the conciliar concept of the church as the People
> of God, the communio concept has shaped the awareness of many be-
> lievers to be responsible members of the church: we are the church!
> Communio has become the *leitidée* too of pastoral planning in many
> dioceses. Communio ecclesiology rediscovered the ancient structure
> of the church universal as a communion of local churches, as com-
> munio ecclesiarum; the local churches have made the experience that
> living the church as communion means to structure themselves and
> their parishes as "communities of communities."[2]

Special Situation in Cuba

There is currently an increasing interest in the role of Christianity in Cuba, especially since the historic visit of John Paul II to the island in 1998. Nevertheless, partially due to the isolation which Cuba has experienced, there are many myths and misunderstandings about both the history and the current reality of Cuban Christianity. Clearly, there is a great need for deeper and more accurate understanding of contemporary Cuban Christianity.

One could easily form the impression that the Cuban Catholic Church was not in touch with the major developments of the Second Vatican Council, and therefore it does not have a biblical understanding of either the preferential option for the poor or liberation theology. In contrast, we

---

2. Hermann Pottmeyer, "The Theology of Communio as a Basis of Spirituality," paper presented at the University of Notre Dame, 2002.

should remember that José Martí was, in a certain sense, a forerunner of the liberating themes of the 1968 General Conference of the Latin American bishops at Medellín, Colombia. Martí both anticipated and supported the preferential option for the poor, and he challenged the dissonance between the Cubans on the island and those in the diaspora. Thus, he promoted a Cuban national identity. In his 2002 book *The Quest for the Cuban Christ: A Historical Search* Miguel A. de la Torre writes:

> The *patria* Martí envisioned is similar in principle and spirit to Latin American Christian base communities known as Base Ecclesial Communities (BECs). BECs were grass-roots organizations fostering lay participation in the liberation theology movement. Martí similarly attempted to erect a grass-roots *patria* in which all Cubans could exercise their duty to participate in their political liberation. He attempted to create *patria* on ethical dimensions of equality, not on economic capitalism.
>
> *Patria* would have freedom of expression, legislative assembly, and a free press, none of which has ever existed in Cuba. Martí's egalitarian Cuba would be a just society without the exploitation of one person by another. He did not uphold a gospel of individual salvation. Rather, he encouraged building a "kingdom" of justice based on morality.

It should be emphasized that the Cuban quest for Christ requires a serious consideration of historical symbols in order to understand how God has communicated to the Cuban people. These symbols are expressed in art, music, and many other venues. The question of the identity of the Cuban Christ needs to be looked at from the "underside" of Cuba's history. This implies a veritable *ajiaco* (a traditional Cuban stew that blends an eclectic array of ingredients into a vibrant whole).

Development of House Churches

Since the late 1980s, and especially since the Special Period, there has been a noticeable growth in church attendance (both Protestant/Evangelical and Catholic) all over Cuba. Due to the lack of church construction during the Revolution, as well as the fact that most churches built during the pre-revolutionary years are concentrated in urban areas, there is a major shortage of churches and temples in rural areas. However, the urban areas also suffer from lack of places to worship, due to closures or deterioration as a result of lack of resources to maintain them. When the number of congregants suddenly rose significantly across Cuba, they thus encountered serious shortages of places to congregate and worship. In response, virtually all denominations developed house churches — congregations that meet in the homes of the members. Given the continuing governmental restrictions on church construction, house churches have come to outnumber more traditional churches and temples, especially in the case of the Pentecostal churches.

What is special about the Cuban house churches? They provide not only temporary accommodations but also a form of resistance to the status quo, i.e., the determination of both the churches and the congregants to find a practical, albeit hopefully temporary, solution to the problem. Furthermore, many house churches are technically illegal since many congregants do not go through the lengthy (and frequently futile) process of seeking the legally required governmental permission. This can also be interpreted as a sign of subtle resistance against the system, and it demonstrates that many of the faithful no longer respect or fear the state as much as they once did.

Given the ongoing shortage of clergy on the island, there are not enough priests or pastors to tend to the house churches whose numbers are rapidly increasing. As a result, laypeople have taken on leadership responsibilities, thus learning to take initiative, lead groups, and gain organizational skills. These are skills and attributes that are new to the majority of Cubans who were born and raised after the Revolution.

New also is the sense of mutual trust, solidarity, and cooperation that is fostered within the community. While house churches (both *casas culto* and *casas de oración*) are communities of faith, they are also *de facto* social service agencies. Members help each other during times of illness or other emergency, assisting each other in obtaining food, medicines, clothing, transportation, child care, and other scarce necessities. Thus, the house churches function as semiautonomous parallel institutions within the still-dominant state system. By doing so, they are sowing the seeds of an alternative civil society.

In short, what make the Cuban house churches special are the context of continuous challenge in which they exist and the growing commitment of their members to meet all such challenges.

What Can We Learn from the Cuban House Churches?

The Cuban house churches provide a wealth of lessons about grassroots Christianity's ability to thrive in the margins of the contemporary church and in the margins of contemporary society. They provide irrefutable evidence that faith can not only survive neglect or oppression by governmental and societal forces, but can actually be strengthened by its strivings to overcome such challenges. They demonstrate that a major expansion of the role of the laity is not merely a necessity in regions where clergy are few, but also a vital step toward the emergence of the people of God as envisioned by the Second Vatican Council. We can learn also the many ways that the same Christian fellowship that empowers the house churches can serve the greater needs of theology and contribute toward fulfillment of the church's social mission in our world.

Perhaps most significantly, the unmistakable parallels between the house churches of contemporary Cuba and the house churches of the first century provide clear evidence that the blueprints for a church that can meet the challenges of the third millennium may well be found in a renewal of commitment to her first-millennium roots.

4

Challenge of Youth to BECs

Mexico, 2004

Compiled by Gerry Proctor

From the moment of our arrival we knew this was going to be an exciting and challenging time. Little did we know just how challenging. The challenge was to come from the young people present at this seventeenth National Meeting of Mexican BECs held in León, Mexico, in September 2004.

Base Ecclesial Communities (BECs) are inevitably small, fragile, even marginal groupings of church, and as such it is quite unusual to be present at a BEC gathering of twenty-five hundred people. Everyone is a delegate, chosen and mandated to attend by the base — ordinary people who belong to their parish BECs. Participants are organized in eleven regional groupings, and each one wears a distinctive T-shirt or neckerchief. The multiplicity of colors at the opening ceremony was magnificent. People came from all different parts of this vast country and demonstrated their regional character by wearing traditional dress. It was a breathtaking vision of unity in diversity.

Each region made a brief presentation to the assembly using a variety of different elements, including drama, dance, song, symbol, and speech. Meanwhile other members of the regional delegation went throughout the arena distributing small gifts, tokens of their desire to share the riches of their area with all those who had traveled from afar. We received sweets, biscuits, cakes, sugar, coffee, traditional crafts, pottery, and embroidery, all made by hand in the homes and small industries of their region. It was a totally unexpected and extraordinary moment. We were literally showered with the goods of the earth, coming from the hands of the poor, revealing in an instant their clear grasp of the true nature of God and the purpose of creation, the fruits of which are to be freely shared and not hoarded or stored away by those afraid that there won't be enough to go around.

It was a countercultural moment and an act of defiance and rebellion in the face of a dominant neoliberal economic model that ensures that the earth's resources are not equitably shared but go consistently to the richest nations. This was an encounter with the reign of God, a living out of its evangelical values and attitudes expressed by the BECs in prophetic gesture and symbol. Unforgettable and definitely repeatable. Another remarkable moment was the feeding of half the five thousand. The people of León had prepared the food, and it was not contracted out to some catering firm but was very much "in-house." Again there was enough for everyone.

At the inaugural ceremonies there were five bishops present, three retired and two active, both auxiliaries, while all 110 members of the Mexico Episcopal Conference had been invited. The numerical insignificance was noted by all participants as a true reflection of where BECs are today in relation to the hierarchical church, but this didn't diminish the warm welcome everyone gave to those bishops in attendance.

The vast gathering then divided itself between eleven centers, each of which had a different theme. I asked to be in the Youth Center. There were over 215 participants, only about half of whom were young people, and of these many had little or no experience of BEC processes. The parish of Our Lady of the Annunciation welcomed us, and responded magnificently to the challenge of receiving 65 more than had been catered for. These local parishioners became the real locus of the felt presence of the reign of God during those three days we spent in the parish.

All the workshops followed the same pattern; first, analysis of the political, social, and economic reality being experienced in Mexico today. This was based upon reports from the dioceses and was discussed (reflected on) in twelve small discussion groups. These groups looked at the impact of globalization, and the advances or otherwise in the national and international political, social, and economic scene. They then moved on to discuss the actual situation of the church in Mexico and then the same for the BECs under the headings strengths, weaknesses, and challenges. Another level of reflection was the role of BECs in the transformation of the social realm. The workshop then moved on to reflect for the first time upon the situation of youth.

Up until this point the reflection and analysis had been beyond the capabilities of most of the youth present, which had led to frustration and boredom. What emerged from the youth at this point was deeply disturbing in its critique of BECs and their inability to attract young people or work with them. All of this took place on Wednesday, and there was more to come! In the evening the workshop had to split again into groups to discuss the diocesan evaluations of the strategic planning program. This was all very well in adult groups that had been working at this for a number of years but totally outside the comprehension of our youth. We were following the tried and true method of many BEC national gatherings; only this year we had a youth workshop for the very first time, and it had not been properly thought through. Young people have their own processes that need to be respected.

The small groups then reformed to tackle three questions, which had been prepared beforehand:

- How do these experiences shed light on our communitarian work?
- What type of youth communities are called for today?
- What challenges does the strategic focus of our identity as church present us with?

Three main challenges were agreed upon. These were:

- Define the identity of youth communities and BECs.
- Begin a youth process that is adapted to the anxieties and needs of young people.
- Establish a friendly dialogue between adults and young people so that together they can build the BECs.

The groups then had to work out specific strategies to achieve each one of these challenges. This done, the BEC National Youth Team made a presentation which was discussed by all, and another set of challenges were agreed upon. Everyone then split into regional groups to define clear lines of action flowing from these challenges. As the meeting has no power to decide on any actions, these proposals will eventually be put to the BECs at diocesan and parish levels for further discussion and action.

On our final morning, Saturday, groups met for the last time. By this stage many of the youth had decided not to participate and formed their own groups, chatting or just walking in the street. The National Meeting concluded back at the arena with a closing mass celebrated by the bishop of León. Thankfully these meetings don't only function at the formal level, but much of the real work is done informally through personal contacts, sharing over mealtimes, working together in small groups from different regions, etc. Because of the tensions in this workshop, many of the advisors present spent quite a bit of time analyzing what was going wrong, and this proved to be immensely helpful in building relationships among a key group of people.

The general consensus was that we had not lived the most basic elements of a BEC church, and so the sense of being where the reign of God was experienced was lost. But the reign is never far away, and for those of us in the Youth Center it was sensed and lived most particularly in the homes and with the families where we were offered hospitality. Once again, the reign of God was at the margins (not at the center where the BEC workshop was) and out in the streets and dwellings of the local people.

5

Analyzing the Present Moment

Latin American BECs in 2004

Compiled by Gerry Proctor

Analyzing the present moment is one of the strengths of the Basic Ecclesial Communities (BECs). It was to this end that advisors of Latin American BECs gathered for their triennial meeting in the city of Aguascalientes, Mexico, in September 2004. Theologians, biblicists, religious, and lay advisors representing twelve countries met to look at the actual situation in which the base communities find themselves and to discover their prospects for the future.

In an opening address Dr. Eduardo Bueno, a Peruvian national, noted the systematic increase in poverty and inequality, the growing culture of violence spreading fear in cities across Latin America, the widespread disenchantment with politicians and the political system, the absence of ethical principles at all levels of society, and the growing demand for greater efficiency and accountability from elected representatives.

This analysis of the socioeconomic background was followed by an analysis of general ecclesial trends both within and without the Catholic Church. It was noted that the Second Vatican Council gave the church an extraordinary breath of fresh theological and ecclesiological life, but failed completely to create the new structures necessary to maintain this development. So not surprisingly the previous ecclesial organization, which had become embedded in the four centuries since the Council of Trent, resurfaced in the years following the Second Vatican Council.

This trend was particularly noticeable in the absence since 1985 of any reference in magisterial statements to church as the people of God. There had been a greater stress on hierarchy, an increase in clericalism, an undermining of the collegiality of bishops, a devaluing of the highest magisterium of the church (an Ecumenical Council), an encouragement to sideline the decisions of the General Conference of Latin American Bishops, a domestication of the local church, the promotion of ecclesial movements rather than the strengthening of diocese and parish, a reversal of the principal of subsidiarity given the increasingly centralized tendency of the Vatican, and the failure to continue a serious dialogue with other churches and religions.

It was a curious moment when the BECs felt themselves to be the ones who were faithful to the council, obedient to the magisterium, and defending the restructuring of the Latin American church achieved at Medellín (1968), Puebla (1979), and Santo Domingo (1992). It is possible that this was the only church to respond to Vatican II by creating new structures corresponding to the new theology. Their ecclesial intuition has been under attack ever since, and yet the BECs continue to be the major source of renewal in the church at the grassroots level. This expression of church at the base is a genuine experience of communion and participation.

Advisors Conclude That BECs Are a Force to Be Reckoned With

On the final morning the participants were presented with the General Conclusions arising from the four days of deliberations. These were discussed, changes suggested, and then accepted. First, looking at the strengths and weaknesses of the BECs in Latin America and the Caribbean, it was agreed that because of the journey they had made and the decades they had now survived, they were a force to be reckoned with. Precisely because of their prophetic and evangelical spirit they had managed to come through crises, conflicts, misunderstandings, and persecutions (oftentimes from within the church), and now were able to glory in an extensive martyrology as they continue their passage through history.

Second, the General Conclusions touched on opportunities and threats that presented themselves to the BECs. They agreed that globalization opened up the possibility of a better and more structured sharing of materials, community experiences, information, and mutual support. There is no doubt that the present crisis in the church reveals the BECs to be an attractive alternative pastoral proposition. They can help the church reach out to the large mass of Christians who have lost contact with their parish community. Another opportunity that presents itself is the massive impact of the World Social Forum and the need being created to form people with a new way of thinking, responding, acting, and organizing in a more communitarian fashion. The BECs of Brazil have already proved themselves to be at the forefront of these forces of hope in the creation of another possible world.

The two main threats identified by the meeting came from capitalist society and the Catholic Church itself. The neoliberal system feeds and sustains a hedonistic, superficial, individualistic, and consumerist culture which obliges people to work more intensely just in order to survive, while at the same time excluding millions from the possibility of employment. All of this works against a communitarian vision of life and a Gospel spirituality that leads inevitably to a social commitment to build a better world in the image of the reign of God.

The other threat comes from within and is the more distressing. Despite the fact that the BECs have been officially recognized by the magisterium as being fully church at the most basic level of neighborhood, a great majority of the hierarchy sees them as just another movement, one more option among many that offer themselves today. This is definitely having an impact on the growth and maturity of the BECs. This is due in large part to the naming of bishops and the formation of priests with a very different model of church from that forged at the Second Vatican Council.

The meeting of advisors has no power of decision, and so the documents from the gathering were to be presented next to the seventh Latin American Meeting of BECs in the Mexican city of Querétaro. There was a tremendous atmosphere in Aguascalientes and a real sense of belonging to a church that was alive and faithful not only to the Gospel but also to the church's magisterium. Despite what many are thinking, this way of being church is not over yet, and any talk of its impending demise is premature!

Analysis Leading to Action:
Latin American BECs Respond

Witnessing to the fact that BECs are not just about the religious dimension of life but embrace the whole of human experience and existence, the gathering that followed of the Latin American BECs Meeting in the Mexican city of Querétaro began with a magnificent Mexican fiesta. The food, singing, mariachis, and dancing expressed a real celebration of life and unity at a continental level. What was noticeable was the total absence of any nationalistic rivalries but instead a genuine recognition of the richness of their unity in the diversity of countries and cultures.

At the first main session the assembly received the document prepared by the advisors a few days earlier, and split into regional groupings to discuss it and make any relevant changes. A brief theological reflection followed focusing on hope, and the comment was made that while it was good to look for and analyze signs of sin and grace, it was also necessary to be aware of structures of sin and structures of grace. Father José Marins, the Brazilian theologian accompanying the BEC process at a continental level, listed four important structures of grace: the lived experience of community which reflects the life, vitality, and being of the Trinity; the Word of God that guides the community and provides it with the divine proposal which is the reign of God; the life, death, and resurrection of Jesus made real again in our times through the presence of martyrs throughout the Latin American church; and the ordained ministry in people like Dom Samuel Ruiz, Dom Pedro Casaldáliga, and many other bishops and priests who give witness to a new style of ministry, as service of the people of God.

Work continued enthusiastically with a further analysis of the BEC reality. In many countries the coordination between BECs at local, regional, and national levels continues to be a challenge, as does the relationship between BECs and the hierarchy. The meeting was reminded that the purpose of the church and therefore the communities is *communion*, and as such it is vital to insist on and maintain good links with bishops and priests. It was agreed by everyone that BECs have been a place where women can break the chains of *machismo* or male domination. One of the great achievements of women in Latin America has been their ability to say to the men, "I'm off to the BEC meeting; your dinner is in the oven!"

Putting Networking and Communication in Place

The assembly then moved into a different gear as delegates began to examine their commitment to being prophetic and to living in solidarity with the poor. A number of workshops were opened that continued to meet over two days, reflecting upon and refining their proposals that would be implemented across the continent during the next four years. These included such subjects as the formation of leaders, migrants, human rights, citizenship, alternative economies, youth, and pastoral processes. The methodology involved meeting first in mixed groups according to the interest of each person. Then the different countries discussed the proposals coming from the workshops and decided how they could best be applied in their situation. Regional meetings followed that placed those decisions in a wider context. And so to the plenary gathering of all delegates where the lines of action were drawn up until the next international BEC meeting in four years' time.

The meeting concluded its exhaustive work with regional and national strategies for action over the next four years. The Caribbean region (Haiti, Dominican Republic, Venezuela) will work on leadership formation, communication, and coordination at the national level in each country, and the alternative economy. They hope to create a network of contacts and communication through the Internet and have called a regional BEC meeting for July 26–31, 2005, in Haiti. The USA/Mexico region focused entirely on the question of migrants and migration and made the decision to establish national BEC teams that will develop contacts and begin to explore the issues surrounding migrants in both countries.

The Central American region (Guatemala, El Salvador, Honduras, Nicaragua, Costa Rica, Panama) realized that first they had to work at improving communication and coordination at the national level, and then if it is possible would move to look at leadership formation and migrants and human rights. They also felt it a challenge to work hard at building relationships with their bishops. The Cono-Sur region (Argentina, Uruguay, Paraguay, Chile, Brazil) wanted to create a team that would help to make links between all the countries and develop levels of coordination and communication within the region. They would then work on leadership formation. Finally the Andes region (Colombia, Peru, Bolivia) decided that their priority was leadership formation and both the quantitative and qualitative growth of BECs, followed by an exchange of resources and materials. The question of migrants also needs to be looked at, and they suggested the formation of a Web site for BECs that would serve the continent.

One issue provoked intense discussion. This revolved around the suggestion from the advisors' meeting to form a BEC team that would be responsible for enabling greater communion to take place between all the participating countries. This would be the first time that the communities had requested another level of support, and some of the older figures cautioned the meeting against moving in this direction. Although the discussion in the assembly hall was brief and polite at lunch afterwards, there was unanimous agreement at a number of tables that it was an essential move and long overdue. The poorer countries were the ones most in favor as they needed any extra help they could get. The caution was about the return of the old Vatican accusation of creating a parallel church and the danger of being seen as a movement and not an integral part of church. Nevertheless, the proposal went ahead and was celebrated liturgically at the end of the closing mass presided over by Don Samuel Ruiz. This was history in the making.

They had decided that they needed another layer of support, which would be at the service of greater continental integration and communication.

Just before the liturgy began in the dying moments of the meeting, a delegate from Honduras proposed that a debt of incalculable gratitude was owed to Father José Marins and Sister Teolide Trevisan for their unstinting work over more than thirty-three years at the service of the Latin American and world church. The Honduran delegate could hardly finish what he wanted to say when everyone rose up to give them a standing ovation amid loud cheers and prolonged applause.

The assembly came to an emotional conclusion. The next assembly will be in Bolivia in 2008. There was a strong sense, commented on by many afterwards, that this model and experience of church, although little understood or accepted by those whose lives are spent maintaining the present order, is the hope of the future simply because it renews the very base of the church, where the mass of the people live out their lives and where the present system is conspicuously absent.

Part Two

North America

These chapters portray the many fruits of Small Christian Communities in North America. There is richness in the diversity. New moments include: the next step after the study by Bernard Lee and others among Catholics in America; parishes and dioceses trying to restructure based on the SCC model of church; small community members living the Gospel by reaching out to others; and the link between SCCs and the Rite of Christian Initiation for Adults (RCIA). High-quality faith-sharing resources are a mark especially of the many national SCC organizations in the United States. The importance of RENEW International is seen in its presence and influence in many chapters of this book. The growing edge and challenge for SCC organizations in North America are more collaboration and networking. This can mean dying to one's own "SCC thing" for the larger good. Creativity is needed to offset cutbacks in personnel and finances.

We are facing different crises in the Catholic Church and the Protestant churches such as the Episcopalian (= Anglican worldwide) Church in North America for somewhat different reasons. For the Catholic Church it is especially the clerical sex abuse crisis, questioning the credibility of our bishops' leadership, the dwindling number of priests, and new forms of ministry. For the different Protestant churches it is questions related to the ordination of openly homosexual and lesbian ministers and same-sex marriages. Many prophetic questions arise: Can SCCs renew churches in America from within? Can the "small church" be an example and model for the "large church"? Can SCCs provide new ways of ministry and service? Can SCCs give new hope to Christians in North America?

39

6

Development of SFCs in the Diocese of San Bernardino, California

Susan DeGuide and Steven Valenzuela

On November 2, 2003, the Diocese of San Bernardino was scheduled to celebrate its twenty-fifth anniversary as a diocese. Plans were carefully made, but then the Old Waterman Canyon and Grand Prix fires started on October 18. Between these two terrible fires more than six hundred homes were destroyed in the area and some people lost their lives. In that same week of the fires, the body of our sixty-two-year-old auxiliary bishop, Dennis O'Neil, was found dead in his home. He seemingly was saying his night prayers and died instantly of a heart attack. Too much sadness happened in two weeks; no one felt like celebrating with so many people displaced from their homes, lives lost, and the fires still raging and not under control, and so the anniversary celebration was postponed until January 18, 2004. Still carrying the grief of the loss of Bishop O'Neil, the diocese looked again at celebrating. What was there to remember and celebrate? Certainly the growth and outreach of Small Faith Communities (SFCs) had to be a part of what the diocese would celebrate.

The Experience of Small Faith Communities (SFCs)

Small Faith Communities (SFCs) have been a part of the Diocese of San Bernardino since its very beginning. One has only to look at the Cursillo movement, the history of over twenty-five years of the Valley Missionary Program, the Base Christian Communities, Buena Vista, and the various other models, such as Father Art Baranowski's "National Alliance for Parishes Restructuring into Communities," that have influenced, impacted, and aroused interest in a new way of being church.

As immigrants from Latin America poured into Southern California in the 1950s, so did they bring with them experiences of Cursillo and Base

41

Christian Communities. These proved to be a source of strength and identity for the Hispanic people as they sought to find their place in American culture. Of particular significance is the Valley Missionary Program (VMP), began some thirty years ago as the dream of Father Jose Pawlicki, C.S.C. Following the call of Pope John Paul II for a "new evangelization," the VMP has sought to bring new life to the Catholic Church of the Coachella Valley. At the heart of the program is the Missionary Encounter Retreat, which is the tool used to provoke a deep conversion to the Lord who then becomes "Jesus Friend" to the people who open their lives to him. This profound conversion to the Lord has led the members of the VMP to live radically Jesus' commandment of mutual love with BCCs as a result of the encounter. There are more than a hundred basic communities in the Coachella Valley right now. Some of them have been meeting weekly for twenty-four years. Following the death of Pawlicki in 1999, Father Pepe Martelli, C.S.C., took on the role of spiritual director of the program. VMP along with the rest of the diocese used the RENEW 2000 material during the five seasons of the program.

Bishop Philip Straling became the first bishop of the diocese in 1978. Being a firm believer in the role of the laity as leaders in the church, he initiated the "Straling Leadership Institute." What was unique to this program was the creation of small faith-sharing groups as an integral part of the leadership formation. For two years people stayed within the same small groups. At the time, however, these groups were seen only as part of the institute but did not directly shape the upcoming vision of seeing the parish as a community of communities.

Diocesan Planning Process

The contemporary story of this diocese can be summed up in two words: pastoral planning. A broad diocesan planning process was begun under the first bishop, Philip Straling, in the mid-1990s. It included all parishes, diocesan organizations, ethnic communities, and ministry groups. After Straling left to shepherd the Diocese of Reno, Nevada, in 1995, the process was completed under the leadership of the new bishop, Gerald Barnes, the former first auxiliary bishop. One of the most significant results of the process was the thirty-three-word *Vision Statement*, promulgated in 1997:

> We, the Church of San Bernardino
> are a Community of Believers

in Jesus the Christ,
called to impact
family, neighborhood, and society
with the Gospel
so that people's lives
are filled with hope

The statement was posted everywhere, and its words of impacting family, neighborhood, and society formed the touchstone for every program and process in parish and diocese over the next five years.

As part of the planning, all parishes, diocesan offices, and organizations developed goals and objectives to be accomplished over the next five years. The goals were written around five main "concerns" that were highlighted in the document *Impact*: family, youth, leadership, organizational structures, and stewardship.

Included in the document was the following statement under the section called Organizational Structures: "Our structures will empower participation, promote networking and facilitate collaboration.... Small Faith Communities will support our commitment to impact family, neighborhood and society." Clearly, the statement imagined SFCs as a new structure that would help create new possibilities for becoming the kind of church that facilitates the growth and transformation of persons and society.

RENEW 2000

In 1998 many discussions were held among the priest and parish staffs about the possibility of bringing the RENEW 2000 process to the diocese. Finally the Presbyteral Council agreed to support this endeavor as one way of supporting the *Impact* statement: "Small faith communities will support our commitment.... We will be open to creative models of parish life that are flexible, supportive and that respect the diversity of our diocese." In the spring of 1999, a director for the Office of RENEW 2000 was hired with the responsibility for the development of RENEW 2000, but also the transitioning that would need to take place from RENEW into SFCs throughout the diocese.

Generally, there was a great feeling of enthusiasm and hunger for what RENEW 2000 had to offer. Most of the pastors and pastoral coordinators were very supportive, saying the RENEW prayer at every liturgy, joining in a small group themselves, and supporting the process from the altar. Training for the parish core teams and group facilitators was given in every one of the six vicariates. All in all, eighty-seven parishes out of a hundred signed the three-year contract for the five seasons of RENEW. Over five thousand people participated in Season 1 in both English and Spanish. As the diocese came to Season 5, the numbers had declined somewhat, yet there remained groups that wished to continue.

St. Paul the Apostle Parish in Chino Hills stood out among the parishes for its total commitment to the RENEW process. The pastor, Father Michael Maher, SS.CC., approached Josie Dumdum, who was about to retire, and asked her to coordinate the process. Josie took on the task wholeheartedly. She began by phoning people one at a time and formed the Parish Core Community, representative of all the ethnic groups present in the parish: Anglo, Hispanic, Filipino, and African American. As Josie says:

> Personal invitation was the most effective way to recruit people to be part of the Small Faith Communities (SFCs). Other effective things done included forming our in-house facilitators-training group, actively supporting the SFCs by visiting them during their meetings, and holding short retreat/reflection sessions and potluck lunches every season for the facilitators. The pastor, deacon and members of the core group made the visits. Above all, a lot of prayers were said for the success of the effort.

In the fall of 2002, the fifth and last season of RENEW, we began our transition time. Speakers came and shared on ways to continue the development of the vision of SFCs apart from the RENEW 2000 model. Over a hundred publishers were invited to come and display their resources. A Web site was created (*www.sbdiocese.org*) and helps were posted there. Now we were on the move from "Uniformity of Structure" (RENEW 2000) to a new "Unity of Vision" for SFCs.

Healing the Body of Christ

As parish and diocesan leaders prepared to launch Season 4 of RENEW 2000 during the winter of 2002, national news broke of a horrific pedophilia case in the Archdiocese of Boston involving several priests and dozens of children. More information began to be uncovered and reported. A larger and ultimately national scandal emerged of the systematic cover-up of clergy pedophilia by bishops throughout the nation The number of cases, the exposure of illegal and immoral behavior of priests and their superiors was unprecedented in American ecclesiastical history.

Locally, the Diocese of San Bernardino already had in place policies and procedures from the previous decade that protected potential victims and prevented such egregious cover-ups. Still, the scandal became a source of pain and anguish for Catholics throughout the diocese as local and regional cases of clergy misconduct were daily news fodder.

Bishop Barnes wanted to help the people of the diocese move forward in the process of reestablishing trust in their church so damaged by the scandal. In a providential meeting, Archbishop Michael Sheehan of Santa Fe, New Mexico, spoke of his diocese's positive experience of RENEW as a way to bring healing to the situation. Barnes shared this testimony in his diocese and his delight that the Diocese of San Bernardino had already completed four seasons of the RENEW process.

So when RENEW International contacted San Bernardino about piloting its new program, "Healing the Body of Christ," as a way to help parishioners deal with the national situation through a faith-sharing format, Barnes, in consultation with the Diocesan Response Team organized to handle the abuse crisis, decided this process could be an excellent strategy in the diocesan response to the scandal. By giving people an opportunity to share their thoughts and feelings in a safe, faith-based context, the hope was that the process of healing and reestablishment of trust could begin. Over the course of Lent 2003, twenty-one parishes reported over forty-two hundred persons participated in "Healing the Body of Christ" faith-sharing groups in both Spanish and English. Other parish and church-based groups used the materials in various settings not reported in the above figures, including parishwide Lenten programs, gender and ministerial groups, and apostolic movements.

Continuing its positive relationships with RENEW International, the diocese then invited parishes to consider using the newly developed "Why Catholic?" program, which draws its reflection content from the *Catechism of the Catholic Church*. This program responded to the expressed desire from many RENEW alum for material that provided deeper and more profound content on which to base their reflections. In fall of 2003, 47 parishes sent 265 persons for training in the use of this material that can be used over several months or years.

Ongoing Development

In order to develop and move forward the vision of Small Christian Communities in our diocese, we needed to root ourselves in a mission statement. In May 2004, we set ourselves to this task and created this statement:

> Grounded in the diocesan vision, the Office of Small Faith Communities is committed to the development, support and networking of parishes and people as small faith communities so as to "support our commitment to impact family, neighborhood and society." To accomplish this mission, each parish must become more and more "a community of communities" with people living deeply committed faith lives. It is the goal of the Office of Small Faith Communities to:
>
> - Provide ongoing education and formation through workshops, consultations and a specialization course in the Ministry Formation Institute program,
> - Assist parishes in the formation of Small Faith Communities,
> - Serve as a resource for parishes on Small Faith Communities, and
> - Support and facilitate the development of leadership and networking of Small Faith Community parish coordinators and other Small Faith Communities in each vicariate.

How best then to begin to address these goals? Starting at the most basic level, we determined that parishes would need a tool in their hands to help with the development of their SFCs. We set to the task of creating a diocesan resource manual, written in both English and Spanish, that could be used by our parishioners. It begins with a letter of endorsement for Small Faith Communities by our Bishop Barnes and a short history of the Small Faith Community experience in our diocese so far:

> In 1998 our diocese visited the concept of Small Faith Communities. Since then we have experienced a renewal among many of our people. We choose this concept as a way of restructuring our local church as cited in the Diocesan Vision statement: *Our structures will empower participation, promote networking and facilitate collaboration ... small communities of faith will support our commitment.* Together, let us vigorously take on this new task of developing each of our parishes into a "community of Small Faith Communities." This will renew our families, neighborhoods and society in hope.

The resource manual continues then with encouragement given for parish staffs and the role of parish leadership in the development of the SFCs. We explain about the specialization course in the diocesan lay leadership training program (Ministry Formation Institute) on SFCs and helps are given on beginning new groups, models of groups, being an effective facilitator, and where to find resources for the groups. We are most grateful to the help that RENEW International and Buena Vista have given to us in this area. Each parish was given a copy and the extras were made available to those who wished one.

In addition to presenting this tool to each parish, PowerPoint presentations were made at vicariate meetings, hoping to stir up within them once again the vision of SFCs and its link with our diocesan vision. Barnes also endorsed this vision with his own words of encouragement. Appointments were then made with pastors and our pastoral coordinators to speak with their parish councils and parish core teams. The important ownership for the process of creating a parish that is a "community of communities" generally lies with the administrators of the parish. They have to buy into the words of Archbishop Raphael Ndingi Mwana'a Nzeki of Nairobi, Kenya, who says: "Small Christian Communities are a priority." When parishes are built with Small Christian Communities, "There are no spectators; they are all players.... Participation is what it is all about."

We plan a big event each year as one way to coordinate the SFCs from different parishes getting to know one another. We have had speakers in both English and Spanish and a retreat in both languages culminating with a bilingual Eucharistic celebration. We gather the coordinators from the six vicariates and plan times for them to be recharged in the vision, develop support for one another, and plan for the future.

One of our greatest needs is to develop leadership on the local level, in the vicariates and in the diocese. We would love to see these leaders taking on more and more responsibility and care for one another in their development of SFCs. This is especially true in the cases where the parish administration does not support the SFCs and yet the people themselves want to maintain or start a group and need to be linked up with someone. This networking will allow them to develop, independent of the administration if it has to be that way. We encourage parishes clustering for retreats and special days of prayer organized and arranged by the local groups. There is much work to be done here.

Ongoing Formation and Growth

The final completion of the resource manual also coincided with the development of a training course for parish ministers called "Ministry with Small Faith Communities." It is offered in both English and Spanish. The course was developed as part of the diocese's basic level of its lay ministry institute. The institute offers two levels of formation. The basic includes a fifteen-hour retreat, thirty-six hours of theological formation, and a specialization course in a particular ministry. The Small Faith Community Course will be one of these specializations offered. Upon completion of the whole program, participants receive a diocesan certification as a volunteer pastoral minister at the parish level.

The SFC Course would cover both theological and theoretical content. The theological areas include church history, ecclesiology of SFCs, and lay spirituality. The theoretical areas include small group dynamics, faith-inspired leadership, and practical skills such as facilitation and the leading of prayer. The plan for presenting the course is to train two teams of three or four persons currently coordinating or facilitating SFCs at their parishes who will then present the course around the diocese.

The way the course is presented is consistent with Barnes's vision for the future. As the diocese grows and parish leadership evolves, more and better-trained lay leadership will be necessary to provide for all the various needs of this vital local church. Local parishes will remain generally large and quite diverse. The presence of active SFCs will offer parishioners in these increasingly populous suburban and urban areas the opportunity for a more personal and direct experience of church, the kind of church where, as the American composer Marty Haugen writes, "Hands will reach beyond the wood and stone, to heal and strengthen, serve and teach, and live the Word they've known" (from *All Are Welcome*, 1994).

7

Communitas Celebrating Twenty Years of Building Community

William D'Antonio

Let us narrate our Communitas journey through the following dialogue:

Friend: Tell me, Bill: Who or what is Communitas?

Bill: Communitas is the name that a group of people chose to show how they feel about themselves and about the world at large. Our story begins in the Newman Center of George Washington University in Washington, D.C., in the 1960s. Like millions of Catholics throughout the world, the roots of the community are found in the events and documents of Vatican II, including recognition of "Freedom of Conscience," that the church is more than the hierarchy, that the laity as the people of God are also a vital part of the church, and that claims to authority are made legitimate in the *sensus fidelium* (sense of the faithful). Through the Newman Center a group of nonstudents gathered to support Catholic student activities and to share the knowledge and excitement of Vatican II, the turmoil of Vietnam, and liberation theology in Latin America.

With the support of a sympathetic priest, the members gradually developed a liturgy that featured dialogue homilies, inclusive language, and a major role for women. In 1984 a change of pastors occurred at the Newman Center and the new priest did not like our communal, participatory style. It soon became evident that if our liturgy service and our commitment to social outreach were to survive, the time had come to form an autonomous community, to pursue the beliefs, values, and goals that now characterize Communitas.

Communitas is a Eucharist-centered community of the Catholic Church. Members come together as equals to form a faith community empowered by the Gospel, and committed to making Christ's teachings on justice, forgiveness, and peace a reality in our own lives, in our larger church, our society, and our world.

Friend: But aren't all Catholic parishes Eucharist-centered? What is different about Communitas?

Bill: We are distinct in the degree to which we exercise autonomy within the canon law of the church. We have organized ourselves independent of any particular diocesan parish or under specific diocesan control. There are currently some eighty Intentional Eucharistic Communities nationwide that have made themselves known to us, and who identify themselves as part of the informal organization we call Intentional Eucharistic Communities (IECs). Actually, the IECs enjoy varying degrees of autonomy along a continuum from total independence to a number of communities that have worked out formal relations with their bishops.

Another feature that makes us distinctive is that we in Communitas select our own priest presiders, true also of the majority of IECs. In our case, during the past twenty years, we have had as few as two or three priests throughout the calendar year, and as many as seven or eight, meaning that we would only see some of them once or twice a year. Currently, six priests rotate the Sunday liturgies, each with his own special talents. Several of these priests can be found in other IECs in the Washington, D.C., area, on alternate Sundays.

Without a doubt, the presence of so many priests in the Washington area who do not have regular parish activities has made it possible for us to grow liturgically and spiritually, even as their homilies have challenged us to relate the "word" to our personal and communal lives. They are in every sense members of our community. Unlike some other communities, we do not offer stipends to our priest members. However, we do make contributions to the organizations they are associated with, or to causes they designate. These donations are our way of expressing our appreciation of their contributions to our communal life.

We are an intentional but not a residential SCC. Since we do not have to provide support for lodging and the realities of everyday life, we are able to use half or more of our annual budget to support social justice programs in which our members participate, and which reflect our commitments to programs in Latin America, Africa, and Asia. Individual members of Communitas are involved in a wide array of peace and justice activities that keep them on the road many weekends.

Friend: Tell me a bit about your Sunday liturgy? What makes it a Communitas liturgy?

Bill: Well, I would begin by saying that our monthly newsletter lists the Sunday readings, and most members read and reflect on them before the Sunday liturgy. A distinctive feature of our liturgy is that by the time we are ready to begin, we have been preparing by setting up chairs; arranging the altar, wine, and bread baked by a member, the candles, the book of readings; setting out the hymnals, etc. In other words, as we arrive we join together to create the setting for the mass, just as we join together at the end of mass to replace the chairs. We even use name tags every Sunday so that now we know each other well by name. Even our priest presiders wear their name tags. In fact, as they arrive, they will usually go right to the place where the name tags are located, and get their own. I would say the spirit of community, of being one, of working together to achieve common goals, begins with the first ones to arrive for mass and ends when we lock up. In between, we greet each other and guests, join in the prayers and in the dialogue homily, and try to make the kiss of peace a vital act of love. The weekly celebration of the Eucharist is the foundation of Communitas. Through our shared reflections we voice our views in ways that confront our faith and the world around us. We also share the conviction that each person present is a co-celebrant.

Perhaps most distinctive of all, about ten of our members have volunteered to rotate as lay presiders at mass. The lay presider has the responsibility to contact the priest who will be presiding at the upcoming liturgy, to collaborate with the priest in all preparations for the mass or any other particular liturgical event. This will include discussion about the theme of the mass, the readings, any special prayers or things to focus on, how to handle the responsorial psalm (whether to sing or chant or read), and other details like that. The lay presider is also responsible for contacting the musician who will be leading the Sunday singing, to help select hymns and other music appropriate for the occasion. The names of the lay presiders and lay readers are also posted in the newsletter, so we all know weeks ahead who will be doing what in the upcoming liturgies. Our priest presiders have never objected to the name and role of the lay presider; in fact, they have encouraged our active participation in the prayers of the mass.

In conformity with local laws, Communitas is registered as a nonprofit voluntary association; we have a constitution and by-laws, and a council of officers. Official meetings are held at least quarterly, and all members are invited to attend. Decision making is as close to consensus voting as we can get.

Friend: Can you tell me a bit about your membership?

Bill: Communitas is a relatively small community, currently with about 50 active members, in a total group of 175 persons, now scattered about the country and even the world. We are students and educators, laity and religious, Defense Department officials and peace activists, artists and bureaucrats, single people, couples, and families with children of all ages. As a community we reflect the mobility and diversity of the greater Washington area.

Less than a third of our active members live in the District of Columbia. Yet throughout the twenty years of our existence, our primary places of celebration have always been in the District. Our current place of worship is the Dignity Center in southeast Washington. Dignity had just bought and renovated an old tile shop near the marine corps barracks at a time when we were looking for a larger and less chaotic place to worship than the friendly but often overcrowded International Youth Hostel in downtown Washington. One of our families had close ties to Dignity and urged us to take a look at their building. One look and we knew it would be just right for us. Dignity makes it available to us for use on Sundays and other days that do not conflict with their own office activity. In appreciation, we make donations to them. Our main gathering room is something like a large living room. Its basic appointments provide a warm, highly spiritual setting which is remarked by all who attend for the first time. The area can accommodate up to forty people. For occasional larger gatherings, we use the upper main room, which can accommodate fifty or more. Usually, however, the upper room is used for Sunday morning after mass brunches, Holy Week services, and pot-luck suppers (especially after Christmas Eve and Easter Vigil liturgies). We feel we have found an ideal place in which to foster the spirit of Christian community.

Friend: Can you tell us a bit more about your life as community apart from Sunday liturgy?

Bill: When Bernard Lee and I began our research project, "The Catholic Experience of Small Christian Communities," one of our major goals was to determine just how mature the small communities were. We took as one indicator of maturity the degree to which communities reached out beyond themselves to live the Gospel. At that time we expected to find that such communities would be characterized by the degree to which the members actively worked together in a common cause.

In the course of our research we learned that the reality is quite different, and Communitas is very much a part of that reality. For example, we see how often the community becomes supportive of its own members, and reaches out to them in times of physical or spiritual need with prayers or visits or food. Thus, it has become our custom to lay on hands and pray over and for members about to undergo serious operations, or facing critical decisions. The primary value of this action as I see it is the feeling of support felt by everyone, not just the direct recipient of the prayers. It is one way the community reaches out to one of its members.

But there is more to this kind of communal recognition of the individual gifts of our members. People like Kevin, a rural sociologist who spends a significant part of each year among the indigenous people of Bolivia to help them organize co-ops, and knows he has the concern and support of the community with him. And we can count on his reports of his work when he returns. The same is true of Sisters Alice and Jeannine, who are often on the road: Alice speaking out against torture and for human rights in Guatemala, and Jeannine continuing her ministry on behalf of gays and lesbians. In some cases our support is prayer, in others financial, in others personal witness. Chris carries medical supplies to Nigeria with funds provided by us and other IECs in the area. Bill works with leaders in Nicaragua to build three-room houses for those dispossessed by recent floods and hurricanes; another member supports a family in Costa Rica, while still another travels back and forth to Haiti to provide a variety of aid. Over time we have developed the habit of simply gathering around informally after mass to hear their stories, and to share their joys or woes.

Several times a year we will be asked by one or another member to bear public witness on behalf of social justice, or in challenging an unjust law. But we never seek to put pressure on everyone to participate. On such occasions we usually find one-half to two-thirds of our members actively involved. We have come to recognize that with so many members involved in their own individual callings, it is difficult to expect that all members can be present at a particular event. But there is no doubt in anyone's mind that we all know and support each of them. Thus I have concluded that as mature communities mature in outreach, they develop a range of ways by which the gifts of individual members are acknowledged and strengthened by the members as a community.

Friend: So, what was your twentieth anniversary party about?

Bill: On May 22, 2004, we celebrated our twentieth year as a maturing Intentional Eucharist-Centered Community with guests from the nearby IECs and alumni from as far away as Boston and New Orleans. It was a great party, celebrated near Pentecost (our official birthday). We recalled our own journey as a pilgrim church. As we look to the next twenty years, we hope to see a few more younger faces to blend with the salt-and-pepper hairdos that dominate our gatherings. Even as we have celebrated memorial liturgies for several members in the past couple of years, so are we encouraged by new and younger people who find our way of being church a way for them also.

8

Imaging Initiation (RCIA) in Small Church Communities

Robert Moriarty

"I see little long-term hope for the [adult] catechumenate unless there is a connection between Small Christian Communities and the catechumenate *before, during,* and *after* initiation." Such was the forthrightly expressed conviction announced by Father Jim Dunning at the beginning of his keynote to the 1994 meeting of the North American Forum for Small Christian Communities (NAFSCC). In the months following the NAFSCC conference, Dunning headed up the design of a Beginnings and Beyond Institute with a particular focus on doing initiation in the adult catechumenate in conjunction with Small Church Communities (SCCs). Scheduled for Rochester, New York, in the fall of 1995, this institute was canceled on account of too few registrations. As it turned out, sadly, Jim was dead by the date that institute would have been conducted.

In 1997, the NAFSCC approached North American Forum on the Catechumenate (commonly known as the FORUM) to suggest a resumption of the conversation about the possibilities of doing initiation in the context of SCCs. How exactly to proceed was not immediately clear, but the shared interest to do so was keen. Subsequently hosted by the National Pastoral Life Center, FORUM and a broad base of SCCs constituencies explored, over a number of meetings, how this relationship might be developed. It was not long before both initiation and small-community specialists jointly acknowledged that there was not a hair's breadth of difference between us on the issue of fundamental vision. Rooted in the parish, we come together under a vision of conversion in community that has for its object *becoming the body of Christ in mission for the sake of the world*. Doing initiation in the context of SCCs offers us major opportunities both to strengthen initiation and to challenge small communities to fuller realization of their ecclesial vocation.

In 1999 FORUM committed itself to collaboration with its dialogue partners for the purpose of developing a new institute. As did FORUM, the three national SCC organizations (Buena Vista, National Alliance of Parishes Restructuring into Communities [NAPRC], and NAFSCC) each committed resources to facilitate the design of an institute. By the spring of 2002, the team had designed a three-day institute for initiation ministers and small community members/leaders to imagine together the possibilities of doing initiation in the context of SCCs. The goals of the institute as initially articulated were as follows:

1. Image the initiation process in Small Church Communities.

2. Provide a process to dialogue about the possibilities and challenges of the initiation process in the Small Church Community context.

3. Deepen an understanding of evangelization, conversion, and discipleship in word, worship, community, and witness/mission.

With a presenting team that involved specialists in both initiation and SCCs we conducted the first institute in July 2002 in the Diocese of Erie, Pennsylvania. About seventy-five people participated, most from the Diocese of Erie, but several also from other parts of the United States. Some came with experience in initiation ministry alone, some with experience just of small communities, some with some experience of each. By the close of the first day, it was already clear, whatever the point of departure of the participants, that all readily embraced the possibilities, even while clearly acknowledging the challenges, of doing initiation in SCCs well.

An adapted celebration of the rites of initiation, followed by mystagogical reflection and critical input, such as might be found in a Beginnings and Beyond Institute, forms the basic structure of the institute. At each stage, correlating experience and reflection on the Small Church Community dimension is introduced. The whole institute begins with consideration of the common overarching goal of both initiation and small communities — a vision of church oriented to the reign of God. Early on, an overview presentation on the vision and workings of parish-rooted SCCs is done for all, but with a special concern for those in initiation ministry who might not be otherwise familiar with small communities. Likewise, a general overview of the rites and process of Christian initiation is presented at the outset to the whole assembly. It is done with a particular concern to orient small-community members who might not otherwise have had a critical introduction to initiation ministry. The overall institute is conducted as a combination of presentation, small-group and large-group process.

With some adjustments the institute as it was presented in Erie was offered again for the Diocese of Oakland, California, in August 2003 and the Diocese of Richmond, Virginia, in June 2004. Having conducted the institute twice already, the team approached planning for the Richmond event with an eye to its evaluation and further development. A full day for evaluation was added on to the Richmond schedule. Several initiation and Small Church Community specialists, not associated with the original design of the institute, were invited to experience the full institute and then gather with the team for the extra day of evaluation. This evaluation process resulted in very valuable feedback and solidified the team's growing sense that we were more than ready to move beyond conducting the institute in the mode of an inquiry about whether or not a fruitful relationship could be developed between initiation ministry and SCCs. The conviction that this relationship is possible and desirable is crystal clear from both the side of initiation ministry and that of small communities. The challenge is how best to go about building this relationship.

As a result of conducting three institutes, it was also clear to the team and our interlocutors that it was time to begin proposing specific concrete alternative steps for doing initiation in the context of SCCs in each of the respective periods of the initiation process. Laying down concrete alternatives and making specific recommendations would begin to offer benchmarks against which to follow up after an institute to assess the kind of implementation that would hopefully follow an institute.

Having had some time to digest the results of the evaluation day, the team gathered in August 2004 to take stock and to refine the design of the institute. While maintaining the exploratory and dialogical spirit of the goals as originally articulated (see above), they have now become more fully defined:

1. To lead participants to a clear understanding of the structure and goals of the initiation process as given in the Rite of Christian Initiation of Adults (RCIA) and the tasks of its various stages and the purpose, structure, and workings of Small Church Communities.

2. To provide opportunities to dialogue about the common elements (word, worship, community, and witness/mission) and the differences between the initiation process and Small Church Communities in carrying out the church's call to be the Body of Christ on mission for the transformation of the world.

3. To lead participants toward identifying and developing concrete possibilities for doing initiation within the context of Small Church
   Communities.

In addition to proposing a number of possible approaches to doing initiation in the context of small communities in the several stages of the initiation
process, the institute design team has also decided at this point to make
one specific concrete recommendation for early implementation. The design team acknowledges that it will take time to develop a thoroughgoing
relationship between initiation ministry and small communities, but it also
wants to encourage parishes to make an early significant beginning. Accord-
ingly, the institute team will explicitly suggest a good beginning can be had by
at least working to introduce catechumens/candidates to the Small Church
Community experience during the periods of Lent and Easter. This new
design was incorporated in the institute in the Archdiocese of St. Louis in
October 2004.

It is understood that SCCs that receive catechumens/candidates during
the time of Lent and Easter will need appropriate orientation to the general
initiation process, to the Rite of Election, the task of the time of Lent, and
the role of the Scrutinies, along with how they may support that experience.
It will also entail appropriate orientation to the Easter Vigil in the life of the
church, the celebration of the sacraments of initiation, and how they might
participate in them in support of the catechumen/candidate who has been
journeying with them during the time of Lent.

The Lenten agenda for the already initiated faithful is intimately related to
that of catechumens/candidates. It is a time of retreat for the whole church.
The period of the catechumenate proper is complete. Lent is a time of intense
spiritual preparation for both the celebration and renewal of the sacraments
of initiation. Connecting catechumens/candidates with SCCs during the period of Lent surrounds them with a very visible sense of support from the
larger church during this special time. Apart from the expectation that the
readings of the previous Sunday, rather than the upcoming Sunday, are the
focus for the community's reflection, it does not require any major adjustment from the ordinary pattern of small community life. At the same time,
this relationship will serve to encourage and challenge SCCs themselves to
enter all the more deeply into the time of Lent.

Surely, small communities who receive catechumens/candidates during
the time of Lent will also join them in the celebration of the Scrutinies
and the Easter Vigil. This being the case, a very solid experiential base is

laid for transition to the time of mystagogy (the reflective period between Easter and Pentecost) and a continuing relationship between the now newly baptized/received and the small communities of which they have been a part. Hopefully, the extended participation of the newly baptized/received with their SCCs during the period of Lent and Easter will lead to their happy continuation as ongoing members of these communities.

Beginning at the initial institute in the Diocese of Erie, participants have been encouraged to share narratives of actual experiences they may have already had connecting catechumens/candidates with SCCs during the various phases of initiation. A more formal effort to collect the stories of actual experience is now built into the institute structure. Institute participants are now encouraged to write out their narratives and appropriate reflective comments. This collection of stories is yet small, but growing. It may eventually serve as a further resource to assess what works and does not work, for imagining new possibilities, and for overall critical reflection on the effort to develop a significant relationship between initiation ministry and the small communities.

Dunning's visionary statement, quoted at the outset, suggests that he was projecting at least the possibility of a thorough, ongoing relationship between small communities and initiation ministry. No one is suggesting at this point, however, that we have all the answers about how to realize fully a complete infusion of initiation ministry in the context of small communities. We do not have to begin with the whole loaf in order to set a course for the future. What animates us at this juncture, however, is a strong intuition about the fruitful potential of this relationship, along with some modest experience throughout the country that encourages that intuition.

The dream that is driving this new institute envisions the incorporation of inquirers into already existing SCCs during the period of evangelization, and the continued participation of catechumens/candidates in small communities throughout the catechumenate and beyond. Realizing this dream will take time; it will be achieved in steps and in multiple ways. There will be many more than one way of doing initiation in the context of small communities.

Not every Small Church Community will be ready, willing, or able to double as a catechumenal community. It will take a relatively mature small community to so serve adequately. The members of a small community will need to be well oriented to the structure and dynamics of the initiation process and their prospective role in the process. The RCIA and critical thinkers about SCCs share a fundamental conviction about the four elements of word, worship, community, and witness/mission. Their substantial cultivation is the critical touchstone by which to test an adequate catechumenal experience and a fully fledged small community. To be an apt candidate to receive inquirers and catechumens a Small Church Community needs for all four elements to be activated in a really cultivated balance.

Happily, completely apart from this conversation about developing a close collaboration between initiation ministry and small communities, there is a clear consensus among people involved with small communities, that the elements of word, worship, community, and witness/mission form the essential measure by which to gauge the ecclesial authenticity of the small-community experience. If sometimes one or the other of these elements is honored more in the breach than in the observance, SCCs are being regularly challenged to achieve a balanced realization of all four elements.

Gathering around the Word of God, usually the lectionary readings of the liturgical year, offers the privileged lens through which small-community members focus on their lives with a view to making concrete connections between life and faith. Making a difference in each others' lives and faith, acknowledging the ties that bind, belonging to one another — these are key themes being cultivated in community. A fundamentally Eucharistic and ecclesial spirituality informs the worship life of small communities. The prayer of the small community both orients members to, and flows from, the weekly celebration of parish Eucharist. If small-community members are typically among the most involved parishioners in the life and mission of the parish, there is a strong effort throughout the United States to underline for small communities the importance of realizing that the call to witness goes beyond an often very laudable involvement with the corporal and spiritual works of mercy. More and more SCCs are being called to a basic engagement with the issues of systemic change that promotes the realization of justice and peace.

To realize this vision for collaboration will call for a spirit of adaptability on the part of both SCCs and catechumenal teams. A small community must be genuinely open to receive inquirers/catechumens/candidates. This openness will be witnessed to by the willingness of the community to adjust its operating style to meet the vision of the RCIA and the needs of those they will be receiving. For instance, small communities typically gather around the lectionary readings in a spirit of preparing for the next Sunday's Eucharist. The initiation process, however, envisions the liturgy as the privileged place of catechesis. There the nourishing word is announced, preached, celebrated. Catechumens/candidates are dismissed from the community to savor the word in the week ahead. Consequently, one simple change that small communities might be called to make would be to gather around the lectionary readings of the previous Sunday, rather than the upcoming Sunday.

The challenge of dealing well with the catechetical component of the catechumenate will be an issue of major importance. How one understands the catechetical task, of course, shapes one's perspectives on what it will take for a Small Church Community to be judged adequate to this task. In this regard, it might be anticipated that over time what is presently understood as the catechumenal team may come to be as much of a resource to small communities doubling as catechumenal communities as to the inquirers/catechumens/candidates themselves.

Presently it is often the case that baptized/received, new Catholics want immediately to become members of the catechumenal team. Having experienced an intense communal experience during the course of their initiation/reception process, they quite naturally want that experience to continue. But, as Dunning was always quick to observe, "We are not initiating people into the catechumenal team; we are initiating them into the church." Tossing people like goldfish into the often relatively anonymous waters of general parish life, however, has led to unsatisfactory results. The retention problems we have experienced can often be traced to the disconnect people experience between the catechumenate experience and that of general parish life.

Drawing prospective Catholics into involvement with mature SCCs before, during, and *after* initiation can capitalize on the bonding experience that develops as a matter of course in small communities. The kind of bonding that happens during the catechumenate does not need to be sacrificed following the completion of the initiation rites. Indeed, preserving it through continuing participation as a member of a Small Church Community will facilitate the transition into the initial mystagogy that has sometimes been found wanting with the newly baptized/received. A continuing communal relationship with the newly baptized/received will also encourage and challenge SCCs to deepen the ongoing, indeed lifelong, mystagogy to which we are all called.

Whether one's entry point in this venture is that of initiation ministry or SCCs, what we are about together transcends the immediate concerns of either point of departure. We come together around a vision of a church oriented to becoming the body of Christ in mission for the sake of the world. Nevertheless, the legitimate self-interest of both initiation ministry and small communities stands to be enormously well served as we cultivate this relationship in the years ahead. Doing initiation in the context of small communities offers new hope for more secure initiation on the one hand; and on the other, it will serve to enhance the ecclesial character of SCCs.

The RCIA makes it crystal clear that the responsibility for initiation belongs to all the baptized. This emerging approach to doing initiation in the context of SCCs opens a path to a deeper embrace of that shared responsibility, a path to a more animating and animated, a more evangelizing and evangelized church at the service of the reign of God.

9

Priority Concerns of SCCs in American Catholicism

Bernard Lee and Michael Cowan

The third national Convocation of Small Christian Communities, entitled "Small Christian Communities, Church, and Society: From Paul's Corinth to North America," took place at St. Mary's University in San Antonio, Texas, August 1–4, 2002. There were over six hundred participants, and representatives from twelve other nations (Canada, Mexico, Brazil, Australia, Kenya, Tanzania, Uganda, Nigeria, Ireland, England, Scotland, and Sweden). They gathered to engage in theological reflection on their experience, and to plan their future.

We describe briefly the multiyear process of research and dissemination that led up to the deliberations at San Antonio. We share the priority concerns of Catholic SCC participants in the United States that emerged from the convocation that help to "read" the contemporary U.S. experience.

How National Priorities Emerged

With funding from Lilly Endowment, Inc., to the Loyola University New Orleans Institute for Ministry, a team of six theologians, five sociologists, and one anthropologist planned and carried out extensive research on small communities.[1] They sought to discover and interpret the real experience of SCCs among Catholics in America: who belongs to communities, what they do, what difference they make, what their concerns are, etc. The grant also provided for a national convocation for the dissemination of the research.

What gave definition to this national convocation was the decision to structure the entire meeting on the model of practical theology: a mutually

---

1. See Bernard Lee, *The Catholic Experience of Small Christian Communities* (New York: Paulist, 2000).

critical conversation between interpretations of faith experience and interpretations of the larger world. The goal of the conversation was to generate strategies for the future of SCCs. The funded study of SCCs was a primary document interpreting the faith experience. The structure of the convocation was developed through extended critical conversation between practical theologians and representatives from the sponsoring organizations.

Qoholeth, chapter 3, is a reminder that for all things there is a time or a season. In Greek there is a distinction between clock time (*chronos* time), and that exquisite sensibility that knows just the right time for something to be said or for something to happen, i.e., to intuit when it's exactly the right "season" (*kairos* time). For SCCs in the U.S. Catholic Church, we believe that this is a *kairos* time for the priorities that follow.

The convocation was the first time that communities gathered at a national meeting specifically to engage in theological reflection together in the mode of practical theology. It seemed to us the *kairos* moment to do this. The San Antonio Convocation was about "where do we go from here, based on our experience, and based on our sense of the life of the Catholic Church?" The outcome of the convocation was a framing of seven national priorities for the proximate future. An eighth priority was added at a follow-up organizational meeting in San Antonio in November 2003.

At the conclusion of the convocation, Dr. Patricia Killen invited participants to respond to this question: "What has your experience at this convocation over the past three days meant to you in terms of your understanding of this gathering and your small community as church?" One of the participants observed, "I leave with the hope that we can create a national agenda for the public life of the SCCs." We have sometimes accompanied these priorities with remarks that SCC folks made in response to Patricia Killen's exit question, because they so often corroborated the general concerns of the priorities.

National Priority One: We recognize our need for better networking of SCCs among ourselves and among our national organizations.

This is a recognition that often we do not know much about what other communities are doing, and multiple national organizations who have interests in the life of SCCs are not regularly in touch with each other. That lessens our possible impact upon the life of the church.

"This experience," wrote one participant, "has affirmed my belief in SCCs and the importance that these groups have on the church. Now is the challenge.... Time is of the essence. Networking and support will be critical."

That networking was the number-one priority is significant. But there were some reservations voiced, for example, that SCCs not lose their grassroots prophetic energy and insight because of too much organization too soon. "I favor a national organization, but only for networking and sharing resources. We must always remember the grassroots base of SCCs." Another said, "I hope that organizing organizations do not attempt to put too much structure in place. It's too early in the movement for that."

Some SCCs did not feel connected beyond their own group. One member wrote, "I was very comfortable with the security, comfort, and closeness of my SCC before this convocation, but now I see a lack of [connection] and a sense of isolation — we have held ourselves exclusive and separate without feeling responsible for the larger church." This reflects the feeling of others too that local networking is as important, or maybe more important for some, than national networking.

One move might be to rethink the structure of current organizations so that what already exists can better mobilize strengths, energy, and people. SCCs recognize the need for better organization for two reasons. Communities themselves need to be in better touch with what goes on in other communities. But also, better organization will help SCCs make a larger, more focused contribution to the church. But they do not want organization that will diminish the freshness and zest of what they do and are.

National Priority Two: We need to forge a much better relationship, a partnership of equals, between Hispanic/Latino and Anglo SCCs.

One of the strengths of the convocation was that its location in San Antonio made possible a large Hispanic participation. Simultaneous translation was available at the gathering. Some workshops were in Spanish, and some small-group processing was in Spanish. But most of the planning came from the Anglo side, although we benefited from the Mexican American Cultural Center.

What became clear in the conference is that there are significant differences between Hispanic and Anglo SCCs, and that there are rich and complementary differences. But it was also clear that most of us from the Hispanic or Anglo experience are not very informed at all about the other's experience. Where we go from here must proceed from a genuine partnership of equals. For that to happen, we need explicit commitments and concrete strategies. It won't just happen.

We will add our own comment here, that implementation of the SCC priorities needs some kind of organization at the national level — someone(s), in this instance, to work systematically with Hispanic and Anglo leaders to devise how this partnership will be formed and energized. It will not, we think, be easy. One participant wrote that "I saw quite a gulf between Anglos and Hispanics in church loyalty and identification. It will make it hard to work together." The second priority speaks from a serious desire to foster deeper collaborative relationships between Anglo and Hispanic communities (and other ethnic communities as well).

National Priority Three: It is important to gain the support of bishops and pastors.

There exists an amazing, and we believe healthy, tension: the desire for strong relationships between SCCs and the hierarchy, and the desire not to have grassroots insights and energies of Small Church Communities coopted.

SCCs know that they can thrive more easily when bishops and pastors are supportive, because we are deeply aware, not only that we are church (already church) and that we deeply want to be church, but we want to be significantly connected. But, along with the desire for organization, SCCs do not want to lose their initiative "from the base." One participant felt that SCCs might not yet be clear enough on their own agenda to present themselves formally. "I also see a large number of small-community agendas raised by a lot of speakers and spokespersons. I suspect that these different agendas will probably interfere with any unified presentation which could be made to governing bodies such as the National Conference of Bishops."

Some of the hopes expressed are for connection with local pastors and local parishes. Another participant said that "our communal experience of faith, life, and mission are an expression of church but needing a deeper connection to the larger gathered church." Still another expresses hope for "the realization that our SCC is part of a larger parish community, diocese community, national community and international community." "The experience ignited in me," said another, "a desire to communicate the importance of SCCs...to church leaders, pastors, priests, etc."

There are similar points raised here as are raised with the notion of greater national organization. One participant put it very well. "The last three days have been energizing, affirming, and stretching. It reminds me of the delicacy of balance we need to keep growing/reaching out and the richness, indeed the essence of personal and communal spiritual growth, which the grassroots of the individual Small Christian Community nurtures."

Victor Turner has described this phenomenon well in terms of *societas*, which is the large organization that cares deeply about continuity, tradition, stability, and order — all of which are critical to an institution; and *communitas*, the smaller units within the larger unit, closer to the concerns of every life and what services their needs, a more local focus of attention. Especially in times of significant change (liminal periods), the dialectic between *societas* and *communitas* is most palpable, where *communitas* breaks in through the interstices of structure. The Catholic Church currently experiences this dialectic in a number of areas: the debates between Cardinals Kasper and Ratzinger concerning the local and universal church, and between bishops and Catholic universities in the context of *Ex Corde Ecclesiae*. No organization, in fact, can be healthy without the dialectic between *societas* and *communitas*. It must be said that even among SCCs there are differences in the tilt towards *societas* or *communitas* in self-understanding.

It is to be hoped that there be somewhere a "home" for the kind of ongoing theological reflection that this dialectic requires to keep the *ekklesia* healthy and open.

National Priority Four: We need to learn better ways to organize SCCs for our public life. This involves both emphasizing peace and justice issues, and learning how to forge links with already existing social justice groups.

This priority comes from the recognition voiced at the convocation that while social concern is a high value, actual social involvement is low. Most of us know this, and do not know quite what to do about it. The research upon which much of the convocation's theological reflection was based made clear that SCCs find it easier to address their inner life (gathered) than their public life (sent), many of the reasons for which are rooted in the individualism in U.S. culture.

In addresses at the convocation, which helped nourish the convocation's theological reflection, Robert Bellah spoke about the impact of individualism, and Patricia Killen addressed the need to focus more intentionally on the relation of faith to the larger world and its needs. Those two presentations helped give many people some words with which to recognize and name their own desire to address social issues more effectively, at the same time acknowledging the difficulty they experience in doing so.

What seemed to capture our imagination at the convocation was naming the power of small groups to help transform the world, especially if it becomes a more conscious intention, and if there is the organization to support it. One person, recently returned from SCC experiences in Latin America, said, "I'm recently back in the country — and am very happy to see SCCs on the increase. These communities have [transformed] and will continue to transform people who can transform the church — and the world." Another said that "there is so much power (in the good sense or the bad) in this movement. If we respond and move forward we are truly capable of changing not just our own lives but the general world."

There is a sense in many of the comments that SCCs may be in a position to do well what the larger church needs to do well and isn't doing well yet. They may help teach the larger ecclesial community some things it needs to know. One writes, for example, "Once we do it well in small groups, perhaps we could teach the larger church community and help all Christians understand the radical message of the Gospel and its call for social justice." We wonder, for example, what might have been the story, or might yet be the story, if U.S. bishops were to ask SCCs to take their pastoral letters on justice and peace, and run with them!

National Priority Five: We need to learn how to welcome youth and young adults into Small Christian Communities.

At the convocation, one had only to look around to see that young adults were few in number. They are also absent from the church, all out of proportion to their numbers in the general population.

On the other hand, the young adults who were at the convocation were very vocal, very present, and deeply appreciated and heard. The appetite for more young adult Catholics in SCCs was clearly whetted by their outspokenness. They also formed one of the caucuses in which national priorities were discussed and formulated.

We would simply say that this is one more example of a priority that is less likely to be addressed effectively without some kind of ongoing effort to evoke continuing theological reflection and provoke strategic pastoral implementations. Just wanting more young adults in this important ecclesial development will not make it happen. Their essential gifts must be identified, invited, and welcomed.

National Priority Six: We need to pay attention to the leadership needs if communities are to respond well to the priorities named at the convocation.

This need, documented in the research as well as expressed at the convocation, is clear. The research on SCCs indicated clearly that community leadership formation deserves serious attention.

One of the major presentations, by Evelyn and James Whitehead, developed a relational, participative model for thinking about leadership. One of the workshops conducted by a young adult presented a structural model that had all members of a small community in one of three committees: the Inner Life Committee, the Public Life Committee, and the Practicalities Committee, that served the life of the whole SCC. This spreads leadership out in focused ways. Patricia Killen's reflections also suggested how important it is that someone has the skill to lead communities in theological reflection. Here again, it would help to have some national organizational help in naming specific resources and in keeping this need to the forefront of SCC consciousness.

National Priority Seven: We must attend to the need to communicate the rich tradition.

The research on SCCs indicates that the major energizing religious practice is correlating scripture and lived experience, and that while there is no negativity toward the doctrinal tradition, it does not enter regularly into SCC processes. In his keynote address, Scott Appleby praised the recovery of scripture in ordinary Catholic life, but challenged SCCs to do a better job of accessing tradition in their dynamics.

This emphasis resonated with many present. Some felt it important, for example, to remember that SCCs were the first form of organized church life. "What happened during this gathering for me was a passing of the tradition of the early church communities to the present day: that we are empowered to renew the real Church of Christ by giving voice to the SCCs." Appreciation of the tradition and the power of SCCs to evoke fidelity to Vatican II is reflected in this observation, that "when we begin to reflect on church tradition in Small Christian Communities the changes will come — and how our culture and worldview dialogue with our tradition will transform us — the emphasis will shift on what we need to teach and what we pass on, our knowledge of Vatican II and what it meant in the context of our tradition. The power we have as laypeople will become known, and Vatican II spirituality will finally have a chance to emerge."

National Priority Eight: The U.S. experience of SCCs must remain in dialogue with the larger international experience.

This eighth priority was later discussed and added, largely responding to recommendations from Father Robert Pelton, who has actively engaged the international SCC experience in theological conversation.

These eight priorities are possible elements of a national strategy for SCCs, and this is a very new development. In the U.S. Catholic Church, SCCs have been very loosely connected or organized. But perhaps it has just taken us time to grow up, as our numbers suggest we have done. Growing up requires a judicious balance of structure and spontaneity. Getting that balance right through "good enough" structures is the challenge now facing SCC leaders in the United States. The research, consultation, and convocation reported here provide one solid base for their response.

The two of us writing this chapter believe that these are coherent and accurate priorities. How responsive small communities will be to some or all of them remains to be seen. Without very effective national organization efforts of some kind, these priorities are less likely to be addressed effectively.

Part Three

Europe

Basic Christian Communities (BCCs) grew throughout Europe in the 1960s and 1970s as a parallel journey to the growth of such communities in other parts of the world. Often these communities were unaware that others existed, although the same sociological and ecclesiastical/theological influences were at work throughout. The scent of liberation was in the air; it was post–Vatican II, and also within Europe new political and social alliances were being formed.

In Europe as elsewhere it was predominantly within Catholic countries that BCCs first appeared. These communities, however, have always had a broad ecumenical dimension. From the start the communities engaged in a biblical/analytical critique of both society and church. Their relationship with the institutional church — both Catholic and Protestant — has been to seek a space on the edge "that allows their experience to have its impact" (Cira Castaldo interviewed by Margaret and Ian Fraser, Naples, 1984). Within this space they have over time developed their own practices, pastoral and liturgical. Within the political context they continue to engage in critical actions that challenge policies considered unjust or discriminatory.

The growth in Britain of BCCs has been more fluid than in other parts of Europe. There are many communities, but Small Christian Communities (SCCs) as written about in this book are not so identifiable. The stories of two developments that do have a connection are told. One is of an ecumenical program, "New Way of Being Church," that came about as a result of workshops animated over a number of years by a team from Brazil led by Brazilian theologian José Marins. The other development, "At Your

71

Word, Lord," is an initiative within the Roman Catholic Diocese of West-minster introduced by Cormac Murphy-O'Connor, the cardinal archbishop of Westminster.

BCCs in Europe thirty years on are finding new energy for the ongoing journey. New Way and "At Your Word, Lord" are newer on the scene. Like one wave following on another, the move to a new model of church is ongoing—slow, often, but sure.

10

A Moment of Revitalization

The European Collective of BCCs

Peter Macdonald

A family holiday in 2004 took us to Collioure in the Pyrenees Orientales at the height of summer. Those of us from northern climes find the guaranteed sunshine, Mediterranean beaches, and vine-patterned hillsides of the South of France the ideal summer destination. On one particularly hot afternoon the seventeenth-century church Notre Dame des Anges provided cool and quiet respite from the twenty-first-century crowds and clamor. The contrast was not lost on my teenage son, who asked, "Why is entering a church like stepping back in time?"

Why indeed! Many Christians have been asking the same question and seeking answers, radically rethinking the meaning of their faith and, through the creation of Small Christian Communities (SCCs), exploring new ways of being the church. They reject ancient prejudices, which are dismissive of other Christian traditions and contemptuous of other faiths. They reject "other worldly" theology that fails to address the sufferings and injustices of this world. They challenge the authoritarian and hierarchical structures of the institutional church with its abuses of power and privilege. They seek to redefine the church as the people of God and to become a prophetic community of faith. As long ago as the 1940s fledgling groups such as the Iona Community in Scotland identified characteristics of such groups: integrating worship and work, scriptures and society, prayer and politics, engagements for justice and peace, the economic, the ecumenical, and the environmental.

The worldwide emergence and evolution of SCCs has been attributed to "the spontaneous combustion of the Holy Spirit."[1] This was a spirit-filled response, begun in the 1950s and 1960s, to rapid social change, including

---

1. Ian Fraser in *Small Christian Communities: Vision and Practicalities* by Jim O'Halloran (Dublin: Columba Press, 2002).

the breakdown in community, greater social and economic mobility, the decline of institutional religion, and the urgent need to reinvent the church to better serve God's purposes. During this period groups emerged, mostly unaware of the existence of other similar SCCs in Europe. Interest in liberation theology and the base communities of Latin America led to the identification and recognition of such groups and the desire to share experiences and concerns. National networks were created most notably in predominantly Roman Catholic countries, the Second Vatican Council having provided the catalyst for renewal.

The first European Congress of SCCs was held in Amsterdam, the Netherlands, in 1983. The need for continuing contact and cooperation resulted in the formation of the European Collective, a body with representation drawn from various regions of the continent. The network created was democratic in its leadership and loosely organized. This gave the collective the lightness of touch necessary to encourage the participation of groups and individuals seeking greater freedom from the authoritarian institutions of church and state.

The European Collective exists to enable us to seek one another out, to spread the word that we are not alone but part of a worldwide movement for renewal and justice. It exists to offer mutual support and encouragement through the exchange of information and ideas, through encounter and joint action, and through the example and experience of exploring new ways of being church. It exists because of an awareness that small communities can become inward-looking, escapist, and self-serving, and are therefore always in need of the reminder of the big picture and their calling to be leaven in the world.

In recent years representatives from SCCs across Europe have shared concerns on major social and justice issues. At a gathering on Iona, Scotland, participants from Central and Eastern Europe concluded that the existence of SCCs was an asset within a new Europe, which "seeks natural forms of integration which will give it a heart and worthy human goals."[2] To this end local groups and national networks have been active in advocating a vision of Europe as a partnership of peoples, affirming the right of every people to its language, culture, history, and geographical territory, campaigning for a Europe which seeks to empower the poor, marginalized, and excluded among its citizens. Other key areas of engagement have been in interfaith dialogue; concern for the asylum seeker, refugee, and economic migrant;

---

2. "Report on Soul for Europe Conference," Iona, August 1999.

and celebration of multiculturalism in the face of growing xenophobia and racism. "The network is important. There is constant exchange, contributing to self-assurance and encouraging solidarity, interchange, critical analysis, and creative inspiration among countries," comments one Swiss member.

Several European national networks have links with SCCs in other parts of the world and express solidarity in the struggle to overcome the injustices and inequities of globalization, in the campaign for the cancellation of international debt, and in demands for the resolution of conflict through the United Nations and the rule of international law.

The collective has struggled over recent years with financial problems and a decline in participation due to difficulties in maintaining communications with existing networks and in developing links with new groups. A recent gathering in Edinburgh, Scotland, in 2003 was an attempt to revitalize the existing membership and to reach out to new communities. Thirty participants representing twelve countries and regions attended with several other national groups requesting to be kept informed of the outcomes of the meeting with a view to future participation.

The gathering exceeded expectations and ended with renewed commitment to strengthening the links between base communities. As a result the Collective agreed on the following objectives:

- To establish/reestablish links with groups in each country

- To encourage representation from each national network

- To organize a "gathering" once a year

- To appoint a secretariat of four representatives drawn from at least three different regions and language groups

- To explore the feasibility of holding a larger event every three years

- To create a Web site with links to national networks

The secretariat meets twice a year and is responsible for overseeing administration and finance, encouraging participation, and planning the annual gathering. The latter is the most significant aspect of the work of the collective as we are bound together not only by common concerns but also by mutual support, inspiration, and challenge — the essence of life in community.

When this summer we visited the church of Notre Dame des Anges, reminders of the troubled history of that region of Europe were all around with commemorations of the crusades against the Cathars and the Moors.

Personal liberty and tolerance which flourished under the Cathars were swept away by twenty years of war; prosperous, cooperative communities were destroyed and their citizens tortured and massacred; the deep connection with the Sufi tradition within Islam and Jewish kabbalism was replaced with the persecution of minorities, and all lay learning was discouraged. The conflict with the Moors was graphically illustrated by an altarpiece that caught my eye — a Christian knight standing over the prostrate body of a black man, a crosslike sword plunged into his belly.

Disturbing reminders of ancient prejudices, religious enmity, persecution, and violence still wound the earth and its weary people. Whenever church authority becomes an obstacle to living the way of Christ or whenever the Christian life is oppressed by political systems, believers will seek one another out to be true to their faith by living it in community, evidenced by the growth of SCCs on every continent.

Three European BCCs
Face Today's Challenges

BCC Members

Italy: The Christian Base Community, San Paolo, Rome

This is a special year for our community. In September 2003 we celebrated thirty years from when we emerged from the Basilica of St. Paul-Outside-the-Walls, where we were born in the postconciliar years. Thirty years — a lifetime, it seems, for all the events that have crowded in since then.

To commemorate this anniversary we reissued Giovanni Franzoni's pastoral letter *The Earth Belongs to God*, which struck a spark and was the cause of Franzoni, then abbot of the Benedictine Monastery of St. Paul, being forced out of the abbey. That was in 1974. He relocated with the fledgling community to a nearby warehouse. The letter documented and exposed Vatican real estate speculation leading to worsening conditions for the poor in the city. The letter sold over a hundred thousand copies and was translated into French, Spanish, and English. This 2003 reissue contains a revision by Giovanni, not a denial of anything but rather new and calm rethinking which, having been taught by life, one can apply to things said, written, or done in the past.

In recent years the community has not drawn up broad documents on social or theological subjects, nor has it done anything to bring itself to the attention of the media, as happened thirty years ago. It has, however, often taken up a position on social or ecclesiastical problems. For instance, when the war in Bosnia was at its height, the community questioned the conflict and its causes at length, looking particularly at the responsibilities of the Catholic Croatians, the Orthodox Serbs, and the Islamic Bosnians.

In 2003 the problem that has caused us most anguish has been the threat, later realized, of the Anglo-American "preventative war" against Iraq. The community, as far as possible, took part in all the big public demonstrations against the war and, in dialogue with the parish priest of Santa Galla and the evangelical Baptist congregation of the Via Pullino (both in the region of Ostiense), prepared and distributed at the metro stations thousands of copies of a leaflet — signed by dozens of groups, parishes, religious congregations — saying, "No to war, Yes to peace." On March 5, 2003, the community took part at Santa Galla in a day of prayer and fasting for peace as proclaimed by the pope on that Ash Wednesday.

During these years, each of us — like everyone else, of course — has faced problems, uncertainties, joys, and sufferings. But along all the difficult roads in life the community has been our little spiritual homeland. Thanks be to God, we are still here in spite of everything. We are the same as we were, and we are different from how we were in 1974. Meanwhile, although Giovanni is always in our midst, the community is increasingly thought and felt to exist in its own right. We are no longer — as we were once labeled — the "Community of Don Franzoni," but for all intents and purposes we are the Christian Base Community of St. Paul, not only in a sociological but also in a theological sense. We have therefore examined closely the ministries of the church and the Eucharist-community relationship, convinced that, without radical rethinking on such subjects, a community like the church as a whole is irremediably destined to be clerical and so in conflict with the Gospel message of freedom from priestly castes.

Consequently, from the biblical-theological point of view and in the consequent praxis, we have overcome the doubts we had in 1973–1976 and emphasize ever more the participation of all the *ekklesia*, the local assembly, in the celebration of the Eucharist. We are, in fact, developing the conviction that the community (every Christian community) is the true "subject" of the divine gift of the Eucharist and that it is therefore the community that holds the office of the right-and-duty to celebrate the Lord's Supper.

Reflection on "the signs of the times" and the Word of the Lord has constantly informed us that we will be in glaring contradiction if we do not know how to "break the bread" like Jesus — that is, to share our lives with others. So we know that we must enter more and more into discussion among ourselves and with other people, seize opportunities and times wherever the kingdom of God may shine and wherever the care, conviviality, and welcome of other people prevail.

Also we reflect on a series of other themes: the lay state of the faith (the "living before God as if God didn't exist," according to the striking statement of the German Lutheran theologian Dietrich Bonhoeffer); rereading scripture according to the historical-critical method and according to feminist theology; the relationship, actual and theological, with other churches and other religions; and bioethics. We have made steps that, thirty years ago, were not even on our horizon.

Certainly, if we look today at some of the statements we made in the 1970s and at some of the arguments then, they seem to us to have faded with the passing of time. We ourselves smile at some of the snippets of presumption that show through some of our operations. If, in the book, *The Earth Belongs to God*, we quoted these facts and documents, it was only to record objectively the road that we have followed, whether direct or tortuous.

Greatly changed from many points of view since 1973, we want the spirit of our commitment to remain identical, to continue to dig deeply into the Gospel, to ask questions of history and of society, of the dramatic North-South problems in the world, of the challenges of globalization, the collapse of the Eastern European regimes and the supremacy of the one "empire," that of the United States, and of everyday life and changing cultural models.

We are not, today, secure in something definitive, in absolute certainties. On the contrary, we feel entirely inadequate in the face of the gravity, complexity, and urgency of impending geopolitical problems, human and ecclesiastical. Yet nevertheless we affirm the legitimacy of the ecclesial and theological experience of the base community of St. Paul.

We do not seem, after all, to be isolated. In fact, if not truly in the "hierarchical communion" delineated by the Code of Canon Law, we feel ourselves part of and reconciled with the wider communion of so many brothers and sisters in the faith with whom we see ourselves in tune in research and outlook, and also profoundly linked to the very many Christians throughout the world who have the grace and the responsibility to proclaim themselves disciples of Jesus, who died and rose again. In fact, we feel ourselves linked with believers in other faiths and with so many people of goodwill everywhere who seek, day by day, to build peace through justice and solidarity.

And this is why we have hope.

(By the Christian Base Community of San Paolo, Rome. English translation by Toni Salmonson.)

Italy: Christian Base Community, Pinerola

The Christian Base Community of Pinerola was born in December 1973 in the midst of that great church renewal movement which took place during the years immediately following the Second Vatican Council. While "political" theology and liberation theology were flourishing in Latin America and Europe, the Christian Base Community movement in Italy was active in drawing up an ecclesial model, a theology, and a spirituality responding to the most fertile seeds rediscovered during the years of the council. But the base church went far beyond conciliar requirements. The reference "hinge" (or "cornerstone") was singled out in scripture and in the world of the poor. The Word of God, the sufferings, struggles, and hopes of the poor of the earth were the historical and theological "place" on which the community was built.

Also on account of its geographical location, in the Waldensian valleys of Piedmont, our base community has always held open discussion with the Waldensian-Methodist and the other evangelical churches, giving life over the years to various occasions of communal study, of celebrations, prayer, and open debate in the city.

In these years, always supported by a free, rigorous (but not dogmatic) reading of the scriptures, our base community has struggled with important issues in the Christian churches: the principle of the indissolubility of marriage, the right to a second marriage, the admission of women to the priesthood, and the right for gays and lesbians to live their condition of life freely in society and in the church.

Central to the life of our community is the weekly celebration of the Eucharist. In turn, one of the community Bible groups (which meet weekly) chooses the biblical texts on which the preaching in the Eucharist will be based, prepares the homily (for two or more voices), and "constructs" the whole liturgical celebration. After the sermon, space is left for the free participation of the brothers and sisters. Next to the moment of spontaneous prayer, which follows the breaking of the bread, the most important moment for us is when we devote ourselves to listening to each other.

In our community the activity of listening to people who turn to us in uncomfortable situations or personal search goes on constantly. Today, our little world is a meeting place where many people come seeking listeners, discussion — a space in which men and women, groups, parishes, and associations pay us visits and share with us their experience, doubts, plans, and hopes. Many who have set aside their search for faith invite us to walk with them for a while. Then there are people who are looking for someone with whom to open a wound, with whom to weep and rejoice, with whom to search for a way out of despair. The ecumenical dimension (people of various Christian churches belong to the community) helps us to cultivate a theological and pastoral opening, which comes from the gift of meeting. We feel that the network of brotherhood and sisterhood which we are living and interweaving with hundreds of people on the way floods the heart with hope.

The active participation of gay and lesbian believers in the life of the community, the celebration of second Christian marriages, and the welcome for those couples who are refused in other places, all this represents for our community an invitation from God to enlarge our hearts. Tensions, setbacks, tiredness, simplifications, errors, and discouragement are interwoven with dreams, joys, growth, profound communion, search, and simplicity.

Now in May 2004 we are full of gratitude to God for our small community experience in the base church. We see its limitations, we recognize and experience its fragility, precariousness, and temporary nature, but we see in this experience an extraordinary gift that God has given us in order to involve us deeply and passionately in our faith.

(By Paolo Sales. English translation by Toni Salmonson.)

Central Switzerland: Base Community, Küssnacht am Rigi

The easiest thing for me to write about is my own base community group, with which I have been involved for some years now. We most likely came together due to our common faith and the fact that we live and work in the same village, Küssnacht, near Lucerne in German-speaking Switzerland. The main initiative was provided by the experience of some of us who had worked as laypeople for Missionary Institutions in South America and Asia for several years. There we experienced life in Small Christian Communities and analyzed liberation theology. All of us in our base community feel linked to the church and touched by the Gospel of Jesus Christ.

Arrangements for the weekly community meeting are made by the host-couple and the gathering begins with a greeting. Then comes a Bible reading with discussion, often done according to the Seven Step Method. Occasionally Thursday meetings also include the ongoing reading of a spiritual book. We sing and pray at these gatherings, exchange our everyday experiences, and thus reflect on social reality through the message of Jesus. Once a month, we hold a Gospel service and an Agape celebration, and sometimes the topic is completely open. Occasionally, we even make an excursion, have a lecture, or hold an all-men or all-women evening.

At present we are nine adults, the majority couples, and most of us belong to the founding core, that is, we have been here since the beginning. Over the course of the years, some moved away or left us, while others joined. Naturally, our children are also part of our base community group, although they seldom attend our Thursday gatherings. They always participate in social events and important services before Easter and on Christmas. Friends of both adults and children also attend these social occasions.

Each and every one of us is involved in various areas of the parish, in the political community, or at the workplace, in favor of the interests of the disadvantaged or the church. We are likewise concerned — though we live in a relatively wealthy country — with leading a simple lifestyle, concretely along the lines of the Ecumenical Movement for Justice, Peace, and the Integrity of Creation. This is embodied, among other measures, by the fact that our children and we almost always use public transport or bicycles as a means of transportation to work or in our free time.

Some of us are active members of progressive political parties or various different sociopolitical workgroups. We participate in activities of other groups — for instance, joining in nonviolent actions for human rights or against the war in Iraq. For twelve years now, a member of the community has been leading an ecologically inspired project: a small, local, and seasonal fruit and vegetable market that helps small growers in the region to sell their produce directly to local consumers. One of our members has been working for a year on a new project to integrate immigrants and the Swiss in our town. This is an important program as tensions here are on the rise.

Our base community is a particularly good place for us to find good listeners for our needs and questions, as well as real support. In discussions, we receive feedback, constructive criticism, and empowerment. We gain insight and, through prayer as well as Bible reading, individuals have always managed to overcome difficult crises.

Is our base community a self-help therapy group or more like a political cell? At a certain point, the term *Kuschelgruppe*, literally "cuddling group," appeared on the Swiss base community scene, and it occasionally had negative and even contemptuous overtones. "Cuddling" has something to do with coming together and with giving and seeking warmth. Groups that were hardly socially or politically engaged and seen by some as almost exclusively involved in spiritual aspects were at times condescendingly designated "cuddling groups." The people who know the history of the last three decades of the Swiss base communities have seen that many groups that fell apart were those that had become too socially and politically active as a group. Those groups, on the other hand, that focused on engagement and reflection, that balanced action with contemplation, are still together today.

We all live in the same district, most of us quite close to one another and one and a half miles apart. This geographical proximity greatly facilitates our collaboration. Many base community groups in Switzerland are ecumenical and therefore also open to members from other religious communities. We are naturally also open to people of other denominations or faiths, but at present we are all Catholic in our Thursday group.

Churches in Switzerland are experiencing a significant exodus, as more and more people are leaving the church and turning their backs on church organizations. Those leaving do so only partially to avoid paying church taxes. The trend away from responsibilities and commitment towards less solidarity in our society is also visible in decreasing participation in church and parish life. The number of people attending Sunday mass falls significantly every year. On the other hand, it is evident that other religious groups such as Buddhism and Hinduism, new religion providers, movements such as New Age, and sects are clearly in high demand. It could well be that the hunger for spiritual nourishment among old and young is just as present as before or even increasing.

It seems as if the representatives of our Christian churches are less and less capable of supplying the necessary answers to the spiritual questions of those seeking — especially today's youth. In this increasingly cold and aging church environment, our base community seems an important place, a home of the church, where we, through our community, can keep some of the fire of faith alive, or as some say, keep the coals burning. In this sense, the above-stated term, "cuddling group," gains positive overtones. Our base community group goes against the trend towards individualism. It establishes and provides solidarity and the hope that another type of church is possible. It gives warmth and security. We are attempting to live in the church through this proximity and friendliness, to practice a form of solidarity that is binding to us and others, to hold services in our small group but also with the larger churchgoing community, as well as to reflect upon the Gospel through our everyday lives and work.

(By Pepe Beerli-Bamberger. English translation by Global Language Services, Cornwall, England.)

12

The Story of Seeds
in the United Kingdom

Jeanne Hinton and Stephen Rymer

Join us as we visit a typical workshop on a "New Way of Being Church." Participants, who have been together for five days now, list what has been helpful:

"The experience of creating a Small Christian Community and working within it."

"Worship that arises out of, and reflects, everyday life and concerns."

"A new approach to using the Bible, bringing the written word and present reality together."

"Use of the pastoral (action/reflection) cycle to encourage the ongoing process of creating the kingdom."

"Ways to look at damaged parts of society and to analyze 'why things are the way they are.'"

"Updating ourselves regularly with news from outside."

"Experiencing the importance of memory and of building continuity."

"Fiesta—times of fun and games!"

Eighteen participants have taken part and are now returning to local churches and neighborhoods to sow some seeds. This notion of planting seeds had come from a Brazilian Catholic priest, José Marins, some years previously.

These outcomes of a workshop will be familiar to members of Small Christian Communities (SCCs) the world over. The Marins team first came to England in the early 1980s to share the story of Basic Ecclesial Communities (BECs) in Latin America. José Marins, who leads the team, is a consultant to the Latin American and Caribbean Catholic Bishops Conferences and closely associated with the development of BECs in Latin America and elsewhere. The team came to share a predominantly Catholic experience within an ecumenical workshop and within a quite different culture, but it captured the minds and imaginations of many who attended. Participants came away talking about a radical reorientation — "from doing church to being church and engaging with a reign-of-God agenda." John Summers, an Anglican clergyman, later wrote, "It was unlike any workshop or course that I had ever done before. It was an introduction to a new process of learning by doing. It was not at all a matter of copying how they did things in Brazil, of taking course notes, or collecting the appropriate do-it-yourself pack to take back to the parish. Rather it was the beginning of a long process of entering into understanding something that was highly relevant and might just be possible here."

But could the experience be transplanted here in Britain? That was the challenge.

In 1990 it was agreed that a local team would take on the work of continuing to nurture this seed. We took the name that linked the two — a "New Way of Being Church," "New Way" for short. The "we" at that time were Derek Hanscombe, an Anglican priest who sadly died of cancer in 1991; Jeanne Hinton, a writer and educator; and Peter Price, at that time general secretary of an Anglican missionary organization (USPG). Others were quickly drawn in to form an ecumenical team that has animated the program over these past fifteen years, led workshops, written publications, and responded to requests from local churches and church bodies to facilitate this work.

Now at the end of 2004 we are both evaluating the last ten or more years and launching out in new directions. What has happened to the seeds that have been sown? Sometimes we feel very little. We have run numerous workshops, accompanied some local churches in their seeking to establish a "new way," written and published booklets, and begun to establish regional support groups. We have shared the concept of sowing seeds at workshops, but we do not always hear what results. When we do, we encourage the sharing of stories.

One Anglican priest writes to say she is "experimenting" with dialogue sermons and discovering how "many people come to church week after week desperate to be able to share how their lives really are." Six women tell their story of how they have formed "not a typical Basic Christian Community," but come together every two months "to share where they are in life, to worship informally together, and to reflect biblically on our experiences." Living some distance from each other, none had found this opportunity in her local church. Another woman writes that engaging with others working for a Debt-Free Start for indebted countries has become her "way of being church"; "campaigning is part of the work of the kingdom of God." A United Reformed Church minister in a rural church tells of the effectiveness of running open-air "pets services." One thing "common to all inside and outside the church" had been identified, and dogs and cats and a variety of other pet animals were brought to an open-air service by their owners, who had heartfelt stories to tell and wanted to give thanks for their pets. A Methodist writes of how he took the step "of enabling church members to listen to themselves and to each other — 'to dream their own dreams.'"

These stories are told in two New Way booklets — *Tapestry of Stories* and *Stepping Stones* — and illustrate again this amazing variety of different types of growth both in mainstream church and on the edge. Not exactly SCCs, but not so different either. These are small groups of Christians connecting life with faith. They are steps along the way, seeds.

We had hoped by now to be able to point to more local churches where SCCs had taken root as the basic units of church. This, however, is proving to be a longer journey than we had anticipated. Often it is more on the edge of the church that seeds for the moment have grown. Two further stories illustrate this point.

St. Barnabas is an inner-city Anglican parish in southwestern England. John Summers, quoted earlier, began in 1995 to share with his small congregation the vision of the local church as a "community of communities." By 1996 neighborhood groups — SCCs — had been established in four areas of the parish, engaging with local issues and enabling reflection and action. For a small congregation the outcome was remarkable. The area was undergoing a program of urban regeneration, but "without the St. B's folk we could not have achieved our goals," commented a city councilor. But John's retirement in 2000 disturbed the continuity and has meant that this is not necessarily an ongoing story. Many readers will know this situation for themselves.

A different story is a group of somewhat disaffected church members in the north of England who in 1992 put an advert in a local magazine inviting those interested to a "bread and cheese" lunch and to the possibility of meeting regularly to discuss topics of interest "where all could freely express their opinion." The lunches drew others in and also led to the group beginning to share in new forms of worship, particularly in the Celtic tradition, where faith and life have always been closely intertwined. Discussion and worship have led also to local actions for justice and peace. For this group — Celtic Spirituality Group — this is their new way of being church. Some continue to attend mainstream church, many do not. Detached from the mainstream, the future of the group is in its own hands.

Here are two different expressions of church — one part of an established structure, the other not. There could be and sometimes is friction. There is, however, a hopeful background to this. We, with others, are aware of a shift that is taking place now in the churches in Britain … "a new moment," a gift of the Spirit surprising us. Much of the impetus, thus far, has come from a steep decline in church attendance and membership, a fall in the number of people offering themselves for ordained ministry, and a predominately elderly priesthood, many of whom will retire in the next five to ten years. All this raises questions about the long-term viability of the church. There is much that is different from even ten years ago, certainly a recognition that as church we need to be out there in the community and need to find ways to be relevant to today's society. There is the recognition that present church structures are mostly a hindrance to this, and it is in the small group or cell that the church is finding ways to be relevant at a local level. While ten years ago we in New Way felt we were plowing a lonely furrow, now this is not so. A whole range of books about new ways of being church has been published. There are different emphases, but all are about the importance of a way of *being* church.

This growth is heartening, but it is also fragile. Some is more on paper than in practice. While the structures of the church remain largely untouched, new developments are always likely to be at risk. There is, however, recognition that mainstream church can learn from what is happening on or at the edge or fringe. In 2004 a Church of England working group produced a report entitled "Mission-Shaped Church." Commissioned by the archbishop of Canterbury, Rowan Williams, it looked at a "fresh expression of church in a changing context." Fresh expressions range from cell church, seeker church, café church, and network church, and include Basic Ecclesial Communities. One of its recommendations is that in every diocese there is a strategy for the encouragement of such new expressions, and that training programs for lay and ordained ministers should include this focus. Rowan Williams, in his presidential address, said: "The Church is renewed as it so often is from the edges, not the center. We need a positive willingness to see and understand all this — and to find the patterns and rhythms and means of communication that will let everyone see the benefits." Other denominations have done similar exercises.

Much of this energy for change, however, appears to be available primarily from within large churches that have the capacity to send "missionaries" to plant "fresh expressions" of themselves. The majority of the denominational churches in Britain have a weekly attendance of fewer than fifty persons, many less. Enabling these churches, which are already close to Small Christian Community size, to find a new way of being in their life-or-death situation, remains a huge task.

We are writing this in December 2004. The future for those engaged in a "new way" is always uncertain but full of possibilities. A year ago we were facing the possibility of closing New Way. Such is the fragility of all grassroots organizations where funding and workers are not easily come by. Since then we have received a sum of money from an anonymous source that has enabled us to appoint a development worker and to continue the program for at least the next three years. Small Christian Communities remain at the heart of what we are about. We aim to nurture communities whose primary purpose is to bring wholeness to their neighborhood; to encourage those who seek to be part of a community of faith to come together; to support communities where doubt can be explored and faith nurtured; to enable ordinary people to make a difference.

In this we are open to working within the mainstream and with groups at the edge. Primarily we seek to work with local churches of all denominations. We also recognize that growth is not only bottom up but also top down, a meeting of the two. Only in this way will structural change happen. As a New Way team we are mostly Anglican, and at present we have a particular opportunity to work for change within the Anglican Diocese of Bath and Wells. Peter Price, who helped to found New Way, is now the bishop of Bath and Wells, and New Way's development worker, Stephen Rymer, works part-time for New Way and part-time for the diocese, where he is engaged to bring New Way concepts into the diocesan "Changing Lives" program and to encourage emerging forms of church.

Much of this chapter has been about church; little of what we have said so far begins to touch the 70 percent of the population who say that they believe in God but do not attend any church or the many people who have left the church in recent times. The church sees its future in "relevance," but that holds enormous dangers of collusion with society's values. Jesus challenged "the system," the forces that maintain the status quo, that keep intact power, wealth, and exclusion. By and large, the church in Britain is middle class; its language is that of the educated; its members are wealthy. Like the rest of society we buy into the consumer culture, are protected by society's high-tech armaments, feast off out-of-season produce grown by impoverished Third

World nations, and pollute the planet with waste gases. At best, the distinctiveness of our Christianity is represented by thoughtful charity, the careful disposal of a portion of our surplus.

For all these reasons we want to encourage ourselves and others to find ways to make a difference in the places where we live and work. Our concern is to contribute to transforming local communities, to making Britain a more inclusive, fairer society to live in. This is how we see the calling to be church — "from doing church to being church and engaging with a reign-of-God agenda" — the perspective that came as a fresh challenge over twenty years ago at those formative workshops led by the Marins team. Seeds of the Gospel!

13

"At Your Word, Lord"

Renewal Program in the Diocese of Westminster

Stuart Wilson

The Catholic Diocese of Westminster began in 1850. It has always been a "welcoming" diocese to peoples from all over the world. Our cardinal, Cormac Murphy-O'Connor, spoke at the mass in Wembley Arena in London, England, in September 2003 to launch the renewal program "At Your Word, Lord," and said, "The reestablishment of our diocese was marked by a large influx of immigrants especially from Ireland and from other countries. They came as well from Italy, from Poland and elsewhere."

The diocese is still very diverse. The many different languages and national groups bring challenges to our unity. Over the last twenty-five years the diocese has had an area system that had been good in many ways but had fragmented the diocese into units which experienced some difficulty in relating to each other. The Diocese of Westminster is part of a vast metropolitan area that embraces inner-city and suburban as well as rural parishes beyond the metropolitan boundary. Each parish has different needs, which again strains our fragile unity. It was also the case that most of our parishes were not well structured in terms of having Parish Pastoral Councils or the existence of small faith-sharing communities.

All the previous nine archbishops have died in office after having made distinctive contributions to the life of the diocese. The present archbishop (Cardinal Cormac Murphy-O'Connor) is making an equally important contribution because new things are happening. The diocese has been challenged by him to find a new unity and purpose through a program of renewal.

With the new millennium there was an urgent call from Pope John Paul II to every diocese to engage in renewal and evangelization. The document *At the Beginning of a New Millennium* meditates on that story in Luke's Gospel when Jesus urges the disciples/fishermen (despite the fact that they had caught nothing) to "launch out into the deep." Cardinal Cormac offered our diocese the same challenge. The diocese sensed that the cardinal is an urgent man, and they sensed the urgency in his call. They made their response using the words that St. Peter spoke to Jesus, "At your word, Lord." These words became the name for the pastoral and spiritual renewal program that is changing the face of the diocese. The "At Your Word, Lord" (AYWL) program did not have the luxury of long-term planning, and this inevitably creates some stress. Yet stress can be exciting and enthusing and good for our program.

The cardinal sent four priests to look at various programs for parish renewal, and they recommended that the RENEW International program would best serve our needs. With this knowledge the cardinal called the clergy together in synod (at a family holiday camp on the south coast of England!). Four hundred clergy listened, reflected, and finally committed themselves to a plan for renewal. Of course, the plan needed to hear the voice of the laity. But how? There are no synods of laity, so questionnaires were sent out to every parish. Over fifteen hundred replies were received. Many topics were mentioned, but the response to the question, "Do you think we need a program of renewal?" was an overwhelming yes! The cardinal went around the diocese to fourteen public meetings to meet the laity and offer the challenge of renewal. Over five thousand came out to those meetings and gave their assent. There were also meetings of the many religious — female and male — who also gave their assent and support to this call for renewal.

Westminster has 214 parishes and 37 ethnic communities, so it needed an effective plan. The first thing we had to do was get a team in place. Our team numbers six people. I am the only priest, but there is also a religious sister, two women, and two men. We are all different in outlook and age but equally dedicated to spiritual and pastoral renewal. Our partners at RENEW International offer a diocesan renewal program based on prayer, Sunday Liturgy, and above all else Small Christian Communities (SCCs). Some such communities already existed in the diocese, having been introduced by various movements. We are convinced that SCCs are important for two reasons. First, they do bring about a personal desire for a deeper life in Christ, and second, they act as a catalyst for a new parish vision and hopefully a new structure. Expressed simply and in the words of the pope, "The parish is to become a 'community of small communities.'" Speaking to the National Conference of Priests in England and Wales in September 2002 Cardinal Cormac Murphy-O'Connor said: "I often think these small communities are the secret for the future of the church.... Any strategy for the future must seek to maintain the parish, perhaps more loosely based, but a parish as a communion of communities. It is within the parish, seen and developed as a community and within which there are small communities, that we equip people to evangelize."

Small communities are formed at the invitation of the Parish Core Community (PCC), whose task it is to develop them. The PCC is made up of the priest, the parish team, and parishioners. Two-thirds of the parishes in the diocese have formed PCCs. Many are effective, but quite a number struggle. The "At Your Word, Lord" program focuses on SCCs that meet twice a year for two six-week Seasons. In November 2004 we finished Season III on the theme "Reaching Out — Through Evangelization." The fifth and final Season will take place in October–November 2005. Each small community has a leader, and built into our program of renewal is the *importance* of trained leaders. Much of our energy is dedicated to this; we have trained over a hundred new leaders who will train others. Each SCC has eight to ten people who listen to God's Word and then share the experience of God in their daily lives. Doing this as a community means that their joint experiences enrich and challenge each one present.

Our feedback tells us that 2,000 small communities had met in over 170 parishes. We also know that sharing has been *deeper*. I was moved by the comment of a businessman who said, "For the first time I have found the courage to share my faith with my business colleagues." The feedback also highlighted the fact that the parishes were becoming more *welcoming*. This was exemplified for me when a woman at a parish meeting said, "The SCCs have turned the smiles at Sunday mass into voices." Every Season, the effect of small communities on the life of the parish grows.

Developing the renewal process has not been without its challenges. Multiculturalism has been a real boon to our program as it allows people who have already been members of small communities in their own country to bring that experience to us. So many different cultures and languages make real demands on our ability to offer resources. Sharing the things of the heart is always done better in one's mother tongue. The diocese supports over thirty ethnic chaplaincies, but they in turn bring vitality for renewal that is infectious. Another challenge for the program is convincing the clergy that it will bring blessing and not extra work. As a priest I recognize the challenge. It really does demand that I think and work in a slightly different way — the way of collaboration. Most of us were not trained for this, and it can fill us with apprehension. Priests in our diocese are well loved by their people. It was great to hear the cheers of the ten thousand people at the Wembley Launch Mass as the priests entered the arena. Yet despite this, priests feel very vulnerable at present. Fewer seminarians, fewer priests, less people at mass, and the few but very well publicized scandals are not a good basis for the challenge to launch out once again.

Yet we believe that this is a good moment to launch out into the deep. Why? Because the feedback tells over and over again that the inspiration to meet in small communities is beginning to make the parishes different. Running alongside our program is another project looking at diocesan and parish resources. It is called "Graced by the Spirit." In a report to the archbishop it said, "We have received numerous direct references to the fact that the consultation is all the more possible because of the increased sense of participation that people feel in their parish and faith through the AYWL initiative." There are very practical changes, like the new sense of the importance of the ministry of welcoming at the church entrances. As Bishop Jim O'Brien, one of the auxiliary bishops, said in a video we produced on "Evangelization": "How can we share with one another if we do not know one another?"

The importance of the small community was highlighted by a journalist in the *Tablet*, Carolyn Butler. She wrote very personally when she said: "The small groups are the powerhouse of the future parish. They are replacing some of the more traditional groups and providing the parish with much-needed foot soldiers." She went on, "There has, in my own life, been a flowering of faith — all of which was triggered by the AYWL program." I suppose one of the measures of the effectiveness of the small groups is that they continue after our renewal program finishes. We have published RENEW's book *PrayerTime* to deal with this demand.

The SCCs help develop new leadership. We see new leaders in all areas of parish life. Not only have we encouraged and trained hundreds of small community leaders, but we also hope to encourage every parish to recognize the potential leadership among the young adults. Many parishes have young adult communities meeting in the five Seasons. One parish became aware of over a hundred young adults involved in small groups. We keep on challenging the parish leadership to ensure that people from this vital group are being encouraged in other areas of parish leadership. Already things are happening. I think of the young man who started off being opposed to the program, but out of loyalty to his priest and parish decided to join an SCC. Today he is the leader of the PCC. In East London (an area that struggles for leaders), a parish has had a "new springtime" in those volunteering to be trained to be eucharistic ministers and lectors.

One of the other fruits of the program is the thirst for knowledge that so many now have. SCCs report a growing desire from participants for a better appreciation of the faith which continues to change their lives. There will be a further development of Adult Formation Catechesis at parish level, and it could be done in small communities. There are regular twenty-four-hour retreats for priests that are appreciated by the forty to fifty priests who come. The program has also brought a new sense of the importance of evangelization as the mission of every baptized person. Well over a thousand people attended the "Share Your Faith" workshop. Many parishes have organized lay-led "come and see" missions. One of RENEW's leaflets called *Everyday Evangelizing for Everyday Catholics* was used by the National Evangelization Department and sent to every parish in the country. The team was heartened to read the report of the Lourdes pilgrimage, where the pilgrimage director wrote, "We had the largest number of pilgrims ever. Many came as a result of finding their faith renewed through the 'At Your Word, Lord' Program."

In the future fewer priests, population shifts, and increasing numbers of Catholics coming into the diocese from all over Europe and beyond will change the look of the diocese. The biggest change will be seen in how parishes operate. Collaboration is the key, and parishes, inspired by the small communities, are being encouraged to build collaboration into their structure. It's good to know that parish councils like the one in Pimlico decided to consult the laity by using the AYWL small faith-sharing groups as described in the July 3, 2004, issue of the *Tablet*.

However, I do believe that SCCs are doing something even deeper. Some liturgy groups now begin with a time of sharing faith. SCCs are hopefully making the parish remember that Christ is the head and heart of every activity. It was good to learn from articles in the *Tablet* how two parishes were moving towards this model of using faith sharing at the beginning of the meetings of the finance committee and claiming the AYWL small communities as the inspiration.

What will the future bring? Small communities are here to stay. Recently we had a brainstorming session about how the future will look, and many people asked for resources to help small communities continue. Maybe there won't be that many, but with good resources we hope to keep 10 to 15 percent of the parishioners in the AYWL program to continue in ongoing groups. Another hope is that the diocese would see the importance of developing a program of formation so that each and every Catholic can be well equipped in the faith.

Without small communities 99 percent of our parishes will have no new plan, no new vision. Parishes of the future must be evangelizing. We hope for the development of a strategy that would equip and renew every parish to become the natural place where faith is deepened and parishioners are enthused to reach out to others. The parish is the natural place for evangelization. I sense that the diocese will need to establish a structure to help parishes reform for this task. Maybe it will need its own Department of Evangelization. Whatever, it will certainly need to respond to the desire for parish formation as well as individual faith formation.

If the "At Your Word, Lord" program helps achieve this, it will show that when a parish struggles to develop itself into a community of small communities, then truly there is a new sense of being church. Wonderfully this new sense of being church is as old as the hills — or at least as old as the apostles! That is good enough for me.

Part Four

Africa

The growth and influence of Small Christian Communities (SCCs) throughout the continent of Africa are mixed. Doing solid research diocese by diocese seems more effective than country by country. In various parts of Africa SCCs have not taken root. But where they are flourishing, SCCs are an important pastoral strategy and even a new way of being a communitarian church. Some places are experiencing considerable growth. While the three chapters in this section document the pastoral priority of SCCs in East Africa (Kenya, Tanzania, and Uganda), SCCs are strong in southern Africa (South Africa, including the worldwide importance of the Lumko materials), West Africa (Ghana and Sierra Leone), and French-speaking Africa (Democratic Republic of the Congo — DRC).

This "new moment" includes the strengthening of parish-based and family-based SCCs that are faith-sharing/Bible-sharing groups based on the scriptures, especially the lectionary readings; building on the implementation of the 1994 Africa Synod and the ecclesiology of the "Church-as-Family"; SCCs that are an essential part of the restructuring process in both the parish and the diocese; and SCC members who reach out to the poor and marginated like people with HIV/AIDS.

The growing edges and challenges of SCCs in Africa include:

- Analyzing justice and peace issues with concrete follow-up on the local level. This encourages SCCs to be more than just prayer groups. SCCs can be a means of bridging the gap between the haves and the have-nots. They can be important catalysts of reconciliation and peace.

- SCCs as a model/example of equality where nobody is excluded. Pope John Paul II states in the *Apostolic Exhortation on the African Synod:* "Above all, these communities are to be committed to living Christ's love for everybody, a love which transcends the limits of natural solidarity of clans, tribes or other interest groups." The *Final Message* of the Synod states: "It is such communities that will provide the best means to fight against ethnocentrism within the church itself and, more widely, within our nations. These individual Churches-as-Families have the task of working to transform society."

- Attracting African youth. Our experience shows that young people want their own small communities where they can discuss and reflect on the issues that concern them.

- Attracting more African men.

- Helping priests to realize the value of SCCs.

- Being open to other models of SCCs that are not parish-based.

The pastoral model of SCC in Africa can help to revitalize parishes and communities in the West. African parish-based SCCs challenge dioceses in Europe and North America where the parish is not a "home" or "community" for people, but only a provider of services. The religious values in family and community can balance the growing secularization of Europe and North America.

14

Pastoral Involvement of Parish-Based SCCs in Dar es Salaam

Christopher Cieslikiewicz

A Series of "New Moments" in the SCCs in Dar es Salaam

"Listen to what the Spirit is saying to the churches" (Rev. 2:7). We see the phenomenon of Small Christian Communities (SCCs) in the Archdiocese of Dar es Salaam, Tanzania, as a great sign of the times and the powerful voice of the Holy Spirit. By the end of the year 2004 there were more than 2,300 SCCs in the 48 parishes of the archdiocese, and their number is ever increasing. There is not a parish without SCCs, and the number of SCCs ranges from 16 up to 117 in a given parish. Structurally it is a large network that truly transforms a parish into a communion of communities. In this way SCCs help the parish to really become a living community. Without any doubt these communities have become a powerful force of renewal of the parish structures, thanks to the pastoral decision in 1995 to make SCCs the pastoral priority in the Archdiocese of Dar es Salaam. However, this new moment goes beyond structures and touches also lay participation in the life of the local church. The implementation of the new Constitution of the National Lay Council in 1998 required that the election of lay leaders in parishes throughout Tanzania start at the level of SCCs and move upwards. This ensured that the parish council leaders would be chosen from those who were already leaders in their SCCs — thus, true representation from below. Such decisions gave full confidence to the faithful and opened new possibilities for the laity in the local church.

This "new moment" includes also a new time of the church at the beginning of this third millennium. The AMECEA (Association of Member Episcopal Conferences of Eastern Africa) bishops at their Fourteenth Plenary Assembly in Dar es Salaam in July 2002 renewed their confidence in

SCCs and gave to them an indispensable role in the new and deeper evangelization in Africa. While discussing the topic "Deeper Evangelization in the Third Millennium," the bishops confirmed SCCs as a key pastoral option. Why is this priority for SCCs so strongly sustained? First of all, in the age of the new evangelization these communities offer a good opportunity to deepen Christian faith, especially where evangelization often stops at the preparatory stage. Moreover, the pastoral agents become more and more convinced that SCCs can help the parish — often perceived only as a *service station* — to really become a living and missionary community. At the same time these communities, in an African continent wounded by conflicts and social injustice, prove to be helpful in the process of fighting against African ethnocentrism by promoting justice and peace.

The pastoral option for SCCs makes them not only an essential object of pastoral concern, but a main and indispensable subject of pastoral life in the parish. Since the parish-based SCCs make clear reference to the territorial principle that includes all the faithful of specific geographical territory in the community, the parish understands itself as one big community made up of a network of many SCCs covering the whole parish area. The advantage of such geographical communities lies in the fact that SCC members gather together around the Bible; they all are parishioners without social, economical, or interest distinctions; and they help the neighboring families to live in the spirit of fraternity and sense of spiritual togetherness.

Visiting St. Charles Lwanga SCC

At 5 p.m. on Sunday, fifteen enthusiastic laypeople gather at Peter Macha's home for the weekly meeting of their St. Charles Lwanga Small Christian Community in the Drive-in Estate of St. Peter's Parish in Dar es Salaam, Tanzania. The SCC members (mainly adults) report on their families' health and local problems in the neighborhood. Then they reflect on one of the Sunday scripture readings: the Epistle of St. James that stresses that faith without action is dead. The SCC members decide to help some of the homeless street children in their neighborhood. They plan a party for the youth in their SCC who will soon be confirmed. The meeting includes lively singing in Swahili with clapping and offering special prayer intentions for the sick in their parish and peace in Sudan. For these SCC members the maxim "We are the Church" is not just a slogan, but a way of life that truly applies to them.

St. Charles Lwanga SCC was officially launched on the feast of Epiphany in 1978 and is the oldest of the thirty-eight active SCCs in St. Peter's Parish, all fully involved in the local pastoral life. The bedrock of this community is the family. Married couples host, organize, and lead the group. Other people drift in and out; some only really turn up when there's a celebration and a meal. But it's the couples who provide the core stability of the SCC. Currently there are twenty-two families with a total membership of ninety-six, including children of all ages. St. Charles Lwanga is a model of a family-based and lectionary-based SCC. The parent SCC started a youth branch, a women's club, and children's activities. The SCC is twinned with the Fellowship Group, a small reflection group in the Anglican Rattery Church in South Hams in Devon, England.

Challenges for the Small Christian Communities in Dar es Salaam

"Closeness" and "Smallness"

In the modern society of Dar es Salaam, over and above their religious significance, SCCs have become social and psychological communities of support. However, it is important to give these communities proper guidelines so that the elements of faith will always prevail over other social and anthropological dimensions. The concepts of "closeness" and "smallness" in the organization of urban communities in Africa remain important and challenging. At present most of the communities in the archdiocese are too large and run the risk of becoming impersonal. Such SCCs cannot provide indispensable bonds of fellowship and a sense of belonging. There is an urgent need to help members of SCCs to be ready even to divide their community into smaller ones so as to facilitate in this way the creation of authentic fraternal relationships. Only in this way will SCCs become centers of authentic Christian communion where people gather to pray, listen to the Word of God, and celebrate the sacraments. Moreover, in such communities life can be celebrated and death can be mourned; people can get to know each other and can feel a sense of security.

Involving Men in the Community Meetings

SCCs, modeled on the church as a communion or as the family of God, cannot reach their genuine scope without full participation of all their members. As a family without a father is "wounded," so are SCCs without the presence of men. One of the greatest challenges for the communities today is to succeed in getting men involved in the life of SCCs. Parish pastoral councils need to understand that SCCs will not mirror the model of family if they are reduced to gatherings of only women and children. Such communities will rather reflect the modern problem of family dissolution. The fact that a small number of men participate in weekly community meetings cannot remain only a complaint, but must become an essential issue to be dealt with in the project of creating SCCs as authentic families of God. SCCs must ask themselves why some members do not participate voluntarily in the weekly meetings, and what is to be done in order to attract them to attend the weekly meetings and participate in the life of the community. It has been noticed that SCCs tend to turn easily into simple prayer groups where the presence of women prevail.

Youth SCCs

The church in Africa is a young church, when one considers that a great percentage of the population is sixteen to twenty-five years old. Nevertheless, only a small number of young people participate in the meetings of SCCs. One of the questions often asked today by pastors and members of the SCCs is how the Catholic Church in general, and SCCs in particular, can offer a greater appeal to young people, especially in large cities such as Dar es Salaam.

First of all, it ought to be remembered that it is precisely on the level of community that we can easily reach young people and recognize their problems, needs, and expectations. As a matter of fact, young people tend to take an active part in associations created specifically for them. In the case of young people, they have a tendency to gather together and to look for their peer groups where they feel at home. There is an urgent need to create Youth SCCs. Although some of the young people belong to other Catholic Youth Movements operating on the level of parish or diocese, Youth SCCs present the opportunity for uniting the young people of the neighborhood for the good of their area and of their community.

Young people must never be looked upon as a problem, but as a resource of great hope for the development and life of SCCs and the young church of Dar es Salaam. Pastoral planning that ignores their presence and role in evangelization is destined to fail. Young people represent a vital force and a source of initiatives which ought not to be neglected. Experiments done by some communities in this area might indicate a way for trying to realize this idea. Young people must be able to find their place in the SCCs' network.

How SCCs can reach out to the young people in urban settings like that of Dar es Salaam constitutes a real challenge for the new evangelization. It must be remembered that the young people initially gather for recreational purposes and social activities and only later become involved in service and prayer. The community should provide an environment in which an individual can find faith attractive and not something forcibly imposed. In such an informal place and time, the first proclamation of Gospel can be done through community or individual witness. The whole process is to lead the individual to the point of a personal decision for conversion — *metanoia* — and an encounter with Christ if faith is to have full meaning in one's life. Here is a very important moment of transition from the faith inherited from one's ancestors to a personal and freely accepted faith. Faith matures gradually when what has been known previously is finally understood in a new light, that of personal conviction — the characteristic so important for young people.

Social Involvement

The actual situation of Dar es Salaam presents a great social challenge because of the widespread injustice, the ever-widening gap between the rich and the poor, the violation of human rights by the powerful, corruption in high places, the poor administration of public funds, and the rapid spread of AIDS. This new social context challenges previous pastoral activities and requires active involvement in the broader problems of society not only on the part of the local church but also of the SCCs. The fact remains that up to now African SCCs have been more effective in prayer and mutual assistance among their members than in the sociopolitical life. We may ask how SCCs can become involved in propagating issues of justice and peace. As charity begins at home, so starting with the current and burning issues of the neighborhood — the promotion of justice, peace, harmony, and unity — can awaken the social conscience of SCCs. In community formation programs, it is necessary to do away with the dichotomy between the spiritual dimension and the secular world because the social concerns of the church and the promotion of justice and peace are constitutive dimensions of the mission of the church.

Mission

SCCs at the beginning of this third millennium have been challenged by the rapidly changing sociocultural context of Africa and in consequence the growing need of deeper evangelization. This kind of evangelization is needed to guarantee solid ongoing formation among the baptized Christians, taking care of the person in his or her totality and aiming at the transforming encounter with the living person of Christ. For a long time evangelization remained at an elementary stage and as a task of missionaries and local priests. Moreover, the faithful can no longer be considered on the first level of evangelization because many of them have already been born and brought up in the context of Christian families. Therefore, their faith needs to be reinforced and deepened. The faithful of the Archdiocese of Dar es Salaam are slowly growing in awareness that all are called to be missionaries and have their unique place in the life of the church. SCCs have a very important role to play in the work of evangelizing first of all by being missionaries to themselves by helping members in their spiritual growth, and at the same time by sharing with others their encounter with Jesus in the Word of God and in the Eucharist. Only in such a way will SCCs become more dynamic, vital, and missionary communities that enable their members to enter in living communion with Christ and feel responsible for the salvation of their brothers and sisters.

Ongoing Formation

The "new moment" for SCCs in Dar es Salaam must be considered in the context of a new and profound evangelization. Increasing numbers of communities demand solid and continuing formation. According to the majority opinion of SCC members, ongoing formation and religious education, especially in the field of Bible study, are urgently needed. Lack of such formation has been seen as one of the principal reasons for the fragility of people's faith and why they choose to leave the Catholic Church for other Christian denominations or sects. Lack of ongoing formation has also caused many Catholics to revert to their traditional religion as they search for answers to the questions of healing, witchcraft, and misfortune. Special attention must be paid also to family catechesis especially in this difficult time of cultural transition for the family. Social issues are still marginal in the life of the SCCs. There is an urgent need to stimulate social awareness in the growing situation of poverty and injustice. The place of youth in SCCs and the pastoral care they require calls for special attention. Such expectations call for a new approach to evangelization that goes beyond simple preparation for the sacraments and their celebration, as has been the case up to the present in the life and activities of most SCCs.

Ongoing formation must emphasize the mission outreach of SCCs and prepare SCC members to extend their activities to the larger community. SCCs will become more and more significant in human involvement if they will reflect on human problems in the light of the Gospel. At present the practice of Bible sharing often remains merely on the level of expressing one's ideas; little else is done in addition to this. SCCs in the archdiocese need to be involved in projects that will guide them towards some concrete prophetic actions. Such programs need to look for the root causes of common problems and their adequate solution. However, correct understanding of the Bible is essential; the leaders of SCCs need to be taught how to relate the Bible to the actual life lived by Christians today.

One of the key values that need to be taught and propagated is *sharing*. This notion is close to good African traditions and to one of the basic characteristics of genuine SCCs. The notion of sharing is very important for the spiritual life of the faithful that expresses itself in sharing the Word of God, faith experiences, ways of living, and joys and sorrows. But it also refers to material aspects such as helping community members in times of sickness, funerals, and celebrations of sacraments. Sharing is needed also in the fight against poverty, injustice, and corruption. This notion of sharing is strongly supported by the traditional value of solidarity but must be purified of its restrictions to one's clan or ethnic group.

The Story of SCCs Has Just Begun

The network of SCCs present in each parish in Dar es Salaam and throughout Eastern Africa gives to the parish a specific character and a new face. SCCs, as a true expression of communion and an instrument of evangelization, turn the parish into a living, fraternal, and apostolic community. These communities represent an attempt to get down to the very place where people live, know one another, love, suffer, work, and die. They are places where God is most truly God-with-us and the church effectively present to the faithful.

We should remember that through our work for the establishment and development of the SCCs we plant the seeds that one day will grow, or we water the seeds already planted, knowing that they hold future promises. Through our animating work for these communities, we provide yeast that will produce effects far beyond our expectations. We cannot do everything, but we can do something. Although our work might be incomplete and imperfect, it is a beginning, a step along the way, an opportunity for God's grace to enter in and do the rest. A new moment has come, and the story of SCCs has just begun.

15

SCC Diocesan Training Team Reaches Out in Uganda

*John Vianney Muweesi
and Emmanuel Mwerekande*

AMECEA (the Catholic Bishops of Eritrea, Ethiopia, Kenya, Malawi, Sudan, Tanzania, Uganda, and Zambia), as early as 1973, issued a declaration that Small Christian Communities (SCCs) "should be" a new way of being church in this part of Africa. Here SCCs are seen as essential to the very structure of the parish, the diocese, and the church as a whole. No wonder that Archbishop Raphael Ndingi Mwana'a Nzeki, archbishop of Nairobi, Kenya, says: "Small Christian Communities are a priority. When a parish is built with Small Christian Communities, there are no spectators, they are all players." This pastoral priority is highlighted in the section on "Living (or Vital) Christian Communities" in Pope John Paul II's *Apostolic Exhortation on the African Synod.*

The Diocese of Kiyinda-Mityana was created on November 21, 1981, and is located forty-seven miles west of Kampala, the capital city of Uganda. SCCs as the focal point of the life of Christians in the Diocese of Kiyinda-Mityana first emerged at the First Diocesan Synod in 1985. A decade later the importance of this SCC pastoral structure was reaffirmed when the Second Diocesan Synod (July–August 1997) invited the people of Kiyinda-Mityana to return to the faith and commitment of the very first Christian communities. Bishop Joseph Mukwaya, the former bishop of the Diocese of Kiyinda-Mityana, after thorough consultation with the whole diocese, declared SCCs as the priority pastoral program in the diocese. The diocese has 23 parishes, 532 subparishes or bush chapels, and 2,815 SCCs. Bukalagi Parish has the largest number, with 246 SCCs, and Kanyogoga Parish the least, with 42 SCCs. From the second synod in 1997 to date, there has been much development, so that every parish in the Diocese of Kiyinda-Mityana now has a model SCC.

Part of the implementation of this SCC priority pastoral program was the formation of an SCC Diocesan Training Team. Under the supervision of the diocesan pastoral coordinator's office, the SCC plan in the Diocese of Kiyinda-Mityana has training teams ranging from the diocese to the sub-parish level. Training programs with special emphasis on training of trainers and community leaders run throughout the year. Support and active involvement of the bishops (the ordinary and the retired bishop), clergy, religious, catechists, parish councils, and other pastoral agents have been vital for the implementation of this program.

Efforts have been made in the intervening years to encourage and stimulate the growth of these small communities, primarily through the training of lay leaders, then the religious and the clergy. The program began in earnest with the specific objectives of establishing a diocesan training team. This was slowly expanded to encompass five parishes: one from each of the then five deaneries of the diocese (today we have six). At this level the parish training teams were formed.

The Diocese of Kiyinda-Mityana, along with the Diocese of Arua, has become one of the model dioceses in Uganda in Small Christian Community development. The diocesan training team is receiving numerous invitations from other dioceses in the country to conduct awareness programs and to train trainers of these local churches.

Relevance of the Small Christian Community Priority

What is the relevance of Small Christian Community priority in the life of the local church of the Diocese of Kiyinda-Mityana?

- In the Diocese of Kiyinda-Mityana, like many areas of our central region, Small Christian Communities can be traced back to the time of the Martyrs of Uganda, St. Charles Lwanga and his companions (1885–1897), who are our Christian ancestors in the faith. The homes of many of them turned into centers where new converts to the Christian faith would meet regularly not only for instructions but also to read and share the Word of God. Small Christian Communities emerged from such centers. Lukka Baanabakintu's home at Mityana, where the cathedral church is located and the spot at which Noa Mawaggali was martyred, gave rise to the first Christian community in Ssingo

County. Many SCCs are named after the Uganda Martyrs, such as Noa Mawaggali, Matia Mulumba, and Achilles.

- In the Diocese of Kiyinda-Mityana Small Christian Communities have a unique and distinguishing name in the main local language Luganda: *Ebibiina by'abasseekimu*, which is derived from John 17:21. The name literally means "people bonded together by love" and signifies "the communities united by faith and love."

- After the Christian family, which is the smallest cell of the church, SCCs serve as the basic structure of the church. Every baptized Catholic is expected to belong to a given community in his or her locality. There is increased awareness among the faithful that "We as baptized are the Church," so we shouldn't be just observers but players. There is joy of the vision that our SCCs are the church at the very basic level.

- One cannot be validly elected to any key position of the subparish or parish pastoral council leadership if one is not among the SCC leaders. In other words, SCCs are represented on pastoral councils at all levels.

- Church pastoral and social services to the people, including administering of sacraments, are organized and channeled through SCCs.

- Small Christian Communities meet on a regular basis. The Second Diocesan Synod recommended that SCCs meet at least twice a month, to pray together, share the Word of God, and discuss matters concerning the community. Many people are becoming more enthusiastic in reading the Bible and cultivating a sense of "owning the Bible."

- Through love and charitable deeds, SCCs are becoming more responsive to the poorest of the poor and sick members of their communities. Today SCCs are playing a big role in pastoral care and support, especially to people with HIV/AIDS and their families.

- Increased involvement of the parishioners is serving to implement a number of church projects that in the past would have taken years to realize; for example, parishioners of Lwangiri Parish built a nice priests' house and contributed tremendously to the construction of their new magnificent parish church, which was built with a small grant. More permanent bush chapels are being built.

Outreach to the Archdiocese of Kampala
and the Dioceses of Kasana-Luwero and Lugazi

Due to the fact that this system of SCCs has brought significant changes in the life of Christians in the Diocese of Kiyinda-Mityana, it has attracted neighboring dioceses to ask our help. The Archdiocese of Kampala asked our diocesan training team to help them with the formation of SCCs (*Obubondo* in Luganda). The team met with catechists and lay leaders from all over the diocese for a one-day seminar in the Pope Paul VI Memorial Community Centre, Rubaga.

In March 2003 the director of catechists in the Archdiocese of Kampala, along with Msgr. Joseph Obunga, the secretary general of Uganda Episcopal Conference, invited our diocesan training team to train the trainers in the Archdiocese of Kampala. The first place was Namugongo Parish. The course was for catechists and lasted for one week. Other parishes that invited the training team were Nabbingo in May 2003, Ggoli in July 2003, Ndeeba in August 2003, and Bweyogerere in December 2003. Later we received invitations from Rubaga Cathedral Parish and Naggulu Parish. A training session for lay leaders took placed in Rubaga Deanery in August 2003.

In February 2003 Bishop Cyprian Kizito Lwanga of the Diocese of Kasana-Luwero invited our diocese to send a delegate to their First Diocesan Synod. One of our SCC Diocesan Training Team, Father Remigius Kintu, was nominated to represent the diocese. At the synod he talked about SCCs and the influence they have had in the Diocese of Kiyinda-Mityana. By the end of his talk everybody had been convinced to begin the formation of SCCs. After the synod the bishop of Kasana-Luwero asked our training team to help them to start the system of SCCs.

In March 2003 our diocesan training team went to Kasana-Luwero and met a group of three hundred people from all over the diocese, including the bishop, priests, religious, catechists, and lay leaders, for a five-day seminar. In May 2003 we went back to form a local diocesan group of trainers who have done excellent work in the formation of small communities in Kasana-Luwero.

In 2004 an outreach program started in the Diocese of Lugazi. At the National Meeting of Diocesan Pastoral Coordinators in 2004 we were invited to explain the SCC plan in the Diocese of Kiyinda-Mityana. We continue to spread our SCC light to others. There is still much to be done in order to keep the fire burning.

16

Small Communities Light Up Neighborhoods in Kisumu

Alphonce Omolo

In Kisumu, the third-largest urban center in Kenya, neighborhood communities started taking shape around 1977 when groups of the Bible apostolate began to establish themselves to further the teaching of the church and as mutual support. They later recognized that the best way to live faith in the world is through sharing and responding to day-to-day challenges. Signs of hope began to emerge among the underprivileged in Kisumu, who were already facing the challenges of urbanization and social change.

Urbanization and social change had pressured and disoriented the African traditional bonding experience in families and extended families. This hastened rural-urban migration, creating peri-urban areas that were not planned to accommodate such large numbers, resulting in insufficient services of sanitation as well as settlement and other problems. The resultant pressure from these spiritual, economic, social, health, environmental, and cultural challenges demanded a neighborhood response.

Popularizing the Neighborhood Work

These emerging neighborhood communities introduced the sharing of life experiences during Bible gatherings, which began to create solidarity and the realization of the commonality of the hardships that afflicted the communities. Community members started acting as counselors in one another's physical, mental, and spiritual life. This became the framework for one another to speak, listen, understand, and take action. They began to realize their own power to change their living conditions and popularized action-oriented Bible reflection. The most asked question in meetings became: "What must we do to practice the teaching of scripture in our life today?" To

110

bring Gospel values or basic human values into their daily activities, Christians began to identify resources that existed among them to enable them to respond practically. A transformation was taking place in their understanding of Christian discipleship and its outworking in proclamation, prayer, and service to those in need. These neighborhood communities became salt and light for one another. Visiting and praying for the sick and those facing hardships became a popular activity of these communities.

The Mill Hill Missionaries had taken up a challenge of urban apostolate during this period. Father Hans Burgman, a Dutch missionary priest, with the support of the archbishop of Kisumu, began to live with the communities in one of the shanty areas known as Pandipieri. This gave encouragement to a community that had already started to rediscover their own potential towards giving one another support and popularizing the works of God.

The Bible remained a key pillar as the community began to seek specialized training and skills relevant to their needs. At this moment an urban apostolate team came into being with a group of local community members and Burgman starting to live together in a model of the African family. Members of this team took up the animation of the community groups, which had developed a strong resemblance to Small Christian Communities (SCCs) and had started activities to support and enable neighborhood regeneration. The communities began to enlarge and include Christians who had stopped going to the church after being overwhelmed by their social challenges.

Most of these communities had barely enough to survive. They needed to meet their basic needs, especially good health and the education, feeding, and clothing of their children. To be able to attend to their needs in an effective way, the SCCs began to assign their members to various ministries (spiritual, pastoral, or social apostolate) to help the needy in their neighborhood. These activities were mainly intended to bring about a sign of hope to sick, dying, and malnourished children; abandoned and runaway children; alcoholics and other substance abusers; the disabled; and the emotionally depressed.

The Caring Neighborhood

In more recent years these caring community ministries have developed in response to the escalating spiritual and social challenges within the peri-urban neighborhood. Migration of people from their rural areas to search for work and livelihood in Kisumu City continues to rise steadily, thus exacerbating neighborhood problems. The number of SCCs has grown to forty-eight from its initial twelve small communities over a short period of time. The community needs have become increasingly sophisticated, demanding a greater community response. The escalation of new adversities such as HIV/AIDS could have not come at a worse time, making the local communities that much more vulnerable. Neighborhood ministries — such as prayer, visiting the sick, counseling the emotionally afflicted, helping the needy, and other services — have been transformed into projects so that they can provide functional and sustainable relief to the growing complexities of the community quandary. These projects were started to give a holistic approach to community challenges over and above pastoral ministry. In 2004 they included community-based health care, home-based health care, voluntary counseling and testing, nutrition clinics, treatment clinics, a community health information center, social counseling, child counseling, street visits, temporary shelter, recreation, and rehabilitation for street children. Other projects are a child rights center, nursery school, nonformal education, art school, girls' domestic training, a community ambulance, plastic waste recycling, textile production, a community savings and credit bank, a community study library, and training in carpentry, masonry, and computer graphics.

The SCCs remain at the heart of these projects. Each community has nominated and sponsored members for specific training to work in an area of immediate neighborhood concern. For instance, this might be as a counselor, community health worker, nutritionist, traditional birth attender, youth development representative, or child counselor. The training is carried out in the homes of the community members and sometimes in the community centers or prayer houses. The other members of the community volunteer to prepare meals during the training workshops. Those trained voluntarily and without any discrimination offer relevant services within their neighborhood. Their voluntary work covers the geographical area of their SCCs, and the services are offered to anyone in need, whether Catholic or not.

When the Neighborhood Church Congregates

Twelve SCCs form a neighborhood church community, and leaders' meetings are held once a month, starting with a visit of a priest in the evening. After a short prayer sick people in the community are visited and prayed for. During such visits the community identifies various neighborhood needs that call for the assistance of the relevant community members who have been trained in those areas. Each case is assessed and referred promptly.

The visit is followed by a leaders' meeting, prayer, and a meal ending at about 8 p.m. The discussion is centered around the community pastoral ministries, catechism for children and adults, infant baptism, weddings, and feedback and review on how the various voluntary service groups have performed. The following day at 7 a.m. the priest comes back to say a mass in the neighborhood and bless pregnant women and anoint infants in preparation for baptism, which is normally a big event in the community that involves over fifty infants and children. The community catechist prepares the infants' mothers by taking them through a series of sessions on how to undertake the spiritual upbringing of their children.

Every two years a house blessing activity takes place that helps to identify new Catholics in the neighborhood as well as taking a census on the number of faithful in each community. The community members organize and make a list of Christians from each community to be blessed that is handed over to the leader to help guide the priest during the blessings. During these house blessings interviews are done to find out if the family are all receiving Catholics, and if not, what steps are required to ensure that they all receive the Holy Communion. If they have not yet joined an SCC, they are encouraged to join in their area so as to ensure that they are in the picture and included in the spiritual activities. Each neighborhood community has a choir that sings during the community masses and other activities such as funerals and infant baptism. During funerals catechists always invite their colleagues from the neighboring community to support them in keeping vigil at night as well as during burials. In these activities the community marshals all its resources towards their fulfillment, and all the members participate actively to ensure success.

Conclusion

SCCs are dynamic in nature and take different shapes as they influence and are influenced by contemporary life. We have realized that SCCs that are not focused towards action easily disintegrate and the members become unresponsive; "faith without good deeds is useless" (James 2:14–23). The significance of the need to reflect on actions and act on reflections cannot be undervalued when establishing a thinking, feeling, and active church. We have seen SCCs lighting up neighborhoods where hope has been a thing of the past. We have seen many joining or returning to the church as a result. This has truly been an empowerment of the laity into being church for one another, in realizing the privileges of finding God in the neighbor-hood and in people's hearts and of neighborhoods transformed through inspiration of the Word of God. God's caring nature has been experienced through simple expression of hospitality, companionship, and spiritual en-couragement leading to the actualization of the original Small Christian Communities articulated in the Acts of the Apostles.

Part Five

Asia and Oceania

Throughout Asia Small Christian Communities (SCCs) and Basic Ecclesial Communities (BECs) are very much alive. In recent years BECs have spread to most Catholic dioceses and parishes in the Philippines. Coordination of SCCs throughout Asia was strengthened in 1993 through the founding of AsIPA (Asian Integral Pastoral Approach). In Asia SCCs/BECs are clearly identifiable and have a corporate strength as a result.

Other stories in this section come from Australia and New Zealand. In these very different societies the expressions of SCCs vary considerably. Home churches, action/reflection groups, and small clusters of homes or teams are three examples shared. There are many others. An issue of the *Communities Australia* newsletter included news of neighborhood communities; Eucharistic groups; a house of prayer; ecofeminist, family, and justice groups, and many others.

What is it that connects such diverse expressions of SCCs? One is a clear understanding that they are about the transformation of church and society. Another is methodology. It is not only the goal that connects, but also the manner of working towards that goal. Again in this section we see how many of the same resources are drawn on for the ongoing life and action of the communities. For this connectedness between communities within developing and developed countries, a strong rope is needed that can take the strain of building the future together. Asia/Oceania is a microcosm of the story told throughout this book.

Here we come full circle, back to where we began this journey. The new moment is not static; the journey continues. The SCCs are here to stay for the long haul. From the Philippines comes the conviction, "The BECs can renew the church and transform Philippine society." From the Canberra Home Church in Australia comes the reflection that "it is still dawning on us what a profound base we have from which to engage a wider world."

It is the future that beckons.

17

BECs in the Philippines

Renewing and Transforming

Amado Picardal

Visiting the Basic Ecclesial Community (BEC) of Sta. Teresita

The Basic Ecclesial Community (BEC) of Sta. Teresita is a neighborhood community in Buhangin, Davao City, Philippines, that is composed of over a hundred families. Most of the Catholic residents in Sta. Teresita are members with varying degrees of involvement. There is an active core group of around forty people, and the others participate in the BEC activities occasionally. The leaders of the BEC come from the core group.

The members of the BEC gather together in the community chapel every Saturday evening for the *Kasaulogan sa Pulong* (Celebration of the Word). Every Thursday evening, the leaders visit the homes of families within the neighborhood and conduct family evangelization sessions called the *Visita Familia* (Family Visit). They pray together with the members of the family and reflect on the Word of God. Recently, they also introduced the *Visita Silingan*, which brings together the families in a neighborhood for prayer and Bible reflection. An evangelization session was also conducted for the men in the community. Every two months the parish priest celebrates the Eucharist with the members of the community. The BEC of Sta. Teresita also sponsors a Sunday mass in the parish church once in a while. They prepare the liturgy and provide the readers and members of the offertory procession every time they sponsor a mass.

Besides praying and reflecting on the Word, the members of the BEC have pooled their resources and set up a Multipurpose Cooperative whose center is located beside the community chapel. The cooperative sells consumer goods to the members at cheaper prices. It also provides credit to the members who are in need of capital for their "income-generating projects" and livelihood program. The cooperative has organized a seminar on food processing. The cooperative sells the goods produced by the members. Whenever a member of the community is sick, the cooperative helps in paying for the medical expenses. The cooperative also provides mortuary aid for the members. Through the cooperative the members help one another address the problem of poverty.

How the BECs in the Philippines Are Developing at Present

The BECs are fully established in all the twenty-eight parishes in the Archdiocese of Davao. The BECs are recognized as the basic ecclesial unit in the archdiocese. The role of the BECs is enshrined in the archdiocesan decrees and statutes. All the diocesan commissions are geared towards helping form the BECs. The Archdiocesan Liturgical Commission produces the liturgical materials used by the BECs. The Archdiocesan Social Action Center provides assistance to parishes whose BECs want to set up livelihood projects and sustainable agriculture.

The BEC of Sta. Teresita is just one of the thirty-five BECs in the parish of the Mother of Perpetual Help, Davao City. The parish has become a network of BECs, and the leaders of the BECs meet monthly at the parish center. The parish priest and his pastoral workers coordinate these BECs.

The experience of the BEC of Sta. Teresita represents a glimpse of how the BECs in the Philippines are developing at present. The following observation may be made about the BECs in the Philippines: They are now proliferating in most of the dioceses in the Philippines and are part of the network of BECs in the parish. They are actively involved with the liturgical celebration and the process of evangelization, and they are becoming involved in social concerns.

The Proliferation of BECs in Most of the Dioceses and Parishes in the Philippines

The BECs are established in some sixty out of seventy-nine dioceses in the Philippines. A survey conducted in preparation for the BEC National Assembly in 2002 revealed that BECs can be found in 70 percent of the parishes in the country. The majority of the dioceses in the Philippines have made the building up of BECs a pastoral priority. In many dioceses, especially in southern Mindanao, the parishes are becoming a network of BECs, and these BECs are recognized as the basic ecclesial unit of the local church.

Many of the BEC programs that were launched over the last ten years were diocesan pastoral programs. These were not just the individual initiative of some parish priests or laypeople but a concerted effort of the whole diocese. This means that the building of the BECs has been accepted as the project of the local church — of the bishop, clergy, religious, and laypeople. The building of BECs has become part of the vision and mission of the dioceses and parishes. Many diocesan synods and pastoral assemblies have adopted the vision of the BECs.

It was not always like this. When the BECs first emerged in the 1970s and 1980s, there was widespread suspicion about BECs. Due to military propaganda, many bishops, priests, and laypeople suspected BECs to be leftist or subversive. Many would not accept or support the formation of BECs. It was very difficult for BECs to grow and expand. It was only after the fall of the Marcos dictatorship and the celebration of the Second Plenary Council of the Philippines (PCP II) in 1991 that the BECs became acceptable. The PCP II promoted the formation of BECs all over the country:

> Basic Ecclesial Communities under various names and forms — Basic Christian Communities, Small Christian Communities, covenant communities — must be vigorously promoted for the full living of the Christian vocation in both urban and rural areas.[1]

The PCP II further viewed the BECs as an expression of the vision of a renewed church:

> Our vision of the Church as communion, participation and mission, about the Church as priestly, prophetic and kingly people, and as Church of the poor — a Church that is renewed — is today finding expression in one ecclesial movement. This is the movement to foster Basic Ecclesial Communities in the Philippines.[2]

The formation of BECs is considered as part of the implementation of the renewal of the church promoted by Vatican II and PCP II.

Thus, the formation of BECs has the support of the hierarchy (Catholic Bishops' Conference of the Philippines, or CBCP) and the laity (Council of the Laity). In 2002 the national conference organized by the Council of the

---

1. *PCP II Acts and Decrees*, no. 109.
2. *PCP II*, no. 137.

Laity supported the formation of BECs and affirmed their role in the process of social transformation. In the early part of 2004, the CBCP established an episcopal body that would continue to promote and oversee the formation of BECs in the country. This body is headed by Archbishop Orlando Quevedo.

Active Involvement of BECs in Liturgical Activities and in the Evangelization Process

The BECs enable the ordinary laypeople to become actively involved in the liturgical activities in the local community and in the parish. The regular Bible service or Liturgy of the Word is presided by a lay liturgical leader. There is active participation among the members, especially in the sharing of their reflections on the readings and in the prayers of the faithful. The Eucharists that are celebrated in the BECs are well prepared and fully participated in, and there is a festive meal that follows after the mass. The BECs take turns in sponsoring the Sunday mass in the parish church.

The BECs are actively involved in evangelizing the families, the neighborhood clusters, and the wider community. There is a missionary dynamism among the core group and the leaders of the BECs. Some of them go house to house on weekdays for the *Visita Familia.* They pray and reflect on the Word of God with the family or household. Others facilitate neighborhood Bible reflection sessions, bringing neighbors to pray together and reflect on the Word of God and their life. Through the men's fellowship the men in the community are evangelized. The young people in the community are evangelized and organized through the Youth Fellowship. During summer vacation, the education committee organizes a catechetical program for the children. The education committee also conducts prebaptismal seminars for parents who want to have their children baptized. Evangelization seminars are conducted for the whole community.

Involvement of BECs in Socioeconomic, Political, and Environmental Concerns

While there are still many BECs that are primarily Bible-sharing groups and liturgical assemblies, an increasing number is involved in socioeconomic, political, and environmental concerns. The survey conducted for the BEC National Assembly in 2002 revealed that 40 percent of the BECs are engaged in social concerns, an increase from the 30 percent figure released by the National Secretariat for Social Action (NASSA) in the 1996 survey.

To address the problem of poverty, there are BECs engaged in livelihood and income-generating projects. Multipurpose cooperatives have also been set up for this purpose. In Lutopan, Cebu, for example, 80 percent of the BECs have also become economic production units. This helped solve the economic crisis precipitated by the closing of Atlas Mining Corporation in the area.

To respond to the problem of the spiral of violence and war, BECs have set up "zones of peace" and "sanctuaries of peace" that have resulted in the cessation of armed encounters in the area. The earliest ones were in Tulunan, North Cotabato, and in Cantomanyog, Negros. The latest ones are in Pikit, North Cotabato, where BECs are engaged in a dialogue for peace with Muslim communities in the area. There are BECs that have joined prayer rallies for peace and caravans for peace to pressure the warring parties to come up with a negotiated peace settlement. Some BECs, like those in San Fernando, Bukidnon, have successfully stopped the logging operations that used to destroy their environment. Some have been involved in reforestation projects and in cleanup and waste management.

BECs: A Dream or Reality?

The final statement of the BEC National Assembly sums up the new moment of the BECs in the Philippines. The following is an excerpt:

> Over the years, we have been actively involved in the building and strengthening of BECs. We came to this assembly asking ourselves the question: are BECs a dream or reality?
>
> As we shared our stories and discussed our concerns we have come to believe that BECs are indeed a dream that is becoming a reality. The building of BECs has become the pastoral thrust of many dioceses in the Philippines. Many parishes are becoming a network of BECs, a communion of communities. These BECs are becoming the basic unit of the local church and a way of life to many lay faithful. Through the BECs, the lay faithful respond to the call to discipleship and actively participate in the life and mission of the church. It is in the BECs that the church is truly the church of the poor.
>
> We know there is still much to be done. The promotion of BECs is a lifetime process. There are still many dioceses and parishes where BECs remain a dream. There were BECs that were established but are now

inactive. Many are struggling for survival. Others are crying for support from their pastors. There are many BECs that need to address the problems of poverty, injustice, traditional politics, armed conflict and the destruction of the environment. We also see the need to dialogue with the lay organizations, movements and associations and encourage their members to actively participate in the building up of BECs in their locality. The BECs have to participate in the inculturation process so that the church in the Philippines will truly become an inculturated church. They must also be involved in interreligious dialogue and interfaith dialogue especially in this time of intensive globalization. The family and youth within the BECs need to be reevangelized.

We believe that the BECs have a vital role in shaping the church of the future. The BECs can renew the church and transform Philippines society. We journey towards the future with confidence, fully aware of the presence of the risen Christ and empowered by the Holy Spirit.

18

Rerooting the Faith in Asia through SCCs

Cora Mateo

Many church workers often start their pastoral planning session asking questions like: How can we make the people more actively involved in mission, in parish activities, and in programs? How can we create an atmosphere where the people feel a sense of belonging in their parish? Some ask further questions with regard to the role of the church in the neighborhood, in interreligious dialogue, and joint efforts. For the bishops of Asia, one very challenging question is: "How can Christianity find its home in Asia?" During the Synod on Asia in 1998, the bishops recognized that Jesus, who was born in Asia, is least known among the Asians. Statistics show that the followers of the Christian faith are less than 3 percent of the Asian population. For many of the baptized Asian Catholics, their colleagues (even members of their families) still consider them as people who have acquired a "foreign" religion.

During the Second Vatican Council, the bishops of Asia met each other and became aware that they had few links with one another. Their desire to "foster among them solidarity and co-responsibility for the welfare of the church and society in Asia" began to crystallize when they met in Manila during the visit of Pope Paul VI in 1970. Here was the "awakening to see the face of Asia at long last coming to birth as a true community of peoples" (Asian Bishops Meeting, 1970) and this is considered the beginning of the Federation of Asian Bishops' Conferences (FABC), the only recognized body that can represent the particular Catholic churches in Asia. FABC has fourteen full members made up of Bishops' Conferences and ten associate members from countries where there are no Bishops' Conferences, like Hong Kong and Nepal. The highest deciding body is the Plenary Assembly that meets once every four years. There are seven offices to implement the recommendations of the Plenary Assembly: Office of Human

Development, Office of Ecumenical and Inter-Religious Affairs, Office of Education and Student Chaplaincy, Office of Social Communication, Office of Evangelization, Office of Laity, and Office of Theological Concerns.

Faith Made Alive in Human Situations

During the fifth FABC Plenary Assembly in Bandung, Indonesia, in 1990, the bishops talked about the challenges to evangelization in Asia in the next millennium and the response to those challenges. The response is not so much "talking about the church" or organizing actions or projects, or establishing institutions, but a response that comes from the core, from *being* church. They then expressed the renewal towards a "New Way of Being Church," a church that is participatory, a communion of communities, a prophetic church, and a church in dialogue. Before that Plenary Assembly ended, the bishops expressed the need to have a formation program that would bring about this renewal, and the Office of Laity of FABC was designated to take this as its special task.

The first international formation workshop took place in Taiwan for the Chinese-speaking countries. It was followed by an English International workshop in Hua Hin, Thailand. Both were in 1991. The materials used were those from Lumko Institute in South Africa. We had more workshops in Taiwan, Malaysia, the Philippines, and India. In 1993 those who were involved in reflecting about this experience came together to share their evaluation. Twelve persons from six countries gathered to discuss their responses to this question: "What method and what materials can we use so that the Asian who uses them will feel it is for him/her, and that it is applicable to their needs and where their life situations can fit in easily?" Looking at the Asian situation, contextualizing the method was among our main concerns. It was then that the acronym AsIPA was coined: "Asian Integral Pastoral Approach."

"Asian" means it is reflecting the life situations and cultures of Asia. It is a formation process that can dialogue with the poor and can integrate the multireligious context and the socioeconomic progress that is taking place in Asia. It aims to give an Asian response to the Gospel challenge and implement the vision of the Asian bishops.

"Integral" refers to maintaining a balance of the so-called secular and sacred, of the individual and the communitarian, of the hierarchy and the coresponsibility of the laity, and of theory and practice. Faith is then made alive in human situations, with its different dimensions.

"Pastoral" gives special focus on the role of laypeople in carrying out the mission, to realize the dream of Jesus by becoming actively involved. It deals with methods to awaken that coresponsibility of the laity and at the same time bring about joint efforts where clergy and laity can work together. It offers ways for a priest to learn how to work in a team and acquire an enabling type of leadership.

"Approach" refers to the specific process of involving the people in searching together for the answer, as adults. It is a very participative learning where the method itself becomes the message. It is Christ-centered and at the same time builds community that does not live for itself but carries out the mission in the world. It raises awareness about the situation where the message of the Gospel is to be lived and brings about a communitarian response to the needs of the neighborhood and the wider society.

Training for a Participatory Church

The basic AsIPA text for training sessions in Small Christian Communities (SCCs) is a booklet that has a code (a story, a poem, a song, or a picture that points to the reality without directly touching it; it is presented to raise awareness without embarrassing any of the participants). It also includes a related biblical text, church teachings when needed, and guide questions for group reflection. It contains a Supplement to complete the answers given by the participants and a Summary. The booklet is a guide. With minimum training, the facilitator can run the sessions. There are four series, as follows:

- A Series: Topics related to Gospel-sharing methods. This series introduces different methods, starting with the Seven Step Method, and reinforces the spirituality behind each step as follows.

- B Series: Topics related to starting and maintaining Small Christian Communities.

  This series gives the theology that supports becoming a faith community and gives the basis for SCCs, the four marks, and the skills to start and maintain them. It also includes leadership topics.

- C Series: Topics to reflect on the vision of a participatory church. The vision is presented as a whole and can be reflected on in parts and it gives the theological background as well as the supporting church teachings. This series is basic to have a good grasp of the vision of what it means to be church as expressed in the Vatican II documents, where the gifts of the Spirit to all are recognized and put to use.

- D Series: Topics for the training of Parish Teams. A team always conducts the training sessions, and this series helps the team give awareness
  programs and training on how to become a team and on an enabling
  leadership.

There are also Library Topics, which list other topics that deal with specific issues not exactly belonging to any of the above series, parenting,
family life, socioeconomic questions, love and service, women's issues, and
interreligious dialogue.

Very essential to SCCs is the coming together to do Gospel sharing, using the Seven Step Method started by the Lumko Institute. Gospel sharing
nurtures the spirituality of SCCs and the vision of a participatory church. It
is the starting point for SCCs and maintains the faith-filled response to the
challenges to be instruments of transformation. In Gospel sharing, SCCs
prepare for Sunday liturgy and reflect on the Gospel message for each SCC
individually and as a community. Putting this message into practice in their
neighborhood brings the Gospel alive in the very culture and milieu where
the people are. Like all AsIPA texts, the A series explains each step in a simplified manner so that a facilitator with minimal training can feel confident
to run the session.

During the pastoral visit of one bishop in Sri Lanka who joined the Gospel sharing of an SCC and listened to the sharing on how the Word of God
touched the members, he exclaimed, "This is the way to make the church
alive!" The Gospel sharing is the basic prayer for SCCs, and in its very
process faith is lived out and becomes rooted.

Aside from the Seven Step Method, we also use Gospel Mirror, Look-
Listen-Love, and Group Response methods. Gospel-sharing methods and all
the AsIPA texts are translated into more than twenty Asian languages.

A Process That Reflects the Face of Jesus

In September 2003, the third General Assembly of Trainers was held in
Korea. Thirteen Asian countries, along with Papua New Guinea and Germany, participated with the theme: "SCCs/BECs: Empowering People to
Serve." The 123 participants, including bishops, priests, lay leaders, and religious, brought along their reflection on how much each national or diocesan
team has achieved since the previous General Assembly in 2000. They also
brought copies of their latest locally produced materials that responded to

specific needs. The first part of the General Assembly was an evaluative session on how much of the vision has been implemented, followed by the subtopics on family, leadership, ministry, and spirituality.

The General Assembly is a very enriching time for sharing pastoral approaches to make the method more effective in varying contexts. Context creates an awareness that brings about the particular expression of the faith response to life. The General Assembly offers a valuable venue for that exchange. It is also a time to renew acquaintances and to offer mutual support. The added exposure/immersion program to the different SCCs in Korea was a source of firsthand learning.

The AsIPA Desk continues to be a section under the FABC Office of Laity, based in Taipei, Taiwan, and it functions with an AsIPA Resource Team (ART), presently with seven members from India (two), Korea, the Philippines, Singapore, Sri Lanka, and Taiwan. The main tasks of ART include facilitating the training of trainers in different countries, designing the texts, following up the process and doing the final editing, and maintaining effective networking among national and diocesan teams.

The composition of the team gives a wide range of pastoral experiences in different Asian countries and on how the method is being used. Each country where the method is applied has a team that prepares local modules specific to their cultural backgrounds and situation of the people. The ART members gather the modules and choose those that are applicable for common use, revise them, and follow up with trial and revision until the final edition comes out. The trial use period is itself a rerooting process as trainers or facilitators attentively listen to the responses of the participants and note where the topic can be misinterpreted or does not achieve the objectives of the session in a particular context. The final edition comes out in the form of statements and guide questions that can be used in any SCC and yet is able to elicit a contextualized response to the topic.

During the fifth ART meeting, in February 2004, the members finalized the draft for trial use of seventeen new modules on "SCCs and Evangelization," "SCCs and the Sacraments," "SCCs and Pastoral Visitation," "SCCs and Associations," "Deepening on the Vision," "Leadership in SCCs," and "Spirituality."

With the AsIPA method, we have a tool so there can be a gradual process of making the Christian faith alive in the family and in the neighborhood, taking root in the very culture the people are living in now. It is not the Asian culture we read about in the media and cultural history books, but the present culture that the people construct as they live, struggle, and celebrate, as they become living witnesses among their neighbors of different religious beliefs, with whom they engage in joint efforts to improve their lives and surroundings. In simple ways, AsIPA aims to contribute in small but constant steps to bring about the Asian face of Jesus, and at the same time, allow a process so Jesus can be reflected in the faces of Asian Christians.

19

Project Linkup

A Model of Adult Initiation in Australia

Irene Wilson

Welcome to Project Linkup! Concluding his detailed account of the history of the Adult Catechumenate, Paul Turner remarks on the changes wrought by the experience of travel, not only in the scenery but in the traveler as well:

> And not just in the traveller but in all those the traveller touches. When the catechumenate rose in the post–Vatican II Church, we were all changed because it invited us into evangelization, catechesis, worship, community and service in a transformed way.[1]

Many of us who have been privileged companions on the Adult Catechumenal journey will readily identify with the accuracy of Turner's observation, recalling how participation enabled our own dying and rising, and inspired and energized us for the furthering of God's reign in our world. Recognizing the enormous potential for grassroots renewal here, Vatican II's Order of Adult Initiation emphasized the role of the local community, and early proponents of the revised catechumenate, Christiane Brusselmans, Father Jim Dunning, and others, strenuously promoted the new order as a way of invigorating entire parishes! Today, however, thirty years on, too many parishioners still remain peripheral to the sublime journey taking place in their midst, with little awareness of, or involvement in, the Rite of Christian Initiation of Adults (RCIA) in their faith community.

Of even greater concern with the present activating of the RCIA is the loss of new members, a subject that people try to avoid mentioning. Too often, after Mystagogia (the reflective period between Easter and Pentecost), new members often find themselves missing the intimate experience of community and close relationships encountered with the RCIA Team during

---

1. Paul Turner, *The Hallelujah Highway: A History of the Catechumenate* (Chicago: Liturgy Training Publications, 2000).

formation, and floundering with the relative anonymity of ordinary parish life. Sadly, too many of them decide that the cost of belonging far outweighs the benefits.

The good news, however, is that there *is* a better way of implementing the catechumenal process — better for new Catholics and better for "old" ones as well! In the Catholic Parish of St. Thomas More, Belgrave, on the outskirts of the Archdiocese of Melbourne, pastoral issues prompted the RCIA team to locate the journey of new members into the welcoming embrace of Small Church Communities (SCCs) dotted around the parish. With the linking of the RCIA and SCCs at Belgrave the initiation of adult catechumens really does take place now, step by step, in the midst of the community of the faithful. Since its inception at Belgrave the paradigm has begun flowering in other parishes in the West. However, in the African church this integrated model has been thriving for a number of years.

Initiated in 2002, Project Linkup is about publicizing the Belgrave model. The Linkup team, having been closely aligned with its evolution and implementation, are convinced of the benefits both for the catechumenate and the local community in every parish. Through the dissemination of information on its Web site and the linking of a "friends" network, Project Linkup opens up the opportunity of stimulating similar developments in other Australian parishes and of supporting the conversation in countries around the world. There is no doubt that as part of this "new moment" many Small Faith Communities are beginning to recognize the catechumenal possibilities for SCCs.

In another Australian parish, that of Douglas Park, in the Diocese of Woolongong, a small faith-sharing group has, for the first time, just accompanied three candidates to Easter initiation. There are also enquirers in the group who have begun the journey but are not yet ready to take the next step. The members of the group are clear about the advantages that this experience has yielded for them in providing rich opportunities for personal growth and formation. Following the North American Forum for the Catechumenate's Institute in the Diocese of Oakland in 2003, called "Imaging Initiation in Small Christian Communities," Small Faith Communities and the RCIA are beginning to come together. At Spirit of Christ Parish in Arvada, Colorado, four catechumens in four different SCCs have made the journey to Easter and beyond. Coordinator Barbara Howard says that it has been "a blessing on both ends." It seems clear that these newly involved SCCs are being touched and transformed by these travelers in their midst, to recall Paul Turner's earlier observation. In the Diocese of Oakland both the RCIA and SCCs have found that they have much in common. Parish facilitators are being encouraged to find ways of promoting a teamwork approach in the initiation process.

With successive presentations, it seems certain that the institute will continue to awaken the vision and possibilities for this unfolding paradigm of Christian Initiation around the United States. You can read more about these and similar stories on the Project Linkup Web site at *http://home.vicnet.net .au/~rciascc.*

Caring for New Catholics

For the Belgrave parish, loosening the reins on the old model and bringing the local community into greater involvement occurred gradually. Up until 1990 the RCIA team endeavored to be all things to all catechumens. It was nothing short of an endurance feat, given the geographical vastness of the locale with its six mass centers. There was also the added temptation to process candidates within a particular time frame to make the program more manageable. In 1991, in order to share the work load, the team under Cheryl Graham's leadership fostered a neighborhood group around each enquirer. These groups gathered in a home setting on alternate weeks to break open the Word of God and to share their lives (there were no SCCs in existence yet). This invitation involved a degree of risk. What if the neighborhood group gave the enquirer a different message? A different vision of church? Out-of-date teachings? But the risk was considered worth taking. Indeed it was a significant step. Catechumens/candidates now felt that they were able to develop closer bonds with the wider parish community, and parish members who became involved no longer felt on the margins.

Graham's later research — on the retention rates of new members and the sociological factors associated with retention or cessation of involvement — confirmed the soundness of this decision. While her project was restricted to the findings in one large Australian parish, her conclusions must provide a starting point for discussion in all Catholic parishes concerned with the care of new Catholics. Indeed it is relevant for any faith community tasked with the care of new members.

Her research showed that significant factors associated with retention included the number and intensity of close ties that new members had with people in their parish, and the degree to which people in their lives were Catholic and supported their concern. She writes:

But probably the most at risk people were those who joined the church "on their own" for some reason — widowed, divorced, not yet married, married but unsupported by their partner. Many of those who were on their own also fell into the category of those who felt they did not fit in.[2]

She reiterates that indifference and opposition from significant people in the new members' lives, especially family members, predisposes them to cease involvement unless significant close relationships with parish members have been formed to counter this:

> My deduction from this observation is that it is not enough for cat-echumens to form close ties with the RCIA team members. After Mystagogia team members have to turn their attention to a new set of enquirers. By the time Mystagogia ends, new Catholics need to have developed several close relationships with community members other than RCIA team members.[3]

Caring for "Old" Catholics as Well

In time SCCs were established in the parish, and steps were taken to situate the RCIA journey squarely into this setting. In recapturing the early church fathers' perception of the faith community as a nourishing and protective womblike environment, the catechumenal journey was once again likened to the process of gestation and birth; precatechumenate corresponded to conception, catechumenate to gestation, baptism to the process of watery birth itself, and Mystagogia to neonatal care. In this long ago and once again story the new Christian would grow in utero and prepare gradually to come into the world.

The way in which the Belgrave parish has chosen to link the two programs has already been the subject of a number of articles (a synopsis is available on the Web site). It is important to emphasize that this particular arrangement is just one way of proceeding, the way that best suits the Belgrave parish. It is also relevant to add that if the enquirer is to begin forging important relationships with the wider community, the journey together should begin with the period of precatechumenate, that first sharing of stories — both personal and scriptural.

---

2. Cheryl Graham, "Caring for New Catholics," *Australasian Catholic Record*, January 1998, 22.
3. Ibid., 24.

So what's in the Linkup model for "old" Catholics — the SCCs who accompany new Catholics all the way to initiation and beyond? At the conclusion of the inaugural Belgrave RCIA/SCC cycle, using criteria drawn from the *NAFSCC Report 1994*, the team, candidates Ron and Jan, and the SCC who had participated were invited to explore aspects of the experience: How had it been for them? What was the impact of the experience on their ecclesial identity as a group? Here is a small sample of the SCC's responses:

- While admitting to feelings of apprehension at first, and wondering earnestly if they were "good enough" or "qualified enough" for the task, once the journey got under way, SCC members found it "was wonderful to be openly supporting adults who made an enormous turn-around." They began to ponder their own Catholicism and to appreciate it anew.

- On the advantages for Ron and Jan in journeying with an SCC, they said, "They see us as warts and all but still Catholic." It would also open them up to a network, "We could introduce them at church."

- Commenting on their own involvement up-front during the liturgical rites, some described being "moved," "touched," "empowered." "It says, 'I'm committed.'" One member was moved by the scrutinies and the dismissals. It prompted his reflection on where he was and where he wanted to go.

- The experience seemed to bond them more intimately as a group. Importantly, it also bonded them with the larger community as they stood with Ron and Jan. "We became aware of the Belgrave community's needs." The journey, they said, was not silent, passive involvement but "open and witnessing. It was a powerful event — we were directly involved." They spoke for all of us who had helped bring to birth this awesome new paradigm when they said, "The Miracle chose us!"

- For Ron and Jan it was "an opportunity to see real church in action."

This SCC has journeyed with other candidates since then, and other SCCs in the parish are quite emphatic that the experience matured and consolidated them. In all cases the new members have become committed SCC members. All of them are passionately involved in a host of activities that contribute in building up the life of the wider parish community.

Small Christian Communities and the New Moment

Change is all about us. In a world bombarding us with images, change, and burgeoning new life, and in a church wrestling with ways in which to be a relevant presence in the prevailing postmodern condition, SCCs, where the world and the Word of God are juxtaposed, are a vital way of making sense of this transition, of negotiating our way through, and of discerning with the openness that only faith brings what the God of Life is up to. Australian sociologist and theologian Gary Bouma states:

> Change is the order of the day. God's utter reliability is discerned in various ways as people of faith continue to live, to identify in the noise of the change the still small voice of calm, the balm of Gilead, and the presence of the kingdom. God's reliability is not found in distance, objectivity, impassibility, but in being with, part of, vulnerable and with us. This is part of the transition from the age of reason to the age of passion.[4]

In this time of change the God of Life who shares our journey has enabled us to retrieve from the wealth of our tradition the jewels of the catechumenate and small faith-sharing communities. Now at last we are invited to rediscover their ability to work together, to link them for their mutual enhancement, and to carry out, with greater fidelity, the directive of the revised rite.

After all, the business of forming new Christians does not belong merely *to* the baptized community, but *in* the baptized community!

---

4. Gary Bouma, "Mapping Religious Contours," *Religion in an Age of Change* (Kew, Australia: Christian Research Association, 1999).

20

Action and Reflection
at the Heart of SCCs in Australia

John Dacey

Many people today are yearning for their faith to be relevant to the everyday realities of their lives. One of the defining characteristics of many Small Christian Communities (SCCs) is that they give priority to connecting faith to life. The way they do this is variously referred to as "see-judge-act," "review of life," "action-reflection," "theological reflection," or the "pastoral cycle/circle."

It was this see-judge-act process that was at the origins of Australian SCCs. The origins of the process itself lie in France in the 1890s with a movement called *Le Sillon* (The Furrow), which influenced Cardinal Joseph Cardijn, the founder of the Young Christian Workers movement (YCW). It is through YCW that the process was first introduced into Australia, and Australian SCCs have this action-reflection process at their heart. This chapter presents stories of SCCs that use, either implicitly or explicitly, some form of this action-reflection process to facilitate their life. These stories display insights that are to be gained with relative ease when people reflect theologically on the everyday issues facing them.

There are many ways to express the action-reflection process. In this chapter we describe a contemporary process that is used in many Australian SCCs and which is summarized from *The Art of Theological Reflection* by Patricia O'Connell Killen and John de Beer.[1]

Process

See: Naming and analyzing our experience

Think of a recent incident or encounter. Tell the story of what happened (without judgment). Write down the basic facts. Try to relive it now;

---

1. Patricia O'Connell Killen and John de Beer, *The Art of Theological Reflection* (New York: Crossroad, 1994).

bring it to the present. Where are you? Who else is there? What are you hearing/seeing/doing? What's really happening here?

Notice the feelings that accompany the story. Name your feelings precisely. Take a deep breath and notice your physical sensations — feelings like apprehension, concern, disappointment, betrayal, guilt, fear, which your body can reveal to you. Identify one or two central feelings that you experience most strongly in the situation.

Let those feelings evoke images for you. List images until one comes that best captures the feelings. The image is a step towards gaining insight. Images can be visual or tactile or evoke any of the other senses, e.g., *can't see the forest for the trees; trapped in a room with the fire alarm blaring; on a roller coaster ride*. In moving towards insight, an image that captures the central feeling of an experience is the clue to its meaning.

Sit with the image and explore it gently. Consider and question it in ways that open up new perspectives:

What is existence like from within the image?

What is broken or negative in the image?

What is life-giving or positive in the image?

What is present or implied in the image that might improve the situation?

Judge: Identify elements from Christian faith and let them speak to our experience

What stories/images/principles from Christian (or other) faiths does your image evoke? Brainstorm a list. Pick one of the pieces of tradition (story/ image/principle) that grabs your attention. Explore it using the same questions that you used to explore the image of your experience, for example, "Consider what existence is like from within the image," etc.

Begin a conversation between the meanings in the "experience-image" and the meanings in the "tradition-image" using the two sets of responses from the questions above:

What are the similarities?

What are the differences?

Is there a theme coming through both of them?

Is there a tension between them that is enlightening?

What emerges for you in this conversation? What insights or questions does it raise for you?

Does anything out of this conversation shed light or provide a new angle or vision on your thoughts, feelings, and actions in the original situation? On how you think or feel about it now?

Act: Apply — Action arising from the insights and meaning in the situation

Think about what you want to change in your own way of working and approaching this situation or life in general by asking:

Are you being called to some concrete action?

The next time you are in a similar situation, what do you want to remember or do differently?

How will you take what you have learned into your daily living? Write down your intention.

Are you ready to take concrete steps to put this intention into practice? What specifically will you do?

When will you begin?

Who will support you?

Who else will you involve?

Some Stories

The following two stories illustrate this process. They are individual reflections, albeit in a group setting, by young adult members of the Young Christian Workers in Granville, Sydney.

SEE: My coworker resigned unexpectedly when I thought she was happy in her work. I felt hurt, betrayed, deceived, confused, even used. The image those feelings evoked is of being halfway through building a house and becoming stuck on a problem. From within this image, life is a lot of hard work — hot and sweaty. On the downside there is wastage of time and resources, and there is the loneliness of the builder. On the positive side there is the vision of the finished house and the knowledge that I can move forward because I've done it before.

JUDGE: My "faith image" that is evoked by this experience is that of Nelson Mandela in jail. Within that image exists determination, belief in justice, and a better way; trust in the capacities of others and the process itself. Of course the downside is the separation from family and friends and being physically broken/worn down. Positively there is the solidarity of people all around the globe who are taking action to change the situation. God is present with the prisoners, the poor, the oppressed. God's Spirit is alive in the movement of people around Mandela.

ACT: This reflection has encouraged me to "rebuild" the project by working closely with coworkers and contacts in the local area and having more personal contact with them. In the short term I'm going to establish a team of people to meet with, and in the long term I'm going to entrust the continuity of the project to the team. (Joe Magri)

SEE: I recently got a part-time job after time out of work due to an injury. I feel satisfied and challenged yet pressured and anxious too. The image I have is of standing on the edge of a cliff. Within that image there is a lot of uncertainty — I don't know what will happen now. Will I fall/fail or won't I fall/fail? It's a moment of truth. On the plus side it is a chance to move forward and go onto something new. On the negative side there's the doubt about whether I'll be OK in the job.

JUDGE: The "faith image" that this evokes is of Jesus setting people free from all sorts of imprisonment. Jesus knows it is the right thing to do, but it is difficult and fraught with danger. He is happy and confident in his decision but at the same time unsure and perhaps afraid of the consequences. He is putting everything on the line and risking his own loss of freedom; loss of life. But it is done in the knowledge that it's the right thing. God is giving him strength to go into the unknown.

ACT: As a result of this reflection I'm going to keep my thoughts realistic and learn my job well at the same time as managing my injury. My short-term goal is to keep my job, and my long-term goal is to reach my full potential in the job. I'm going to involve my friends and my rehabilitation support person in achieving this. And I'm going to keep a diary of my thoughts and acknowledge what I'm doing is a process and I shouldn't expect instant results. (Cris Jackson)

The more often this process is used, the easier it becomes. The process draws on the natural human capacity to reflect on experience, making what is often unconscious and unguided, conscious and connected to the rich source of the divine which is our faith. Other expressions of action-reflection emphasize the cyclical nature of the process — every action leads to another reflection — and some have four while others have five basic steps. Some expressions emphasize social analysis as part of the "see," while others emphasize biblical exposition as part of the "judge," and still others emphasize the role of planning as part of the "act."

The following story tells how an SCC in Australia used theological reflection to deal with the grief of a number of its members:

> Within a very short space of time, several people in our community suffered the death of a parent. The resulting grief needed to be not only acknowledged but processed in some way in our group setting. We used a reflection process to give each person an opportunity to tell their story about the death of their parent. As this was done we noted the main "feeling" elements of each story on a large piece of paper.
>
> After the last story we chose what we saw as the most important element to come out of the stories. We then asked a question about what this said to us about how we must live. We continued in this way — choosing an image, selecting a relevant piece of scripture, looking at our culture — in each case asking what does this image/scripture/culture tell us about dying? What does it say about how we must live?
>
> We ended with several minutes of reflective silence during which each person wrote a short prayer about life or death, which was then shared during a beautiful and emotional prayer time. By theologising the group experience in this way, we did far more than give our people a chance to share their grief. We created a context in which this grief could be integrated into our faith. It was an emotional, beautiful and healing evening. (Lorraine McCarthy)

Another narrative example is about dealing with grief, but this time the deaths are distant and on a large scale:

> Our group met just two days after the September 11, 2001, terrorist attacks in the United States. We were numb with shock and fear as we recounted our experiences of the last forty-eight hours. It quickly became evident that our planned scripture reflection for the evening needed to be abandoned in favor of a reflection on this enormous experience.

We started by allowing everyone to briefly recount where they were and how they felt as they heard the unfolding events. The main "feeling" elements were noted on a large piece of paper. We then agreed on an image — and examined our reactions and fears in the light of this. We did similarly with scripture and with some newspaper articles. We asked ourselves, what are we being called to as Christians in these times?

Our group felt a strong aversion to the "revenge" which was being called for, even in those early times; we felt for Muslim people, we felt sympathy for the many thousands of grieving people. Our night ended in prayer — for both sides of the conflict — something which certainly would not have been possible at the start of the evening. It was the first time I had felt peaceful since hearing of the attacks. (Lorraine McCarthy)

The last story comes from an SCC in South Australia that has been together since 1983. Several of the foundation members continue as members of the group.

The meeting structure has certainly changed since we first formed in 1983. At that time it was a formal structure with an agenda. It began with prayer, followed by a Gospel discussion, business, finance and finally an activity or sharing. The sharing involved the use of the see-judge-act method. Not all current members are familiar with the see-judge-act process, but those of us who are feel that we use it implicitly in our lives and in our meetings.

We feel that belonging to our group has encouraged us to think and be involved in justice and community actions. It has given us the support of others in dealing with issues that affected us individually and as a community. We use the see-judge-act method during the sharing by helping each other to look at personal issues, reflect on what is happening and use this reflection to decide on an appropriate action if that is required. At the next meeting we often follow up on this issue with the person concerned. We have learned leadership skills from each other and have benefited from the unique gifts that belong to each of us.

Two recent group actions have been to go on the peace march against the continuing war and occupation of Iraq, and to lobby for high-chairs in a local cafe. As a group, we also support the Venny Girls Group, an outreach of the Venny Playground in the Melbourne suburb of Kensington. The girls in the group are aged 10–12 years and live in the local high-rise public housing units. (Lyn van der Borch, Kingswood, South Australia)

While action-reflection is not new to SCCs, it is not often explicitly spoken of and possibly remains, as someone has said, "the best-kept secret of the church." Its use, however, is indispensable. As Killen says: "Without a critical and conscious theological reflection on the part of the adults in the church, the church's faithfulness to the Gospel and authentic witness to that Gospel in the world diminishes, and can become counter productive of Gospel values."[2]

---

2. Killen and de Beer, *The Art of Theological Reflection,* 139.

21

Canberra Home Church Cluster

Richard Begbie

In the late 1960s it was unclear what "home churches" were. Few regular churchgoers had even heard of the concept. To a tiny group gathered in 1967 in a Canberra, Australia, suburban home, 2005 would have been a remote dream. Yet the home churches now clustered in and around the Australian national capital began with that group, and are still evolving and growing in this new century.

The home church vision was kindled by several factors. Small-group experience at that time was opening new doors of honesty, relevance, and mutuality for many Christians. All of the core reasons for meeting — praise, prayer, teaching and understanding, mutual service — took on fresh life in these groups, and any reading of the New Testament revealed close similarities with the early churches. Many of us found this way of doing church more fulfilling, more stimulating, and more pertinent to our world. We still do.

There are currently seven such groups in the Canberra cluster. The term "cluster" is used because while a warm fellowship exists within the larger grouping, it is not in any way a centralized organization. Each group is an autonomous church, responsible for itself as well as its engagement with a wider world. Numbers within groups vary considerably, though this is not primarily what we mean by "growth." Ours is not a story of success or failure as these things are measured by secular and increasingly by Christian groups alike. It is the tale of ordinary Christians who want to serve as well as be served, to grow together in understanding, and to refract God's love in practical ways.

So where are we up to, and how are these home churches approaching the challenges and problems of contemporary life? In early 2004 some of us gathered to look at these questions, and the resulting discussion was worthwhile, rich in content, and chaotic in structure! For convenience, our responses are synthesized into three sections: "Meeting and Learning," "Giving and

Doing," and "Generational Change." As far as possible the story unfolds in a range of voices from across the members of the seven groups.

Meeting and Learning

> One of the delights of this group has been to see how people who ap-peared restricted — hidebound almost — by a conservative background have not only embraced folk with different views, but in time have come to genuinely appreciate difference, and to expand their own hori-zons.... The "regular" churches most in danger seem to me to be those with very strong leaders, who exude such confidence in their own or-thodoxy that they diminish the possibility of people thinking seriously for themselves, or listening genuinely to each other.

The Canberra home churches emerged from an often-rigid Protestant tradi-tion. For many, home churches meant liberation from structures which tend to establish and entrench the relations of power. As well, we began to discover the extent to which paternalistic hierarchies had muffled the expression of those individual and diverse gifts of which the Apostle Paul had made so much. We gained many new insights from studying the church communities of the first Christians.

We were fortunate to begin with a tradition of open-minded teaching on these and other themes central to the biblical narrative. Trained theologians Geoffrey Moon and Robert Banks laid a firm foundation for a generation of home churches, while Julia Banks provided a deeply committed model and catalyst for pastoral and practical action within the churches and beyond.

> We began with a simple arrangement. The weekly church meeting was central, but also vital were the teaching periods, which might last for twelve to fifteen weeks, and the weekly pastoral meeting, primarily for practical and prayer-based encouragement.

These elements have persisted in many guises to the present day. The church meeting (usually weekly) remains central, teaching courses remain a regular feature, and the pastoral meeting is enacted informally in many smaller groupings, as well as every few months on a clusterwide basis. The developing understanding of home churches owed much to books like *The Church Comes Home: A New Base for Community and Mission* (Robert and Julia Banks) and *Paul's Idea of Community* (Robert Banks).

The idea of community is central. Older hierarchical values and more fashionable contemporary views of leadership seem irrelevant. From the start the culture has been informal, open, and honoring of each member as servant to all. This spirit has taken many forms, and because it lies at the root of our theological narrative, it remains strong. It does mean time, and a level of listening that tests the more opinionated. But it yields a quality of relationship rare in today's world outside of family.

> You can't pretend to get on with people in our group. Once you're really in a church you know relationships are real. There is a strong sense of belonging to a caring community. We know with utmost certainty that we will be listened to and supported by all members. One of the really good things about home church is that we've come to a place where we have a comfortable balance between men and women. There's no power struggle, with men or women winning. Our church is a workshop in relationships!

From a rather monochrome early constituency, the Canberra churches have become colorfully diverse in recent years. People from many social strata, from unusual or "alien" religious traditions, the "nonreligious," gay couples—all are embraced as part of the regular fellowship.

> In our group an ex-Quaker, two Roman Catholics, and a woman of great insight but with no personal belief in the supernatural are able to find encouragement and insight from each other. The practice of prayer and worship needn't be a stumbling block to those who for one reason or another are unable to contribute directly. Even though I often find this huge theological range uncomfortable, I don't feel the freedom we enjoy has led to the "dangerous" theology people warned against. I haven't seen any "bad" fruits.

We have our problems too. Busyness, the struggle for survival of smaller churches, and conflicts of personality and opinion have all been recurring themes. The level of commitment is often an issue in a group where a couple of absences leave a discernible hole. One church confronting the contemporary malaise of busyness consists mainly of adults at similar life stages, while a second of rather wider constituency has a different experience.

> This—all the other things we adults fill our lives with—has an impact on the regularity of meetings. I'm always impressed by the fact that despite everything we manage to meet together every week, year after

year. Others looking at the churches find this commitment of three or four hours hard. For us who have learned its value, it's much easier.

Some of our strengths can also be the source of vulnerability. One hurdle we face is encompassing a huge range of theologies and beliefs. This is an ongoing challenge, but it also provides us with riches we otherwise wouldn't experience. Churches with a strong profession- ally trained core can become cerebral. Our group can often become academic and intellectual in discussion.

Yet despite problems and the process of diversification, the core elements and values of 1967 remain strong. One reason for this, identified by several members, is the continuing association between the churches, particularly expressed in pastoral meetings, larger combined gatherings at Easter and Christmas, and in a conference which includes other home churches from across the country, usually held every two years.

Giving and Doing

Most members of the Canberra home churches make little distinction be- tween practical action within the groups and similar responses to a wider world. The churches have usually welcomed the frail and disabled, the dis- turbed and the lonely. In smaller groups this can be difficult, and requires sane love and understanding. The paradox is that often everyone is enriched by the experience.

> I remember a really powerful meeting when our two [disabled] kids were present, and we talked about how God honors the people who aren't always honored within society. They, and we, all felt honored by the experience. Over many years we have attempted to support quite a lot of people with significant physical and medical problems — not always successfully! We get involved in a lot of celebrating — departures and arrivals, births and birthdays, starting high school and university, weddings, deaths. It's terrific to share joys as well as struggles.

Beyond our own gatherings the Canberra churches have initiated some very fruitful "Search for Meaning" groups, to engage folk not yet ready for "church." We have also been involved in an endless array of projects, protests, and causes. The initial lobby for East Timorese independence was served at its core by one or two home church members in particular. Our presence in the federal capital offers great scope for supporting the voiceless and the dispossessed.

> Members of our cluster are currently very strong organizers for social justice issues like challenging the mandatory detention of illegal immigrants and improving the conditions for aboriginal people. We took part in the push for reconciliation with aboriginal Australia. I remember one protest outside Parliament House, where home churches were pretty well represented, and they read out a list of supporting organizations.

Various members have been involved with mainstream organizations from World Vision, the Bible Society, Médicins Sans Frontières, through to the Bush Heritage Society, Australian Conservation Foundation, and Greenpeace. We have been active in protesting the insanity in Iraq, supporting and working with homeless youth, and backing the Yuendumu petrol sniffing project. One group provides substantial support to a small, independent project in Tanzania.

> We've become involved through two Australians working with the orphans and young adults displaced by the Rwandan genocide of 1994. There's an exciting directness of contact with individuals who are being trained and equipped for a new life. One member of our church has spent time at the project, and all of us have been enriched through this involvement.

Generational Change

The involvement of children and young people is an oft-raised question within the Canberra cluster, particularly as it affects survival into the future. Group experiences vary widely. Some of the groups sustain a three-generational age range without apparent difficulty.

> A new generation of young adults is coming into our church. Thoughtful young families are joining the group, keen to raise their children within a committed Christian community.

Other churches find later teenagers are leaving, often moving into other Christian groupings. Most parents are relaxed about the new generation testing their wings, especially when something worthwhile is being explored instead.

As a generalization, the group has not been successful in engaging our adult children in the ongoing activities and values of the group, which is not to say that particular values and attitudes from the group have not been assimilated by individual children.

Partly in response to this trend, one member, Jill Crisp, began a separate group about six years ago. On the Edge (OTE) is an apt title for a group in a loose affiliation with home church and which invites exploration in a climate of openness and acceptance. It is also attractive to the very age group which does not seem to be settling within some churches. Responses from that group are suggestive.

[OTE] shows me how other people live their lives in a thoughtful way. I would not say role models; that is so crass. OTE was really valuable when I started having a crisis of faith. It was a safe place to explore difficult ideas without feeling judged. I don't think Christianity is all bad. They knew about relationships back then.

Will young people like these form the nucleus of a continuing home church cluster? The answer is about as clear as the future was in 1967, and remains as securely in God's hands. The wind blows where it will, and for now we know that the Spirit of God has found willing hearts and open minds in our home churches for nearly four decades.

For many who have thrown in their lot with the Canberra Cluster, it has become uniquely for us the body of Christ, the company of the committed. We share the struggles of an imperfect world. But within these home churches we support and encourage, worship and learn, and share gladly in each other's lives. And beyond them, it is still dawning on us what a profound base we have from which to engage a wider world.

22

Building Prophetic Community in Aotearoa

Michael Mawson and Justin Duckworth

Our purpose is to share a few insights on building and sustaining Christian communities in a Western context. We begin by outlining our situation: First, the economic and political environment of Aotearoa (Maori name for New Zealand), that is, the governing principalities and powers; then the demographics and model of the community we have formed in response to this; and finally, in light of this situation, we share some key insights that have helped make community possible for us.

Aotearoa/New Zealand

For the last two decades Aotearoa/New Zealand has been deeply affected by what has been infamously dubbed the "New Zealand Experiment."[1] From the mid-1980s successive governments have led the world in integrating our country into the so-called global free market. Hot on the heels of the United Kingdom and United States, the N.Z. government eagerly embraced economic structural adjustments, resplendent with all the privatizations of state assets, reduced funding for the health sector, slashing of welfare and benefits, and hiking costs of education. The speed and voracity with which our government pursued such reforms assured its place as an international exemplar of free-market integration.

Less trumpeted is the devastating effect of these reforms for many New Zealanders, particularly those identified as being within the "lower socioeconomic bracket." Predictably the reforms have resulted in a substantial increase in poverty — whether measured in pure economic terms or in related indicators such as social instability, marital breakdown, crime, and

---

1. See Jane Kelsey, *The New Zealand Experiment: A World Model for Structural Adjustment?* (Auckland: Auckland University Press, 1995).

mental health consumption, but also in the further entrenchment of those already deemed poor. Within this broad environment, and more specifically within the capital city of Wellington, our community has sought to respond to the prophetic call to live with and alongside those who struggle.

The Urban Vision Community

Our community, dubbed Urban Vision, is organized practically through four clusters of homes, or teams, each of which is located in or alongside a particular area of need. There are: (1) homes in high-density housing blocks alongside predominantly Somali and African refugee communities; (2) homes in the inner city that offer hospitality and friendship to working women, adult mental health consumers, and those living on the street; and (3) homes in the south Wellington region that primarily provide accommodation and support for at-risk youth. More recently (4) some members of the community have managed to purchase land a short distance out of the city, and this provides a much-needed space for all those living in the city to come for time out, and to bring various friends and groups. This follows the Catholic Worker model, with its symbiosis between inner-city community and outlying forms.

The nature of our community makes its size difficult to convey, but currently there are around fifty people living in approximately fifteen homes throughout these clusters. The homes, however, would better be understood as the beginning of the community rather than as its boundaries. These homes of hospitality provide places from which, or within which, much wider networks and groups are built and maintained. In day-to-day functions the four teams operate relatively autonomously, and thus more as small distinct communities in and of themselves. Despite this degree of independence, the maintenance of a strong community-wide identity remains crucial to longer-term health and sustainability.

On average those currently living in homes tend to be in their mid- to late twenties, although much of the continuity of the community is provided by the presence of slightly older married couples, many with children. Those who move into the community are typically in their early twenties, and are often either studying at the local university or just beginning work. This is probably due to students and young workers being at the stage in life that is more open and available to experimentation. An experiment in community for a young single contains nowhere near the same risk or adjustment as that for a family. Many stay involved for a couple of years and then move on because of typical pressures of career, family, or just plain normality. Some settle and stay for the long term.

The majority of those who join the community tend to be Pakeha (white). Given this, and despite having a number of Maori (indigenous people) central to the community, we would tend to identify the community as a Pakeha community. This identification is not intended to discourage heterogeneity, or participation from non-Pakeha, but rather drops the pretense that Christian community (or Christianity more generally) exists within a neutral cultural space. Acknowledging the basically Pakeha organization and intentionality of our community becomes a way of allowing the Maori Christian group a greater space to claim a specifically Maori identity. Also the more subtle identification of the community as Pakeha — as opposed to "white," "European," or just "New Zealanders" — implicitly entails a commitment to biculturalism.

Religiously the community is fairly ecumenical, and people involved come from a variety of church traditions and backgrounds. Earlier in its history many of those involved came from fairly standard evangelical backgrounds, and the community theology was often articulated through a departure from/development of the basic evangelical framework. To some extent, though, the community — with its own rhythms of prayer, reflection, and engagement — tends to fulfill many of the normal functions of church, and this (along with increasingly different theological emphases) means that many people struggle to find space for, or meaning within, the mainstream church.

Sustaining Prophetic Community in a Western Context

Over the last decade we have developed a number of pragmatic insights for building and sustaining our community and its alternative vision for the world:

- *For community to remain healthy, it must be constantly looking outside itself.*

This is what keeps personal and ideological differences in check, and provides the impetus for commonality of vision and purpose. Most people these days would be well familiar with living situations where flat mates or family members simply can't negotiate personal space and differences in temperament. Riots erupt over whose turn it is to do dishes, or over who keeps leaving their socks on the bathroom floor! Without denying the importance and healthiness of periodic conflict and tension, for relationships to survive such issues must be kept in perspective. This is made somewhat easier by the experience of having a teenager staying who has just made a third suicide attempt in two weeks, or having a friend pop over to disclose difficulties in an abusive relationship. Those living in community homes, regardless of background, are best drawn together through responding to the pain and suffering of the hurting world. Sadly, many Western attempts at community (Christian or otherwise) seem to lose sight of this and, by focusing first on getting the community functioning properly and then engaging with the world, inevitably implode.

- *Community requires caring* with, *and not just* for, *others.*

Those of us engaging with the margins from relatively privileged backgrounds tend to begin with a paternalism that is ultimately disempowering. To move beyond just providing a service of some kind and to arrive at some sort of genuine community, it is necessary to create spaces for learning and receiving as well as teaching and serving. A recent example here was found in the homes working with at-risk youth. A teenager who had been in care for a few months recounted to the wider group his childhood experience of being moved between foster homes (averaging more than one a year for his fifteen years) and resultant insecurities. His story helped those present to reflect on their own backgrounds and experiences (both the good and the bad). Our fumbling attempts to fix the world have resulted in our own deeper understanding. Many of those we relate to are struggling, broken, and difficult people, who have underacknowledged insights and abilities to contribute. Giving dignity to those who struggle requires seeing and acknowledging who they are and what they have to offer.

- *Community requires openness to chaos.*

Closely related to this last point is the need for building communal spaces, which can be owned by everyone. Building such spaces is central to how belonging and identity are created. An example here is Stillwaters Church, a church service run by the Urban Vision team in the inner city and attended by the wider Wellington street community. At the end of each service anyone present can volunteer to take responsibility for the next week's tasks, ranging from preaching the sermon (or sharing their reflections on life) to picking the songs or bringing something for supper. This principle of "anyone can do anything" also translates into "anything can often happen." Through all this, however, the sense of genuine ownership by the group creates both spiritual depth and connection. In the past the most organized and tailored programs and messages often failed to rouse much interest, the reality being that most young people simply don't want to be at church (in any form). This is particularly the case for many at-risk youth, who again often have an engrained negative identity. Again, encouraging young people to be running the show, or at least contributing in significant ways, tends to create a greater sense of involvement and connection.

- *Community should entail sacrifice and cost.*

Community requires a renewal of Christian notions of self-sacrifice and service, and a related rejection of mainstream Christian values, which still give preference to personal autonomy and individual choice. To remain involved in community for any length of time it must be given priority, and other options and opportunities will inevitably be sacrificed. Thus, if community is advertised solely on the basis of its attractive features (friendship, connection, identity, etc.), then when life does begin to become too busy or difficult (as it inevitably does) it is likely that community will be the first thing to suffer. Our practice for combating this has been to set the standard of entry as high as possible. For instance. within the youth homes we encourage, and even require, those wishing to become involved that they move into the more intensive residential homes. While the intensity of living in such an environment straight off discourages some, it ultimately tends to give those who move in a far more genuine experience of the costs and joys of community life and thus places them in a far better position to make serious longer-term decisions about lifestyle and values.

- *Why build Christian community specifically in the West?*

Within the Western church the biblical mandate to give dignity to the dispossessed is most often fulfilled through an engagement with poverty as it exists overseas. While this in itself is important, it also allows a gap for avoiding making the connection between the causes of poverty and our own actions and lifestyles as Westerners. The economic causes of poverty — i.e., the exploitative and forced nature of most trade agreements, foreign debt, the actions of multinationals — remain largely unacknowledged, and poverty is instead stereotypically explained in reference to natural disasters or localized ethnic/religious conflict. Maintaining such simplistic explanations is made easier given our distance from the international poor, and thus our inability to connect to the poor outside the representations of the mainstream (corporate-owned) media. What such solutions implicitly don't require is any deep or fundamental self-reflection, any costly change in lifestyle and activity, or any structural or political engagement or critique. This is in part why Western Christianity, through its prioritizing of overseas poverty, often fails to make the connections inherent to the radical and political character of Jesus' teachings and ministry. To some extent this gap is also what gives *prophetic* character to communities and missionaries operating within a Western context.

There is an inherent and prophetic challenge to forming community in the West, and through doing so proclaiming the reality of local poverty and marginalization within our various churches, families, and places of work and study. The presence of the poor within what is clearly a prosperous country cannot so easily be explained without more serious reflection on our own participation in structural causes of poverty (which are clearly not the result of war or natural disaster). Proclaiming poverty in this way, usually done quite simply through living and serving in the way we do, implicitly challenges current political and economic structures, and the dominant assumptions that these remain compatible with the call to follow Jesus.

Part Six

International

In January 1986 Joe Healey participated in the South African Missiological Conference in Pretoria, South Africa. The keynote speaker of the congress was Hans Küng. Joe gave a lecture on "Basic Christian Communities: Church-Centered or World-Centered?" mainly from the pastoral experience of SCCs in Eastern Africa. After his talk he received a message that Hans Küng wanted to see him at the next coffee break. Küng explained that in his latest research he had been studying different paradigms of the church: house churches in the first century, monasteries in medieval times, the parish in recent centuries. He wondered if the parish model was no longer appropriate in different places in the world, and if the model or paradigm of the future is the Small Christian Community (SCC)? Joe has often wondered if this was prophetic, prophetic in the sense that Yves Congar's quote in the foreword by Cardinal Murphy-O'Connor is prophetic.

One particular sign of the times is that SCCs are a "new way of being local church," "a new model of church," "a new paradigm in the history of the church" as Hans Küng calls them. The concept of Small Christian Communities developed as a result of putting the ecclesiology of Vatican II into practice. Latin America, Africa, and Asia (especially the Philippines) all pioneered the development of an SCC model of church or a BCC model of church. After considerable research and debate, many feel that quite independently of one another these three areas of the Catholic Church in the Third World *simultaneously* experienced the extraordinary growth of SCCs that stress a theology of incarnation and communion ecclesiology.

We have visited all six continents on our "New Moments in SCCs" journey. We have met many parish-based SCCs and other types of SCCs on the margins. We now experience the internationalization of SCCs and the international SCC model of church. Each chapter portrays a special face of global SCC networking. We discover what Irene Wilson felt: "Growing global communion through the sharing of life and faith stories is an awesome privilege." During this twenty-first century, e-mail, the Internet, and other forms of communications will propel this sharing and networking in even different and more exciting ways.

23

Reenergizing International SCC Twinning

Rita Ishengoma and Joseph Healey

Rita Ishengoma's mother in Bukoba, Tanzania, cooked in a clay cooking pot on three cooking stones. Every night after cooking supper she made sure that the fire in the fireplace was preserved until the next morning. The used firewood was kept very close together under the charcoal and covered with ashes with a stone placed on top so that the fire continued to burn inside until morning when it was used for preparing breakfast. This can be called the process of the "sleeping fire."

This process of the sleeping fire symbolizes the challenge of giving new energy to our international or global SCC twinning program. Some SCC twinning relationships have been very active. Others have slowed down. Others just drift along. Others are inactive. Others have gone to sleep. Others have stopped. Others are waiting to be born. What we are discovering is that the idea of SCC twinning is very appealing, but the time it takes to get letters back and forth is often long, and the actual reality of keeping up the relationship is more difficult than the original excitement anticipated.

The difference in the analogy is that my mother kept the fire unlit "on purpose" while SCC twins mainly went into the sleeping period because the communications were not successful or not a priority. If we decide, we can turn our twinning network into the Third Millennium SCC Twinning Program, an energized SCC twinning, an awakened SCC twinning. This needs our collective strength and our working vigorously.

Meaning of International SCC Twinning

International or global Small Christian Community (SCC) twinning (also called Sister SCCs, Sister Communities, and Partner SCCs) is a recent development in the worldwide Small Christian Communities experience and

157

an important form of international networking. Twinning, the setting up of "sister dioceses" and "sister parishes" on a higher level and "sister Small Christian Communities" on a grassroots level, is a practical, proven, and enriching experience of involvement in the global church. SCC twinning has developed rapidly in the last five years. It is a concrete expression of how SCCs are a new way of being church. The heart of SCC twinning is sharing mutual pastoral experiences between local churches on the very grassroots level. It is a group pen-pal friendship rather than an individual pen-pal friendship. The twinning relationship is joint and reciprocal. It is a two-way, mutual relationship. This is a partnership of local churches on all six continents expressed on the local level. This partnership is a special way for laypersons to participate and to say, "We are the church," and to reveal a unique face of sharing and collaboration. Twinning is an important means for SCCs to develop a broader viewpoint and a wider vision.

Barb Darling states: "The global SCC twinning program helps to provide links between Small Christian Communities in the United States and many other countries. These links are meant to form mutual common bonds between Christians in communities at the grassroots level.... SCC Twinning is one way that communities can look outside themselves to the larger experience of community and church. The twinning process introduces SCCs to a community in another culture and country. It is a mutual giving and sharing."

The SCC in a Third World country is not just a receiver (for money and material goods, as an example), but also a giver and better a sharer. Small Christian Community "twins" enter into a mutual, reciprocal relationship. The communities each have something valuable to give and also to receive. The twinning relationship provides a forum to exchange our gifts and talents in order to build a better life and human dignity all around the world. Rather than the "old" idea of twinning, where the rich Westerners just help poor Third World people financially, SCC twinning focuses on exchanging the local personal and pastoral experiences of each SCC partner, such as family events, visiting the sick, youth activities, and justice and peace advocacy. We are all both sending and receiving churches. What is really new is that the Small Christian Community twinning program reaches the parish to involve Christians at the very local, grassroots level, thereby enriching the world church. Brother Robert Moriarty, S.M., states: "In an era of economic globalization which threatens to make the rich ever richer and the poor ever poorer, *twinning*, based not on an exchange of material goods, but on an exchange of experiences of Christian life and mission, offers an approach to the globalization of solidarity, a globalization from below, as it were."

Recent History of International SCC Twinning

Some of the first permanent seeds of international SCC twinning were presented in the video on the Second International Consultation on Small Christian Communities at the University of Notre Dame, Notre Dame, Indiana, in October 1996. In answer to the question, "Is there a simple way that an SCC in America could begin to live out a public life in light of the universal church?" Father Bob Pelton, C.S.C., of Notre Dame explained the tradition of twinning in the Catholic Church on the diocesan and parish levels. Then he described international Small Christian Community twinning as a *new* way of experiencing church — from small community to small community.

Starting in 1996 we received letters asking for an East African SCC twin from the following places: United States of America (total of twenty-four states); Canada: Alberta, Ontario; England; Scotland; India; Australia: Melbourne, Enfield; and Hong Kong.

Four types of twinning relationships or partnerships developed:

- Parish-based SCC to parish-based SCC.

- Parish-based SCC to school-based SCC.

- Youth SCC to youth SCC.

- Children SCC to children SCC.

The first wave of SCC twinning relationships included among others:

- 1996: Twinning between the St. Jude Thaddeus SCC in St. Augustine Parish in Mwisenge, Musoma, Tanzania (coordinated by Simphroza Chacha and Father Joe Healey, M.M.), and the Circle of Friends SCC in St. Joseph's Parish in Golden, Colorado (coordinated by Bernie Moore).

- 1997: Twinning between St. Maria Goretti SCC in Geita, Tanzania (coordinated by Sister Rita Ishengoma and local lay leaders), and the Oilers SCC in Arvada, Colorado (coordinated by Barb Howard and Barb Darling).

- 1998: Twinning between the SCCs of St. Michael's Parish in Kawe, Dar es Salaam, Tanzania, especially St. Michael's SCC (coordinated by Father Jude Shayo, A.J., and local lay leaders), and the SCCs of Our Lady of the Lakes Parish in New Milford, Connecticut, especially Ladies for the Lord SCC (coordinated by Joan Bell and Vicky Miller).

- 1998: St. Clare SCC in St. Joseph's Parish, SCC, Kisumu, Kenya (set up by Alphonce Omolo), and Esperanza (Spanish for "Hope") SCC, University of Notre Dame and St. Mary's College, South Bend, Indiana (set up by Bob Pelton).

The second (and present) wave of SCC twinning relationships in the first years of the twenty-first century included, among others:

- Kandulo Small Christian Community, Chinkombero OutChurch, Njuli, Malawi, and Upwey Small Church Community, Belgrave Parish, Melbourne, Australia (part of the Global Small Christian Communities [SCC] Research and Consultation Project).

- Three SCCs in El Salvador (Oasis, Agua Zarca, and Nueva Jerusalén), and three SCC counterparts in Chile (Luz y Esperanza, Paz y Amor, and Carlos Camus — part of the Global Small Christian Communities [SCC] Research and Consultation Project). *Note:* See chapter 2, "Fruits of El Salvador–Chile SCC Twinning from Within."

- Twinning relationships between four SCCs in the Diocese of Kiyinda-Mityana, Uganda, and four SCCs in Illinois, Montana, Ohio, and Texas (set up by Father John Vianney Muweesi).

- Twinning relationships between six SCCs in western Kenya and six SCCs in Indianapolis, Indiana, and Oneida, New York (set up by Barb Darling).

Theological Foundations of International SCC Twinning

Praxis is prior to theology. Reflection on the theological foundations of international SCC twinning begins with the life, experiences, and reflections of the SCCs themselves. These reflections presuppose, and build upon, the praxis of grassroots case studies and other concrete examples of international SCC twinning around the world (an inductive approach). Reflecting on examples especially of solidarity between SCC twins in East Africa, North America, South America, Australia, and England and their shared biblical reflections and real-life stories leads to five theological foundations:

- Biblical theology
- Communion theology and solidarity theology
- Local or contextual theology
- Narrative theology
- Mission theology

Voices of International SCC Twinning

Listen to the voices of people who are involved in SCC twinning around the world.

"SCC partnering validates and pushes SCCs to a new level of connecting and relating" (United States).

"We believe our partnership will help in mutual spiritual, social, economic, and psychological growth and development" (Kenya).

"We are glad to have you as our overseas sister community. We pray for God's blessings that this sisterhood and brotherhood in Christ grows stronger and bears fruit" (Uganda).

"We are inspired by your community, and we found that the things that unite both our communities are prayer, good works, doughnuts, and a love for one another" (Australia).

"We here in Uganda are happy to know that you got involved in SCC Twinning though the reference in *Quest*, the booklet from the Archdiocese of Hartford. From Connecticut to Montana to Mityana. Wow, that covers a lot of ground" (Uganda).

"We are enclosing some maps of Montana, a photo of our SCC (see the snow!), and a letter from each group member" (United States).

"If you have anything in particular that you are celebrating, or if you have any problems, we would like to share them with you" (England).

"We've traded photos and stories of holiday traditions and observances. We've introduced our families to theirs and shared news of deaths and illnesses" (United States).

"We have been sharing our stories of faith experiences and pictures. We marvel at the similarity of the way we live and do SCC even though many miles away" (Kenya).

"Since starting twinning we in East Africa have true friends in the United States and other places. Twinning has brought about changes in our life. We regard SCCs in America as our sisters and brothers" (Tanzania).

"We are members of one family though far apart. Sometimes we feel that our SCC twin is just in the neighborhood and we can just walk in and say 'Hi'" (Kenya).

"Even though you dear friends live far from us, we want to express our deep sympathy on the tragic events of September 11, 2001" (Tanzania).

"The beautiful African cultural gift from your St. Noa Mawaggali SCC in Uganda arrived safely. We continue to be in amazement that we are connected to Catholics so far away" (United States).

Challenge of Today's Moment

We sowed a mustard seed. We enjoyed its growth and ate its fruits for a few years. Then we went into a kind of sleeping period. Some of the communities are not dead, but covered with ashes. Jude Shayo of St. Michael's Parish, Kawe, describes the SCC twins as "dormant." The fire is there. It needs to be rekindled. We need a Third Millennium spirit, walking together as children of God. Reenergizing our twinning means enhancing ways of the ongoing formation of SCC partnerships. We have to awaken the fire — the faith, faith in the risen Christ who is always in our midst. We have to start afresh from Christ by renewing our commitment to God and to our neighbors. Pope John Paul II in *Starting Afresh from Christ* states: "The church counts on the continual dedication of this chosen host of her sons and daughters, on their yearning for holiness and upon the enthusiasm of their service to foster and sustain every Christian's striving for perfection and to enhance the common welcoming of neighbors, especially those most in need. In this way, witness is given to the love of Christ among all people."

The most important question is who is to start this work of reawakening and reenergizing SCC twinning? Taking the example of Rita Ishengoma's mother, the work of lighting the fire in the morning was done by the one who woke up first. But with twinning we are all called to take a role and not only to listen. Let us all start communicating, sharing the message of love, breaking all barriers. We need active coordinators of SCC twinning: first, national coordinators to start the twinning process and link SCCs together; second, local coordinators in the individual SCC twins to keep the two-way communications process going. Each has a distinct but essential role. An essential part of coordination is to record the names of our SCC twins and their history. This could be shared in an annual newsletter (paper and e-mail).

Let us hear from examples of communities twinned all over the world. Sharing our experiences, our joys and sorrows, our real-life stories with our brothers and sisters must be our priority. By using multimedia communication, letters, e-mails, cards, photos, audiotapes, videotapes, and cultural gifts, we can cross oceans and mountains. The Internet is now more widely used than when we started SCC twinning in 1996. Training and updating workshops and seminars must be ongoing activities in our SCCs in order to widen our understanding and interest. Personal and community commitment is very vital. Prayer and sacrifice strengthen and sustain our small communities.

24

Global Communion on a Face-to-Face Level

Barbara A. Darling

Small Christian Communities are church in the fullest sense at a basic grass-roots level, on the streets and in the neighborhoods of our parishes. The broadest level of church is global. Our church is universal, the concept of which is often difficult to grasp. But when we think of the universal church as a communion of small, local Christian churches rooted in their own society but connected through mission toward one another, the picture becomes clearer. Our challenge, as SCCs, is to connect the large and small by creating communion through global, grassroots relationships.

Face-to-Face Meetings

In the last fifteen years SCCs and their members have established successful global relationships that began with face-to-face meetings. Some of these meetings have been spontaneous events, while others were planned specifically by those who understood early on the significance of this type of networking.

Father Robert Pelton, C.S.C., professor of theology, University of Notre Dame, and Kellogg Institute for International Studies Fellow took to heart what Cardinal Paulo Arns of Brazil said shortly after Vatican II: "Our church is now being called to an ecclesiological shift from power to communion." Pelton brought life into the suggested emphasis toward relationships in and among smaller communities by coordinating four large international SCC conferences between 1991 and 2002, as he describes: "These events were meant to help us all as we strive to deepen relationships in the context of an even more profound commitment to the rich tradition of our faith. This is a pastoral work in progress. There is much hope in the ongoing struggle to build the kingdom among us."

In 1991 and again in 1996, the Institute for Pastoral and Social Ministry, University of Notre Dame, Indiana, hosted international gatherings based in the experience of small church. Participants reflected on the theology of SCCs, shared concrete ideas, and contemplated the impact SCCs have made on their civil and ecclesial worlds.

One enduring relationship has forever connected small-church members in the United States and Tanzania. Sister Rita Ishengoma, STH, and Barbara Howard attended both gatherings, bonded face-to-face, and began heart-to-heart relationships between extended members of their SCCs. "These meetings pulled together the divided world, broke barriers of tribes, colors, languages, and confirmed the people of God to be truly a family of God. My global SCC participation has left me with an impression of the unity of the Catholic Church," writes Rita. "When I returned home, photos and videos of my new friends helped me to express to my Tanzanians this new way of being church."

Reflecting on her experience, Barbara realized:

It's so easy for me to be caught up in a parochialism that tends to see my experience, my small community, my parish, my spirituality, my lifestyle as normative. As a U.S. citizen, that notion is reinforced through the media that often presents the "ideal" of a homogenized world vis-à-vis economic globalization which directly impacts lifestyle. The international gatherings, and subsequent relationships developed as a result of them, have not only expanded my awareness but have challenged me to broaden my understanding of God, of faithfulness, of justice, and of spirituality. "Love your neighbor as yourself" has taken on a whole new meaning as the notion of "neighbor" has become concretized in real faces and real stories from locales and circumstances far different than my cultural experience.

In 1999 Small Christian Community people from six continents met in Cochabamba, Bolivia, to process specific references to SCCs in the Catholic Church's continental synodal documents and their possible future consequences for our church.

In 2002 two opportunities surfaced for international face-to-face networking. In August the third National Convocation of Small Christian Communities in San Antonio, Texas, although meant primarily for American participants, was made richer by the inclusion of representatives from twelve other nations (Canada, Mexico, Brazil, Australia, Kenya, Tanzania, Uganda, Nigeria, Ireland, England, Scotland, and Sweden).

In November theologians and social scientists from Europe, Africa, Latin America, and the United States explored the current and future possibilities of small church hosted by the Helen Kellogg Institute for International Studies, University of Notre Dame, Indiana. This meeting was based on the January–July 2002 international electronic consultation and informal research conducted by Latin American/North American Church Concerns at University of Notre Dame and The Center of Research and Study, Maryknoll, N.Y. Letters exchanged between grassroots communities from fourteen countries provided a snapshot of the spirituality of these communities, how that spirituality affects our church and vice versa.

Gunnar Widforss, a Swedish pastor, described the long-term consequences of his participation in the San Antonio congress and other multinational small-church conferences in the United States and Europe:

> [My experience] has totally changed my way of being a Christian, theologian and pastor. In my country there are few who have ever heard of this way of being church. Global contacts provide [me] with the experience of a new reality, not accepted, not seen, nonexistent in my region. When I discuss with bishops and pastors here, I can refer to living experience in the majority of Christian churches on all continents, besides my own. My international contacts give me credibility in these matters.

On the other hand, Gunnar points out that as a Lutheran and European he felt both privileged and lonely in the compact Catholic and North American context:

> I felt privileged and noticed as a person, but would the US people really feel they needed the experience from other parts of the world or from other churches and denominations? I would like to make a contribution to the life of US SCCs alongside the contribution others have made to our life in Europe and the Lutheran Church of Sweden.

In July 2003, hosted by Maryknoll's Center for Mission Research and Study, participants from Korea, India, Kenya, Peru, Brazil, Argentina, Guatemala, the Dominican Republic, and the United States spent two weeks brainstorming successful strategies for global partnering in a variety of circumstances. Donald Kabara of the United States played a part in this conference, along with Ignacio de León de León, of the Dominican Republic. They represented their respective parishes, which have been partnering for many years. "Perhaps the greatest benefit I have seen from [face-to-face global conferences] is a grassroots theology and ecclesiology that benefits a global community," states Kabara. "This leads to a practical yet dynamic application of the Gospel and the development of a Gospel-based spirituality that promotes growth and meaning to life. So, indeed, they are an effective tool in developing my ministry, spirituality, and my work as a global partner."

Participants from ten countries on five continents participated in the RENEW International Institute in East Rutherford, New Jersey, in July 2004. The liturgies and prayer services celebrated the rich diversity of language and culture. Connected to his workshop and PowerPoint presentation Pelton said:

> In the past I have spent much energy and prayer in supporting the "internationalization" of small Christian communities. I continue to be convinced of the importance of this effort. In view of my current research commitments I find it important to focus more precisely on the emerging "house churches" of Cuba. Many others are now picking up the baton in this effort of "internationalization." I welcome those efforts, and I look forward to cooperating with them.

RENEW International is to be applauded for its current efforts to include an international component in their U.S.-based conferences. "Participants from other countries have been a rich and welcome addition to our agendas, and we hope to continue this practice and enlarge on it," states Michael Brough, director.

One-on-One Travels and Small-Group Global Interaction

At this writing, however, no intentional long-term plans for specific international SCC conferences are on the agenda of SCC organizations in any country. It seems the tide has turned from large gatherings of participants to one-on-one travels and small-group global interaction.

Brother Bob Moriarty, S.M.'s, SCC-related global travels took him to the 1999 Bolivian conference and, more recently, on personal trips to Tanzania and Australia. "Whether it's to Australia or Africa, your entire horizon for church is broadened by seeing people in another country and culture put together a meaningful experience of life through Small Christian Communities," notes Moriarty. "Since I've been back from my travels I've been speaking to others about my encounters. In that way many people get a vicarious experience and come to understand that this Small Christian Community thing is not just a few nice, small groups in American suburbs."

"Bob's visit was a great shot in the arm for the SCCs he connected with here in Australia," commented Irene Wilson, pastoral associate in Sassafras, Victoria. She emphasized:

> As an international practitioner with links to small church around the world, he enlarged the perspective of local SCC participants who heard him speak. His visit offered both support and motivation for the growth and maturing of small groups as a force for shaping a better locality and a better world. It also helped to consolidate networking between the SCC movement in the States and Australia.

Wilson, herself a universal church connector through her work with RCIA and Small Christian Communities, said:

> In recent years I gained a sense from both American and Australian friends that the African church is so alive and vibrant and yearned to experience the blessing of these Christians in order that my own sense of hope and trust for the future could be underpinned and supported. I knew I just had to taste this energizing exuberance for myself, especially as I am currently undertaking some graduate study in the area of the RCIA and Small Christian Communities.

So in March 2005 she visited Msimbazi and Kawe Parishes in Dar es Salaam, Tanzania, which are very involved in adult baptism programs. When asked about the long-term benefits of her visit, she replied that the Dar es Salaam experience enabled her to "gain purchase" on the way the adult catechumenate process has been developed over many years in East Africa:

> This provided valuable perspectives not only for my own research, but also for many parishes in the West, particularly in Australia and the United States who are also imaging ways in which to link the RCIA and SCCs. This African model is a work in progress, but the lessons they have learned and the wisdom gained thus far need to go into the mix. On a personal level I am, of course, now blessed with new friends, new dialogue partners for life. I hope my visit might encourage further connections with the African church, maybe twinning between Australian SCCs and SCCs in Dar es Salaam so that others here may in some personal way also benefit from interaction with our African brothers and sisters.

Wilson summed it up by saying, "Growing global communion like this through the sharing of life and faith stories is an awesome privilege."

New Moments in the Future

International Small Christian Community conferences and small-group or one-on-one visits to SCCs in other countries offer different strengths to a communion way of thinking. Moriarty related the difference between the large conferences and the one-on-one or small-group encounters, saying one is the art of collecting concentrated information and wisdom from many cultures while the other is a thoroughly experiential thing that invites total participation in another's culture. Both, he feels, are essential to the task of nurturing our universal church.

Having experienced several of the international conferences as well as one-on-one intercultural exchanges and the global SCC twinning program, I believe our church needs global dialogue partners for life to grow beyond a parochial understanding of God's plan for salvation. And our civil world needs the links our church can provide through these grassroots relationships.

So the question is, in this world of virtual relationships, how will we, as small church, rise to the challenge of meaningful, global, face-to-face interactions in the future? What group(s) will take up the mantle of coordinating international conferences where grassroots people of many cultures can make connections? How can we ensure that people from every corner of our church have access to this sending and receiving kind of hospitality in one-on-one and small-group travel?

How will you and your SCC respond to these important challenges?

25

Sant'Egidio

Prophets of the Poor and of Peace

Austen Ivereigh

Maputo Central Hospital, Mozambique, November 2001. In a room in the pediatric ward, Dr. Gloria Denga explains that, before the year is out, the three children in here will be dead. Floidi, a few-months-old baby, and Elena, who is two, will die of pneumonia; the six-year-old Armindo of TB. Antibiotics? Dr. Denga lowers her voice so their mothers cannot hear. "Antibiotics require the cooperation of these children's immune system," she whispers over her clipboard. "But theirs never had the chance to develop."

The mothers sit by the beds of the children they gave death to. One holds out a comforting arm, resting a hand on a bandage on a forehead. There are tubes and a rusted, old oxygen tank. The children's bodies are so shrunken that their unblinking eyes seem huge. The scene — the dying children, the solemn dignity of their infected mothers — is one of total patience.

Floidi, Elena, and Armindo were born with AIDS. The shadow that is sliding across Africa, devouring its citizens, covered these children while they were still in the womb. And now there is nothing their mothers, or Dr. Denga, can do but make their brief existence a little more comfortable. These gorgeous little children will soon be dead because antiretroviral therapy is a privilege that the world has reserved for its rich.

How does it feel as a pediatrician, I ask Dr. Denga, not being able to help them? She smiles shyly. In all these years in her dying wards, no one has ever asked her that question. She struggles to single out some emotions and give them names. "Frustration," she says eventually. "Impotence."

AIDS has numbed the West into compliance with a strategy based wholly on prevention. The assumption is worthy in itself, but devastating in its implications, for it writes off the 25 million sub-Saharan Africans in whom the virus is already ticking away. Who decided Africa cannot be cured?

170

Mozambique, a green nation of 18 million people — 20 percent of whose young people are dying of AIDS — unfurls from an old Czech twin prop that rattles its way north up the country's stunning coastline. On board is a team of doctors who belong to the Rome-based Community of Sant'Egidio. The Community is well-known in Mozambique for its role in brokering the 1992 peace agreement that brought to an end the African country's brutal decade-long civil war. That war claimed a million lives, a figure already surpassed, in Mozambique, by HIV.

Sant'Egidio has always put friendship with the poor at the heart of its charism. Its members' first friends were the immigrants on the outskirts of Rome; nowadays they are throughout the developing world. The Community's relationship with Mozambique began when famine struck that country in the 1980s: food was sent, visits were made, bonds forged. That is how the mediation began. When your friends are dying in a war, you try to end it; hence the peace treaty. Then came AIDS. When your friends in Africa are dying of AIDS, it is natural to want them to have the kind of anti-retroviral treatment your friends in Europe enjoy; hence the Community's anti-AIDS program.

Both ventures seemed quixotic at the time. Both have succeeded because years of patient communication learned through friendship with the poor around the world have given the Community a talent for boundary-hopping and conflict mediation. They made contact with a guerrilla chieftain hidden away for years in the heart of Africa, brought him out of his isolation, and persuaded him to negotiate. After a few years the warring factions signed a peace accord in Rome.

Almost ten years after that agreement I am accompanying the Community's AIDS team led by Dr. Leonardo Palombi, an immunologist at Rome's Tor Vergata University, as they attempt another triumph of hope over realism: Africa's first nationwide AIDS testing and treatment program. As in the peace negotiations, there was no shortage of people who said it couldn't be done. But the exclusion of Africans from antiretroviral treatment, the Community insisted, is simply due to an absence of will to deal with the poor hygiene and nutrition that people have long considered would undermine an antiretroviral program.

Sant'Egidio community members have since been proved spectacularly right. After raising some money from a motley assortment of backers, they have spent the past five years building special laboratories to test blood and training small groups of health workers to administer antiretroviral therapy to pregnant women in their homes. It was too late for Floidi, Elena, and

Armindo. But the first treatments, which began in 2003, had by early 2004 saved the lives of a thousand mothers and children whom the Community had placed on HAART (Highly Active Anti Retroviral Therapy), the gold standard of European AIDS treatment. Some 97 percent of the children have been born healthy from the wombs of HIV-positive mothers. Supported by many of the five thousand young people and adults who belong to the Sant'Egidio Communities in Mozambique, the rate of compliance with the therapy is 95 percent. That is a higher rate than in Europe and North America — proving, at long last, that there is nothing about Africans that make them averse to the same treatment that Europeans receive. The numbers are impressive. But even more significant is the beginning of the reversal of the cycle of despair, stigma, and denial which have fueled the spread of the virus through Africa.

With the AIDS team I visit Pemba on the north Mozambican coast. Pemba's Sant'Egidio Community has about forty members, led by Anita, a convert from Islam in her forties. They give us a rapturous welcome: at the church outside town they treat us to the standard Sant'Egidio prayer — a kind of vespers, with readings from the Psalms, the Gospel, a reflection by Anita, songs — but this is the "Prayer with a Difference." We tap, tap our feet, swing our hips, and sing with the sweat pouring down our cheeks for hours. Over and over we chant the song that Sant'Egidio in Mozambique wrote to celebrate the 1992 peace treaty: "A paz do senhor, esteja connosco, a paz do senhor esteja em todo o mundo" (The peace of the Lord be always with us, the peace of the Lord be spread around the world) runs the chorus. Amidst the dust and the hardship, the prayer is a stream of pure joy.

The next day Anita and the others take us to Pemba's prison. "No one is so poor that they cannot help another who is poor" is one of Sant'Egidio's well-known refrains. In Pemba I saw this. The community members have few coins to rub together, and yet every day they come to the jail to supplement the tiny portion of *mielie* the prisoners are given. They come, too, to befriend and give hope to the prisoners, who sit in a concrete yard under the baking sun.

The communities of Sant'Egidio in Mozambique are young, vibrant, flexible, and impressively dedicated. The Sant'Egidio model — committed small communities, wholly inculturated, but tied to the universal church through the Community worldwide — suits Africa, which is increasingly an urban environment.

But it is also a model that suits Europe. A wise religious once told me that Western young people sought three things from religion. They wanted deep, liturgical, contemplative prayer, and to know Christ, she said; they wanted a community of friendship; and they wanted practical justice that made real God's option for the poor, and that transformed the world around them. Her words struck home, because they were three things I was looking for. Later I found them combined in Sant'Egidio.

I met the Community, as most people do, in Rome, in the Basilica of Santa Maria in Trastevere, at 8:30 one evening. The dome of the apse shimmers with Cavallini's gorgeous twelfth-century mosaics. A huge icon of Christ dominates the altar. Even more remarkable is that the basilica fills with young people, mostly in their thirties and forties, the so-called "lost generation." Here they are, hastening in with a seriousness of purpose I have only ever seen in monasteries. They chant a heart-cracking Vespers, which feels monastic yet which is modern, and which includes a Gospel reading and a reflection — one night by a layman, another night by a cardinal.

Sant'Egidio Communities around the world — they were present in sixty countries at the last count and include about forty thousand people — pray like this, at least once a week, before a copy of the same icon. The members do not live together, but in their own homes; they are mostly lay, but there are a few priests and one bishop. There are no vows or pledges; a person just gets involved, and commits himself or herself to the prayer and service of the poor. The central administration is threadbare; communities are, in essence, autonomous, each with a leader — an abbatial figure, unelected, who guides the Community. Most Communities have strong bonds with Rome: Easter in Trastevere brings together members from all over the world for three days of liturgies and talks; Christmas, too, is a time when people travel to take part in the celebrations at the Basilica of Santa Maria. Members are encouraged to help with the yearly gathering of religious leaders organized by Sant'Egidio and/or promote the Community's campaign against the death penalty.

But mostly what members do is spend their time crossing boundaries between religions, between cultures, between rich and poor, young and old, mentally disabled and mentally able. Whichever city they are in, the Communities have a special relationship with its poorer parts. In Antwerp they work around the port areas; in San Salvador, the slums. In New York, as in London, the Community looks out for the hidden poor, the elderly who live alone in high-rise blocks, attended to materially by social services, but in human terms as abandoned as lepers in Calcutta. In Buenos Aires, the Community's service is in La Boca, an area of the city where the destitute end up in houses on stilts to avoid the flooding river. In Havana, Community members take the ferry across to Regla, where among the poor in the tin-shack houses they are greeted as good friends, friends to chat to, friends to offer mouth-burning homemade rum to. These friendships are very normal, as friendship always is. But what is extraordinary and quite abnormal is that the friendship exists between people who in contemporary urban society are separated by hidden chasms.

The Community's founder, Andrea Riccardi, speaks of the deception of the bourgeois city, the lie of prosperity that can only be maintained by hiding away the poor. The Community crosses the river, becomes friends to the friendless, and unmasks that deception.

In London we are a small community, just a few years old, made up of both Anglicans and Catholics — about fifteen in all. Apart from praying to-gether — once a week — and being together, we really only have one kind of work, which is to walk with our elderly friends. At least once a week we visit them on an estate near Clapham Junction, in south London. We don't do it out of pity or duty. We do it because if we stopped doing it, we would all be worse off. It would be as if someone had turned off a tap we had all begun to rely on to slake our thirst.

London is not built for listening. It's not a place where we can easily sit gently at each other's side. Some of us have jobs, some of them good jobs that satisfy us. But all too often we feel like items on supermarket shelves. People take us off the shelf and put us back. And that's just what our el-derly friends often feel. But when we're all together, we don't feel like that. When we spend time with each other, helping each other or just listening, we realize how we're all important to God and we're all important to each other. Our elderly friends show us how to be gentle, and how to listen. They share their wisdom and their incredible strength. Suddenly, we find life matters.

It's the way we were made. God sets us up so we're full of yearning. That's why life is often so painful. What we yearn for, we often don't seem to find. But Jesus knows we all need visiting, because we're all in our own kind of prison. There's a big thirst inside all of us. And we only stop being thirsty when we offer others something to drink.

The Community, then, is the evolving answer to the universal question posed by the students who gathered in 1968 at the Chiesa Nuova in Rome: solitude — how can we get out of it and discover others? What has developed since then is the answer: prayer, fraternity, and friendship with the poor in an urban context. The contemporary city is the place out of which Christian community, a glimpse of the kingdom, can be born, through prayer and friendship with the poor.

When he addressed the Community some years ago, the pope singled out its two vital characteristics: on the one hand, its *filoxenia* — its love of the outsider — and on the other its openness to the universal. The Community tries to live "without walls," conscious of the tendency in both society and the church to build a fortress around itself and to create scapegoats. To the temptation of the church as refuge and the nation as fortress, the Community responds with a counterlogic of concern for the one who is outside and far away. It refutes a false idea of peace in which the East is regarded as fanatical and the Arab world as fundamentalist because it understands that these barriers of the mind contain an inherent violence that can explode at any time.

Peacemaking, therefore, is simply another expression of Sant'Egidio's border-dissolving charism. Its model is the famous story of St. Francis of Assisi taming the wolf of Gubbio. Like Francis, the Community comes to conflicts without any agenda or vested interest except peace with justice; like Francis, they come unarmed: their weakness is their strength. They start from the assumption that no one can be defined as so barbarian or evil as not to deserve even a word; and they embark on a dialogue which some regard — as the townspeople of Gubbio at first regarded Francis's dialogue with the wolf — as madness and possibly treason. But "only peace is holy," the Community insists. Just as Jesus was not put off by the violence of the Gerasene demoniac, or Francis by the wolf that terrorized the village of Gubbio, Sant'Egidio believes that if a person has a gun in his or her hand there is even more reason to stretch out your hands to him or her. If the Community discovered the whereabouts of Osama bin Laden's cave, they would be loading up a Land Rover tomorrow to go and have a dialogue with him.

For the same reason, the Community has organized a yearly "Religions and Peace" meeting of religious leaders in the spirit of the famous 1986 Assisi gathering. The meetings transmit to the world a resounding rejection of the pessimistic Samuel Huntingdon vision of the world as increasingly divided by conflict along religious lines. The clash of religious civilizations, the Community endlessly demonstrates, is no more inevitable than the class struggle was a hundred years ago.

But to avert it will require a new spiritual humanism of the sort which Sant'Egidio lives. It will require the kind of friendship the Community does so well. It will require the kind of hope that children in the Community's slum school outside Maputo sang for me, using upturned pots and pans for drums, when I visited it. "Nós queremos um povo sem doença," they bellowed, "nesta terra, terra moçambicana." (We want our people to be well again. In this land, our Mozambican land.)

26

Promoting SCCs via the Internet

Joseph Healey

I live in Dar es Salaam, Tanzania. I wonder how many people could find it on a world map. I get comments like: "You mean Tasmania." "One of fifty-three countries in Africa. You got to be kidding!" Here in the Archdiocese of Dar es Salaam alone we have over twenty-three hundred Small Christian Communities (SCCs) in forty-nine parishes. Yet as I travel around the world people often ask, "Do you have SCCs in Africa?"

How can we get this message out? How can we share our good news of SCCs with people in other continents? The young people in Dar es Salaam tell me: "That's easy. Use IT [information technology]." It's true! E-mail, Internet, Web sites, online PowerPoint presentations, online education, and so on open up an exciting window of opportunity to mutually share our experiences of SCCs in our global society and world church. If we are convinced about SCCs, we must also be convinced about the importance of the Internet — especially in reaching young people today.

When it comes to promoting SCCs through the Internet a good adage is: *Think outside the box.* Try this example: Enter the words "Small Christian Communities" (using the quotation marks) in the Google search engine (*www.google.com*) and see how many results (hits) and useful information you get. I just tried it and got 17,300 results! Most Web sites listed include links to many other Web sites with similar SCC concerns. Browsing through these Web sites can yield many surprises and facilitate new connections.

SCC Web Sites around the World

Marins Team
www.cebs.ws/english/english.htm (English)
E-mail: *Teamtrema@aol.com*
Includes sections on the José Marins Itinerant Team, services, calendar, books and articles on BECs, and photos.

Adital (Agencia de Información Fray Tito para América Latina)
www.adital.com.br
E-mail: *agencia@adital.org.br*
News service on CEBs across the Latin American world originating in Brazil. In Portuguese and Spanish with English as an option.

Consejo Episcopal Latinoamericano (CELAM)
www.celam.org
E-mail: *celam@celam.org*
Web site in Spanish of the Latin America [Catholic] Episcopal Conference. Various resources on Comunidades Eclesiales de Base (CEBs) known by the English translation Basic Ecclesial Communities (BECs).

Parish without Borders
www.parish-without-borders.net
E-mail: *paa2000@n-jcenter.com*
Variety of SCC material. Section on "Twinning Resources for Small Christian Communities" includes general resources, SCC twinning stories, articles, documents, and Internet links.

House Church Central
www.hccentral.com
E-mail: *hdrake@hccentral.com*
The house church movement is an attempt to get away from the institutional church, seeking instead to return to the small gatherings of peoples that constituted all of the churches of the New Testament era. This U.S.-based, nondenominational Web site is dedicated to the growing house church movement. It offers a Bible-centered doctrinal base for home church and endeavors to provide house churches with: (1) a channel for the interchange of ideas, (2) a source for solid Christian theology, (3) a catalog of resources for the house church, and (4) a (necessarily incomplete) worldwide directory.

New Way of Being Church
www.newway.org.uk
E-mail: *info@newway.org.uk*
Web site is designed to provide information about New Way, its underlying principles and method of working. It has sections covering New Way Resource Publications, its *Newsletter,* book reviews on related subjects, and stories of new ways of being church that are appearing across the United Kingdom. Includes an effective online PowerPoint presentation that is also available by e-mail file attachment. Questions for the immediate future are

whether the Web site could: (1) create a forum for the exchange of ideas, (2) provide resource material to enquirers and generate income, and (3) provide a "Virtual Community" for scattered Small Christian Communities presently existing in isolation.

At Your Word, Lord

www.aywl.org.uk

E-mail: *aywl@rcdow.org.uk*

A pastoral and spiritual renewal program in the Catholic Diocese of Westminster, England, based on Small Christian Communities — weekly faith-sharing groups.

Iona Community

www.iona.org.uk

E-mail: *ionacomm@gla.iona.org.uk*

An ecumenical Christian community of men and women from different walks of life and different Christian traditions that is committed to seeking new ways of living the Gospel of Jesus Christ in today's world. Wild Goose Publications features books on small communities around the world.

Fresh Expressions: Helping to Build a Mission-shaped Church

www.freshexpressions.org.uk

E-mail: Contact is made by submitting a message form on the Web site.

A resource of a growing movement of mission across every tradition — fresh expressions of the Christian Churches all across Britain. Over the last fifteen years local churches have been trying out fresh expressions and experiments of church life. Often these churches have borrowed ideas from churches in other parts of the world. All around the edge of the traditional churches (such as parishes) good things are growing. The Web site is connected to the report of the Church of England, *Mission Shaped Church: Church Planting and Fresh Expressions of Church in a Changing Context*, published in January 2004. It includes examples and case studies of Base Ecclesial Communities, Café Churches, Cell Churches, etc.

European Collective

A Web site presently under construction.

Lumko Institute

www.catholic-johannesburg.org.za/dms/contacts/dms_contact-view?contact_id=3011

E-mail: *lumko@global.co.za*

Pastoral Institute of the Southern Africa Catholic Bishops' Conference
(SACBC) — pastoral and mission research and training through workshops,
seminars, and courses. Produces a wide range of audiovisual and printed materials on SCCs, including the famous Seven Step Method for neighborhood
Gospel groups.

AMECEA
www.amecea.org/index.htm
E-mail: *amecea@amecea.org*
Acronym for "Association of Member [Catholic] Episcopal Conferences in
Eastern Africa." A service organization for the National Episcopal Confer-
ences of the eight countries of Eastern Africa, namely, Eritrea, Ethiopia,
Kenya, Malawi, Sudan, Tanzania, Uganda, and Zambia. Somalia and Dji-
bouti are affiliate members. Part of its mission is revitalizing Small Christian
Communities and emphasizing the role of the SCCs in evangelization.

Maryknoll Fathers and Brothers Africa Region
www.maryknollafrica.org
E-mail: *AfricaRFO@Maryknoll.org*
Part of the history of SCCs in Eastern Africa together with a variety of case
studies and concrete examples of this pastoral priority and its pastoral and
missionary outreach. Includes resources such as books and videos on SCCs.

AsIPA (Asian Integral Pastoral Approach) Desk
www.asipa.net
E-mail: *asipa@ms78.hinet.net*
A desk in the Office of Laity of the Federation of Asian Bishops' Conferences
(FABC). The Asian Integral Pastoral Approach (AsIPA) is a tool towards
the new way of being church in Asia through SCCs as envisioned by the
Vatican II and as emphasized by FABC 5. Facilitates training programs on
international and national levels (for pastoral leaders, priests, and laypeople
with exposure to BCCs) that have proved to be effective tools to see the
vision and to acquire the skills needed in a participatory church (for example, new leadership style, Gospel-based communities, and participative
formation programs).

SAMBAYANIHAN: The Basic Ecclesial Communities in the Philippines
http://frpicx.tripod.com
E-mail: *frpicx@hotmail.com*
Sambayanihan is a Filipino word that captures the essence of BECs as a
way of being church. Contains information, stories, and reflections about

the Basic Ecclesial Communities (BECs) in the Philippines, including on-line PowerPoint presentations. It answers the questions that are frequently asked: What are BECs? What are the approaches in building BECs? What is happening in these BECs?

Project Linkup

www.home.vicnet.net.au/~rciascc
E-mail: *noola@alphalink.com.au*
Web site designed to publicize the model of adult initiation developed in St. Thomas More's Catholic Parish, Belgrave, Victoria, Australia. There is compelling evidence for linking the Adult Catechumenate and SCCs. Project Linkup describes stories of some of the people who have been brought into the Catholic Church through a program of initiation.

Archdiocese of Adelaide Basic Ecclesial Communities

www.adelaide.catholic.org.au/Services/BEC/default.htm
E-mail: *becs@adelaide.catholic.org.au*
Covers history, information about BECs, comprehensive lists of resources (books, booklets, videos, CDs, posters), and a newsletter.

Australian Home Church

www.users.tpg.com.au/kgoodlet/homechurch
E-mail: *kgoodlet@tpg.com.au*
User-friendly site which explains home church in clear language, accessible alike to the already-churched and the unchurched. Includes sections on FAQs, getting started, resources and a directory for many Australian home churches.

OIKOS

www.oikos.org.au
E-mail: *oikos@optusnet.com.au*
Provides friendship and encouragement to anyone involved in new ways of church. This includes those within denominations, independent groups meeting outside the traditional church, and individual Christians who do not attend any church. *OIKOS* (the Greek word for "household" used in the Bible) is a resource for home churches and is also the name of the quarterly newsletter sent to home churches and interested individuals. The Web site includes sections on "Home Church Happenings," "Resources for Home Church," and the *Australian Home Church Directory.*

Small Christian Communities in North America
Collaborative Web Site
Barbara A. Darling

The United States is blessed with numerous organizations that support and network the small church experience. Most of them came into existence in the 1970s and 1980s about the time when lots of church folks were discovering and developing a passion for SCCs.

In this new moment early in the third millennium, most folks in the United States are feeling a financial pinch, and the church is no exception. As a result, parish and diocesan staff people are wearing several different hats and need to consider numerous ministries a priority. They and parish volunteers as well as grassroots SCC members are balancing personal and department budgets with the need to interact with like-minded people and learn more about keeping their SCCs healthy and lively. No longer is it possible for most folks to keep up memberships in several national organizations, much less travel to more than one conference annually to meet with others face to face.

Thirteen U.S. and Canadian organizations are exploring creative answers by looking at ways they can collaborate in their service to SCCs. There was always a loose relationship among these organizations but little in the way of an inclusive working affiliation. As a result of the Lilly-financed SCC study carried out by Bernard Lee and others (see chapter 9), six hundred members and representatives of these organizations convened in San Antonio, Texas, in August 2002. At that gathering and at a subsequent summit of leadership in 2003, it became apparent that a more collaborative model of North American SCC support and networking was crucial. The decision was made not only for financial reasons, but because this mutuality of purpose and effort reflects the model of Small Church Community among the groups. Yet this metamorphosis of SCC support in North America is intentionally a slow process. Particular emphases among the groups such as evangelization, resource development, the connections between SCCs and the catechumenate, leadership training, multicultural church, scriptural literacy, young adults, and the diversity of parish-based and community-based small church must be recognized, included, and respected by the whole.

The first concrete result of this loose confederation is a Web site that displays links to individual Web sites of the organizations. Web surfers in North America will find a multitude of services available to SCCs and can easily choose those that fit their current needs. Those outside North America will likely find resources and wisdom to complement their small church experiences as well. Strategies are being developed to work collaboratively in other areas so that there is little overlap of services, yet no needs go unmet in North American SCCs.

To find out more about these organizations, go to the Small Christian Communities in North America Web site at

www.smallchristiancommunities.org

Or go directly to:

Buena Vista
www.buenavista.org
E-mail: *bv@buenavista.org*

Celebrating the Word
www.celebratingtheword.com
E-mail: *fjruetz@celebratingtheword.com*

Diocese of Oakland Small Christian Communities Office
www.oakdiocese.org/pastoral/SCC
E-mail: *npetersen@oakdiocese.org*
With related SCC Web site in Spanish:
Oficina de las Pequeñas Comunidades Cristianas de la Diócesis de Oakland
www.oakdiocese.org/pastoral/Comunidades.htm

Good Ground Press
www.goodgroundpress.com
E-mail: *editor@goodgroundpress.com*

Latin American/North American Church Concerns
www.nd.edu/~kellogg
E-mail: *Robert.S.Pelton.1@nd.edu*

Loyola Institute for Ministry, Loyola University, New Orleans including the LIMEX Program and LIM On-Campus Program
www.loyno.edu/lim/index.html
E-mail: *lim@loyno.edu*

Mexican American Cultural Center
www.maccsa.org
E-mail: *register@maccsa.org*

With related SCC Web site in Spanish:
Centro Mexico Americano de la Cultura:
www.maccsa.org

National Alliance of Parishes Restructuring into Communities (NAPRC)
www.naprc.faithweb.com
E-mail: *naprcoffice@ameritech.net*

National Pastoral Life Center
www.nplc.org/smallcommunities.htm
E-mail: *smallcommunities@nplc.org*

North American Forum for Small Christian Communities (NAFSCC)
www.nafscc.org. Inclusive for English-, French-, and Spanish-speaking members.
E-mail: *DMK@dosp.org*

North American Forum on the Catechumenate
www.naforum.org
E-mail: *amanda_drago2005@yahoo.com*

Pastoral Department for Small Christian Communities in the Archdiocese of Hartford
www.sccquest.org
E-mail: *info@sccquest.org*

RENEW International
www.renewintl.org
E-mail: *renew@renewintl.org*
With related SCC Web site in Spanish:
RENEW International en Español
www.renewintl.org/Espanol/index.htm

An Experiment in Online Education
for Small Christian Community Leadership
Barbara J. Fleischer

In 2000 Rev. Bernard Lee and fellow researchers published the results of the first national study on Small Christian Communities in the U.S. context (see chapter 9). The study recommended two primary areas for leadership development to enhance the life and direction of SCCs in the United States.

It called for strong attention to the biblical literacy of SCC leaders and a systemic development of group leadership skills.

The Loyola Institute for Ministry of Loyola University, New Orleans, has developed both a Master of Pastoral Studies and a Certificate of Pastoral Studies with an area of concentration in Small Christian Community Formation for both its on-campus program and its distance learning program. It offers both grounding in scripture and Catholic theology in its "theological core" and specific courses in Small Christian Community development. The off-campus program, the Loyola Institute for Ministry Extension program (or LIMEX, for short), operates in sponsoring dioceses by forming small learning communities that are guided by faculty and a Loyola-certified facilitator through the four-year curriculum.

Since the completion of the national study, the Loyola Institute for Ministry has experimented with a new way of two focus courses in Small Christian Community Formation. The two courses, entitled the "Inner Life of Small Christian Communities" and the "Public Life of Small Christian Communities," are offered online through the formation of a learning community in cyberspace.

Students register for the semester-long courses either as graduate students or as continuing education students (graduate students complete term papers in addition to their weekly assignments). The course Web site lists required textbooks, supplementary readings and bibliographies, audiotapes for each session, and weekly assignments. Each week students complete the readings and listen to the Web-based presentation. The instructor then assigns each student to post a beginning reflection on an assigned discussion question on the "Discussion Board" located on the course Web site. Other students in the class then post their own reflections in response to the discussion question and their peer's lead, and an online conversation develops. The advantage of the discussion board is that students can post their responses at any time during the session "week" and do not all have to be online at the same time. Typically, three in-depth discussions will occur for each week's class, and the instructor will comment on both student responses and course material.

While some may object that online courses do not have the richness of face-to-face communication, they do allow participants to come together to reflect on their SCC leadership and life in ways that would not otherwise be possible. One recent student, for example, lives in Panama where her husband was transferred. Her graduate education was interrupted at the point where she needed to complete her ministry focus courses. By participating in the online class she was able to share her various experiences of SCC life

with others in the class who were similarly involved in fostering the development of SCCs in their locations. The online courses have not only provided
these students with resources, content, and verbal communication skills development, they have also offered them a glimpse of what might be a new
venue for SCC life in the twenty-first century. For more information, go to
www.loyno.edu/lim.

Connecting through a Variety of Internet Resources

There are a wide variety of e-mail mailing lists and e-mail discussion lists on
SCCs. Some Listservs are restricted to a specific network or core group. Chat
rooms, discussion boards, and message boards on SCCs on popular Web sites
such as Yahoo and Hotmail tend to come and go. Blogs (private and public)
with SCC content are becoming more popular. There are daily and weekly
logs on SCC Web sites. Text messaging on cell phones is a popular form
of communication. All these examples are part of what are called the new
media that can promote SCCs in different ways.

Some ongoing examples are:

Faith-Sharing Newsletter:
www.goodgroundpress.com/index.asp?PageAction=Custom&ID=54
An interactive newsletter for small groups of people who gather as a faith-
based community. The small communities might be parish based, multiparish
based, ecumenical, or nonparish based, including RCIA groups, RENEW
groups, and post-RENEW groups.

World RENEW Newsletter
www.renewintl.org/NewsEvents/Pages/WorldRenewNewsletter.htm
Covers the spiritual life with behind-the-scenes stories and updates on
RENEW International's work with parishes and small communities across
the United States and abroad. The RENEW International Web site includes
an online community in English and Spanish.

Buena Vista
www.buenavista.org
E-mail, mailing list, and chat room.

North American Forum for Small Christian Communities (NAFSCC)
www.nafscc.org
E-mail, mailing list.

What are the possibilities in the future? Already virtual or online parishes (also called "Online 3D Churches" and "Churches on the Net") exist. What about virtual or online SCCs?

It is important to keep in touch with changes and updates by going through Google and other search engines regularly and checking SCC Web sites for changes and updates in content as well as new links. For promoting SCCs via the Internet the future is now.

Appendix

How to Use This Book
Suggestions for SCCs

We have tried to make this book user-friendly for a readership of SCC members and interested people from all six continents. There is plenty of practical, pastoral content with many examples, anecdotes, stories, case studies, quotations, references, etc. At the same time we have tried to back up the chapters with solid academic content and references. Our goal is what Cardinal Cormac Murphy-O'Connor says in the foreword: "To bring together the varied, prophetic experiences of Small Christian Communities around the world, and allow them to speak to each other." We hope that you will speak to each other and learn from each other's SCC experiences in furthering this new way of being church. Here are a few suggestions for an SCC reading of this book.

1. **Choose** one or two appropriate chapters to reflect on. In your SCC you might take a chapter from a different continent than yours or over a period of time work through all six sections of the book. Prepare by having each person read the suggested chapter in advance (photocopying for such use is permissible), or have one person summarize the chapter and read selected extracts.

2. **Consider** the following questions:

   - What are some similarities to your experience?
   - What are some differences?
   - What is helpful for you and also thought provoking?
   - What of your SCC story would you like to share with the writer(s) if the opportunity is given?

3. **Contact**. You could send a response to the writer(s) by e-mail (see addresses in the list of contributors) or c/o Joe Healey or Jeanne Hinton.

4. **Twin.** Is your SCC twinned with another SCC elsewhere? If not, would it be helpful for you to twin, and where would you choose?

5. **Learn** from one or more of the Web sites mentioned in the book. These can provide excellent discussion material for your SCC. One person could give a summary and some printouts of a particular Web site of interest. The questions above could be helpful here too.

(With material supplied by Richard Begbie, Michael Brough, Barbara A. Darling, Robert Moriarty, James O'Halloran, Robert Pelton, Irene Wilson, and others.)

Resources and Annotated Bibliography

(including "How to Use This Book")

Editors' Note: Many e-mail and Internet resources are found in chapter 26, "Promoting SCCs via the Internet."

Resources

Newsletters and Magazines

Electronic versions are available. Web site and e-mail addresses are provided in chapter 26.

Buena Vista Ink. A six-times-yearly newsletter for people devoted to the formation and support of Small Christian Communities. Produced by Buena Vista, Inc., a Catholic network of people devoted to the formation and support of SCCs since 1987. Includes a wide variety of SCC articles and resource material. Contact: P.O. Box 745475, Arvada, CO 80006-5475.

Gatherings. A quarterly newsletter published by the Pastoral Department for Small Christian Communities of the Archdiocese of Hartford, Connecticut. Quality reflection articles with questions and a roundup of SCC happenings. Contact: 467 Bloomfield Avenue, Bloomfield, CT 06002.

New Way of Being Church Newsletter. Published by New Way of Being Church. The New Way Network provides a wide variety of small community information, news about meetings and workshops, special articles, and SCC resource material in the United Kingdom. Contact: Wells, Somerset BA5 2PD, United Kingdom.

OIKOS. A quarterly newsletter originating from Victoria, Australia, that is designed to encourage, network, and provide resources for home churches across Australia. Contact: Bessie Pereira, Editor, 10 Viviani Crescent, Heathmont, Victoria 3135, Australia.

Re-gather the Parish. A newsletter of the Melbourne, Australia, SCC Network. Includes examples and case studies of specific SCCs, ongoing support for SCC facilitators, and SCC resource material. Contact: Una Melville, St. John the Baptist Parish, 21 Forest Road, Ferntree Gully, VIC 3156, Australia. E-mail: *UnaMelville<saintjb@ozemail .com.au>*.

Twist in the Tale: Parables from the Neighbourhood Church. A quarterly newsletter from the Basic Ecclesial Communities Office in the Archdiocese of Adelaide, Australia, that links faith with the stories and experiences of people in their neighborhoods. Contact: Coordinator, BEC Office, 39 Wakefield St., Adelaide, South Australia 5000.

Bible-Sharing and Faith-Sharing Resources

Additional resources are found in the annotated bibliography. Many resources are also found on Internet Web sites.

Bible and Practice. Sheffield: Urban Theology Unit (UTU). How does the Bible lead to and provoke contemporary action, politics, and lifestyle, particularly in an urban context? UTU also provides resource material, booklets, and training material of practical value to those developing SCCs, in particular on the use of the pastoral cycle and biblical reflection. *www.utusheffield.fsnet.co.uk.* E-mail: *office@utusheffield.fsnet.co.uk.*

Bible Study and Sharing on the Gospel of Matthew — Year A/Gospel of Mark — Year B/Gospel of Luke — Year C for Christian Communities (English and Swahili). Produced by Richard Baawobr, M.Afr. Published by the AMECEA Pastoral Department and BICAM, Nairobi, Kenya. 1999–2001.

C.T.W.: a weekly process for small faith-sharing groups, based on Sunday's scripture readings *Celebrating the Word.* Weekly publication (excepting July–August). By paper mail or e-mail. A user-friendly process to help people of faith to break open Sunday's Word. It is a weekly faith-sharing experience that participants worldwide find life-giving and Spirit-filled and an effective process for reevangelizing. Contact: Celebrating the Word, 265 Westmount Road North, Waterloo, ON, Canada.

Connecting Faith and Life, written by Paul O'Bryan. A "Gathering Format" to foster a spirituality of Christian Community. Depending on the time available there are different components for a long ninety-minute or short twenty-minute prayer gathering such as for an SCC. It links the cycle of Sunday Gospels with current issues, both local and global. It is available free online and can be downloaded in PDF format from the Diocese of Maitland-Newcastle, Australia, Web site: *www.mn.catholic.org.au/diocesan/connecting_life_faith.htm. Editors' note:* In doing research for this chapter we found that more and more Bible-sharing and faith-sharing resources for SCCs are available only online. This is one example.

Disciples in Mission — An Evangelization Experience. A ministry of the Paulist National Catholic Evangelization Association (PNCEA). English and Spanish materials for Lectionary-based faith-sharing groups (adults, teens, and families with young children) especially in Lent. Group Study Guides for Lectionary Cycles A, B, and C including African American editions. Contact: Paulist National Catholic Evangelization Association, 3031 Fourth Street, NE, Washington, DC 20017-1102. E-mail: *pncea@pncea.org.*

Disciples on the Journey: Faith-Sharing Booklets for Small Groups. Cycles ABC (English and Spanish). Victoria, Texas: Faith-sharing publications. Separate sections for each group: adult, teen, family. Contact: Faith Journey Publications, Diocese of Victoria, P.O. Box 4070, Victoria, TX 77903-4070. *www.victoriadiocese.org.*

Education for Ministry (EFM). A well-designed four-year training program in biblical studies, church history, theology, and liturgy. With Episcopalian/Anglican roots, it is not home-church specific, but in Australia at least is home-church friendly. Based at the University of the South in the United States, EFM operates in many countries around the world. To check if EFM has a base in your country, or for further details: *www.sewanee.edu/EFM/EFMhome.html.* E-mail: *efm@sewanee.edu.*

Faith Sharing for Small Church Communities: Questions and Commentaries on the Sunday Readings. Edited by Art Baranowski and the National Alliance for Parishes Restructuring into Communities (NAPRC). Cincinnati: St. Anthony Messenger Press, 1993. Life focus commentaries and questions on Cycles ABC from seventy-five hundred members of SCCs around the world.

Healing the Body of Christ (English and Spanish). Faith-sharing booklet produced by RENEW International, Plainfield, New Jersey. Mahwah, N.J.: Paulist Press, 2002. Designed to help people work through the impact of the serious sexual abuse crisis and scandal in the church and to invite Christ to heal us in the midst of suffering.

PRAYERTIME: Faith-Sharing Reflections on the Sunday Gospels. Cycles ABC (English and Spanish). Produced by RENEW International, Plainfield, New Jersey. Mahwah, N.J.: Paulist Press, 2002. Adapted by Westminster Diocese for the United Kingdom in the AYWL Program. An important resource for adult faith formation. RENEW International also sponsors a subscription Web site specifically designed for Small Church Communities. Faith-sharing material on the Sunday Gospel and a variety of topics is updated weekly. *www.parishlife.com.* E-mail: *Subscription@ParishLife.com.*

Quest — A Reflection Booklet for Small Christian Communities. Published three times a year by the Pastoral Department for Small Christian Communities of the Archdiocese of Hartford, Connecticut. Week-by-week reflection booklet based on the Sunday readings of the three-year lectionary. *Quest* is used in small communities throughout the United States and in about a dozen countries around the world.

Resource Booklets for Small Christian Communities. Reflections on all four Gospels by Peter B. Price. Wells, Somerset, England: New Way of Being Church (variable dates). Four booklets based on readings for each Sunday throughout the year. A resource for daily living and transforming communities.

Sunday by Sunday. A four-page weekly newsletter published by Good Ground Press, St. Paul, Minnesota. It invites adults, groups, or individuals to reflect on the Sunday readings. Perfect for group reflection and a very good resource for all kinds of SCCs.

Videos

20/20 Vision for the Parish: A Clear Direction for the Future. A three-part video: Part I — "Is the Church Working? Why Change?" Part II — "The Basics of the Called to Be Church Vision for Parish." Part III — "Implementation in Several Parishes." 35 minutes. Three-part process guide included. Produced by and available from the National Alliance of Parishes Restructuring into Communities (NAPRC), 310 Allen Street, Dayton, OH 45410.

Bridges to Build. 29 minutes. Insights into churches seeking to engage effectively with the communities around them. Ties into the book *Changing Churches: Building Bridges in Local Mission.* Produced by and available from the Churches Commission on Mission/CTBI, 35–41 Lower Marsh, London SE1 7SA, England. E-mail: *bbh@ctbi.org.uk.*

The Church in the Neighborhood. 43 minutes in the PAL System. A very instructive video showing how to develop and animate/facilitate Small Christian Communities within the parish in East Africa. It has two parts: (1) shows the basis and formation of Small Christian Communities; and (2) shows the different services that can be established within the community. The life and activities of several Small Christian Communities in Kenya are shown. Produced by and available from Ukweli Video, P.O. Box 14465, Nairobi, Kenya. *www.geocities.com/UkweliVideo.* E-mail: *ukweli@wananchi.com.*

Church: Past, Present, Future. Three-set video: (1) "Insights from the Past, Discovering Our Biblical Roots." (2) "Gift for the Present, Being Church Where We Are." (3) "Legacy for the Future, Living into the Reign of God." The internationally known SCC team led by Father José Marins invites viewers to discover the sense of where history is going in our church. Facilitator guide and participant material are included. Produced by and available from Buena Vista, Inc., P.O. Box 745475, Arvada, CO 80006-5475.

Imagine That: Small Christian Communities. Video on the "Second International Consultation on Small Christian Communities" at the University of Notre Dame, Notre Dame, Indiana, in October 1996. 22 minutes. In answer to the question, "Is there a simple way that an SCC in America could begin to live out a public life in light of the universal church?" Father Bob Pelton, C.S.C., of Notre Dame (13 minutes into the videotape) explains the tradition of twinning in the Catholic Church on the diocesan, parish, and SCC levels. He describes the international Small Christian Community (SCC) twinning program as a new way of experiencing church — from small community to small community. Produced by Fatima Media Ministry and Buena Vista, Inc. Available from Buena Vista (see above).

It's a Small Church After All (Spanish version is *Ven Con Nosotros*). Video on the "Third International Consultation on Small Christian Communities" in Cochabamba, Bolivia, in November 1999. English and Spanish. 46 minutes. Under the section on "Local and Global Networking for Small Christian Communities," twinning is explained as an important means for SCCs to develop a broader viewpoint and a wider vision. Sister Rita Ishengoma, STH, of Tanzania (36 minutes into the videotape) describes the characteristics of the International Small Christian Community (SCC) twinning program that involves sister or partner communities around the world. Produced by Fatima Media Ministry and Buena Vista, Inc. Available from Buena Vista (see above).

Parish Core Communities: Renewing the Face of the Earth. Two hours. A four-part video series to help the Parish Core Community for Small Community Development: (1) *Community: As It Was in the Beginning and Is Now.* Stresses the importance of the Core Community as a permanent structure in the parish and highlights its responsibilities. (2) *Conversion: The Heart of the Matter.* Proclaims Christ as truly at the center of Small Christian Communities and at the center of the lives of its members. (3) *Small Communities: Reaching Out.* Inspires Core Communities to reach out in evangelization and social action. (4) *Core Communities: Charting the Course.* Enumerates the challenges facing Core Communities as they form SCCs: planning, evaluating, inviting others, nurturing parish ministries, developing leaders, pastoring, etc. Produced by and available from RENEW International, 1232 George Street, Plainfield, NJ 07062-1717.

Rediscovering Community — International Perspectives. Video on the "First International Consultation on Small Christian Communities," at the University of Notre Dame, Notre Dame, Indiana, in December 1991. Participants came from Africa, Asia, Europe, Latin America, and North America to promote the communion between the local churches of the various regions of the world. Produced by and available from

Fatima Media Ministry, P.O. Box 929, Notre Dame, IN 46556. *www.nd.edu/~fatima/mediaministry.html.* E-mail: *fatima@nd.edu.*

Sharing Faith across the Hemisphere. English and Spanish. 28 minutes with discussion guide. What happens when North meets South? This video portrays the story of the relationship of the church in the United States and in Latin America — a mutual sharing of faith come alive. Men, women, priests, religious, and laypersons tell their amazing story of the dynamic faith that is present in the church. Portrays the context for the development of SCCs. Washington, D.C.: United States Conference of Catholic Bishops (USCCB), 1997. A book (English and Spanish) by the same title is available.

Small Community Basics in a Nutshell. 30 minutes. The "nutshell" contains basic steps to consider before implementing Small Christian Communities in a parish or diocesan setting. The video, easily divided into four sessions, is an excellent tool for pastors, staff, parish leaders, and SCC facilitators. Produced by and available from Buena Vista (see above).

This Is the Moment. Celebrating the Launch of the "At Your Word, Lord" (AYWL) Spiritual and Pastoral Renewal Program in the Diocese of Westminster, England. Wembley Arena, London, September 2003. 14 minutes. Stresses the importance of the weekly small groups in the five seasons of the AYWL Program. Participants share what the Gospel means to them. The Holy Spirit does the work. Produced by and available from At Your Word, Lord (AYWL), Archbishop's House, Ambrosden Avenue, London, SW1P 1QJ, England.

Three Videos from the Archdiocese of Adelaide, Australia: An Interview with Pat Edwards (No. 10). Pat Edwards, a former BEC Key Leader, speaks about the experience of starting BECs in Glenelg Parish. *Stories of Neighbourhood Visiting* (No. 11). Neighborhood Pastoral Team Leaders Joe and Vicki Dall'Armi speak about their experience of BECs visiting. *Marins Lectures* (No. 12). José Marins, Teo Trevisan, and Robert Mueller speak during a BEC Conference in Adelaide in April 2001. Topics include "The Early Church," "The Reign of God," "Miracles," "Exorcism," "The Good News," and "Prayer" (2 hours, 53 minutes). Available from the Archdiocese of Adelaide: The Coordinator, BEC Office, 39 Wakefield Street, Adelaide, South Australia 5000.

We Are the Church — Lay Involvement in the Church. 45 minutes in the PAL System. A timely video showing in so many ways how the Catholic laity in Kenya are involved in proclaiming "the Word of God." Their work is portrayed through preaching, teaching, hymns, vibrant liturgies, healing ministries, dramas, youth activities, Small Christian Communities, nonviolent marches, and peace and justice initiatives. Produced by and available from Ukweli Video (see above).

International SCC Twinning Coordinators

(See chapter 22, "Reenergizing International SCC Twinning")

East Africa:
    Kenya: Mr. Alphonce Omolo: *alphonce@pandipieri.org*
    Tanzania: Sister Rita Ishengoma, STH: *rishengomak@yahoo.com*
    Uganda: Father John Vianney Muweesi: *weekembe@hotmail.com*
El Salvador: Mrs. Irma Chávez: *renelsal@navegante.com.sv*
United States: Barbara A. Darling: *badarling@juno.com*

Annotated Bibliography

Africa Faith and Justice Network. *The African Synod: Documents, Reflections, Perspectives.* Maryknoll, N.Y.: Orbis Books, 1996. Of the 211 interventions during the first two weeks of the African Synod in 1994, there were 29 interventions on SCCs (the fourth largest number after the topics of justice, inculturation, and laity). In the *Final Message*, Section 28 on "The Church-as-Family and Small Christian Communities" states: "The Church, the Family of God, implies the creation of small communities at the human level, living or basic ecclesial communities.... These individual Churches-as-Families have the task of working to transform society."

AMECEA Study Conference. "Conclusions of the 1973 AMECEA Study Conference on 'Planning for the Church in Eastern Africa in the 1980s.'" *African Ecclesial Review* (AFER) 16, nos. 1–2 (1974). "We have to insist on building church life and work on Basic Christian Communities in both rural and urban areas. Church life must be based on the communities in which everyday life and work take place: those basic and manageable social groups whose members can experience real interpersonal relationships and feel a sense of communal belonging, both in living and working."

AMECEA Study Conference. "Conclusions of the 1976 AMECEA Study Conference on 'Building Small Christian Communities in Eastern Africa.'" *African Ecclesial Review* (AFER) 18, no. 5 (1976). "Systematic formation of Small Christian Communities should be the key pastoral priority in the years to come in Eastern Africa."

AMECEA Study Conference. "Conclusions of the 1979 AMECEA Study Conference on 'The Implementation of the AMECEA Bishops' Pastoral Priority of Building Small Christian Communities: An Evaluation.'" *African Ecclesial Review* (AFER) 21, no. 5 (1979). "SCCs are an effective way of developing the mission dimension of the church at the most local level, and of making people feel that they are really part of the church's evangelizing work."

Andrews, Dave. *Building a Better World.* Sutherland, NSW: Albatross Books, 1996. A set of realistic, tested strategies for changing the world — and us — for the better.

Andrews, Dave and David Engwicht. *Can You Hear the Heartbeat?* Sydney: Hodder and Stoughton, 1989. Describes the radical alternative to a me-first lifestyle in which the strong get power and the weak go to the wall.

Azevado, Marcelo, S.J. *Basic Ecclesial Communities in Brazil.* Washington, D.C.: Georgetown University Press, 1987. A thorough investigation of the "fascinating reality of Brazilian Basic Ecclesial Communities." The book is geared to the academic.

Background Papers and Final Statement of the 1991 International Consultation on Basic Christian Communities on "Rediscovering Community — International Perspectives." Notre Dame, Ind.: Institute for Pastoral and Social Ministry, 1991. Later published separately in various newsletters and journals. Includes "Final Consultation Statement" and Joseph Healey, "Evolving a World Church from the Bottom Up: An Analysis and Interpretation of 3,500 Different Names, Titles, Terms, Expressions, Descriptions and Meanings for and about Small Christian Communities/Basic Christian Communities in the World with 11 Case Studies from Six Continents." Participants came from Africa, Asia, Europe, Latin America, and North America to promote the communion between the local churches of the various regions of the world.

Banks, Robert. *Going to Church in the First Century.* Blacktown, NSW: Hexagon Press, 1985. A historically accurate fictionalization of one pagan's encounter with a first-century house church. Helps peel away our cultural misconceptions of church by seeing what things were like in the early church. Interesting and provocative.

——. *Paul's Idea of Community: The Early House Churches in Their Historical Setting.* Grand Rapids, Mich.: Eerdmans Publishing, 1980. A fantastic rereading of the New Testament which will change your view of church! Scholarly in tone yet easy to read, this book lays a solid biblical and theological foundation for church as community.

Banks, Robert and Julia. *The Church Comes Home.* Peabody, Mass.: Hendrickson Publishers, 1998. A visionary and practical handbook by two deeply experienced people for those interested in home churches. An excellent read.

Baranowski, Arthur R. *Creating Small Faith Communities.* Cincinnati: St. Anthony's Messenger Press, 1988. A methodology for establishing Small Christian Communities in parishes written by one who has had considerable experience in the field.

Barret, Lois. *Building the House Church.* Scottsdale, Pa.: Herald Press, 1986. A valuable guide to starting home churches by an experienced leader of a network of home churches in Wichita, Kansas. Deals with questions such as written covenants, worship, relationships, decision making, growth strategies, and so on. The book's only flaw is an overemphasis on structure and order.

Barret, Tony. *Seeking Gospel Justice in Africa.* Spearhead 69. Eldoret, Kenya: AMECEA Gaba Publications, 1981.

Barriero, Alvaro, S.J. *Basic Ecclesial Communities — The Evangelization of the Poor.* Maryknoll, N.Y.: Orbis Books, 1982. This simply written book shows the power of the poor for evangelization, particularly when this power is harnessed in basic ecclesial communities.

Bauman, Clarence. *On the Meaning of Life: An Anthology of Theological Reflection.* Evangel Press, 1993.

BCCs/BECs Empowering People to Serve. Report of the AsIPA General Assembly in South Korea, September 2–9, 2003. Topics, proceedings, evaluation, and reports of participating countries and dioceses. Taipei: AsIPA Desk, 2003. *Belonging, Believing, and Serving: The Stories of Small Christian Community.* Hartford: Pastoral Department for Small Christian Communities, 1995. A variety of first-person accounts of SCCs in the Archdiocese of Hartford, Connecticut. Some of these SCCs are twinned with SCCs in East Africa.

Biagi, Bob. *A Manual for Helping Groups to Work More Effectively.* Amherst: University of Massachusetts. A book that reads easily and may be adapted for use by Small Christian Communities. It has useful suggestions for group dynamics or exercises.

Bisgrove, Margaret. *Where Two Are Gathered.* Winona, Minn: St. Mary's Press, 1997. This book is important because it offers an assortment of stories about real people who candidly share their successes and failures as they build the reign of God.

Boadt, Lawrence. *Reading the Old Testament: An Introduction.* New York: Paulist Press, 1984.

Boff, Clodovis. *Feet-On-the-Ground Theology: A Brazilian Journey.* Lima, Ohio: Academic Renewal, 2002.

Boff, Leonardo. *Ecclesiogenesis: The Base Communities Reinvent the Church.* Maryknoll, N.Y.: Orbis Books, 1986. The author explains how the Brazilian Basic Christian Communities are a new way of being church.

———. *Jesus Christ, Liberator.* Maryknoll, N.Y.: Orbis Books, 1978. Refreshing insights on Jesus.

Bonhoeffer, Dietrich. *Life Together: A Discussion of Christian Fellowship.* New York: Harper and Row, 1954. A perceptive analysis of the biblical reasons for residential community and for the style of community. A classic.

Bouma, Gary D. "Mapping Religious Contours." In *Religion in an Age of Change.* Kew, Australia: Christian Research Association, 1999.

Brown, Raymond E. *The Churches the Apostles Left Behind.* Mahwah, N.J.: Paulist Press, 1984. In New Testament times the church was not a monolith. There were various models operating.

———. *An Introduction to the New Testament.* New York: Doubleday, 1997. A monumental piece of scholarship that speaks to experts and novices alike. If a person could only have one book on the New Testament, this is the one to have.

Buena Vista's Four Essentials of Church Series. Seeking Justice: The Public Life of Faith in Small Christian Communities by Peter Eichten, Michael Cowan, and Bernard Lee, S.M. (1995). *Creating Community: Where There Is Love and Caring for Others, There Is God* by Barbara Howard and William V. D'Antonio (1996). *Designing Ritual: Celebrating the Sacred in the Ordinary* by James Telthorst, Richard White, and Felicia Wolf, O.S.F. (1997). *Living Scripture: Small Christian Communities and the Great Story* by Rick Connor, S.M., Nora Petersen, and Richard Rohr, O.F.M. (1998). Arvada, Colo.: Buena Vista, Inc. The whole series was revised and republished by Living the Good News in 2003. This four-booklet series is designed to help Small Christian Communities carry out the essentials of church.

Burke, Harriet, et al. *People, Promise, and Community: A Practical Guide to Creating and Sustaining Small Christian Communities.* New York: Paulist Press. Deals with the nuts and bolts of being a Small Christian Community, step by patient step. Useful for beginners.

Byrne, Tony, C.S.Sp. *How to Evaluate.* Ndola, Zambia: Mission Press, 1988. A practical guide for evaluating the work of the church and its organizations.

———. *Working for Justice and Peace: A Practical Guide.* Ndola, Zambia: Mission Press, 1988. A practical and easy-to-read guidebook for people who wish to encourage and motivate themselves and others to take action for justice and peace. Byrne is very experienced in the field.

Cardenal, Ernesto. *The Gospel in Solentiname.* 4 vols. Maryknoll, N.Y.: Orbis Books, 1976–1982. Records the creative Bible reflections and commentaries of small communities of fisherfolk and farm workers in Solentiname, a remote archipelago on Lake Nicaragua, on the Sunday Gospel readings. The true author is the Holy Spirit who inspired these commentaries.

Carroll, Denis. *What Is Liberation Theology?* Cork: The Mercier Press. Many people ask this question. This book provides an excellent answer.

Center for Conflict Resolution. *Building United Judgments: A Handbook for Consensus Decision Making.* Madison, Wis., 1981. Although not a "Christian" book in itself, this is an invaluable how-to guide to the form of decision making most appropriate for Christian community: consensus. Extremely practical and thorough. Highly recommended.

Cieslikiewicz, Christopher, O.F.M.Conv. *Small Christian Communities: Pastoral Priority and a Vital Force for Evangelization in the Archdiocese of Dar es Salaam, Tanzania. An*

Evaluation and New Perspectives. Rome: Lateran University, 2004. Thorough doctorate dissertation based on current SCC surveys, an in-depth questionnaire, and extensive field interviews with extensive bibliography and appendices.

Clark, Stephen B. *Patterns of Christian Community: A Statement of Community Order.* Ann Arbor, Mich.: Servant Books, 1984. Useful overview of what constitutes Christian community from the perspective of a Roman Catholic live-in community, but with an attempt to be ecumenical.

Claver, Francisco, S.J. "The Basic Ecclesial Community: Vehicle Par Excellence for Inculturation." *Discovery* 3 (May 1993): 15–82.

Come and See: A New Vision of Parish Renewal. Dublin: Veritas Publications, 1993. An account of a parish cell system pioneered in Ballinteer, Dublin.

Cook, Guillermo. *The Expectation of the Poor: Latin American Basic Ecclesial Communities in Protestant Perspective.* Maryknoll, N.Y.: Orbis Books, 1985. The most complete treatment of this theme, adapted from a doctoral thesis.

Cowan, Michael A. and Bernard J. Lee, S.M. *Conversation, Risk, and Conversion: The Inner and Public Life of Small Christian Communities.* Maryknoll, N.Y.: Orbis Books, 1997. Gathers reflections on the likely future of the SCC phenomenon. A must read, especially for those interested in Small Christian Communities.

Crosby, Michael H. *House of Disciples: Church, Economics. and Justice.* Maryknoll, N.Y.: Orbis Books, 1988. Through an in-depth exploration of Matthew's Gospel and its socioeconomic milieu, this book shows how the world of the early church continues to challenge Christians today. It makes a unique contribution to both New Testament scholarship and the practice of contemporary spirituality.

Cruden, Alexander. *Concordance of the Holy Scriptures.* London: Epworth Press, 1969. Most useful in helping resource persons to locate scripture passages.

Cunningham, Loren, with Janice Rogers. *Is That Really You, God?* Seattle: YWAM Publishing. The Youth with a Mission (YWAM) story. A spellbinding book that describes how YWAM was formed. Community is an essential component of the organization.

Darling, Barbara A. *Getting a Grip on Your Group: A Guide for Discerning Priorities in Your Small Christian Community.* St. Paul: Good Ground Press, 2002. Emphasizes the significance of SCC members understanding their very important role in the church. We have responsibilities for church, both small and large. Good resources section at the end of the book under "Connections to the Larger Church."

Darling, Barbara A., and Jack Ventura. *Creating Small Christian Communities: Minimum Structure, Maximum Life.* St. Paul: Good Ground Press, 2003. Chapter 1 describes how SCC twinning is one way that communities can look outside themselves to the larger experience of community and church. The twinning process introduces SCCs to a community in another culture and country. It is a mutual giving and sharing.

Dearling, Alan, and Howard Armstrong. *The Youth Games Book.* Renfrewshire, Scotland: I.T. Resource Centre, 1980. Useful exercises for youth.

De la Torre, Ed. *Touching Ground, Taking Root.* Quezon City, Philippines: Socio-Pastoral Institute, 1986. This book gives an account of Small Christian Communities in the Philippines.

Donders, Joseph G. *Empowering Hope: Thoughts to Brighten Your Day.* Mystic, Conn.: Twenty-Third Publications, 1985. This simple, down-to-earth book is a collection of inspirational radio and television presentations broadcast in many parts of the world. Provides excellent material for small community meetings.

Donovan, Vincent, C.S.Sp. *Christianity Rediscovered.* Maryknoll, N.Y.: Orbis Books, 1982. An account of a missionary endeavor among the Maasai people in Tanzania which makes one think about the church in a wonderfully creative way.

Dorr, Donal. *Mission in Today's World.* Dublin: Columba Press, 2000, and Maryknoll, N.Y.: Orbis Books, 2000. Dorr explores the meaning of "mission" for today and comes up with some absorbing insights. Dialogue and openness to different religions and spiritualities are important. He insists on serious religious dialogue with the value system of the modern world.

———. *Option for the Poor: A Hundred Years of Vatican Social Teaching.* Maryknoll, N.Y.: Orbis Books, 1983, and Dublin: Gill and Macmillan, 1983. An excellent scholarly survey of the period under consideration.

Drane, John. *Introducing the Bible.* Oxford: Lion Publishing, 1990. A simple introduction.

Dublin Diocesan Committee for Parish Development and Renewal. *Parish Development and Renewal.* Dublin: Veritas Publications, 1993. An account by the diocesan committee of attempts being made to animate parishes.

Dujarier, Michel. *A History of the Catechumenate.* New York: Sadlier, 1979.

Dulles, Avery, S.J. *Models of the Church.* Dublin: Gill and Macmillan, 1976, and New York: Image Books, Doubleday and Company, 1978. This book shows us that the church is not just one simple reality, but can express itself in various forms or models.

Eagleson, John, and Philip Scharper, eds. *Puebla and Beyond.* Maryknoll, N.Y.: Orbis Books, 1979. Includes the opening address of John Paul II to the Latin American Bishops' Conference in Puebla.

Earley, Ciaran, OMI, ed. *Parish Alive Alive O!* Dublin: Columba Press, 1985. This is an account of efforts to establish Small Christian Communities in a variety of (urban and rural) Dublin parishes.

East African Participants in the "1996 International Consultation on Small Christian Communities," eds. "Our Five-Year Journey of SCCs from December 1991 to October 1996: The Evolving Sociology and Ecclesiology of Church as Family in Eastern Africa." In Robert S. Pelton, ed., *Small Christian Communities: Imagining Future Church.* Notre Dame, Ind.: University of Notre Dame Press, 1997: 89–110, and *African Ecclesial Review (AFER)* 29, no. 5 (October 1987): 266–77.

East African Participants in the "1999 International Consultation on Small Christian Communities" (in Cochabamba, Bolivia, November 1–6, 1999), eds. *African Continent Report for the 1999 International Consultation on Small Christian Communities.* Nairobi, Kenya: Printed Paper, 1999. 45 pages. Sections of the report are published in *Omnis Terra* (April 2000) (English, Spanish, and French).

East African Participants in the "2002 National SCC Convocation" (in San Antonio, Texas, on August 1, 2002), eds. *Talks at Workshop on International SCC Twinning.* Dar es Salaam, Tanzania: Printed Paper, 2002. 42 pages.

East African and El Salvadorian Participants in the "RENEW International Institute 2004" (in East Rutherford, N.J., on July 10, 2004), eds. *Talks at Workshop on International SCC Twinning: A New Way of Living Global Church at the Grassroots Level.* Morristown, N.J.: Printed Paper, 2004. 22 pages.

Edwards, Denis, and Bob Wilkinson. *The Christian Community Connection: A Program for Small Christian Communities.* Adelaide, Australia: Community for the World Movement, 1992. This book introduces small communities to the changing world, changing church.

Ela, Jean Marc. *African Cry.* Maryknoll, N.Y.: Orbis Books, 1986. A profoundly prophetic voice from the African church. Strong on issues of justice and inculturation.

Ellsberg, Robert. *All Saints.* New York: Crossroad, 1997. A wonderfully ecumenical collection of saints — not all are officially canonized, not all are Christian. Each fascinating vignette carries some intriguing reflection on its subject. Excellent material for Small Christian Communities.

Evans, Alice Fraser, Robert A. Evans, and William Bean Kennedy. *Pedagogies for the Non-Poor.* Maryknoll, N.Y.: Orbis Books, 1990.

Figueroa Deck, Allan, Yolanda Tarango, and Timothy M. Matovina, eds. *Perspectives: New Insights into Hispanic Ministry.* Kansas City: Sheed and Ward, 1995. A work that probes the tensions, issues, and options facing the church as Hispanic ministry continues to develop and deepen in the United States.

Flannery, Austin, ed. *More Post-Conciliar Documents.* Dublin: Dominican Publications, 1982, and New York: Costello Publishing Company, 1982. Excellent resource.

———*Vatican II: Conciliar and Post-Conciliar Documents.* Dublin: Dominican Publications, 1975, and New York: Costello Publishing Co., 1975. Excellent resource.

Fraser, Barbara, and Paul Jeffrey. "Base Communities, Once Hope of Church, Now in Disarray." *National Catholic Reporter* 41, no. 4 (November 12, 2004): 12–13, 16. Up-to-date, realistic assessment of BCCs in Latin America. Despite the present crisis, these grassroots communities remain a strong model for an effective church.

Fraser, Ian M. *Living a Countersign.* Glasgow: Wild Goose Publications, 1990. Enormously experienced author seeks to explain Basic Christian Communities in terms of their historical roots, their distinctive features, and their experiences of struggle.

———. *Many Cells, One Body: Stories from Small Christian Communities.* Geneva: WCC Publications, Risk Book Series 101, 2003. Includes stories that reveal the lifestyles of SCCs, how SCCs stand up to the criteria of the traditional marks of the church, and reflections on the form of the church to come.

———. *Reinventing Theology as the People's Work.* Glasgow: Wild Goose Publications, 1988. Shows how theology is not just the project of the academic world, but of the entire Christian community.

———. *Strange Fire: Life Stories and Prayers.* Glasgow: Wild Goose Publications, 1994. This work brings together ninety stories from Ian Fraser's many years among Christian communities around the world. Inspiring, well drawn, and always thought-provoking. These stories bring to life the profound faith of ordinary people, often in extremes of hardship and danger. Each finishes with a prayer or reflection that lets us link the stories with those of our own daily lives. The volume is an invaluable resource for meetings of Small Christian Communities.

Fraser, Margaret and Ian M. *Salted with Fire: Life-stories, Meditations, Prayers.* Edinburgh: St. Andrew's Press, 1999. An ideal resource book for church and pastoral work, and for use within the field of religious education.

———. *Wind and Fire: The Spirit Reshapes the Church in Basic Christian Communities.* Dunblane, Scotland: Basic Communities Resource Centre, 1986. This book gives us the opportunity to feel the life of Small Christian Communities. In the book the communities speak for themselves.

Fung, Raymond. *Household of God on China's Soil.* Maryknoll, N.Y.: Orbis Books, 1983. A refreshing collection of firsthand experiences of fourteen Chinese Christian communities during the turbulent Cultural Revolution years.

Gaba Publications. *African Cities and Christian Communities.* Eldoret, Kenya: *Spearhead* 72 (1982). A good study by people with local knowledge.

Galdámez, Pablo. *Faith of a People — The Life of a Basic Christian Community in El Salvador.* Maryknoll, N.Y.: Orbis Books; Melbourne: Dove; and London: CIIR, 1986. An account of a basic community in an area that has suffered much.

Galilea, Segundo. *The Future of Our Past.* Notre Dame, Ind.: Ave Maria Press, 1985. One is struck by how relevant the spirituality of the great Spanish mystics is to modern times. It is particularly suited to Small Christian Communities.

Gilkey, Langdon. *Message and Existence.* Minnesota: Seabury Press, 1972.

Gill, Athol. *Life on the Road — The Gospel Basis for a Messianic Lifestyle.* Scottsdale, Pa.: Herald Press, 1992. An in-depth study of the Gospels, emphasizing their differences from each other and the necessity of breaking with cultural chains if one is to truly follow Jesus.

Gish, Art. *Living in Christian Community.* Scottsdale, Pa.: Herald Press, 1978. An excellent book on Christian community. Written from an Anabaptist perspective, it comprehensively addresses the important theological and organizational issues. Both solidly theoretical and extremely practical.

Graham, Cheryl. "Caring for New Catholics." *Australasian Catholic Record* 25, no. 1 (1998): 21–26.

——. "Retention of Converts in a Catholic Parish." M.Min. thesis, Melbourne College of Divinity, 1995.

Green, Laurie. *Let's Do Theology: A Pastoral Cycle Resource Book.* London: Mowbray, 1990.

Guiney, John. "Comparing BCCs in South America and Africa." *African Ecclesial Review (AFER)* 30, no. 3 (June 1988): 167–80. Detailed comparison of the reflection methods of BCCs in Latin America and SCCs in Eastern Africa.

Gutiérrez, Gustavo. *A Theology of Liberation.* Maryknoll, N.Y.: Orbis Books, 1973. A most important book that created a watershed in theology.

——. *We Drink from Our Own Wells.* Maryknoll, N.Y.: Orbis Books, 2002. Local gatherings of SCCs reflecting on their daily lives in light of the Gospel can be a real theological locus or theological moment. This can lead to a communion of local churches theologizing on the grassroots level.

Harper, Michael. *A New Way of Living — How the Church of the Redeemer, Houston Found a New Lifestyle.* London: Hodder and Stoughton, 1973. A description of household communities with Harper's perspective of their biblical basis.

Healey, Joseph G., M.M. "Basic Christian Communities: Church-Centred or World-Centred?" *Missionalia* (April 1986): 14–34. Case studies of a BCC in Chile and SCCs in Kenya and Tanzania. In comparing the Latin American and Eastern African experiences some clear differences emerge, but they can learn a great deal from each other and mutually enrich the world church.

——. *A Fifth Gospel: The Experience of Black Christian Values.* Maryknoll, N.Y.: Orbis Books, 1981, and London: SCM Press, 1981. Chapter 4 is on "Small Christian Communities." Gives valuable insights into the workings of SCCs in Eastern Africa.

——. "Praxis Is Prior to Theology: Theological Foundations of International SCC Twinning." *Mission* 11, no. 1 (2004): 29–43. International Small Christian Community (SCC) Twinning (also called Sister SCCs and Partner SCCs) is one form of international networking. Reflecting on the praxis of SCC Twins especially in East Africa and North America and their shared biblical reflections and stories leads to six theological foundations: biblical theology, communion theology, solidarity theology, local or contextual theology, narrative theology, and mission theology.

——. "Twelve Case Studies of Small Christian Communities (SCCs) in Eastern Africa." In *How Local Is the Local Church: Small Christian Communities and Church in Eastern Africa*, ed. Agatha Radoli. Eldoret, Kenya: AMECEA Gaba Publications, 1993. *Spearhead* nos. 126–28 (1993): 59–103.

——, compiler. *Once Upon a Time in Africa: Stories of Wisdom and Joy.* Maryknoll, N.Y.: Orbis Books, 2004. African stories in the chapters on "Family" and "Community" describe the underlying values of participation, consensus, and solidarity that are so important in African SCCs.

Healey, Joseph, and Donald Sybertz. *Towards an African Narrative Theology.* 3rd ed. Nairobi: Paulines Publications, Africa, 2000, and Maryknoll, N.Y.: Orbis Books, 5th printing, 2004. Contains over a hundred pages on SCCs, especially chapter 3, "Church as the Extended Family of God." Case Study of St. Jude Thaddeus SCC in St. Augustine Parish in Mwisenge, Musoma, Tanzania, called "The Story of the Journey of St. Jude Thaddeus SCC" (157–60). This SCC is twinned with the Circle of Friends SCC in St. Joseph's Parish, Golden, Colorado. For those interested in the church in Africa and beyond. Well received in Africa.

Healy, Sean, S.M., and Brigid Reynolds. *Social Analysis in the Light of the Gospel.* Dublin: Folens and Co., 1983. A useful volume that emerged from a series of workshops. From the Justice Desk of CORI (Conference of Religious of Ireland), these authors have produced a series of publications that deal with Irish and European issues mainly.

Hebblethwaite, Margaret. *Base Communities — An Introduction.* London: Geoffrey Chapman, 1993. A recommended resource.

——. *Basic Is Beautiful.* London: Fount Harper Collins Publishers, 1993. Deals with the issue of how to translate Basic Ecclesial Communities from the Third World to the First World. Includes valuable accounts of, and reflection on, practical experiences.

Hennelly, Alfred T., S.J., ed. *Santo Domingo and Beyond.* Maryknoll, N.Y.: Orbis Books, 1993. Documents and commentaries from the historic meeting of the Latin American Bishops' Conference.

Hinton, Jeanne. *Changing Churches: Building Bridges in Local Mission.* London: Churches Together in Britain and Ireland (CTBI), 2002. Stories of Christian communities that took part in a three-year ecumenical learning experiment. A record of changes in local situations as people have reflected on what being church for their local community really means.

——. *Church at the Most Local Level: A Pastoral Priority Shaping the Catholic Church in East Africa.* Plymouth, England: Printed Paper, Revised August 7, 2002. 16 pages. Report on visiting SCCs in East Africa.

——. *Communities.* Guildford Surrey, Eagle, 1993. Gives the instructive stories and spiritualities of twelve European communities. The volume is enhanced with photographs by Christopher Phillips.

————. *Walking in the Same Direction.* Geneva: WCC Publications, 1995. The author, who has considerable experience, examines the new church that is emerging in the world largely through the vision and action of small communities.

Hinton, Jeanne, and Peter B. Price. *Changing Communities: Church from the Grassroots.* London: Churches Together in Britain and Ireland (CTBI), 2003. Models of church that are about participation and transformation. The authors draw on the experience of the New Way of Being Church's program in seeking to create processes for change in church and society.

Hirmer, Oswald. *How to Start Neighbourhood Gospel Groups.* Delmenville, South Africa: Lumko Missiological Institute. A kit with posters and textbook for learning a method of Gospel sharing by a person very experienced in the field.

————. *Our Journey Together: Catechetical Sessions for Christian Initiation for Adults (RCIA)* 47. Kampala: St. Paul Publications–Africa, 1988. The Swahili version is *Safari Yetu Pamoja. Vikao 47 vya Ukatekesi Kwa Kuwaingiza Watu Wazima Katika Ukristu (RCIA).* Nairobi: St. Paul Publications–Africa, 1990. A guide for the Christian community to accompany adult catechumens on their journey of faith. Promotes regular meetings of Catechumen Communities that consist of the catechumens, their sponsors, and other members of the local Christian community.

Holland, Joe, and Peter Henriot, S.J. *Social Analysis: Linking Faith and Justice.* Maryknoll, N.Y.: Orbis Books, 1983. A valuable book by two experienced practitioners. Suited for animators of small groups.

Hoomaert, Eduardo. *The Memory of the Christian People.* Maryknoll, N.Y.: Orbis Books, 1988. This excellent work reveals striking similarities between the church's first communities and the grassroots communities transforming the church today. It puts us in touch with useful documentation from the early church, thereby providing a sound historic base.

Hope, Anne, and Sally Timmel. *Training for Transformation: A Handbook for Community Workers.* 3 vols. Gweru, Zimbabwe: Mambo Press, 1984. These volumes are excellent for justice formation and provide useful group exercises and group dynamics.

Huelsmann, Peter, S.J. *Pray — An Introduction to the Spiritual Life for Busy People.* Mahwah, N.J.: Paulist Press, 1976. Comes with a Moderator's Manual. A "course" in prayer to be used alone or in groups. Some communities in the United States have found this book most helpful.

Hug, James E., ed. *Tracing the Spirit: Communities, Action and Theological Reflection.* New York: Paulist Press, 1983.

Hurley, Michael. *Transforming Your Parish: Building a Faith Community.* Dublin: Columba Press, 1998. An excellent introduction to a creative way of living the Gospel as a community employing the cell system.

Icenogle, Gareth Weldon. *Biblical Foundations for Small Group Ministry.* Downers Grove, Ill.: InterVarsity Press, 1994. We must begin with the Word of God. This book gives the biblical foundations for small-group ministry.

Imboden, Roberta. *From the Cross to the Kingdom.* San Francisco: Harper and Row, 1987. Basing herself on the philosophy of Sartre, the author says much that is of interest to Small Christian Communities. Brilliant and original.

Jackson, Dave and Neta. *Living Together in a World Falling Apart.* Altamonte Springs, Fla.: Creation House Publishers, 1974. This book sparked much interest in Small Christian Communities when first published. Years later it is still relevant. Deals

with the most basic questions — from the theology of community to issues of who
does the housework — in a very readable way.

Janzen, David, et al. *Fire, Salt, and Peace: Intentional Communities Alive in North America.* Evanston, Ill.: Shalom Mission Communities. Explores the narrative method
by profiling twenty-nine communities. There is an ecumenical mix "chosen from
thousands of such communities worldwide."

Jenkins, Philip. *The Next Christendom: The Coming of Global Christianity.* New York:
Oxford University Press, 2002. Provides an important context for the development
of SCCs with the southward shift of the center of gravity in global Christianity. "The
era of Western Christianity has passed within our lifetimes, and the day of Southern
Christianity is dawning."

John Paul II. *The Mission of the Redeemer.* Nairobi, Kenya: Paulines Publications Africa,
1990. No. 51 treats the theme "Ecclesial Base Communities as a Force for Evangelization."

———. Post Synodal Apostolic Exhortation *The Church in Africa.* Nairobi: Paulines Pub-
lications Africa, 1995. See also *The African Synod Comes Home — A Simplified Text.*
Ed. AMECEA Pastoral Department. Nairobi: Paulines Publications Africa, 1995.
No. 89 treats the theme "Living (or Vital) Christian Communities." Small or living
Christian communities should "reflect on different human problems in the light of
the Gospel."

———. Post Synodal Apostolic Exhortation *The Church in America.* Washington, D.C.:
United States Conference of Catholic Bishops (USCCB), 1998. English and Spanish. Pope John Paul II calls for a renewal of the church since "the encounter with
the living Jesus Christ is the path to conversion, communion, and solidarity." He
mentions SCCs in No. 41 in the context of renewing parishes so that each might become a "community of communities" and in No. 73 in the context of SCCs "being
capable of interpersonal bonds of mutual support within the Catholic Church."

———. Post Synodal Apostolic Exhortation *The Church in Asia.* "The Synod Fathers underlined the value of *basic ecclesial communities* as an effective way of promoting
communion and participation in parishes and dioceses, and as a genuine force for
evangelization. These small groups help the faithful to live as believing, praying,
and loving communities like the early Christians (cf. Acts 2:44–47; 4:32–35). They
aim to help their members to live the Gospel in a spirit of fraternal love and service,
and are therefore a solid starting point for building a new society, the expression
of *a civilization of love.* With the Synod, I encourage the Church in Asia, where
possible, to consider these basic communities as a positive feature of the Church's
evangelizing activity."

———. Post Synodal Apostolic Exhortation *The Church in Oceania.*

———. *This Is the Laity* (Simplification of *Christifideles Laici*). Pinner, U.K.: The Grail,
1989.

Justice and Peace Commission of the Kenyan Bishops' Conference. *We Are the Church.*
Lenten Campaign 1994. Nairobi: St. Joseph's Press, Kangemi, 1994.

Kalilombe, Patrick A. "From 'Outstation' to 'Small Christian Communities': A Comparison between Two Pastoral Methods in Lilongwe Diocese." Ph.D. diss., University
of California, 1983.

———. *From Outstation to Small Christian Communities.* Eldoret, Kenya: Gaba Publications, *Spearhead* 82–83 (June–October 1984). A study, adapted from a doctoral

thesis, by a person who was himself one of the pioneers in fostering Small Christian Communities in Africa. Shows how having a small number of people doesn't necessarily constitute an SCC.

Kinast, Robert L. *What Are They Saying about Theological Reflection?* Mahwah, N.J.: Paulist, 2000.

Kleissler, Thomas A., Margo A. LeBert, and Mary C. McGuinness. *Small Christian Communities: A Vision of Hope for the 21st Century.* Rev. and updated. Mahwah, N.J.: Paulist, 2003. Covers the foundational history of SCCs and provides a step-by-step guide for their implementation and development.

Latin American Bishops. *The Church in the Present-Day Transformation of Latin America in the Light of the Council* (Medellín Documents). 3rd ed. Washington D.C.: Secretariat for Latin America, National Conference of Bishops, 1979.

Lee, Bernard J., and Michael A. Cowan. *Dangerous Memories.* Kansas City: Sheed and Ward, 1986. Explores home churches in the United States. Includes a valuable discussion of mutuality, political action, and servant leadership. Contains an especially useful treatment of the role and potential of communities in the context of American individualism.

———. *Gathered and Sent: The Mission of Small Church Communities Today.* Mahwah, N.J.: Paulist Press, 2003. Indicates that there are forty-five thousand to fifty thousand SCCs in the United States with an estimated one million members. The two main reasons that Catholics join SCCs are that they are looking for more religious nurture than the parish is providing and a hunger for community with relational depth.

Lee, Bernard J., S.M., with William V. D'Antonio. *The Catholic Experience of Small Christian Communities.* Mahwah, N.J.: Paulist Press, 2000. Results and reflection upon a valuable, wide-scale sociological study of Small Christian Communities in North America.

Lernoux, Penny. *Cry of the People.* Middlesex: Penguin, 1981; New York: Doubleday, 1980. An excellent resource book regarding the justice issue in Latin America. Particularly good on the National Security State and the role of multinationals.

"Letters, Reports and Essays from Small Christian Communities around the World." Part of the Global Small Christian Communities (SCC) Research and Consultation Project sponsored by the Latin American/North American Church Concerns (LANACC) of the University of Notre Dame's Kellogg Center that began in January 2002. Available on the Buena Vista Web site. See also Imperatori, Maria Natalia. "Report on Global Spiritualities for Small Christian Communities Conference." Notre Dame, Ind.: Unpublished Report, 2002. 11 pages.

Lobinger, Fritz. *Building Small Christian Communities.* Delmenville, South Africa: Lumko Missiological Institute, 1981. A kit with large posters and textbook for starting Small Christian Communities. Widely used, especially in Africa. Part of the excellent pastoral materials of Lumko.

———. *Like His Brothers and Sisters.* Quezon City, Philippines: Claretian Publications, 1998. This book takes a constructive look at a possible means of renewing the priesthood.

Lohfink, Gerhard. *Jesus and Community: The Social Dimension of Christian Faith.* Philadelphia: Fortress Press, 1984; New York: Paulist Press, 1982. Implementing the Christian ethic must be done by groups of people who consciously place themselves under the Gospel of the reign of God and who wish to be real communities of brothers and sisters. A challenging book.

Lumko Institute. *Training for Community Ministries Series.* Delmenville, South Africa: Lumko Institute, and Nairobi: St. Paul Publications–Africa, 1979. Important series of awareness program booklets for pastoral workers, trainers and facilitators of church groups such as SCCs, women, youth, workers, etc. Highlights the Seven Step Method of Gospel Sharing for neighborhood groups. Used worldwide to help groups and parishes to move towards a life of participation and communion.

Lwaminda, Peter. "A Theological Analysis of the AMECEA Documents on the Local Church with Special Emphasis on the Pastoral Option for Small Christian Communities." In *The Local Church with a Human Face,* ed. Agatha Radoli. Eldoret, Kenya: AMECEA Gaba Publications, 1996. *Spearhead* 140–41 (1996): 67–99.

Marins, José. *Church from the Roots.* Quito: Technical College of Don Bosco, 1979; London: CAFOD, 1989. Proceeding from modern day parables, the author and his team, who have shared worldwide on Small Christian Communities, draw valuable conclusions for small groups.

McCarthy, Flor, S.D.B. *Windows on the Gospel: Stories and Reflections.* Dublin: Dominican Publications, and Mystic, Conn.: Twenty-Third Publications, 1992. This simple collection of stories and reflections is offered to all who are searching for a spirituality based on the Gospel. Excellent material for meetings.

McConnell, Frank. *Find Quickly in the Gospels.* Sevenoaks, Kent: Petrus Books, 1990. An extremely user-friendly guide for locating Gospel texts — an ordinary person's concordance.

McDonagh, Sean. *The Greening of the Church.* Maryknoll, N.Y.: Orbis Books, 1990. Effectively highlights the crucial environmental issue.

McGarry, Cecil, S.J., ed. *What Happened at the African Synod?* Nairobi: Paulines Publications Africa, 1995. A must for anyone interested in the church generally and the African church in particular. The priority of Small Christian Communities is at the core of African pastoral concerns.

McGowan, Phelim, S.J. *Welcome Home.* Dublin: Dominican Publications, 1998. A prayerful reflection on the sacrament of reconciliation, including a section containing excellent "Services of Reconciliation."

Mejia, Rodrigo. *The Church in the Neighborhood: Meetings for the Animation of Small Christian Communities.* Nairobi: St. Paul Publications–Africa, 1992. Shows how to develop and animate Small Christian Communities in the parish.

Mellis, Charles J. *Committed Communities.* South Pasadena, Calif.: William Carey Library, 1976. A very insightful evaluation of the importance of community in mission presented historically. Gives the implications for today.

Mesters, Carlos. *Defenseless Flower.* Maryknoll, N.Y.: Orbis Books, 1989. Shows a marvelous use of the Bible in the Brazilian Small Christian Communities. A significant contribution to methodology in scripture reflection.

Miller, Hal. *Christian Community: Biblical or Optional?* Ann Arbor, Mich.: Servant Books, 1979. A solid theology of Christian community demonstrating from the scriptures that community was part of God's plan from the beginning and that Jesus restored community through the kingdom.

Mission-Shaped Church: Church Planting and Fresh Expressions of Church in a Changing Context. London: Church House Publishing, 2004. A report from a working group of Church of England (Anglican)'s Mission and Public Affairs Council. A good overview of present developments.

Moriarty, Robert K. *The Catechumenate and Small Christian Communities: Building Church Together.* A Report on the 1994 Conference of the North American Forum for Small Christian Communities. Louisville: NAFSCC, 1994.

——. *An Experience of World Church in Miniature: A Report on the 1999 International Consultation on Small Christian Communities.* Cochabamba, Bolivia, November 1–6, 1999. Hartford, Conn.: Pastoral Department for Small Christian Communities, March 2001. 52 pages. Forty-five delegates from seventeen countries spanning six continents reflected on the worldwide experience of SCCs.

——. "Parish and Small Church Communities." *America* 184, no. 15 (May 7, 2001): 14–19. The article reports and reflects on the Loyola/Lilly research on Small Church Communities in the U.S. Catholic context.

——. "Small Church Communities and the Pastoral Formation of the Seminarian as a 'Man of Communion.'" *Seminary Journal* 9, no. 2 (Fall 2003): 68–73. The article offers a specific proposal for a worldwide concern: the formation of future priests to work with Small Church Communities.

Mringi, Augustine. *Communio at the Grassroots: Small Christian Communities.* Bangalore: Indian Institute of Spirituality, 1995.

Murphy-O'Connor, Cormac. "Fired by the Spirit." *The Tablet* (May 31, 2003): 11–12. An influential article in which the cardinal of the Diocese of Westminster, England, emphasizes how small groups hold the key to parish renewal. Small communities are an integral part of the communion of the church and an important spur for renewing the mission of the church.

Mwoleka, Christopher. *Do. This! The Church of the Third Millennium — What Face Shall It Have?* Ndanda-Peramiho: Benedictine Publications, 1988.

Mwoleka, Christopher, and Joseph Healey, eds. *Ujamaa and Christian Communities.* Eldoret, Kenya: Gaba Publications, 1976. *Spearhead* 45 (1976).

Myers, Ched. *Who Will Roll Away the Stone? Discipleship Queries for First World Christians.* Maryknoll, N.Y.: Orbis Books, 1994. A thought-provoking book.

NACCAN (National Association of Christian Communities and Networks, Britain). *Directory of Christian Communities and Networks.* JAS Print, 1993.

National Secretariat and Hispanic Teams. *Basic Ecclesial Communities.* Ligouri, Mo.: Ligouri, 1980. Simple, theologically rich, and practical.

——. *Guidelines for Establishing Basic Christian Communities in the United States.* Ligouri, Mo.: Ligouri, 1981.

"New Way Publications" has produced a very useful set of booklets related to the life of Small Christian Communities: *Living Faith in the World through Word and Action: Reflections on St. Matthew's Gospel for Small Christian Communities* and others in the same series by Peter Price. *Small and in Place: Practical Steps in Forming Small Christian Communities,* by Jeanne Hinton. *A Tapestry of Stories: A New Way of Being Church,* by Jeanne Hinton. *Stepping Stones: Small Steps Pave the Way to a New Way of Being Church,* by Jeanne Hinton. *Fresh Start — The Story of NEW WAY in an Anglican Parish,* by John Summers. Wells, Somerset: New Way of Being Church (variable dates).

New Wine into Fresh Wineskins: A Report on Pastoral Planning. Diocese of Maitland-Newcastle, Australia, 2000. 58 pages. A report on pastoral planning in the diocese that sets out the results of a cooperative diocesan effort "to create a new way of being church together." Encourages the development within parishes of Neighborhood Church Communities (NCCs) and Small Church Groups (SCGs).

Ndingi, Raphael. "Basic Communities: The African Experience." In *A New Missionary Era*. Maryknoll, N.Y.: Orbis Books, 1982. In East Africa a new approach to ecclesiology is evolving. It is based on the concept of the church as a communion of communities, a two-way sharing between communities.

O'Brien, David J., and Thomas A. Shannon. *Renewing the Earth*. New York: Image Books, 1977. The single most comprehensive available collection of primary documents on Catholic social thought from Pope Leo XIII's *Rerum Novarum* (1891) to John Paul II's *Centesimus Annus* (1991). Documents are accompanied by introductory essays and helpful notes.

O'Brien, John, C.S.Sp. *Seeds of a New Church*. Dublin: Columba Press, 1994. Deals with twenty-two group experiences in the Irish context and their implications for the church of the future. Important and challenging reading for anyone connected with the church, particularly in Ireland.

O'Brien, Timothy. *Why Small Christian Communities Work*. San Jose, Calif.: Resource Publications, 1996. Useful documented information.

O'Bryan, Paul. *Growing the SCC Vision*. Melbourne: Southern Cross and Communities Australia, 1998.

———. *Leadership in the SCC Parish*. Melbourne: Southern Cross and Communities Australia, 1999.

———. *Regathering the Parish: A Beginning Program for the Parish SCC Core Team*. Melbourne: Southern Cross and Communities Australia (Revised Edition), 1997. Useful material from an experienced team.

———. *The SCC Gathering Format*. Melbourne: Southern Cross and Communities Australia, 1997.

Obunga, Joseph. "The Small Christian Communities in the AMECEA Region Today and Tomorrow Particularly in Kampala Archdiocese, Uganda." Ph.D. diss., Catholic University of Louvain, 1993. Treats grassroots SCCs in East Africa.

O'Connell Killen, Patricia. "The Practice of Theological Reflection in Small Faith Communities." *Chicago Studies* 21, no. 2 (August 1992).

O'Connell Killen, Patricia, and John de Beer. *The Art of Theological Reflection*. New York: Crossroad, 1994.

Ó Donnchadha, Proinsias. *A Stack of Stories*. Dublin: Night Owl Early Bird Bureau, 1995. Beautiful short reflections that could provide valuable materials for meetings of SCCs.

O'Gorman, Frances Elsie. *Base Communities in Brazil: Dynamics of a Journey*. Rio de Janeiro: FASE-NUCLAR, 1983. An account of Brazilian Small Christian Communities by one who has been deeply involved with them in the favelas of Rio de Janeiro.

O'Halloran, James, S.D.B. *The Least of These*. Dublin: Columba Press, 1991. A book of short stories, some of which have been used in catechetical programs and courses on peace and justice.

———. *Signs of Hope: Developing Small Christian Communities*. Maryknoll, N.Y.: Orbis Books, 1991; Dublin: Columba Press, 1991. This book developed from *Living Cells*

(1984) that was for some years one of the best introductions to Small Christian Communities.

———. *Small Christian Communities: A Pastoral Companion.* Dublin: Columba Press, 1996; Orbis Books, Maryknoll: N.Y., 1996. Builds on the two previous volumes.

———. *Small Christian Communities: Vision and Practicalities.* Dublin: Columba Press, 2002. Includes a historical profile of SCCs covering biblical and premodern times, North America (United States and Canada), Latin America, Africa, Asia, Oceania, and Europe. With "Passages for Bible Sharing" and an "Annotated Bibliography."

O'Hanlon, Joseph. *Beginning the Bible.* Slough (England): St. Paul's, 1994. A user-friendly, integrated introduction to the Bible. The general reader will find this helpful.

O'Regan, Pauline, and Teresa O'Connor. *Community, Give It a Go!* Christchurch, New Zealand: Allen and Unwin, 1989. The authors describe their work in building community: how to establish networks, how to start a coffee group, ways of arranging childcare, kinds of celebrations, relationships between local community workers and professional groups.

Parker, J. Palmer. *The Promise of Paradox: A Celebration of Contradictions in the Christian Life.* Notre Dame, Ind.: Ave Maria Press, Notre Dame, 1980. The section on community is worthwhile reading.

Paul VI. Apostolic Exhortation *Evangelii Nuntiandi (Evangelization Today).* Dublin: Dominican Publications, 1977. Commentary by Bede McGregor OP. Section No. 58 on "Ecclesial Base Communities" states that BECs are "a place of evangelization and a hope for the universal church."

Paulian Association. *A Storybook of Australian Small Christian Communities.* Sydney: Paulian Association and Communities Australia, 1998.

Pelton, Robert S., C.S.C. "Can Communities Survive — in the Margins?" *Doctrine and Life* 51, no. 4 (April 2001): 235–43. "Marginal" is a metaphor for fertile new venues of growth. New approaches can be developed and tested. The best elements of many paradigms can be integrated into synergistically vital new ways of being church.

———. *From Power to Communion: Toward a New Way of Being Church Based on the Latin American Experience.* Notre Dame, Ind.: University of Notre Dame Press, 1994.

———. *Small Christian Community: Imagining Future Church.* Notre Dame, Ind.: University of Notre Dame Press, 1997. A thought-provoking book edited by a man of vast experience in SCCs.

Perkins, Pheme. *Reading the New Testament: An Introduction.* New York: Paulist Press, 1977.

Picardal, Amado, C.Ss.R. *Building BECs: Ecclesiological Vision, Strategic Framework, Implication for Priestly Ministry.* Davao, Philippines: Redemptorist Publication, 2000.

———. *The Local Church with a Human Face.* Eldoret: AMECEA Gaba Publications. *Spearhead* 40–141, 1996. Second volume of the publication of a research project, "The Reception of the *Communio*-Ecclesiology Theology of the Second Vatican Council," that focused on the local church in the context of Germany, Papua New Guinea, and Tonga. With a paper on the history and guiding theological principles of the AMECEA region.

Picardal, Amado, C.Ss.R., Estela Padilla, et al. *BECs in the Philippines: Dream or Reality — A Multi-disciplinary Reflection.* Antipolo, Philippines: Bukal ng Tipan, 2004.

Prased Pinto, Joseph, O.F.M.Cap. *Inculturation through Basic Communities: An Indian Perspective*. Bangalore: Asia Trading Company, 1985. Describes the emerging types of base communities in India. The author explores the potential of basic communities to create a church that will be "deeply rooted in the Indian values of religiosity, poverty, joy, and festivity."

Price, Peter B. *Seeds of the Word: Biblical Reflections on Small Christian Communities*. London: Darton, Longman and Todd, 1996. This book brings an originality and realism to Bible reflection in small groups that will inspire practical action and enable the footprints of God to be seen in the life of the local community. An excellent resource.

Proctor, Gerry. "BECs/SCCs Both Spirit and Law." Part 1: *Buena Vista Ink* 18, no. 5 (September–October 2004): 1, 3–4; Part 2: *Buena Vista Ink* 18, no. 6 (November–December 2004): 1, 3. Also posted on the Marins Team Web site: *http://aolsvc.news.aol .com/news/main.adp*. While there is no explicit mention of Base Ecclesial Communities in the *Code of Canon Law*, there are a number of significant references in the code to give some solidity and juridical basis to this local level of being church.

Radoli, Agatha, ed. *How Local Is the Local Church: Small Christian Communities and Church in Eastern Africa*. Eldoret: AMECEA Gaba Publications. *Spearhead* 126–28, 1993. First volume of the publication of a research project, "The Reception of the *Communio*-Ecclesiology of the Second Vatican Council," that focused on the local church in the context of the AMECEA countries.

Rahner, Karl, S.J. *I Remember*. London: SCM, 1984. An autobiographical account, taken from an interview, of one who has been described as the "quiet mover" and "ghostwriter" of Vatican II, and even as "the father of the church in the twentieth century." The volume gives his thinking on the council.

Raines, John C., and Donna C. Day-Lower. *Modern Work and Human Meaning*. Philadelphia: Westminster Press, 1986. This work deals with social problems in the United States. It has the considerable merit of allowing the poor to speak for themselves. Listening to their voice is even more critical in the present political climate.

Reichert, Richard. *Simulation Games for Religious Education*. Winona, Minn.: St. Mary's Press, Christian Brothers Publications, 1975. Useful resource material.

Research and Development Division. *Training Volunteer Leaders — A Handbook to Train Volunteers and Other Leaders of Program Groups*. New York: National Council of Young Men's Christian Associations. Contains helpful resource material and group exercises. "Renewing the Parish" Series (2003) and "Parish Practice" Series (2004–2005) in *The Tablet*. A whole variety of examples and case studies of SCCs and other kinds of small groups mainly in the context of Catholic parishes in England.

Saxby, Trevor J. *Pilgrims of a Common Life: Christian Community of Goods through the Centuries*. Scottdale, Pa.: Herald Press, 1987. A review of intentional residential Christian communities from New Testament times to the twentieth century and of the biblical principles indicating sharing of possessions.

Scharper, Sally, and Philip Scharper, eds. *The Gospel in Art by the Peasants of Solentiname*. Maryknoll, N.Y.: Orbis Books, 1984. This book shows how the Gospels can be used effectively by ordinary people.

Schreiter, Robert, C.PP.S. *Constructing Local Theologies*. Maryknoll, N.Y.: Orbis Books. A systematic study of the nature and theology of indigenous churches. Local theologies can be constructed with the "local community as theologian," or more accurately, "the local Christian community theologizing." The contextual model of local theology concentrates on the real problems experienced by local people. An excellent read.

Shea, John. *The Art of Theological Reflection: Connecting Faith and Life.* Sound Recording. Chicago: ACTA Publications, 1997.

Slattery, Hugh, MSC. *HIV/AIDS, A Call to Action, Responding as Christians.* Nairobi: Paulines Publications Africa, 2002. A thoughtful volume on the subject of AIDS by one who is actively involved with the issue in southern Africa. He emphasizes the crucial work of SCCs in providing solutions to the problem.

Sluss, Amy. *Family Faith Communities.* St. Paul: Good Ground Press, 2003. Provides both vision and practical steps for starting family-based Small Christian Communities. Each of the ten gatherings presented in this book mixes the basic ingredients of prayer, faith sharing, activities, and social time.

Smith, Adrian. *Tomorrow's Parish.* Essex, England: Mayhew McCrimmon, 1983. Based on the experience of the Movement for a Better World, the parish is best described as a communion of Basic Christian Communities.

Smith, Christian. *Going to the Roots.* Scottsdale, Pa.: Herald Press, 1992. Smith is very knowledgeable and experienced in Small Christian Communities.

Snyder, Howard. *Community of the King.* Chicago: InterVarsity Press. 1977. On alternative church models as agents of the kingdom. Interesting reading about Christian community based on practical experience in the Irving Park Free Methodist Church in Chicago.

Special Assembly for Africa of the Synod of Bishops. *Final Message and 64 Propositions.* Rome: Vatican City, 1994. Strong emphasis on the pastoral model of SCCs.

Special Issue on "Small Christian Communities." *Catholic World* 234, no. 1402 (July–August 1991). With articles by Barbara Darling, Richard Long, Rosemary Bleuher, Carol Quinn Hirt, John J. Fitzpatrick, Bernard J. Lee, and Joseph G. Healey.

Sybertz, Donald. *Hadithi za Kisukuma Zinazofanana Vikao (Sukuma Stories Following the Themes of the RCIA Catechetical Sessions).* Bujora, Mwanza: Kituo cha Utamaduni wa Usukuma, Printed Materials, 1991–2005. Swahili materials for "Small Adult Catechumenate Communities" in Tanzania that use the Lumko Method.

Torres, Sergio, and John Eagleson, eds. *The Challenge of Basic Christian Communities.* Maryknoll, N.Y.: Orbis Books, 1981. Papers from the Ecumenical Association of Third World Theologians in São Paulo, Brazil, from February 20 to March 2, 1980, on "The Ecclesiology of the Popular Christian Communities." Reflections on Small Christian Communities by some of the most eminent people in the fields of theology and pastoral practice from the Third World. Chapter 16 by Carlos Mesters includes information that is most enlightening on the use of the Bible in small communities.

Turner, Paul. 2000. *The Hallelujah Highway: A History of the Catechumenate.* Chicago: Liturgy Training Publications.

United States Conference of Catholic Bishops. *Called to Global Solidarity: International Challenges for U.S. Parishes.* Washington, D.C.: United States Catholic Conference, 1997. Statement has important implications for international SCC twinning. The "new" idea of parish or SCC twinning focuses on sharing of life experiences of parishes or SCCs and networking in building a world church.

Vanier, Jean. *Community and Growth.* Rev. ed. London: Darton, Longman and Todd, 1989. A veritable gold mine of reflective and practical ideas on community by the founder of L'Arche.

Veling, Terry. *Living in the Margins: Intentional Communities and the Art of Interpretation.* New York: Crossroad, 1996. A gifted theologian sheds light on the meaning and value of intentional faith communities on the margins of parish life.

Weber, Hans-Ruedi. *The Book That Reads Me.* Geneva: WCC Publications, 1995. A worthwhile handbook for Bible study enablers.

Whitehead, Evelyn Eaton and James D. *Community of Faith: Crafting Christian Communities Today.* Mystic, Conn.: Twenty-Third Publications, 1992. An enormously valuable book which creatively employs the insights of modern psychology and sociology to help understand the nature and dynamics of Christian community. Strong as both a theoretical analysis of community and a practical guide to life in community.

Whitehead, James D. and Evelyn Eaton. *Method in Ministry: Theological Reflection and Christian Ministry.* New York: Seabury, 1980.

Wilson, Irene. *Report on a Ministry Project: Interfacing the RCIA and Small Church Communities in the Catholic Parish of St. Thomas More, Belgrave.* Melbourne: Yarra Theological Union Project Report for graduate diploma in Pastoral Leadership, 1998.

Winter, Derek. *Communities of Freedom.* London: Christian Aid, 1988. A useful resource.

Wuthnow, Robert. *Sharing the Journey: Support Groups and America's New Quest for Community.* New York: Free Press, 1994. A thought-provoking account of the new impetus towards community in not only religious, but also civil society in the United States.

Contributors

Pepe Beerli-Bamberger works in the field of vocational counseling and the integration of migrant families from the Balkans and southern Europe. He lives in Küssnacht, Switzerland. He is married to Heidi and has one daughter and two sons. Currently he is the chairperson for the European Collective of Basic Christian Communities. *beerlipe@hotmail.com.*

Richard Begbie moved from Sydney to Canberra, Australia, in 1972 to set up a project for people needing time out at a change point in their lives. Previously a member of an Anglican church, he then became closely involved with the Canberra Home Churches. He has worked as a journalist for the *Canberra Times. rb@clearmail.com.au.*

Alicia Butkiewicz is a codirector of the Maryknoll Lay Missioners (MLM) based at Maryknoll, New York. For twenty-two years she served in a variety of mission activities in Bolivia, many focusing on the leadership training and on the creation of faith-based communities and grassroots organizations. From 1987 to 2003 she served as a coordinator of Basic Christian Communities for the Archdiocese of Cochabamba and in the same capacity on the national level from 1989 to 1999. *Abutkiewicz@mkl-mmaf.org.*

Irma Chávez is a doctor of philosophy and theology and has been Dean of the Faculty of Theology at the University of Don Bosco in El Salvador. For more than twenty years she has worked to promote SCCs in the United States and Central America. She has written on various theological topics and published many materials for reflection in SCCs. Currently she implements RENEW in El Salvador and Honduras. *renelsal@navegante.com.sv.*

Christopher Cieslikiewicz, O.F.M.Conv., is the Polish Franciscan Conventual priest. He has worked in parishes in Arusha and Dar es Salaam, Tanzania. In 2004 he completed his doctorate at the Lateran University in Rome on "Small Christian Communities: Pastoral Priority and a Vital Force for Evangelization in the Archdiocese of Dar es Salaam, Tanzania. An Evaluation and New Perspectives." At present he is working in Segerea Parish in Dar es Salaam. *krzcie@yahoo.com.*

Michael Cowan is a psychologist, theologian, and organizer. He serves as Executive Director of the Lindy Boggs National Center for Community Literacy, Loyola University, New Orleans. He is a founding leader of three interracial community organizations seeking justice in New Orleans and beyond. He is coauthor with Bernard Lee, S.M., of *Dangerous Memories* (Sheed and Ward, 1986); *Conversation, Risk and Conversion: The Inner and Public Life of Small Christian Communities* (Orbis Books, 1997); and *Gathered and Sent: The Mission of Small Christian Communities Today* (Paulist Press, 2003); and the scribe/editor of *Roots for Radicals: Organizing for Power, Action and Justice* by Edward T. Chambers (Continuum, 2003). *mcowan@loyno.edu.*

John Dacey is a Deacon of the Uniting Church in Australia and works ecumenically in adult education and formation in the areas of peace, justice, mission, and community building. John has been passionate about SCCs for twenty years. For five years he was the editor of *Communities Australia*, a national newsletter for the SCCs in Australia. *animate@palms.org.au.*

William D'Antonio is a Visiting Research Professor in the Department of Sociology, The Catholic University of America, Washington D.C. His interests and writings include religion, ethnicity, politics, and family. He has served as editor of the ASA journal *Contemporary Sociology*. He is the coauthor of seven books and coeditor of four books including *The Catholic Experience of Small Christian Communities* (Paulist Press, 2000) and *American Catholics: Gender, Generation, and Commitment* (Rowman and Littlefield, 2001). He is a member of the Communitas Intentional Community in Washington D.C. *lorrandbill@msn.com.*

Barbara A. Darling cherishes and nurtures Small Christian Community whenever and wherever she can. She has accompanied SCCs locally, nationally, and worldwide in her work with Buena Vista and the Latin American/North American Church Concerns at the University of Notre Dame. Good Ground Press, St. Paul, has published two of her books about and for SCCs. She is a founding member of Buena Vista, Inc. After thirty years with the Oilers' SCC in Arvada, Colorado, she and her husband Rusty are currently members of a fledgling faith-sharing group on Pine Island, Florida. *badarling@juno.com.*

Susan DeGuide, R.S.M., is a member of the Congregation of the Sisters of Mercy and the Director of the Office of Small Faith Communities in the Diocese of San Bernardino, California. She considers herself a multinational person, having lived and ministered in Ireland, Peru, and at home in California. Her pastoral experience in Lima, Peru, introduced her to the lived reality of SFCs and has strongly impacted her pastoral vision for this new way of being church. *sdeguide@sbdiocese.org.*

Justin Duckworth is Youth Education Officer for the NGO Global Education Centre in Wellington, New Zealand, a role that involves both writing resources and facilitating seminars. This has enabled him to travel around Aotearoa/New Zealand to see what is happening with young people and community development He has an M.Phil. in development studies and a B.D. from Melbourne Theological Seminary.

Joseph G. Healey, M.M., is a Maryknoll missionary priest and the former Coordinator of the Mission Awareness Committee (MAC) of the Religious Superiors' Association of Tanzania (RSAT) based in Dar es Salaam. He has written extensively on SCCs, mission, and African proverbs and stories. His books include *Once Upon a Time in Africa: Stories of Wisdom and Joy* (Orbis Books, 2004) and *Towards an African Narrative Theology* (Paulines Publications Africa, 1996, and Orbis Books, 1997). He is a member of the St. Charles Lwanga SCC in Dar es Salaam and the St. Jude Thaddeus SCC in Musoma. *JGHealey@aol.com.*

Jeanne Hinton is an Anglican laywoman who has worked in various fields including journalism and youth work, and in developing training materials and workshops in personal growth and spirituality and the development of SCCs. She is a member of the New Way of Being Church Team, an ecumenical program in the United Kingdom. She has written a number of books including *Communities* (Inter Publishing Service, 1993), *Walking in the*

Same Direction (WCC Publications, 1995), *Changing Churches: Building Bridges in Local Mission* (Churches Together in Britain and Ireland, April 22, 2002 and *Changing Communities: Church from the Grassroots* (Churches Together in Britain and Ireland, 2003). *Jeanne@hinton.wanaloo.co.uk.*

Rita K. Ishengoma, STH, is a sister of St. Therese of the Child Jesus Congregation, Diocese of Bukoba, Tanzania. Presently she is working at the Msimbazi Center in the Archdiocese of Dar es Salaam. She a journalist by profession and has written extensively on SCCs and pastoral topics. She participated in international SCC meetings in the United States and Bolivia and is a contact person for international SCC twinning. She is a member and animator of several SCCs in Tanzania. *rishengomak@yahoo.com.*

Austen Ivereigh is the press secretary to the archbishop of Westminster, Cardinal Cormac Murphy-O'Connor. Until last year he was Deputy Editor of *The Tablet*, a London-based international Catholic weekly. A member of the Community of Sant'Egidio, he is also leader of a parish small faith-sharing group taking part in the "At Your Word, Lord" renewal program in the Diocese of Westminster, England. He is the editor of *Unfinished Journey: The Church Forty Years after Vatican II: Essays for John Wilkins* (Continuum, 2003). *austenivereigh@rcdow.org.uk.*

Bernard Lee, S.M., is a Marianist priest and the Assistant Chancellor and Professor of Theology at St. Mary's University in San Antonio, Texas. Several of his driving concerns have been the life practices and ecclesiological foundations of base communities. He is the author of *The Catholic Experience of Small Christian Communities* (Paulist Press, 2000) and the coauthor with Michael Cowan of *Dangerous Memories: House Churches and Our American Story* (Sheed and Ward, 1986); *Conversation, Risk and Conversion: The Inner and Public Life of Small Christian Communities* (Orbis Books, 1997); and *Gathered and Sent: The Mission of Small Christian Communities Today* (Paulist Press, 2003). *bleesm@STMARYTX.EDU.*

Peter Macdonald is a member of the Iona Community serving as a Church of Scotland minister in Edinburgh, Scotland. He is married to Lesley Orr and has two sons, Callum and Lorn. He the representative of Scotland on the European Collective of Basic Christian Communities. He is a member of the secretariat of the collective. *petermacdonald@blueyonder.co.uk.*

Cora Mateo is the Coordinator of the AsIPA Desk of the FABC Office of Laity based in Taipei, Taiwan. She was the former Executive Secretary of the FABC Office of Laity (1993–1999) and presently is on the General Council of the Teresian Association, an international Catholic lay association of professionals. *asipa@ms78.hinet.net.*

Michael Mawson is a writer and researcher for the Anglican Social Justice Commission of Aotearoa/New Zealand. At the same time he lives in and runs the e Pringa (Shelter) home for at-risk teenagers in Wellington. He helps Christian young adults to engage with the political and social dimensions of their faith. He has an MA in the implications of postmodern theory for issues of theology from Victoria University of Wellington. He has written widely on this subject and also helped to put together seminars developing and aiding church engagement with political/policy ideas. *just_mike@clear.net.nz.*

Robert Moriarty, S.M., is a Marianist brother who directs the Pastoral Department for Small Christian Communities in the Archdiocese of Hartford. In addition to serving as an on-site pastoral resource to the parishes of the archdiocese, the department publishes *Quest* and *Summer Reflections*, lectionary-based resources for Small Church Communities. He is a board member of the National Alliance of Parishes Restructuring into Communities (NAPRC). He is the author of *An Experience of World Church in Miniature: A Report on the International Consultation on Small Christian Communities* (Pastoral Department for Small Christian Communities, 2001). *RkMoriarty@aol.com*.

Cormac Murphy-O'Connor is the cardinal archbishop of the Diocese of Westminster, England. He experienced the power of small faith-sharing communities in his first two parishes in and near Portsmouth from 1957 to 1966. He actively promoted SCCs when he was bishop of the Diocese of Arundel and Brighton, which was the first English diocese to initiate the RENEW program. He has written widely on many pastoral subjects including the theology and praxis of SCCs. *archbishop@rcdow.org.uk*.

John Vianney Muweesi is a secular diocesan priest of the Diocese of Kiyinda-Mityana, Uganda. He has served as pastor in three parishes and six years as pastoral coordinator of his diocese. He is very involved in promoting SCCs, which are a pastoral priority in his diocese. He has an M.A. in Pastoral Studies with a focus on small community formation from Loyola University, New Orleans. He is a contact person for international SCC twinning. *weekembe@hotmail.com*.

Emmanuel Mwerekande is a secular diocesan priest of the Diocese of Kiyinda-Mityana, Uganda. He served as pastor of Mwema Parish. As the pastoral coordinator of his diocese he was very involved in promoting SCCs, which are a pastoral priority in his diocese. Presently he is doing graduate studies in the United States. *mwerekan@bc.edu*.

Alphonce Omolo is manager of the Kisumu Urban Apostolate Programmes-Pandipieri (KUAP-Pandipieri). As a community educator and a facilitator of community and organizations development, he has worked with grassroots neighborhoods for twenty years. He participated in international SCC meetings in the United States and Bolivia and is a contact person for international SCC twinning. He is a member and animator of several SCCs in St. Joseph Parish in Kisumu, Kenya. *alphonce@pandipieri.org*.

Robert Pelton, C.S.C., is a Holy Cross priest on the faculty of Theology at the University of Notre Dame and currently the Director of the Latin American/North American Church Concerns and a fellow of the Kellogg Institute. He has coordinated many international SCC meetings and research projects. He is the author of *From Power to Communion: Toward a New Way of Being Church Based on the Latin American Experience* (1994) and the editor of *Small Christian Communities: Imagining Future Church* (1997) and *Monsignor Romero, A Bishop for the Third Millennium* (2004), all published by the University of Notre Dame Press. He is a member of the Esperanza SCC in South Bend. *rpelton@nd.edu*.

Amado Picardal, C.Ss.R., is a Redemptorist priest who has taught theology at the St. Alphonsus Theologate in Davao, the Philippines, since 1995. He gives talks and seminars on BECs and helps to organize BEC national assemblies. His books include *Building BECs: Ecclesiological Vision, Strategic Framework, Implication for Priestly Ministry* (Redemptorist Publication, 2000); *Building BECs: Case Studies from the Philippines*, coedited with Bishop Antonio Ledesma (NASSA, 2001); and *BECs in the Philippines: Dream or Reality — A Multi-Disciplinary Reflection*, coedited with Estela Padilla et al. (Bukal ng Tipan, 2004). *frpicx@hotmail.com.*

Gerry Proctor was ordained priest for the Archdiocese of Liverpool, England, in 1977. He then spent six years working with the Society of St. James in Ecuador and Bolivia, where he was strongly influenced by Base Ecclesial Communities. In 1991 he was appointed parish priest of St. Margaret Mary's, Knotty Ash, Liverpool, where he encouraged a "neighborhood church" to develop. In 2004 he spent a year as part of the José Marins Team, facilitating workshops for churches of Latin America and the Hispanic community of the United States. *proctorgerry@hotmail.com.*

Stephen Rymer has wide experience of church life and of being a member of a Christian community. He was Administrator in a Bristol UPA (Urban Priority Area) church from 1986 to 1990, Parish Resource Adviser for the Diocese of Bristol from 1990 to 1997, Lay Chaplain at Scargill House from 1997 to 2002, and is now Development Worker for New Way of Being Church. *newway@stbr.co.uk.*

Paolo Sales is a chemistry graduate and a graphic artist. He is one of the leading spirits of the Christian Base Community of Pinerola, Italy, and responsible for the production of graphic art for the community's publications and for the management of its Internet Web site.

Steve Valenzuela is the Associate Director of the Office of Small Faith Communities in the Diocese of San Bernardino, California. He is presently completing his MA in Pastoral Theology at Loyola Marymount University in Los Angeles. Over the past sixteen years as a professional lay ecclesial minister he has held various positions, including being a coordinator in the diocesan lay ministry formation institute, a parish pastoral associate, and campus minister at a state university. Throughout his career he has been involved in various forms of small groups and small communities as both a participant and facilitator. *svalenzuela@sbdiocese.org.*

Irene Wilson is involved in pastoral ministry in a number of parishes throughout the Archdiocese of Melbourne, Australia, including her own parish of St. Thomas More, Belgrave, Victoria. She is currently exploring, in a postgraduate thesis, the implications for Australian parishes in linking the Adult Catechumenate and Small Church Communities. She is a member of the Project Linkup Team. She and her husband John continue to be involved in a local SCC. *noola@alphalink.com.au.*

Stuart Wilson is a priest of the Diocese of Westminster, London, England. He was ordained into the Anglican (Episcopal) Ministry in June 1974. In 1996 he was ordained a Catholic priest. For most of his ministry he has worked in parishes in the London area, most recently as the parish priest in Kentish Town and Dean in the Camden Deanery. Presently he is the director of the "At Your Word, Lord" program for Pastoral and Spiritual Renewal in the diocese. *stuartwilson@rcdow.org.uk.*

Index

Of Related Interest

Once Upon a Time in Africa
Stories of Wisdom & Joy
Compiled by Joseph G. Healey
ISBN 1-57075-527-2

Soul-inspiring and heart-warming tales from every part of Africa.

"Enchanting . . . Healey has done us all a service by retrieving
these gems and putting them together in one collection."
—Spirituality and Health

"Must reading for any one who appreciates things African and
interesting and well-told stories."
—*Joseph Kariuki, Assistant Moderator,*
African Proverbs, Sayings and Stories Website,
Nairobi, Kenya www.afriprov.org

"What a joy it is to read *Once Upon a Time in Africa.*
These stories of wisdom and joy help us become wiser, holier,
happier people. This collection is a must read for everyone who
loves a good story!"
—*Beverly A. Carroll, Executive Director,*
Secretariat for African American Catholics,
United States Conference of Catholic Bishops

This rich collection of nearly a hundred stories—legends and
folktales, myths and parables, poems, prayers, and proverbs—
probes deeply into the mystery of being and our relationships with
God and one another.

Whether myths from the past or accounts of life today these
stories teach every human heart about compassion, forgiveness,
joy, peace, and community—indeed, about the value of harmony
within all creation.

Of Related Interest

Towards an African Narrative Theology
by Joseph G. Healey and
Donald F. Sybertz
ISBN 1-57075-121-8

"Carve with your friends; alone you cut yourself."
(Luvale, Zambia)

Shows how the wisdom sayings and proverbs
of Africa offer a new way to look at and understand
the Christian mysteries.

"These authors have succeeded in drawing on the rich
oral literature and cultural symbols of many ethnic groups
in different parts of Africa . . . The book expounds
vividly with practical examples. [The authors are]
transmitting the theological insights and reflections
of the African people from grassroots . . ."
—*John P. Mbonde in* The Sunday Observer

Please support your local bookstore or call 1-800-258-5838.
For a free catalog, please write us at
Orbis Books, Box 308
Maryknoll, NY 10545-0308
or visit our website at www.orbisbooks.com

Thank you for reading *Small Christian Communities Today.*
We hope you enjoyed it.

A Complete Guide to
Surviving in
the Wilderness

Everything You Need to Know to Stay Alive and Get Rescued

Terri Paajanen

A COMPLETE GUIDE TO SURVIVING IN THE WILDERNESS: EVERYTHING YOU NEED TO KNOW TO STAY ALIVE AND GET RESCUED

Copyright © 2014 Atlantic Publishing Group, Inc.

1210 SW 23rd Place • Ocala, Florida 34471 • Phone 800-814-1132 • Fax 352-622-1875

Website: www.atlantic-pub.com • Email: sales@atlantic-pub.com

SAN Number: 268-1250

Library of Congress Cataloging-in-Publication Data

Paajanen, Terri, 1971-

 A complete guide to surviving in the wilderness : everything you need to know to stay alive and get rescued / Terri Paajanen.

　　p. cm.

Includes bibliographical references and index.

ISBN 978-1-60138-581-9 (alk. paper) -- ISBN 1-60138-581-1 (alk. paper) 1. Wilderness survival. 2. Survival. I. Title.

　GV200.5.P236 2012

　613.6'9--dc23

                              2012015627

Printed on Recycled Paper

INTERIOR LAYOUT: Antoinette D'Amore • addesign@videotron.ca

COVER DESIGNS: Jackie Miller • millerjackiej@gmail.com

A few years back we lost our beloved pet dog Bear, who was not only our best and dearest friend but also the "Vice President of Sunshine" here at Atlantic Publishing. He did not receive a salary but worked tirelessly 24 hours a day to please his parents.

Bear was a rescue dog who turned around and showered myself, my wife, Sherri, his grandparents Jean, Bob, and Nancy, and every person and animal he met (well, maybe not rabbits) with friendship and love. He made a lot of people smile every day.

We wanted you to know a portion of the profits of this book will be donated in Bear's memory to local animal shelters, parks, conservation organizations, and other individuals and nonprofit organizations in need of assistance.

– Douglas & Sherri Brown

PS: We have since adopted two more rescue dogs: first Scout, and the following year, Ginger. They were both mixed golden retrievers who needed a home.

Want to help animals and the world? Here are a dozen easy suggestions you and your family can implement today:

- *Adopt and rescue a pet from a local shelter.*
- *Support local and no-kill animal shelters.*
- *Plant a tree to honor someone you love.*
- *Be a developer — put up some birdhouses.*
- *Buy live, potted Christmas trees and replant them.*
- *Make sure you spend time with your animals each day.*
- *Save natural resources by recycling and buying recycled products.*
- *Drink tap water, or filter your own water at home.*
- *Whenever possible, limit your use of or do not use pesticides.*
- *If you eat seafood, make sustainable choices.*
- *Support your local farmers market.*
- *Get outside. Visit a park, volunteer, walk your dog, or ride your bike.*

Five years ago, Atlantic Publishing signed the Green Press Initiative. These guidelines promote environmentally friendly practices, such as using recycled stock and vegetable-based inks, avoiding waste, choosing energy-efficient resources, and promoting a no-pulping policy. We now use 100-percent recycled stock on all our books. The results: in one year, switching to post-consumer recycled stock saved 24 mature trees, 5,000 gallons of water, the equivalent of the total energy used for one home in a year, and the equivalent of the greenhouse gases from one car driven for a year.

Author Dedication

I wouldn't have been able to write this book without Mike Wilson, who shared a great deal of his own wilderness knowledge while I was working on it. And of course, I have to thank my daughter Emily who happily tagged along on so many of our adventures.

I also greatly appreciate the help from those who supplied their own wilderness survival stories that contributed to the content of this book.

Table of Contents

Chapter 3: Starting and Maintaining a Fire.....................................65

Chapter 4: Finding Water........................81

Introduction

The idea of being prepared for any type of disaster is not new, but with reality TV shows such as *Survivorman* and *Man vs. Wild* bringing the importance of wilderness survival into the public eye and making it glamorous, people are becoming aware of wilderness skills they should have, even in this modern world. It is no longer only crazy mountain folk who can make fire with flint or learn how to eat wild roots. These are skills anyone can master, and even a small kit of gear can help you survive an unexpected problem in the woods.

In the past, it was generally common knowledge how to start up a fire or read a map. Today, our lives have changed, and these skills are no longer commonplace. We travel with GPS units in our cars and rarely have the need to start a fire. Modern technology has made our lives easier, and yet it has also caused us to move away from these basic hands-on type of skills. Unfortunately, technology can fail at any time. Your learned skills, on the other hand, are always ready to use.

There are many potential disaster situations, but the most common ones are covered here, and their respective chapters offer specific gear requirements and skills you will need to survive each particular catastrophe. Overall, the techniques and skills presented should help you survive any possible scenario and be ready for anything. You will be able to make a fire, find water, forage for food, and take the right steps to getting rescued. Seem extreme? The fact is that these basic needs can be at risk in an emergency, and it might be up to you and you alone to provide for the needs of yourself and your family.

Campers, hunters, hikers, and fishermen are not the only ones who might find themselves in a wilderness situation. Anyone can have a car breakdown or even slide right off the road after an accident.

In May 2011, tornadoes ripped through the town of Joplin, Missouri, and left 160 people dead. A thousand more were injured. Nearly a quarter of the town was razed, and the hospital had extensive damage. Power was out for up to a month is some areas, and cell phone communication was severely disrupted. Though shelters were quickly set up and established, many people were left helpless in the wake of the disaster. Having some good skills under your belt along with basic equipment can go a long way to help you built quick shelter or find water. Never assume that it cannot happen to you. Always be prepared.

If you ever watched an episode of *Lost* and started thinking about all the "what if..." scenarios in your own life, then this is the book to get you on the right path to being prepared.

Chapter 1

Preparation and Avoidance

Being prepared for a disaster can save your life, but knowing how to prevent it in the first place is an even better skill. Having some talents under your belt, as well as some basic survival supplies on hand, can go a long way toward keeping you and your family safe. Staying out of disaster is the first step to surviving it.

Avoid the Disaster

Many disasters are going to be unexpected regardless of what you do. But staying on top of things and taking a few extra steps when going out can really reduce your risks. Basically, preparation is your biggest survival tool.

Plan ahead

Never get into a situation, even if it might seem benign, without some pre-planning. A little spontaneity is a great thing as long as you are not getting into serious circumstances without any preparation at all. Because getting stuck or lost in the wilderness is going to be an outdoor event, do your most serious planning when you are heading out into nature, even if it is not going to be a long stay. A trip to the mall, in which you stay secure in civilization the entire way, would not count.

Some things to consider before your outing would include:

- Where are you going?
- How do you plan on getting there?
- What is an alternate route there (or back)?
- What should you take in a best-case scenario?
- What should you take in a worst-case scenario?
- What are some problems that could arise?
- How can you best prepare for these problems?

If your trip will include several people, go over the possible issue with everyone, and give this short list to everyone as well. See if anyone else can think of possible outcomes that should be planned for. Establish within your group who will carry what supplies or equipment so nothing accidentally gets left behind or forgotten.

Communicate your plans to others

Knowing what is going on within your group is vital, but so is letting people outside your group in on your plans. If something goes awry when no one is expecting you back, you are going to have an even longer wait for any assistance. Let someone at home know where you are going, when you expect to be back, and what route you are planning to take.

You can make these arrangements with anyone, not just people you see regularly near your home. As long as you call in when you are home safe, you could even have your great-aunt who lives across the country as your backup. Arrange with him or her (or them) how much time to wait before hearing from you, and ask him or her to call the authorities if you fail to return or call in. If you find yourself running late due to non-disaster reasons, do not forget to let your contact person know so you do not wind up on the receiving end of a missing-persons manhunt.

Pack appropriately

This is not just about pack-ing survival gear. Be prac-tical and do not worry too much about traveling light. Do not see how little you can get away with or skimp on bringing what is necessary for your spe-cific trip. Do not go hiking in flip-flops or decide you "probably" will not need any bug repellent. Weath-er can always get cold or

wet, no matter what season you are traveling in, so a light jacket and umbrella might be a good idea.

Have gear on hand

This is more about survival gear. Aside from the typical equip-ment you need for your specific outdoor activity, always have a good kit of survival equipment with you as well. Even if it seems unlikely that a real disaster is going to hit, survival gear will help no one if it is left at home. Find a little room in the car or backpack for a decent kit of emergency equipment. That also means to keep it with you at your destination. Having a kit in the car while you are off hiking is not a smart approach. *More about these kits and their contents is in Chapter 2.*

Potential Disaster Situations

Some situations are more prone to problems than others. Your average afternoon across town to the movies is unlikely to present any serious problems. Whenever you are going to be in an area with high traffic and lots of people, you are going to be fine. It is when you leave the city and head out into the wilderness, even just out to a well-marked nature trail, that problems arise.

Road trouble

Road trouble can happen to anyone at any time. Having an automotive kit of gear is important to tackle car troubles. Usually if your car breaks down, you can flag someone down for some assistance or call your auto club for a tow. However, if you have road trouble in a remote area or during bad weather, or if you have been injured, you can have more serious problems and have to fend for yourself. Unless you are taking a short drive within the city, always prepare for potential road trouble.

The most serious road problems will happen in winter. Car trouble in the summer usually means (at worst) a long walk — albeit a sweaty one — to the nearest house. Of course, for children or the elderly, being stuck on the side of the road in the summer can be as deadly as during the winter if you have no shade or water. In the winter, you will have snow to contend with, and that will complicate your situation. If you cannot get back to the road due to heavy snow, you can be trapped in your car, and your kit will be vital.

Real-life scenario: In 2009, a couple took their 4 by 4 out into a remote area in the mountains near Medford, Oregon. They got stuck in the snow and were trapped in the woods for more than two days until they were able to free their vehicle and drive back to town.

Hiking and camping

Wilderness survival is more likely to come up if you are out in the wilderness to begin with. Getting lost or injured during a hiking or camping trip is the most common way people end up needing wilderness survival skills. You do not have to be in a distant or remote location for disaster to strike, so even a short hike in the woods can become more serious. People lose their way on a trail all the time and can easily get disoriented. Unexpected weather can hamper your movements, also leading to your group taking a wrong turn.

Real-life scenario: Also in Oregon, a woman was hiking with her boyfriend but took a fall from a cliff. She broke her leg and had to survive on berries and insects for four days until she was found and rescued by helicopter. This event was in 2011.

Boating

Being out on the water poses a whole other realm of potential disasters. Equipment failure can leave you stranded, damage to your boat can leave you struggling in the water, and you can get lost easily once you are out of sight of land. Being trapped on the water is a unique situation because of the lack of movement options to get yourself to safety. *Chapter 11 covers many of the special skills needed for survival in a boating situation.*

Real-life scenario: Off the coast of Key Largo, two men went on a boating trip to the Bahamas, but debris struck their boat and it sank. Stranded with minimal supplies in a dinghy, they survived on the water for three days until they managed to row to Boca Raton.

Plane accident

This might seem extremely unlikely, and it is. Even so, a plane crash is the one scenario that can put you at the greatest risk and the farthest from rescue when it occurs. It will be the least likely to happen and yet the one time you most need your survival skills.

Traveling on a commercial airplane is not going to be the problem. If such a plane were to go down, there would be signal beacons involved and a rescue crew quickly dispatched. But any small flight such as a private charter will be another matter. Anyone who flies to remote areas for work or for other outdoors activities (hunting, camping) will fall into this category. Fly with your kit handy, not stowed away, and be prepared should the plane go down.

Real-life scenario: In a more dramatic event, a small plane went down in the Kalahari Desert in 2000, and two survivors had to survive a 200 km walk to civilization while scrounging for water and avoiding local wildlife in order to lead rescuers back to the rest of the injured survivors.

Disasters at home

A disaster at home is not exactly a wilderness situation, but if you are going to be conscious of your own safety and security, you do need to keep it in mind. Many of the same skills and equipment will come in handy, so these situations should be part of your survival plan. Prolonged power outages, earthquakes, snow storms, tornadoes, flooding, and even simple economic hardship can all put you in danger right at home. *This subject is covered in more detail in Chapter 13.*

The Survival Mindset

Survival gear and even skills are only part of staying alive in a bad situation. Having the proper frame of mind can be a huge advantage.

Have a plan

By thinking ahead, you will already have a good idea of what to do when faced with the unexpected. This type of plan goes beyond the typical travel planning mentioned above. What has been discussed so far is intended to keep you *out* of trouble. But you also need to know the proper steps when that fails and you *are* in trouble.

When your situation gets out of hand, it is easy to lose your head and forget important survival steps. Even general common sense can go out the window if you are not careful. Have a printout of the following list of steps so you can stay focused.

Assess the Situation – Before you can determine what needs to be done, you need to have a clear and complete picture of exactly what state you are in. Check on everyone to make sure no first aid is needed, double-check your available equipment, and see what natural resources you have around you.

Administer First Aid – Even small injuries should be dealt with immediately. There is no sense worrying about foraging for food if someone is bleeding. Injuries and wounds are always the top priority. Starting a fire might come before this if the weather warrants it, so use your best judgment.

Establish Your Immediate Needs – If your disaster situation has taken place during the winter or any other type of inclement weather, then put together some kind of shelter and start a fire.

Establish your Location – Once the immediate needs are addressed, you have to figure out where you are. When your emergency involves a car accident or breakdown, this task should be relatively simple unless you were lost on the road to begin with. A good road map should help narrow down your location. When lost in the woods, it will be a much tougher problem.

Try to Signal – An accident on the road might not progress any farther than this point if you have a cell phone and can call for assistance. Same principle applies if your boat breaks down and you can call the shore on the radio. Flares or flags can also be used to see if you can make contact right away.

Decide on Moving or Staying – This decision is probably one of the most difficult parts of your plan and one that only you can decide upon. Do you stay where you are and wait for rescue, or get on the move and find your way back to safety? Ideally, stay where you are and wait for someone to find you. Unfortunately, if no one is expecting you for several days or if you have not established a contact person, you might end up waiting for a long time.

Also, if you feel you have a good sense of your location and are confident that you can back to safety, plan on moving. If you are completely lost, trying to get back to safety will be a riskier bet. You could end up traveling farther away from your destination and making matters worse. When hiking, you might be able to follow your trail backwards, especially if you are traveling with a group of people. This is a good option if you think you are close to your original known trail.

If you are going to stay, think about getting a shelter in place. Even if it is early morning, do not wait until the chill of night starts to arrive. It can take a lot longer than you think to build something, so do not put it off. If you are near a car, you can use the car for shelter, and you can also pitch your tent if you are carrying camping gear with you. If you are on the move, stop to make camp early enough to allow for proper shelter. Building a fire, looking for water and food will all come into play at this point.

Stay positive

Nothing gets accomplished by negative thinking. Of course, do not be unrealistically optimistic in the face of a bad situation, but keep your mind positive in order to get through things. Operate under the assumption that you will get out of this alive and unharmed, and you need to keep everyone in your group on the same positive page.

Work at getting rescued

This might seem obvious, but if you start getting distracted by too many things, you can lose sight of your ultimate goal — getting rescued. Everything you do should work toward the goal of being rescued, or keeping you safe and healthy until that time. Focus on signaling, establishing your location, and finding your way to safety. Your camp should keep you warm and dry, but it is not going to be your next permanent home.

CASE STUDY:
JUST KEEP CALM

Shannon Morrigan
www.shaylamyst.net

Though not a die-hard survivalist, Shannon enjoys spending time outside. At home, she is always out in the garden, and when she and her family go camping, they always stick to primitive methods with facilities.

Her current skill-set includes knowing how to set snares and handle the animals once caught, to establish direction for navigating, to build a shelter, to forage for edible and medicinal plants, to get a fire started, and to stay calm in an emergency. She has learned most of her skills from her mother since she was a young girl, and she has more recently become CPR and First Aid Certified.

When outdoors, she regularly forages for edible plants to add to their menu of packed food. So far she has yet to use any of her skills in a true survival emergency, but she does practice many of her techniques while camping or canoeing.

Aside from her range of survival skills, she also keeps a chest of supplies whenever they go camping. She also keeps this gear on hand whenever she travels farther than walking distance from home. In this box are her general camping supplies (pots, silverware, dishes, potholders) as well as extra supplies such as an extra tarp, package of sealed matches, fire-starters, can opener, 2 gallons of fresh drinking water, and several dehydrated meals.

She also carries a first-aid kit with a collection of bandages, tea tree oil (a natural antiseptic), cotton swabs, powdered milk, sewing needles, tweezers, and an informational booklet on medicinal plants.

If she was going to be stranded with just one survival item, she would choose a multi-tool with a knife blade. According to Shannon, "I could create the other items I'd need. It would be hard, of course, but I believe I could do it."

What new skills are on the horizon for Shannon? She would like to learn archery to expand her hunting options and also how to tan hides.

And when asked about sharing one piece of advice for our readers, she said, "Keep your head. I'd be willing to bet that every person who had to survive stayed calm. Panicking will get you seriously injured or even killed."

Chapter 2

Your Survival Gear

Surviving with only your wits and bare hands is possible, but you will need a great deal of knowledge, skill, and experience to pull it off. For the average person, a proper kit of equipment and supplies is the better way to go. Of course, when you account for all the potential situations and emergency needs, you are going to need an additional vehicle to lug it all around with you. The trick is to establish which ones are the necessary items and find any tools that can serve several purposes. It is not as easy as you think. Your kit of survival supplies can be a simple kit that could be carried on a belt or in a fanny pack, or it could be a more complete bag of gear in a large

nat is the approach taken here: a small all-purpose kit
have with you, and then a larger array of supplies that
be tailored to your specific outings.

Basic Survival Kit

This is a kit providing the basic survival needs that can arise in
any situation. It makes a good everyday kit that can be carried
when you are out. It is the core of your survival gear arrangement. You can pack a small kit like this in a metal tin or fanny
pack. Or pack everything in the watertight metal tin, and carry
it in a fanny pack for better portability. First, here is a list of the
contents, and further explanations for all of the items will follow.

- Matches
- Small candle
- Flint fire starter
- Needle and thread
- Fish hooks and length of line
- Compass
- Mini flashlight
- Whistle
- Mirror
- Large garbage bag, tightly folded
- Wire saw
- Pocket knife
- Foil emergency blanket
- Protein bar
- First-aid kit
  - Bandages in various sizes
  - Scalpel blades
  - Butterfly sutures
  - Roll of gauze or gauze and tape

o   Water purification tablets

o   Antihistamine tablets

o   Pain relief tablets

o   Diarrhea treatment tablets

This is not a concrete list, and you can always adapt this to suit your circumstances and carrying capacity. You can leave out the blanket and protein bar if you have to conserve space, for example. If you have certain medical conditions, adapt these basic supplies to suit what you may need.

Though most of the items will seem straight-forward, further explanation can help you understand how to make the most of your kit.

Matches

Matches are the easiest and quickest way to start a fire and should never be left out of a survival kit. A book of paper matches is better than nothing, but pack better quality ones to make sure they are useable when they need to be. Wooden matches are much more durable, and waterproof ones are even better. They are coated with a soft wax you scrape off before you strike the match. If you are tight on space, snip off part of each matchstick. As long as you can still grip it, it can be used.

Because fire is such an important survival tool, there are other methods for making fire in this kit. Never rely on just one.

Small Candle

An inexpensive tea-light candle is ideal for this. Although a candle will not start a fire on its own, it can be a great help for keeping one going. If you are having trouble getting a fire started, or suspect you will, use your matches to light the candle first. Once it is burning, it can provide a more stable flame while you work to build a larger fire. In a car or other enclosed space where you cannot build an open fire, a candle can provide some warmth and light.

Flint Fire Starter

A number of variations on this item exist, and the exact one you choose is up to you. Matches are the best option for fire, but a flint starter will work in almost any condition and does not run out like a pack of matches can. It is a good idea to practice so you are prepared in an emergency. *More details on using fire starters are included later on in this chapter.*

Needle and Thread

Mending small tears in your clothes is not going to be a big priority when you are in an emergency situation. Nonetheless, you can use a little sewing kit for more than just clothing. Serious cuts can be stitched up temporarily even by the most novice sewer, and sometimes doing repairs (such as on a backpack) can mean the difference between keeping your gear and losing something on the trail. You can also use the needle to remove splinters.

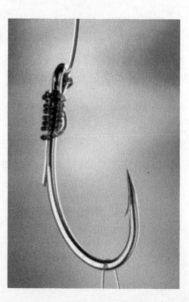

Fish Hooks and Line

Even a small stream can be home to fish worth catching for a meal. Unfortunately, you will have to be near water for this to be of any use. Package together three different sizes of hooks, a few lead sinkers, and several feet of fishing line. Do not settle for fine line, or you run the risk of it snapping at a bad moment. Try to have at least 30-pound test. *More information on how to fish in an emergency can be found in Chapter 5.*

Compass

You might already carry one of these with you when you are out, but keep a good-quality one in your kit for that rare occasion when you have forgotten to bring one. One that has glow-in-the-dark arms can be the most helpful.

Mini Flashlight

Many small LED flashlights on the market these days will produce a bright light and have a long battery life to them. Not only will a flashlight provide light for you to find your way on a trail or when you are trying to do a task in the dark, it can also make an excellent tool for signaling to potential rescuers during the night.

Whistle

A loud whistle is a classic and effective signaling aid when you are lost. If every member of your group has one, they can also be used to help everyone stay within hearing distance if you are not within sight of each other. Any whistle will do, though there are some survival whistles designed to produce a particularly loud sound.

Mirror

A small mirror is another option as a signaling device. Obviously, only pack one of the unbreakable varieties. *The best ways for using a mirror as a signal are further outlined in Chapter 7.*

Garbage Bag

A large heavy-weight garbage bag can be a little bulky in a kit, but it has so many possible uses. It can help keep you and your gear dry if it rains, and it can also be used to help catch rain if you need fresh water. Sleeping on it can keep you warm and off the damp soil, and the bags can be used to hold any food you forage or even as a place to dispose of bodily waste. One of the orange bags can make a good signal as well.

Wire Saw

This item might not be that necessary in shorter-term emergency situations, but if you are out in the wilderness for several days, you will be happy to have it. These saws are made with a chain on a flexible wire, with two handle rings on the ends. You can use one to cut through branches or even small trees. If you have to build a shelter, this will make the job faster and less energy intensive.

Pocket Knife

This will be covered in more detail further down in this chapter, as many variations to the standard "pocket  knife" exist. A blade alone is handy, but a knife with additional tools is a more practical choice as long as you are not compromising the blade. A good Swiss Army style knife is a popular choice because their models have good quality blades as well as a decent array of handy little tools. You might also want to carry a simpler knife and then a separate multi-tool.

Foil Emergency Blanket

These are also known as "space blankets" or "solar blankets." If you are not familiar with them, they are large sheets of thin flexible foil material that hold in heat well. They fold up not much thicker than a deck of cards but can open up to cover your body.

Protein Bar

Given the size of this basic kit, carrying many food supplies is not feasible. But a small protein bar can be added, which will provide some immediate nutrition. These bars will last a long time without going bad or stale, so you can keep one in your kit without having to worry about replacing it frequently.

First-Aid Kit

The items all listed for the first-aid portion of the kit are self-explanatory. The number of items you pack will depend on how much room you have available. For the medications, make sure their containers are well marked and carry at least three or four doses worth of tablets. There is more on first-aid supplies later in this chapter, and *Chapter 9 handles the techniques for applying first aid in an emergency.*

This simple kit contains items that can help you create fire, navigate your location, signal for help, acquire food, stay warm and/or dry, and take care of any wounds or injuries. That will go a long way in any emergency.

You can easily put together a kit like this or purchase a pre-assembled one. By getting all the components yourself, you can make sure you are getting good quality items for everything. Pre-made kits might not have exactly what you want or the specific items to suit your needs.

More Complete Kits

What has been so far described could be considered your "core" kit that has all the bare bones necessities for survival. But that does not really accommodate too many situations and certainly does not provide much comfort. You will really be roughing it if you have to rely on those kits. So when you have the space or carrying capacity, you might want to expand on that core kit with some additional supplies.

Once you start expanding your kit, you can tailor it to suit your circumstances. You might want to create larger kits for more than one purpose and then toss in your core kit when you need to take it with you rather than duplicate the items. If you fear you might forget the core portion, have extras to keep in each type of kit you maintain.

These larger kits usually are kept in a backpack or duffel bag for easier portability. But plastic tote boxes will also work well, particularly for a kit that is not going to be carried any distance. Car or boat kits would be fine in a sturdy box.

General kit expansion

Many extra items that deserve a place in your larger kit are going to be the same regardless of your situation. These items are listed here and would be ideal for any survival kit. More details are expanded below the list.

- Larger flashlight
- Additional matches (as per the core kit)
- Additional emergency candles
- Additional first-aid supplies
- Folding camp stove with fuel
- Lightweight camping pot

- Bottle of fresh water
- Additional food supplies
- Map book
- Hat and gloves (winter)
- Chemical heat packs (winter)
- Sunscreen and bug repellent (summer)
- Waterproof poncho or jacket
- Roll of duct tape
- Parachute cord
- Roll of toilet paper
- Bottle of hand sanitizer
- Tarp
- Comfort activity

Larger Flashlight

The flashlight in your core kit is going to be small to save space. Because you have more room in a car kit, you might want to upgrade to a larger model. This is not 100 percent necessary and will depend on the type of flashlight you are already keeping in your core survival kit. *More on choosing a flashlight will come later in this chapter.*

Additional Matches and Candles

These are for the same purpose as in the core kit, but having more is always better when you have the extra space for them. Also include some kind of holder or stand for a candle. Even a small candle can put off enough heat within a closed car to keep you reasonably comfortable.

Additional First-Aid Supplies

This will depend on how thorough the first-aid portion of your core kit is. Besides adding more bandages and gauze, you can also include alcohol wipes, elastic bandages, latex gloves, and more. The list of possible first-aid items is extensive. *You can read more on this part of your kit later in this chapter.*

Folding Camp Stove

You can find these at most outdoor stores, and they come with their own brand of solid fuel pellets. When open, they make a stand where you can put a small pot with the fuel underneath. You can use these with regular firewood (small pieces), and they can be useful for heating water or making simple soups while stuck on the side of the road.

Lightweight Camping Pot

This can be used with the camp stove. They will hold water for drinking or making coffee, tea, or soup. A light set of cutlery would be a good addi-

tion, though it would only be useful if you are keeping food supplies in your kit that would warrant their use.

Bottle of Fresh Water

Usually too large for the core kit, the car kit should have the space for a 500 mL or a 1L bottle of drinking water. Even pure water can get stale over time, so you need to rotate this out of your kit twice a year to keep it fresh. If you are going to be storing your kit anywhere that will drop below freezing (such as the trunk of your car), leave this out and remember to bring water with you when you pack for your trip. The bottle can split or crack when the water freezes, and then it will leak everywhere when it warms up again.

Additional Food Supplies

This can vary greatly, and all that matters is that you pack food that will stay edible in your kit for a while and that provides a high level of calories. Protein bars or meal replacement bars can be a good option for dense nutrition in a small package. Peanuts, meat jerky, dried fruit, granola bars, or even some chocolate will all give you energy when you need it. Dehydrated camping food is another option that will last a *long* time in a kit, though you will need to have access to heat and water to prepare it. The other items can be eaten instantly in any condition. Packets of tea, instant soup, and even chewing gum would help round out your supplies.

Map Book

Carrying a bound book of maps for a large region is better than trying to man-age a collection of smaller maps that can get lost or misplaced. Because you never know when a disas-ter can strike, have a book  that covers a fairly large geographic region. Your entire state is a good place to start. A GPS unit can be helpful, but it is usually too expensive a piece of equipment to purchase for an emergency kit. It can also malfunction or have its batteries go dead. If you carry a GPS when you travel, all the better to keep you on track. But you will want to have a reliable backup in your kit.

Seasonal Supplies

The list indicates a few important things to have depending on the season. If you have the space, you can carry them all the time and then never have to think about it. But it would be reasonable to switch out the winter and summer gear between seasons to help save on space.

Chemical heat packs are a must-have in the winter months. They are sealed in a tight package, and they react with the moisture in the air to produce instant heat. Some are constructed so you have to bend them or twist them sharply to snap open a chemical capsule inside. Either way, once you have activated them, you cannot turn them off. They can get quite hot. Never use them right up against your skin, or you can burn. Make sure to supervise any children using these heaters.

Waterproof Jacket

When you do not have adequate shelter, it can be a challenge to stay dry. Even so, it is important that both you and your gear can get out of the rain if the weather is a problem. A lightweight jacket can fold up tightly for storage in a kit. As long as it is large enough to cover your existing clothing and your backpack, it will be fine. You do not need to worry about having something with a precise fit.

Duct Tape

This is a universal item that does not have a specific purpose, but it has been known to help out in a variety of situations. You can use strips of it to waterproof other items, to join nearly any two things

together, to seal something, and even to close up a wound if you are desperate.

Parachute Cord

This can really be any type of comparable rope, though parachute cord (also called paracord or 550 cord) is the most typical for a survival kit application. A length of 20 to 50 feet should be sufficient, and you can also buy tightly woven survival bracelets or lanyards that compress another 10 feet or so into a wearable item. You can use rope like this to string up tarps for shelter, lash together branches, hang gear from a tree to get it off the ground, tie additional pieces of gear to your pack, or even tie large bandages in place. It is a multi-purpose item to have in your kit.

Toilet Paper

The use for this is self-explanatory. Remove the cardboard roll and squash the roll a little flatter to save space in your pack.

Hand Sanitizer

These alcohol-based hand cleaners are an excellent product for a kit. Because you probably will not have a lot of water to spare, keeping your hands as clean as possible will be a challenge. These cleansers are perfect for this use. In a pinch, you can even use a few drops to help your fire get started (there is enough alcohol in these gels to burn).

Tarp

A sturdy woven plastic tarp can suit a number of purposes, namely to create a quick shelter. Have at least one, 10 by 10

feet in size, with heavy-duty metal grommets for attaching rope. It can also be a ground cover for sleeping.

Comfort Activity

Depending on your situation, you can find yourself with a lot of time to kill. If you are stuck in one location and waiting for assistance, you will can get bored and anxious in the meantime. A deck of cards is sufficient and can help pass the time for one person or several. A crossword or similar puzzle book is another option. You could also bring along a favorite book.

For the car

Keeping a kit in your car is a wise idea, especially during the winter months, which are more likely to lead to inclement weather and finding yourself stuck off the road. All of the items listed above should be included, as well as the following:

- Jumper cables
- Red or fluorescent signal fabric
- Flares
- Basic toolkit
- Quick tire patch
- Blanket
- Work gloves
- Shovel
- First-aid kit
- Additional supplies

Jumper Cables

A common problem when an automotive breaks down is the battery. If someone stops and offers to help you, a sim-

ple jump-start can get your car going again. Having your own jumper cables will ensure someone can help in case your rescuer is not carrying any cables. Make sure you know how to use them so you do not do further damage to the battery of your car.

Signal Fabric

If your car is off the side of the road, it might not be obvious that you are in trouble. Adding a signal flag of some kind will let anyone going by know you need assistance. This is doubly true if your car is farther off the road or is obscured by snowfall.

Flares

Have a few of these with you because they do not last long (ten minutes to an hour, depending on the make and brand). They are lit the same way you would strike a match along the pavement or with a pull-tab, and they will provide a bright flame and light to clearly signal oncoming traffic that you are in the lane. You can also buy LED versions of these that will last much longer, though you then have to worry about battery life while the lights are stored in your kit.

Basic Toolkit

This part of your survival equipment should not be ignored just because you do not know anything about car engines. Many people do not bother to carry tools because they do not know how to repair a car, but you want to be prepared if someone more knowledgeable than yourself happens to stop. Have a pack with a socket set, a screwdriver set, a hammer, electrical tape, and pliers.

Quick Tire Patch

Quick Tire Patches come in different brands (Slime, Fix-a-Flat), but they work the same way. An aerosol can with a liquid sealant is attached to the air valve of a flat tire. The compressed air inside helps to re-inflate the tire, and the sealant will temporarily seal up the hole (within reason). These can get you back on the road if a nail or something punctures your tire but will not help with large holes or splits.

Blanket

Unlike most other wilderness scenarios, you do not have to supply shelter because you are already in your car. But a thick wool blanket will help keep you warm and comfortable if you have to sleep in your car.

Work Gloves

Having to work around a car can be hard on your hands and fingers, so keep a sturdy pair of work gloves in your size. The last thing you need is an additional injury when the situation is getting tough.

Shovel

A full-size shovel is a little bulky even in a car, but there are some with shorter handles or even folding models intended to be kept for emergencies. You can use one to dig out of soft mud or snow if you are stuck.

First-Aid Kit

You should have a good first-aid kit in your complete survival kit, and you might not feel you need a separate one in your car, but given the odds that most automotive problems can mean injuries, have an extra one. Being prepared for larger injuries is a good idea. Add in larger packs of gauze, surgical tape, and bandages.

Additional Supplies

To keep your car running on the road and to avoid an unexpected pit stop on the side, keep some additional supplies on hand as well. Keep a jug of windshield washer fluid and a pint of oil with you. An empty gas can will make a huge difference if you have to walk a few miles to a gas station and find they do not sell containers. In cold weather, a bottle of gas line antifreeze should be added to your kit.

All of these items can be packed in a secure container and simply left in your car at all times. When going on a trip or for any extended travel time, you can grab your usual complete survival kit and toss it in the car. You could also leave your main supply kit in the car as well if you have the space. That way you always have it when you leave the house.

For the hiking or camping trip

When you are in a car, you will almost never find yourself truly in the wilderness because you will always be right near a road no matter what has gotten you stuck. You also will have the vehicle itself for shelter. For true situations of wilderness survival, you

need to be out in the wilderness. A hiking or camping trip gone wrong is the most common situation that can do this to you, so these are the situations that require the most serious survival kits.

If you are hiking on urban trails where you would be able to find your way out of the woods no matter which direction you go in, you should be fine carrying only the core kit. However, while on any trips in which there is a substantial area you can get lost in, the full kit is a much better idea. "Camping" in any kind of trailer or recreational vehicle would be closer to a road scenario, so you can work with the kits described for use in a car.

For a true camping trip away from any vehicles, you will already have a full assortment of gear with you, including a tent and sleeping bags, which will make some of your survival kit extraneous. But a situation can arise where you get lost and separated from your campsite or your regular gear can get damaged in severe weather, so you should still pack a complete kit with these extras.

- An additional tarp (or emergency tent)
- Blanket
- Extra socks
- Moleskin or other blister protection
- Small hatchet
- Snare wire
- Topographical maps
- Additional food supplies
- Binoculars
- Canteen

Another Tarp or Tent

If you have your regular camping gear with you, this will not be necessary. But if you do not, you can fashion a decent shelter with a couple of tarps. There is already one in your standard kit, and this one makes two. One can be tied above you as a shelter, and you can sleep on the second one to keep you dry. A small emergency tent or "tube tent" can also be used and put up with just a few pieces of rope. Either one will keep you dry when away from your campsite and gear.

Blanket

Unlike the car situation where you have a vehicle for shelter, you are going to be roughing it if you are stranded out during a camping trip. An extra blanket is vital. Your core kit already contains a foil space blanket for insulation, but a heavier one will add more comfort to your nights. A wool or fleece blanket is ideal for this, though it will take up a large amount of space in your pack.

Extra Socks

Getting lost in the wilderness means you will be doing a lot of walking unless you are rescued quickly. A spare pair of sturdy socks can keep your feet warm, dry, and blister-free.

Moleskin or Blister Protection

This goes along with the last point about having to walk. A typical first-aid kit might already have this included, but soft adhesive material you can use to cushion sore spots on your feet can help keep blisters at bay.

Small Hatchet

A hatchet can be used to quickly cut up large branches for shelter making and firewood. Always have a sturdy sheath for it in your pack. A sharpening stone is also a good addition so long as you know how to use it.

Snare Wire

This one item can be used for several applications, though its prime purpose is to rig snares for trapping small animals. *Chapter 5 will outline this in more detail.* You will have to have the right wire in your kit. Most hunting or outdoors stores will carry it, and the roll can be added to your pack. You can use the wire in place of rope for some situations as well. This is not something you will need during a short-term emergency, as you should have some food supplies with you already. But if you are out in the wilderness for more than a few days, you will have to start looking for your own food.

Topographical Maps

The map book included in the basic kit would be for street maps, but if you are hiking away from the roads, a local topographical map is also vital. These are the maps that show all the details of the terrain rather than the roads. You will want to make sure you know how to read them before you head out, though they are not complicated. Types of landscape are marked (bodies of water, types of terrain) as well as lines showing elevation. The elevation lines that are close together would mean a steeper path to follow, which can be important to know if you are trying to establish a route back to safety. *You can read more on how to interpret a map in Chapter 8.*

Additional Food Supplies

This has been mentioned in every kit grouping so far, and it bears repeating. Though the main complete kit already has a store of food, augment that for a hiking or camping expedition. These are the trips that can result in long unexpected stays in the outdoors more than any other, and your need for food will be greatest. All the previous commentary on food items applies, though you could expand your options to include more dehydrated meals to save on space and weight.

Binoculars

Getting a better view on things can help when you are lost. Binoculars help scope out a safe trail or look for landmarks. They should be sturdy as well as lightweight, but you do not need to get a model so clear that you could check out the tail feathers on every passing bird. At a minimum, have 7X magnification, though 10X would be better.

Canteen

Water is unfortunately heavy, so you are going to be limited on how much of it you can carry with you. In a survival situation, any packed water will run out soon enough, and you will have to rely on other sources. Keep any empty water bottles from your supply; having an extra empty canteen or bottle can help a great deal in establishing new stores of water when you find a source. What good is locating water if you have nothing to put it in?

These lists can be helpful in deciding what items you want to have in your various survival kits. The next sections will elaborate and more fully explain what you need for the vital survival tools.

For the boat

A potential disaster on a boat can mean two things: either you are stranded out on the water but secure in your boat, or the boat is damaged in some way and you are going to sink. You are going to have to handle these situations differently, so your boat kit should be just as diverse. Many of these items are going to be standard safety gear, so you might not need anything new.

- Floatation devices for each person on board
- Paddle
- Flares and/or flare gun
- Signaling flags
- Basic set of tools
- Bilge pump (hand-powered)
- Fishing net
- Length of rope

Flotation Devices

These should be typical gear on any boat and should not be something you need to acquire specially.

Paddle

Unless you are traveling in a large boat, a paddle can be a vital tool when you are stranded due to motor failure. Two paddles are best to help paddle straight, with one on either side of the boat, but that might not work if you are alone. It can take a lot of time and muscle exertion to get around this way, but the alternative of staying where you are might not be any better.

Flares and/or Gun

Unlike a car scenario, a boating emergency can put you much farther from civilization when disaster strikes. Carry extra flares so you can signal passing planes or other boats. Signaling flags are carried for the same reason. An air horn is another vital signaling device to keep on board. You could also carry one for other emergencies, but they are bulky for a backpack.

Basic Set of Tools

This is the same requirement as with the car kit, though tailor the tools to apply to the engine and mechanics of your particular type of boat.

Bilge Pump

If you are taking on water, a way to quickly and effectively bail can mean the difference between getting to shore or sinking. A bucket is a simple option, but a hand-powered pump can work better.

Fishing Net

Being lost in the woods allows for several options when foraging for food. If you are stranded on a boat out on a body of water, you are going to be limited to getting fish. A good net on hand can help with this, as you already have basic fishing gear in your core kit. Of course, if you do catch a fish, you will only be able to cook it if you have a functioning stove unit on board. *You can learn more about getting food on a boat in Chapter 11.*

Length of Rope

Rope can be particularly important when on a boat, so have more on board than what is in your kit. Being able to tie off the boat, help pull it out onto shore, or tie onto another boat that has come to help are all examples of when rope will be vital. Unlike the rope in your kit, you will want something a little heavier for these purposes. Try to have at least 50 feet of ½- or ¾-inch thick rope on your boat.

For a plane

Because a potential plane accident was mentioned in Chapter 1 as a possible disaster scenario, it should be mentioned here even though there really is not

a special list of gear unique to this event. When traveling on a small private plane or charter, you will probably have no problems keeping your gear with you. Keep at least a core kit if not your full kit on hand rather than having it stowed away somewhere else in the plane. It could be lost several miles from you if the plane breaks apart before coming down.

If you want to carry a kit with you on a commercial airline, you could run into trouble with some of the contents. A knife most certainly would not be permitted, and even a flint/steel tool might be disallowed. Though being stranded somewhere without a knife is not ideal, it can be done. Carrying a kit without these items is better than no kit at all. A magnifying lens is a good "plane-safe" alternative as a fire-starter.

Unfortunately, the regulations for air travel vary and tend to change due to world events. Always check to see what is allowed or prohibited on a plane before carrying any kind of survival kit on board.

Knives

Knives are often one of the first things that come to mind when you think of survival equipment. A reliable (and sharp) blade can be used in so many circumstances; consider this to be one of the most versatile tools in your kit. A multi-tool knife is even doubly so. For the purpose of outfitting a survival kit, knives are broken down into two groups: utility knives and hunting knives. The first group include the Swiss Army style knives that include tools along with a blade. The second group is strictly for single-blade knives.

Utility knives and multi-tools

These knives can be a whole tool box in your hand. For a general survival purpose, these are more important than the hunting knives, and if you only have space for one knife, choose one of these. Multi-tools are a little different as they focus on the tool component rather than the blades. *More on those later in this section.*

Utility Knives

Swiss Army is the most popular brand of utility knife, and they have the best quality knives in this category. You can choose from a simple knife with just one blade to large units with a dozen tools and multiple blades. These knifes are built so all the tools fold down into the handle, and they fold out from a single pivot at the end. Each item will lock in place when extended so it is relatively solid for use.

It can be a little awkward for some of the smaller tool portions to be attached to a large handle, but you can usually manage with a little practice.

Depending on the specific knife you choose, you can have the following tools at your fingertips:

- Various sizes of knife blade
- Corkscrew
- Bottle opener
- Scissors
- Saw blade
- Tweezers
- Nail file
- Screwdriver (various tips)
- Magnifying lens
- Toothpick
- Pliers
- Wire strippers
- LED flashlight
- Ballpoint pen

Although not all of these tools will have important uses in a survival setting, you never know when a particular implement will be necessary. Remember that these tools are small, sometimes under 2 inches in length. That might not be enough in a serious emergency situation.

It might be tempting to choose the knife with the most tools possible. You can easily spend several hundred dollars on a top-of-the-line knife with every tool imaginable. However, that might not be the best way to spend a limited budget. And the heavily laden knives can be even more awkward to use than the smaller ones because the handle portion is so thick. It would be best to determine which tools you want to have with you and find a model of knife that contains only those.

Multi-Tools

On the other hand, you have the multi-tools. They operate on same principle, but instead of being built around a knife blade, they are made with a pair of pliers as the central piece. Each part of the handle then has its own collection of mini-tools inside. The overall shape is different, and these can be a bit more practical if you are looking for an item that is more about the tools than the knives.

Leatherman makes some great ones, and there are many cheap variations on the market. Stay with the quality tools if you want them to last and stand up to use in an emergency. These tools have the same basic options as the Swiss Army style knives, though usually there are more tools in each unit and only one knife blade.

Hunting knives

Hunting knives are much larger than the multi-use knives and have only one blade. These are the knives you carry because  you are going to need a knife and nothing else. Do not be fooled by the simplicity of a blade. There are many different situations where a cutting edge can be helpful. Cutting rope, bandages, trimming wood for tinder or kindling, and killing and skinning an animal for food are just a few obvious examples.

Within this category, you will have the choice of a fixed blade knife or a folding blade. A fixed blade knife will take up more space in your kit and have to have a sheath to protect the blade, whereas a folding knife is more compact and will not need a sheath. A fixed blade is a little more secure because there are no moving parts and it is a solid piece. This is the better knife for serious hunting, but a good quality folding knife is usually the better option for a survival situation because it can be folded up for portability and safety.

You can also purchase fixed blade knives that have a hollow handle where you can store many small survival items (like you would find in the core kit described in the first section of this chapter). These are a particularly nice item if you are already a hunter and travel with such a knife when you are in the wilderness.

Regardless of which knife you carry, keeping a small sharpening stone and knowing how to use it will mean you always have a sharp blade when you need it.

Flashlights

Flashlights are a simple addition to your kit and will not need much explanation. Standard flashlights come in many sizes, and you can almost always find the right one for your kit whether you are building a fanny-pack core kit or a larger duffel bag survival package. Larger flashlights will provide more light, but they are heavier than small ones. Always pack fresh batteries with you.

Standard flashlights can be a little delicate, so take care not to break the glass or the bulb inside. You can find more rugged versions that can take more of a beating and would do better in an emergency situation. A water-resistant model would be even better.

Another option is one of the newer LED flashlights. They are much brighter than those with a typical bulb, and they use less battery power.

If you have room in your kit, you could augment your lighting options with a free-standing lantern or a lamp that straps to your head. These will provide light for you while you keep both hands free for a task.

To make the light source in your kit the most reliable, you could even go with a model powered by a crank or by shaking. These lights can be charged anytime and anywhere without any concern for batteries. They are bulkier than some of the standard ones and probably would not fit in a little core kit. But in a larger bag, they are a great asset. They need to be shaken or cranked for several minutes to develop a charge for lighting, so they might not be able to light up instantly. Depending on the situation, this could be a significant drawback.

One final mention for lighting is the glowstick. They will work in almost any weather or situation, and batteries are never a problem. Snap the stick in the middle and shake up the chemicals inside to create a steady glow of light. They are best for task lighting, as they do not project a beam of light outward far (down a path, for example). You can also use them as signals during the night to help identify your position to others, or just to mark a trail. They are not reusable, so once the light goes out, they are done.

Inexpensive children's glowsticks are even worth having, as they can put out light for several hours. For a more robust option, you can get larger ones intended for survival situations. Be careful not to bend them enough to snap their inner capsule, or they will light before you need them. Try any outdoors or camping store and look for brands such as Omniglow® and Cyalume. Some of the non-branded (usually Chinese made) sticks can be a little unreliable, though they can be a much cheaper option if you are on a tight budget.

Fire Starters

Now this is one part of your gear that will not be quite so commonplace or as well known as knives or flashlights. Nonetheless, have at least two different ways to make fire in a survival situation. Knowing your options is crucial. Some are easy to use, and some are going to take some practice to use them properly. This section outlines the equipment for starting fires, but Chapter 3 will have more information on how to use them and how to get a fire going.

Matches

You might be surprised at the number of options you have even with a simple match. Typical paper matches in their little fold-over books are practically free and can be added to any type of kit or just kept in a pocket or purse. They are handy, though not all that reliable. They do not always light well and can be ruined by just a little moisture.

Wooden matches are more durable, and waterproof matches are even better. The waterproof ones have a coating of wax over the flammable head to keep them usable after having gotten wet. A little of your own heated wax could be used to do a similar waterproofing to standard wooden matches.

Survival retailers might also have what are called "stormproof" matches. They are considerably longer than standard matches, and there is a longer, thicker flammable portion (not just the tip), so they will burn for 15 to 20 seconds. This extra time can be valuable if making a fire in a bad situation.

Matches offer the most basic of fire-starting capabilities, though you are limited by the number of matches you are carrying. Also, their flames do not last long once you light the match. Other options are worth exploring for emergencies.

Lighters

This is another simple method that can be better than matches in some instances. One lighter takes up little space in a kit and can produce a lot of fires. It can also hold a flame going for a much longer time than a match, though that will use up fuel. A cheap disposable lighter has butane inside, but a Zippo model has lighter fluid. If you are keeping a non-disposable type like a Zippo, you will need to have the right fuel on hand, though you likely will not need to carry that with you in your kit.

If you are going to carry a lighter as a fire starter, you can also find rugged versions intended for survival situations. One of the best is the Windmill Stormproof lighter. It is rubberized and water-resistant, and it can keep its butane flame going in 70 mph winds. Brunton® also makes a similar type of lighter that should get your fire going in nearly any weather conditions.

Flint and steel

Scraping a steel edge along flint will create some powerful sparks. It is not quite the same as a flame and will take a bit of practice to get tinder to burn, but this type of fire starter will last for thousands of uses. These items have been packaged a number of ways, so you can find many different products that use a flint/steel combination. The BlastMatch™ is one particular brand that works well in adverse conditions and is easy to use.

Magnesium blocks

This is similar to the flint and steel but with an added benefit of the magnesium. You do need to have a knife or other sharp implement to make this one work because they generally do not come with a flint striker. First, you scrape the silver block of magnesium to make a pile of shavings, and then you strike the flint to make a spark. The shavings will light up almost instantly and will hold a hot flame while you get your tinder lit.

Fire piston

This is an outdoors tool that takes a sparkless approach to starting a fire. A small tube with a piston is pressed to compact the air within the sealed compartment. That generates heat and should ignite a piece of tinder placed inside. These are a little less reliable than the other items, and the gaskets that seal the tube can wear out or split.

Magnifying lens

This is not a method for the amateur and really would only be used if you ran out of all the other items first. By focusing sunlight through a lens, you can create a hot point of light that is enough to set fine tinder on fire. Needless to say, this will only work in the sun. Night or even just a cloudy day will make this impossible.

Tinder

Though not actually a way to start a fire, having good tinder on hand in your kit can make the creation of a fire easier. There are commercial products available that have chemicals to help create a hot, fast fire once you get your flame going with a fire starter (WetFire™ tinder is one example). You can make your own by soaking cotton balls in liquid petroleum jelly, and then store in your kit in a waterproof container. These will burn longer but might not catch a spark as well.

Clothing and Footwear

Clothing is not a huge component in a survival kit because it takes up so much space. For the most part, you can wear whatever you are already wearing for many days without much problem. However, there are still some things to consider about clothing. First and foremost, dress appropriately for the outdoors in the first place. Sturdy shoes or hiking boots should be worn even for a short walk in the woods. Getting stuck somewhere in light sandals can be a real problem.

Even if the weather is hot, be somewhat covered up to minimize sun exposure. Light breathable clothing that still covers is the best choice. Various brands of synthetic fabrics are ideal for the outdoors, such as GORE-TEX® and Polartec®, each with its own qualities. You want something that will draw moisture (sweat) away from your body and provide the best protection without being bulky.

First-Aid Supplies

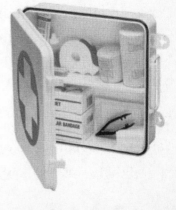

As mentioned, quite an array of potential first-aid supplies can go in a kit. *Chapter 9 covers the techniques of first aid, which you should be familiar with so you know how to properly use all the items in your kit when the time*

comes. Here are the basic items that can be kept in your kit along with a quick explanation on what they are for.

Band-Aids®

These are the self-adhesive strips that come in either plastic or fabric, and they are used for small cuts and abrasions. They come in various sizes, and some are uniquely shaped for fingertips or knuckles. Band-Aids are a crucial part of any kit. Pack a couple dozen, though they are not really a "life or death" type of item. Except for possible infection, small cuts are not going to be a disaster on their own.

Gauze Pads and Tape

These two items go together and are used to treat larger wounds or injuries when a sticky Band-Aid will not suffice. Pads of gauze are placed over the wound and held in place with a strip of adhesive tape. The tape is specifically for first-aid purposes and will peel off the skin without too much damage when the dressing has to come off. Average pads are around 3 by 3 inches, but you can get larger ones as well.

You can also get long strips of gauze in a roll that you can wrap around a limb instead of using adhesive tape.

Butterfly Sutures

These are also called butterfly stitches, and a popular brand is Steri-Strip™, though Band-Aid also makes them. They are used to close a cut rather than cover one. They are quite small and a common item in a first-aid kit.

Scalpel Blades

You can pack complete scalpels if you wish, but the blades alone will save space. They can be used fairly well held in your fingers.

Handles can also be packed separately so you only have to carry one to fit any of the blades. Minor surgery situations can occur, though you will want to have a good knowledge of first aid before you start cutting anyone.

Elastic Bandages

This is what you will use to help stabilize a twisted or wounded joint like a wrist or ankle. They are wrapped snuggly around the joint and fastened with a metal clip.

Antiseptic or Alcohol Wipes

To help reduce the chance of infection in a wound, you can purchase individual-packed wipes that are saturated in alcohol or any other antiseptic solution. They are just like the little "wet-naps" you sometimes find at fast food restaurants. Wiping a wound thoroughly before wrapping a dressing is a sound idea.

Latex Gloves

Although not a "must-have" in a kit, they also take up little space. If someone is injured, it can make treatment a lot easier if you can keep your hands clean while you bandage a wound. When water is in short supply, it can be hard to get blood off your hands.

Medications and Tablets

There are several of these that can be carried in a first-aid kit, as long as you have them well labeled and kept in a waterproof container. Water purification tablets are a must, and carrying a full bottle of them is the best idea. *Chapter 4 has more details on how to use these to create safe drinking water.* The other medications are all optional. Antihistamines are used to relieve allergy symptoms and are more for individual comfort than anything else. Of course, trying to survive a bad situation while you sneeze and have blurry eyes is not a good idea either. Pain relief medication can be whatever type works best for you, whether it is ibuprofen or aspirin. Anti-diarrhea medication (such as IMODIUM®) is vital if you are going to be in a situation when you might be drinking questionable water. Uncontrolled diarrhea can be fatal, so do not overlook this item.

GPS Units

We have not discussed these popular navigation tools so far because their cost makes them impractical to store in an emergency kit. But anyone who spends time outdoors should think about getting one.

The fundamental function of a GPS unit (GPS stands for global positioning system) is to contact satellites above the Earth and use that information to establish your location. They work in any location and are not dependent on any kind of broadcast service (like radio signals or cell phone reception). However, you can sometimes have trouble connecting to the satellites if you are indoors or under heavy tree cover.

Maps and a compass are still vital tools for navigation, but you cannot ignore the benefits of a piece of technology like a GPS when it comes to trying to find your way out of the wilderness.

You can choose from a number of models, though the general features are going to be the same across the board. Some will take standard AA batteries, and some will have their own internal lithium batteries. The lithium ones will last longer, but the AA ones will be easier to replace. These hand-held units are intended for outdoor use, so they will all be rugged and water-resistant to some degree.

The most important differences between models will be their mapping capabilities. Some will show your position as an X on the screen, along with an illustration of your recent movements as lines. This is a bare-bones type of model and will only be helpful for you to place your location in reference to where you have just been. That can often be good enough for you to figure out how to get back to your camp or the road if you are not too deeply lost. If you plan your trip ahead of time, you can program in the GSP coordinates of landmarks around your planned hiking or camping location. These are shown on the screen and add more helpful details to the display.

A better model would have actual maps programmed into the unit so you can see your position in relation to roads and landmarks. Depending on the memory capabilities of your unit, you can have street maps, topographical maps, marine charts, or satellite images at your fingertips. Some unit will have these pre-programmed when you buy the device, and with others you will have to upload the maps yourself afterward. Know which is which so you do not end up lost and assume that there are maps at the ready, only to find a blank screen instead.

Some extra bells and whistles that can be found on GPS units include: color monitors, touch screens, cameras, barometer, or wireless data transfer. Your own needs and budget will determine whether you include any of these features.

Garmin™ and Magellen are the two largest makers of GPS units, and they both carry a wide range of devices so you can make an informed selection with any combination of features.

Chapter 3

Starting and Maintaining a Fire

his is the first section that delves into the techniques and skills you will need when out in the wilderness. It only makes sense to begin with the most important aspect of survival: creating fire. A fire will provide light and heat, and it will also give you the means to cook food or boil water. You can also use a fire as a signal to show your location (light at night and smoke during the day)

Find a Safe Location

Knowing where to light your fire is nearly as important as knowing how to light one. Consider several things. You need to make sure you do not accidentally start a serious forest fire, nor do you want to set your own shelter ablaze. Starting a fire under tree boughs can seem like a good idea until wet leaves or snow fall through and smother your new fire. Plan your fire out properly from the start, and you will have better success. Depending on your gear, you might not have many chances to do this right.

Choose a dry and sheltered area that does not have any immediate brush hanging directly above. Beside large rocks or boulders is a good idea, as your fire will be safely sheltered and the stone will help absorb and spread the heat. Clear away as much ground brush as you can, and gather up some rocks to help contain your fire.

If you have the means, dig a shallow hole. This is a good safety precaution, and it also helps protect your growing fire from prevailing winds.

Starting Your Fire

Before you try starting a fire, gather up a large pile of tinder, kindling, and firewood so you are able to quickly capture that brief spark or flame. Start with fine light tinder, then progressively larger twigs until your fire is big enough to handle large sticks and branches. Once you have your fuel handy, you can start.

Methods for starting a fire

These methods have all been touched on briefly in the gear section, but that was to introduce the equipment. Now you will see more detail on the various methods and how to make the most out of them when it comes time to start that fire.

Matches and Lighters

This is the most common way of starting a fire, though using a lighter is easier than matches. Both matches and lighters are simple to use and do not require much instruction. They work easily when starting a fire because they create a flame for you to work with. Just light up your tinder and get started. The other methods usually start with a spark and can be much harder to manage until you have more experience. Have at least one open-flame tool (matches or lighter) as well as a sparking device in your kit.

Flint and Steel

As discussed in the gear chapter, a flint and steel is a reliable way to create fire that will last longer than your supply of matches. Unfortunately, it only creates hot sparks, which will mean a little more expertise to turn that into a roaring fire. It works by dragging a steel edge along a piece of flint, which creates a shower of sparks. Some types of starters have their own steel striker portion, but you can also use a knife blade. To save the edge on your knife, use the opposite side of the blade.

The sparks will fly off from the flint, down and away from the direction of motion of the steel edge. With some practice, you can aim these sparks at your ready pile of tinder for it to catch fire.

Magnesium Starter

This item is a step above the plain flint and steel, and you will create your sparks in the same way. The bar of magnesium has a flint edge to it and you will have to strike your metal blade against it to create sparks. But before you do so, use the sharp edge of the knife blade to scrape away a small pile of magnesium shavings. These shavings should be clustered together amidst your tinder and small kindling. Once a hot spark hits the magnesium shreds, they will light up into a hot flame and give your fire a boost.

If your fire is waning, add more shavings to keep the flames going.

Fire Piston

A fire piston can be a good choice in windy or wet conditions because it creates a red-hot ember from tinder right within itself. It operates on the concept that compressed air will get hotter as it is compressed. This principle can be enough to get a piece of tinder to light up just by pressing down on a small plunger.

You place a small bit of tinder inside the piston and fit the plunger in place. Give it a quick hard push to compress the air inside. When you open it back up, the tinder should be red-hot and ready to be used to light more tinder into an open flame. These little devices are handy given the right circumstances because they keep the tinder enclosed. But the rubber gasket within the cylinder that keeps the air out can wear or become damaged with use. A fire piston should not be your only or main source for fire-making.

Steel Wool and Battery

Not quite as primitive or traditional as some of these other methods but a fairly reliable one nonetheless, a battery used with steel wool can also be used to create a decent fire when nothing else is working. A 9-volt battery is the usual way of implementing this technique, though any type will do. A 9-volt has the negative and positive poles close to each other for easier handling. Pull a tuft of steel wool and place it over both poles of the battery. The charge will heat the metal; it will turn bright red and ideally burn.

The wool will heat up fast, so be quick about putting it to your tinder without getting your fingers burnt. You do not need to worry about getting a shock; there is not enough power for that. A battery will only have enough charge to use this method two to four times, so you might not want to have it as your only source of potential fire.

Benefits to this method are that it works well in stormy conditions and steel wool does not absorb moisture, so you do not have as much worry about keeping it dry in your kit.

Magnifying Lens

This should not be your main way of starting fire in an emergency, as it can be difficult and un-reliable. The idea is that you can focus the sun's rays through the lens to create a hot point of light on the ground. With enough power and the right tinder, you can get a fire going. Any type of magnifying glass lens will work for this, and you can buy small ones designed

specifically for this purpose. In a pinch, you might even be able to use your binocular lenses.

Hold your lens at a right angle to the sun and watch the spot of light that is created. Slowly move the lens to get the smallest and brightest spot you can produce. If the angle is wrong, you get a larger (and cooler) circle of light. Place your fine tinder in that spot, and it should not take long for it to start smoking. Ideally, it will catch and you can get your fire going.

You will only be able to get this to work in sunny weather, so you must have an alternative for night or even just a cloudy day.

Friction Methods

Everyone has seen the classic "rubbing two sticks together" method for getting a fire started in dire circumstances. This is a valid technique and can work, but it is by far the least reliable and not really worth considering if you already have a decent survival kit with you. The amount of time it would take to build a proper fire bow is extensive, and the skill to use it will require a great deal of practice. Certainly, it is an impressive ability to have, but a more practical idea would be to keep supplies with you that would do a better job in an emergency.

Tinder

Having a great spark or flame to start with is vital, but unless you have some material ready to take that and burn, you will never have a fire going. Tinder is the finest material that goes into starting a fire, and it can be the toughest to find in an emergency situation. Finding simple wood is one thing, but tinder is quite another. It needs to be easily flammable, light, fine or fluffy, and dry.

Materials for Tinder

You can pack pre-made tinder in your kit, either homemade versions or commercial products. For packed tinder, you can use dryer lint, cotton balls, or sawdust.

Tinder found in the wild could include cattail fluff, milkweed fluff, dry grass, fine shreds of birch bark or cedar wood, dry moss, or a specific type of mushroom called "tinder fungus" among outdoor enthusiasts. Tinder fungus grows on birch trees from an injured point in the bark and resembles a large black lump. It does not have the same type of form as a standard mushroom. When you cut it open, it should be reddish brown inside and made up of powdery fibers. This makes excellent tinder. It will take some luck finding it in the right moment, but you can always be on the lookout for tinder fungus when out hiking. Harvest some when you find it for your survival kit.

Dry leaves are not that great for tinder, but they can be used as light kindling once you have a flame going.

Char cloth is another popular tinder material for kits that you have to prepare beforehand. Many survivalists will swear by it as the best option. It is small pieces of fabric that have been partially burned and will catch fire easily when exposed to sparks.

To make char cloth, start with some natural fabric such as cotton or linen. Cut up several 1-inch square pieces and put them in a metal tin (a small cookie tin with a tight lid would work great) and punch a small hole or two in the lid. Get a fire going and set the can in the coals once they have burned down some. Gases from the charring fabric will force out the air in the tin, and you will see small flames come from the holes as the gas burns off. Then there will be smoke coming out. When the smoke starts to taper off, pull the tin from the coals.

Plug the hole and let the cloth finish charring. Air would probably set it alight given how hot it still is inside. After 15 to 20 minutes, open up the can, and there should be black pieces of charred cloth inside. Pack several pieces of this cloth in your survival kit, and it will work as excellent tinder that picks up a spark almost instantly.

If you do not carry tinder with you, you might not be able to find anything usable when you need it. When conditions are bad, you can even exhaust your supply of tinder material when you do carry it. It is a good idea to have a small candle with you to help keep a flame going longer. You cannot light a candle with any type of sparking device, but with a match or lighter, you can create a longer flame that will get small kindling going and help eliminate your need for good tinder. Tea lights are good, and you can even keep a flame going nicely with a birthday candle (if you are low on carrying space).

How to Use Tinder

Once you have your tinder material on hand, you need to know how to coax it into flame. This can take a little practice if you are using a sparking method for starting a fire. You should work at using your survival kit supplies to get a fire going before you have an emergency so you have the proper skills in place.

Bundle up your tinder into a bowl-shaped pile, and keep extra on hand to help feed the burgeoning flames. It is a terrible situation when you finally get a spark to take, only to watch it die because you did not gather enough fuel. If you are using a flame-method, you simply have to light up the pile. Otherwise, direct your sparks into the center of the pile (hence the bowl shape) and keep sparking until it catches an ember. Gently blow on the red-hot sparks until the tinder catches fire. At this point, add more tinder and get your first pieces of kindling ready.

Kindling

The next step of fuel after the tinder is your kindling. Having a good mix of small pieces as well as thicker ones means you should be able to coax the fire to fine size in a short period of time. Trying to rush a fire by adding overly large pieces of wood to hot tinder will usually end up with a smothered out flame and a lot of frustration.

The first level of kindling should be quite small, not much larger than your original tinder. Dry pine needles, toothpick-sized slivers of wood, and larger pieces of birch bark will all work well with a newly born fire.

After you add some of these, you want larger pieces of wood that are closer to pencil thickness. Pile them on without smothering your flames by keeping them staggered in a tee-pee type of formation. You have to leave plenty of air between the pieces so the flame can survive. Keep adding the pencil- to thumb-sized pieces until they are burning cheerfully, then move up to slighter larger pieces. Make sure all the kindling you use is as dry as possible. Soon you should have a sustainable fire going. At this point, you are no longer starting a fire but maintaining one.

Maintaining a Fire

Granted, getting a fire started in an emergency is one of the most important steps to surviving a disaster, and it will take some skills to do it right. But once it is going, you will have to also know how to keep it going. Tinder will be in relatively short supply, so you do not want to have to keep starting and re-starting a fire unnecessarily.

Getting and using firewood

Your firewood will need to be as dry as your kindling and tinder was, though if your fire is going strong, a little bit of moisture will not kill it. Try to gather your wood from dead trees that are still standing. Fallen trees will be wet due to the moisture they absorb from the ground.

Once you have graduated up from thicker kindling, most of your firewood will be around wrist thickness. That means branches for the most part. Larger pieces of wood will have to be split, but you will not have the means to do so in the wild unless you are carrying a hatchet. Dead wood should snap fairly easily if you can bend the branches down but having a flexible wire chain saw can also go a long way in making your wood collecting chores a little more efficient.

At any point when you leave your base camp area, scout out additional fuel to keep your supplies ample. Always carry a bit of wood back with you, no matter where you are headed at that time.

When you do have a stack of wood at your camp area, keep it off the ground on a layer of rocks and preferably under some cover if you can afford the extra supplies (such as one of your emergency tarps).

Once your fire has been going awhile and you have a good bed of red-hot coals, you do not have to worry as much about how you stack your wood onto the fire. Alternate your pieces so airflow will make sure any wood placed right in the coals will light up and burn.

Preparing the fire for the night

Leaving your precious fire overnight can be a nerve-wracking problem to anyone who is new to this type of survival activity.

Can you afford to have a dead fire in the morning and have to dig up more tinder again?

As long as you have a roaring fire going and you do not sleep for 14 hours, odds are good that you will have some red coals waiting for you in the morning that can be brought back to life with some light kindling. That is even if you do not do anything in particular to maintain the fire. To play it a little safer, make a few plans to keep it going.

Before you go to bed, add a few large pieces of wood to the fire. The longer it has fuel to work on, the hotter your fire will be in the morning. Also before going to sleep, stock up on extra firewood and kindling. If you do have a weak fire in the morning, the faster you can revive it, and the better success you will have.

If you happen to wake up in the night, take a few minutes to refuel the fire. Needing to relieve yourself will often wake you, but setting a watch alarm might be a good idea as well for a midnight addition of fuel if you are not experienced at bringing a fire back to life from coals.

Reviving Your Fire

In the morning, you will have to revive your campfire. Even if you do not need the fire right away, you must get it started again while you still have hot coals to work with. Otherwise, you will waste valuable time and tinder if you have to start from scratch again later.

When you get up, you are most likely going to find a pile of coals. Red hot ones are the best, but even a pile of white ash can hold a red gem or two, so do not despair right away.

You will want to treat your red coals a lot like your first sparks when you started your fire and add fairly small kindling to get a flame started. You should not need fine tinder at this point though. With enough good coals, you should even be able to use larger pieces of wood and just settle them into the coals.

Gently blowing on your coals and materials will help bring it back to a flame.

Cooking Over a Fire

A fire is primarily needed as a source of vital heat and light in a bad situation, but if you are out in the wilderness long enough, then it can also take on a cooking purpose as well. Unless you have a whole range of camping gear with you, you are not going to have the proper cooking pots with you to make this easy. So that means you will have to do some improvising.

For those not familiar with open-fire cooking, the first thing you need to know is that you do not cook over an open flame. The heat is down in the coals, and that is where you want to focus your attention.

One of the best ways to cook any food in the wilderness is to boil it. Of course, you will have to be carrying a heat-proof container with you in your gear for this to be a practical solution. This method will work with meat, fish, and any plant material you forage. Most pre-packed survival foods that require cooking can either be boiled or reconstituted with boiling water.

All you need to do is fill your cup or pot with water and then add in chunks of whatever you want to cook. If you will be cooking for at least five minutes at a boil, you will be sterilizing the water at the same time, so you can save your clean drinking water. You can suspend your pot over the fire if you have a few branches and wire, but you can also set it down right in the coals for a more stable approach.

If you do not have a pot or are trying to cook something that is too large for what you do have, you can give spit-roasting a try. This is the type of cooking you would use if you have a fish or game animal to prepare. Trim a green branch (one that is still living and moist inside) from a tree and sharpen one end with your knife. Green branches work better because they will not catch fire themselves quite as easily.

A single branch as a skewer will work, but larger items can end up spinning on the stick as you try to turn your food over in the fire. A better method is to use 2 sticks so your food item cannot rotate. Spear your food in two places, then angle both sticks together so you can hold them in one hand. When cooking something large (perhaps a rabbit), your arm will probably give out before it is cooked. Use another forked stick or a few rocks to prop up your spit but do not leave so far as to not be able to watch and frequently turn your food.

The precise art of cooking food this way is something that only practice can teach. Keep your food over hot coals and not right in a flame. That will just burn the outside and leave the inside raw. The coals will create a much more even and intense heat. If you have to pull some coals out of the fire to make a cooking area away from the main flame, it can work a little better.

Take care when handling hot food or pots. Even a small burn can be a problem when there is little medical care available.

More specific instructions for cooking different types of food over a fire can be found at the end of Chapter 5.

Portable Fire for Light

Having a good fire at your base camp is going to be your main priority. When moving around beyond your camp, you might need to bring some fire with you for light. A good flashlight will usually suit this purpose, as long as it is still functioning with good batteries. The minute you lose your flashlight, you lose all portable light. So that is when a torch can be used.

Any burning stick can give off light if you are not traveling a long away from your base camp. For something that lasts a little longer, wrap the end of your stick with some scraps of cloth or flexible bark.

When walking with a burning torch, be careful not to accidentally set the forest on fire as you go.

Chapter 4

Finding Water

ire will fill your immediate need for heat, which means getting water will be your next area of concern. You can last only a few days without drinking water and even less if you are exerting yourself hiking through the woods.

Locating a Natural Water Source

The easiest way to get water is to find a natural source, such as a stream or pond. Even water in marshes or swamps can be usable, so do not discount these sources (especially if they are your only options).

Topographical maps can be helpful because water features are marked on them. On the other hand, if you had a good topo map with you, then you probably would not have gotten lost in the first place. Nonetheless, it might be of some assistance even if you cannot exactly place yourself on the map. A large lake or river can give you a direction to head and can provide a decent chance of success because you are aiming for a large "target." Without a map, you will have to rely on what you can see around you.

Following animals

Animals can sense water far better than we can, not to mention they are more familiar with your immediate terrain. You can trust them to know where the nearest water source is, provided you know how to properly follow them to it.

However, you cannot take this literally. Animals are not going to quietly walk along to their favorite watering hole with you trailing behind them. This is where you have to do a little tracking.

Your first sign should be trails through the woods. The local terrain can make this easy or difficult, so it is not a guaranteed tactic. Watch your surroundings carefully, and look for any trampled grass or bent branches. Trails to water are going to be more frequently used by many animals, so they should be more visible than a trail used by a single animal just walking through the forest. Unfortunately, there is no way to tell which direction you need to go once you locate a trail. Choose a direction that most closely fits where you are heading and hope for the best.

Another way to take your cues from the animal population is to focus on the smaller creatures. Look for insects that normally stay around bodies of water, such as dragonflies. Even mosquitoes are more plentiful when water is around. Also watch (and listen for) frogs or moisture-loving lizards such as salamanders. Keep an eye on the sky for ducks, geese, gulls, or other water birds, too. All of these are subtle and are not a direct sign of where water is. But if you are hiking along and see lots of frogs, and then there are none, you can backtrack to see if you can locate the water source.

Using terrain

Water always follows basic laws of physics, which can help you in an emergency. Follow the landscape to the lowest points you can to find small pools or even puddles.

Plants can also direct you toward water. If you see willow trees in one direction, that should be where you head first. Also look for ferns and cattails, which grow close to a source of water.

Finding Other Water Sources

A water source such as a pond or stream is the most convenient way of getting water, but with a little effort, you might have to "find" water in other ways. Ironically, some of these other sources might be cleaner for drinking.

Capturing rain

Rain can be a big problem when stuck in the woods, but it does present a good opportunity to harvest some clean drinking water.

Try to create as large a catchment area as possible using plastic bags or tarps. Tie them between the branches of a tree forming a slanted area or a funnel that will lead all the collected water into a clean container. You can use empty water bottles or even plastic bags if that is all you have. Water is a vital resource outdoors, so gather it as strenuously as you can.

Set up your capturing area in an open spot so you are getting as little debris in with your water as possible. If no tree branches will allow for this, you will have to use sticks and rope to fashion a collector.

Capturing dew

Dew will form on every open surface during the night when there is a quick drop in temperature and warm, moist air to begin with. Not all nights will produce a decent crop of dew. It is usually something you will be able to use mainly in the spring and fall. You can usually only gather a small amount of water this way, so ideally it will not be your sole source for water. Nonetheless, it is an approach that can be tried.

An area with long grass is the best place to get a dew harvest. You can soak up the tiny drops with fine fabric and then wring it out into a container.

Collecting condensation

During the spring and summer, you can also collect some small amounts of water from plants. Plants breathe out water vapor much like animals do, particularly at night. Cover the end of a healthy leafy branch with a plastic bag (something that will not let air seep out), and tie it tightly to the branch overnight. In the morning, condensation should be on the bag's inner surface. You might only gather a tablespoon or so this way, but with a few bags set out each night, you can end up with a decent drink of water.

Digging for water

There are two approaches to digging for water. One is when you dig in a spot where there is likely to be water close underground. Low-lying areas with ferns and lots of moss can indicate a shallow water table. In that case, dig until water starts to seep into the bottom of your hole. Unfortunately, this can expend a lot of your energy with not a huge chance of success. Only use this approach if you are certain of water.

You can also dig a hole with the intention of harvesting condensation from the moist soil below. This technique is often called building a solar still, though it is simpler than the name implies. The first step is to dig a hole, at least 3 feet across and 1 ½ feet deep. Ideally, the soil will be moist by the time you dig this far down.

Now set a can or other container in the middle of the hole (something with a wide mouth like a cup will work best for this). Cover the entire hole with plastic or a light tarp, and place rocks around the edge to keep it still. Now, gently place a small rock in the center so that the cover is pushed down. You are basically making an upside-down cone over the hole.

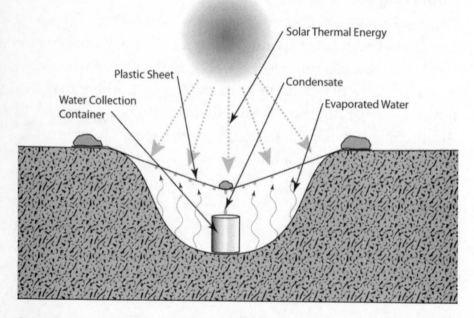

Set this up early in the morning, and water will evaporate out of the soil as the day warms up. It will condense on the plastic because the vapor has no place else to go, and then slowly start to run down to the point of your cone. From there it will drip off the plastic into the container you placed in the hole. If there is enough moisture in the earth, you can collect a cup or two each day with this method.

Tapping plants

When trapped in a desert environment, you can have some success getting water from the local plant life because these plants have evolved to hoard water. Even cacti and succulents that are not edible on their own can be good sources of water when used in conjunction with a solar still because they have a great deal of moisture within their fleshy parts. Put cut pieces of plant inside your hole to add to the moisture caught overnight.

Large baobab trees have trunks filled with water that can be tapped, though the larger trees do have thick bark to contend with. Many cacti have juicy fruit, which can provide you with a lot of water along with being a food source. The prickly pear is one good example. *You can find more on foraging for desert foods in Chapter 5.*

In temperate regions, plants generally do not have the same types of large water storage as desert plants do.

Water Safety and Purification

Rain and dew are going to be your cleanest sources of water, and any water collected from a vapor source (condensation or the solar still) will also be clean and can be consumed without a problem.

However, any water from a ground source can be contaminated no matter how clean and clear it might look. Even when you are miles from civilization, the water can be impure. An animal might have died nearby or defecated near where you are collecting your water. Always treat water as potentially dangerous.

If you are lucky enough to have your choice of more than one water source, go for moving water over still water. A stream is more likely to be cleaner than a marsh for example.

Even out in the wilderness, you have a few options for purifying your water.

Simple straining or filtering

This alone will not remove any bacteria, parasites, or toxins from your water, but by taking out any larger dirt particles, the other methods will be more effective. If you are trying to purify cloudy water, this should always be your first step. Water can be poured from one container to another through clean fine-woven fabric, or a paper coffee filter (if you have one in your kit for this purpose).

Purification chemicals

A well-stocked survival kit will have a bottle of tablets for this purpose. These commercial tablets are usually made with some form of iodine and will kill most (not all) possible pathogens in an unclean water source. Not all brands will work the same way, so read the instructions before you use the products. You have to add a tablet to a certain volume of water and then wait a period of time (30 minutes or so) to let the chemicals work.

You also have to know the right amount of water you are treating, so it is a good idea to have a container in your survival kit with a known volume. Even if it is not marked on the cup, knowing your cooking cup holds 14 oz. of water will make using these tablets safer. Brands will vary. Most tablets will each purify from 1 to 2 quarts of water.

Boiling

If you are without any chemical tablets, you can resort to the time-old tradition of boiling your water. You will have to have a heat-proof container for this, but that is the only piece of gear you will need. A lid of some kind would help keep the heat in and allow less water to be lost as steam. Either hang your container over the fire by a wire, or set the container among the coals.

Let it boil hard for at least five minutes. Most pathogens will be killed by that point, and boiling it for long periods of time will result in lost water due to escaping steam. Once it has finished its boiling time, let it cool down, and you can consider it drinkable.

Boiling does not make all problems disappear though. Any toxins or chemicals in the water will still be there. This method only kills bacteria and other living contaminants.

Solar still

This is the same technique mentioned in the last section for acquiring water, and the explanation on how to build it can be found there. To use such a contraption to purify water just means you have to put an open-topped container with impure water in the hole along with the clean collection vessel. Only the collection container should be placed under the drip-point. You can put the dirty water container anywhere else in the hole.

Few contaminants are able to evaporate along with the water, so your dirty water will slowly lose vapor within the sill and leave the dirt and bacteria behind. It will condense on the plastic and run down into the collection bottle as drinkable water.

You can also use this process if you are trying to purify salt water into drinking water.

Portable water filter

This is not really a standard survival tool, especially because the tablets work well and will fit in most people's budgets. But if you have the money to spend or find that you are at risk for getting lost more often because you spend a lot of time in the outdoors, think about investing in a good-quality water filter.

Cheap water bottles with filters in them will not suffice in a real survival situation. They are intended to filter out some sediment and perhaps the chlorine in tap water. You need a more serious filter in order to make unknown ground water drinkable. Katadyn® and MSR® are two well-respected brands that make small filters for backpacking use.

Most small filters like this operate with a hand-pump mechanism that draws dirty water in through the fine micro-filter, and then the clean water is collected as is pumps out of the hose. Each model is different, so always read the instructions before you pack it away in your kit. Most filters will last for thousands of gallons, so keeping extra filters handy is not necessary. Do your research before choosing a specific model. With Katadyn, for example, their Hiker Pro unit only has limited purification ability, whereas their Pocket Filter is much better at truly cleaning water to a significant degree.

Drinking contaminated water can lead to various illnesses, the most serious in a survival situation being vomiting and diarrhea. Longer-term parasite infections can be treated after you are rescued, but other symptoms can be fatal. You cannot ignore any water purification tasks when in the wilderness. Even so, if you are unable to use any of these methods, you are going to have to take that risk because drinking no water at all is going to be fatal.

Survival Water Requirements

The following section should be considered only a guideline on how much water is necessary in survival situations. Everyone has their own unique physiology, and the altitude, temperature, and terrain will make every survival situation different from the next. Fundamentally, higher temperatures and more exertion will mean your body needs more water (at least for drinking).

Even so, knowing just how much water you are going to require can help guide your efforts in rationing what you have and knowing when you must search for more water supplies.

Aside from drinking, do not forget that having water for hygiene and cooking purposes is also important.

Drinking water

A rough baseline for your daily water requirements is between 3 and 5 quarts per day. Basically, you need a gallon of water for drinking only. When water is in short supply (or no supply at all), this volume can seem daunting. Even so, do not skimp on your

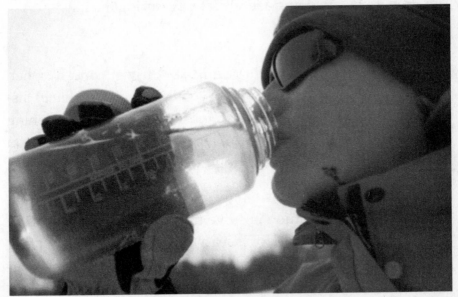

water consumption if you can avoid it. The physical toll it will take on your body is significant and goes well beyond just "feeling thirsty." You can start to suffer from nausea, depression, lack of attention, fatigue, and poor judgment. All of these can turn your survival situation from bad to worse.

To keep yourself in top condition, force yourself to drink even you are not feeling immediately thirsty. Your body only triggers a thirst sensation when it is already starting to dehydrate.

One additional factor in how much water you will need is what your diet is. Getting by on dense protein bars, jerky, or packs of salted peanuts is going to increase your water needs, compared to a situation where you have plenty of wild fruit or even leaves to eat.

Going without water for even 24 hours will start to diminish your physical state, and you will be in serious trouble after about three days. There have been accounts of people surviving for a week without water, but that usually involves little movement (such as being trapped in earthquake rubble). Do not expect that kind of duration if you are doing a lot of activity during the day.

Water for hygiene

Though keeping clean might seem like a trivial concern when you are fighting for survival in the woods, do not completely disregard the need for hygiene. If you must choose between cleaning yourself and drinking, then drinking must come first. But if you have a decent source of water, you can accommodate both needs.

Staying somewhat clean is a huge morale booster and can really help keep your attitude positive until you are rescued. Aside from that, you run the risk of disease if you are frequently eating and drinking without being able to wash your hands, particularly after going to the "washroom."

One way to lower your water needs in this area is to have a bottle of alcohol-based hand sanitizer with you. That will kill off most of the bacteria on your hands, though it will not do much for any accumulated dirt.

Do not assume that impure water is fine for washing just because you are not consuming it. That can be the case if you are rinsing off your feet or armpits, but your hands need to stay as germ-free as possible. When washing off some parts of your body with potentially contaminated water, still re-wash your hands with cleanser or water you know is clean.

Water for cooking

This one will depend on what you are going to be eating and how you plan to cook it. Roasting a bit of meat over your fire will not take any water, but boiling dandelion greens will. The same goes for any dehydrated survival food you might have in your pack. Exact volumes for cooking cannot really be estimated, so you are on your own for this one. The point is to keep cooking in mind when managing your water supply.

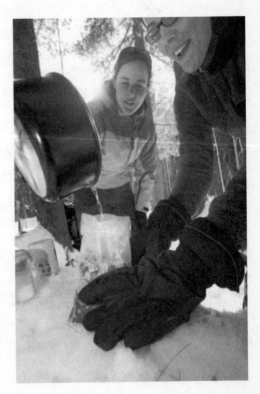

As mentioned earlier, water that is boiled for five minutes will be pure enough for drinking. So if you are going to be boiling food for cooking, you do not have to use clean drinking water to do it. The boiling period while you cook will be enough to sterilize the water.

CASE STUDY:
LIKE FATHER, LIKE SON

John and Joe Smith
Ashland, KY

John and Joe are a father and son team that enjoy the outdoors and consider themselves well versed in many good survival skills. They both go shooting and enjoy going out on the boat for sea fishing.

Between them, they can set snares and traps, shoot, skin and dress any small game animals, and build rough shelters. John is very handy when repairing small engines, and Joe is looking to pick up that skill as he gets older. They both use and practice their skills whenever they are on a trip outdoors.

Whenever they go out, they carry a basic kit with them. It currently includes a flashlight, set of bandages, headache tablets, reusable handwarmers, a knife, a wire saw, and a flint with tinder.

The only survival situation that John has come into was a day when his boat engine failed out at sea. He kept the boat in position with the spare paddles he keeps on board. When the tide shifted to the right direction, he paddled back to shore. The weather was not very good that day, so he used an old sailcloth for some quick temporary protection.

The one tool that John would want with him in an emergency would be his knife, but Joe said he would rather have a good multi-tool on hand. Each also had their own pieces of wisdom to share. John says that if you have to ask how to do something, then you probably shouldn't be doing it until you have some training. Joe wanted to remind people to always carry a good kit of supplies with you wherever you go.

Chapter 5

Finding Food

Finding water is more of a priority than finding food, as you can easily go for several days without any food and you should have some basics supplies in your kit to start with. But if you are stuck for longer than your supplies last, you will have to look to your surroundings to provide additional nutrition.

Packing Survival Food

A good kit will have some food supplies in it, which will provide quick sustenance at the beginning of any disaster situation. Ideas and suggestions for this have already been covered in the various gear sections, so you should have a good idea of what can be packed.

For any short-term emergency or for your food requirements when you first realize that there is a problem, have some supplies that can be eaten immediately and without any cooking. Packages of peanuts, meat jerky, trail mix, dried fruit, chocolate, protein or granola bars, and packages of snack crackers are good choices for this.

A kit can be filled out with only these types of food, which will make your cooking chores simple, though these foods are not the

most nutritious on their own over a long period of time. Add in some foraged greens, and you will do better.

If you want to be prepared for a longer stay in the wilderness, packing dehydrated camping food is your next option. Meals that can be reconstituted with the addition of boiling water are common for campers and are easy enough to find at most outdoor stores to add more substantial food supplies to your

kit. There are many brands available, and you can choose from different styles of soup, pasta, rice, beans, and more. This is a more nutritious option, but it will require a source of water and heat in order to be used.

Even the light dehydrated food will take up space in your pack, so these supplies are going to be limited. Unless you are back home in a few days, you will probably need to forage in the woods for additional supplies.

Foraging for Plants

Though there are always going to be plants to shy away from, you can also find many edible options out in the wilderness. Some environments are going to offer more food plants than others, so it will depend on where you are. A thick forest will have many more choices than a barren mountainside or harsh desert. Knowing your local plant species can mean you are able to locate something edible no matter where you are.

Berries and leaves are the most common edible parts of wild plants, but do not forget the roots as well. Mushrooms can be eaten, though the number of poisonous ones can make this a riskier proposition if you are not well versed in identifying them. This book has a good selection of edible plant references, but a complete book on edible plants would provide a more detailed and thorough collection.

The main section below is divided by the parts of the plant you can use for food, and it includes the most commonly found edible plants in North America. But there are some less common ones in more unique regions, and they are mentioned separately in this section.

Berries and fruit

Berries can be the easiest to find and identify because they are colorful and will stand out in a forest of green. One of the best benefits of fruit is that you can eat them raw without any preparation, and they provide a lot of water to your diet. Take care that you do not overdo eating wild fruit, as it can induce diarrhea due to the high water content.

Though they are the easiest to eat, fruit has the most limited time span. In other words, fruit is only available during a short portion of the year unlike roots or leaves that are present for a much longer time.

Just because they are a fruit does not automatically make them edible. Many are distasteful or poisonous. Here is a breakdown of many edible berries found in various climates.

Raspberry or Blackberries

These are easy enough to identify because they are such a familiar fruit to begin with. They look like commercially grown berries. Both fruits grow on long prickly branches that tend to bend back down toward the ground in an arch. They are not vines, but the branches are flexible and the older ones are slightly  woody. Blackberries that are not quite ripe are bright red and are often mistaken for ripe raspberries. They will be hard to the touch if that is the case. Either type of berry will be soft and come off the plant easily when they are ripe. Avoid unripe berries as they can cause intestinal problems if you eat too many of them.

Habitat: Found in both wooded and open areas
Range: All through North America as well as in Europe and northern parts of Asia
Preparation: Eaten raw right off the plant
Season: Late spring to late summer

Blueberries

Blueberries are another common type of berry, though they can be mistaken for other similar wild berries. The berries are blue or purple when ripe, but the insides are still green. Unripe blueberries are pale green on the outside as well. Ripe ones will also have a white waxy-looking film on the outside.

Because there are several different species of blueberry, you will find that blueberry plants are not all identical. They grow on leafy shrubs; some that are low to the ground (lowbush blueberries) and some that are waist-high (highbush). The leaves will be small, smooth-edged,  and oval in shape in either case. The berries themselves are found in small clusters along the branches.

Habitat: Forested and wooded areas
Range: Through most of United States and Canada, and other temperate regions around the world including Europe, Asia, and South America.
Preparation: You can eat them raw from the plant.
Season: Summer

Wild Grape

Compared to commercially grown grapes, the wild fruit is quite a bit smaller and might not immediately be recognizable as grapes.

The plants are easily identified by their creeping vines that grow along other tree trunks or branches up off the ground. The leaves are quite large, with heavily serrated edges that look similar to a maple leaf. Just like cultivated grapes, the fruit will grow in hang-ing clusters from the newer tendrils of the plant. Grapes can be confused with Virginia Creeper, which is not edible. If the small stems holding the grapes are red, then it is a Creeper rather than a grape vine.

Clarence A. Rechenthin
@ USDA-NRCS PLANTS Database

Each fruit will have a sizable seed inside, and it can be quite sour. These might look quite a bit like blueberries, with the ripe ones being blue and the unripe ones being pale green. Though grapes are most useful as a fruit, you can eat the young leaves as well.

Habitat: Usually forested areas but also some open fields
Range: Across United States and Canada, as well as Europe and northern Africa
Preparation: The fruit can be eaten raw, but cook the leaves for about five to ten minutes before eating.
Season: Leaves can be picked from spring until autumn, and the fruit is usually ripe in the fall.

Pin Cherry

These berries are also known as bird cherries in some areas, and they look much like commercial cherries. Each bright red fruit is on a long stem, and they grow in clusters at the ends of the branches. Pin cherry trees are fairly small and can even be more like large shrubs. The bark of the tree is smooth with some horizontal splits to it, and the leaves are oval and have only a faint bit of serration to the edges. The fruit is usually sour and there will be one large seed inside each one.

Habitat: Pin cherries grow in open fields and sunny areas.

Range: Found in most of southern Canada and northern United States. Closely related bird cherries are found in Europe

Preparation: You can eat the fruit right from the tree.

Season: Midsummer to early autumn

Chokecherry

Chokecherries are a close relative to the pin cherry, though the berries are different. These small black berries hang in clusters, and the leaves are more pointed than the pin cherry. The trees are quite similar otherwise. Buckthorn trees do resemble chokecherries, but those plants have noticeable thorns on their smaller branches where the chokecherries are smooth. Ripe chokecherries are deep purple or black, and the unripe berries are red.

Sheri Hagwood @ USDA-NRCS PLANTS Database

Habitat: Open areas, usually near bodies of water
Range: Most of North America and farther north in Canada than
most others Preparation: Fruit is eaten raw
Season: Berries are ripe in the late summer.

Apples

Few people will have
trouble identifying ap-
ples in the wild, and
finding a tree can pro-
vide quite a bit of for-
aged fruit if you are
in the wild during the
right time of year. The
problem will be dis-
tinguishing between
true wild apples and
crab apples. Granted,
you can eat either one
in a survival situation,
but crab apples will be
sour and quite unpleasant compared to the wild apples that
would taste much like regular store-bought apples. Some crab
apples are small, about the size of a marble, and can be eaten
though they are unappealing. These are found with ornamen-
tal or flowering crab apples, which are not a common tree in
most wilderness areas.

Habitat: They grow in open as well as more heavily forested areas.
Range: Throughout North America and in temperate areas
around the world
Preparation: Usually eaten raw from the tree
Season: Late summer through most of the autumn

Nannyberries

These are probably a little less well known than the other berries, though they can be common in some areas. The berries are similar to chokecherries but are usually more oblong and tend to look a little wrinkled. The stems for each berry cluster are bright red and the ripe berries are black. The unripe berries are hard and green. Each berry has an odd shaped flat seed inside. The trees are fairly small and more like large shrubs, with finely serrated leaves.

Habitat: These berries grow in wet or swampy areas.
Range: Northeast United States and eastern Canada
Preparation: Like the other fruits, just eat them raw.
Season: Late summer to early fall

Persimmon

The fruit of the persimmon tree look a lot like small tomatoes, though they can be found in shades of yellow and orange as well as red. The leaves on the tree are oval and pointed, with a smooth edge. You can also tell a persimmon tree by the deep blocky cracks in the bark.

The unripe fruit is astringent (will make your mouth feel puckered and dry) and inedible. You have to wait for it to ripen, and that means it will be soft. If you are not familiar with persimmons, it will seem like they are overripe. For the fruit to be sweet and edible, the flesh will be a jelly-like texture. You will likely find the best choices on the ground after they have fallen from the tree.

Habitat: Sunny open fields

Range: Southeastern United States, and some varieties can be found in Mexico and Southeast Asia.

Preparation: Eat the fruit raw as long as it is soft and ripe.

Season: Most trees will have fruit in late fall.

Leaves

After berries, the next easiest parts of the plant to harvest for food are the leaves. They are above ground for easy harvest though they are seldom edible when raw. Most of these will require at least a short period of cooking (boiling in water) before you can eat them.

Some of these plants are only edible at certain times (the younger leaves can be eaten but the older ones cannot), so be careful when harvesting.

Fiddleheads

"Fiddlehead" is a generic term that applies to newly sprouted fronds of many species of ferns. Ostrich ferns are the most common and the one most frequently eaten as a fiddlehead. They come up as a thick green stalk with a tightly wound curl at the top, and they are found in marshy wet areas.

You can break them or cut them off at soil level, and remove any light brown covering that might still be on the stalk. That is how you know it is an ostrich fern. If it has a white fuzzy covering, do not eat it. Once the coiled part has started to open, they are past the point of being edible.

Habitat: Shady wet areas often near standing water
Range: Across the northeastern United States, most of Canada
and other temperate parts of Europe and Asia
Preparation: They must be cooked in boiling water for 15 minutes
until they start to soften. Changing the water half way through
(if you have enough water to allow for it) will reduce the bitter-
ness further. Only eat the coiled portion of the stalk.
Season: Early spring

Dandelion

This is one plant that
should need no intro-
duction, though you
might be surprised to
hear that it is edible. The
fine-petaled blossoms
are almost feathery, and
their leaves are long
and deeply toothed.
The most edible parts
of the dandelion are the
leaves, though only the small young ones are palatable. You can
eat the root, but it is bitter and usually roasted as a coffee substi-
tute. In a survival situation, the leaves are a better option.

Many people feel that the leaves are too old once the flowers
bloom, but as long as you choose the smaller new leaves, they
should still be fine to eat. You can also eat the still-closed flower
buds before the yellow petals are visible. Cook them in the same
way as the leaves.

Habitat: Open sunny areas
Range: Across North America and most of the world except for
extreme desert regions

Preparation: Young leaves can be eaten raw, but the larger ones should be cooked in boiling water.

Season: Spring into late autumn

Milkweed

Paul C. Lemon @ USDA-NRCS PLANTS Database

Best known for its large fluffy seed bundles, the milkweed has many edible parts, which means you can forage them at many times of the year for something to eat. The plants have large wide leaves all coming from a single stalk. If you break open the stalk, you will find a thick milky fluid.

Milkweed plants are similar to dogbane, so you need to be able to distinguish them. There are fine hairs on the milkweed stalk where the dogbane is smooth. Also, milkweed plants have their largest leaves at the bottom while dogbane leaves are smallest at the bottom.

You can eat the new shoots (smaller than 6 inches) as well as the tight flower clusters before they blossom. For a more substantial "meal," you can eat the large bumpy seed pods while they are still hard to the touch. Once the seeds inside develop their fluff, they cannot be eaten. They will be green and about 1 to 2 inches long.

These plants are the main food for the distinctive Monarch butterfly, so if you see many butterflies in the area, it is a safe guess that there are mature milkweed plants nearby.

Habitat: Usually found in fields or open sunny areas

Range: Eastern North America, the UK, and parts of northern Europe

Preparation: Any of the parts need to be cooked, typically boiled in water for five to ten minutes.

Season: New shoots in the spring, flower clusters in the summer, and the seed pods usually come out in the fall.

Nettle

Various species of nettle are edible, and that does include the notorious stinging nettle. Oddly enough, sometimes the best way to identify stinging nettle is to see if it stings you when you touch it. Other types of nettle will not have this effect. All nettles are covered in fine hairs even if they do not sting.

If you are collecting nettle, use gloves or wrap your hands in fabric to protect them. A few stings will not cause much damage to your hands, but in an emergency situation, you want to stay as injury-free as possible. The hairs have a chemical in them that causes the sting.

Aside from that, the leaves are heart-shaped and evenly toothed around the edges. The leaves grow in pairs, opposite each other across the stem. You will want to pick any small young leaves and stalks for eating, and they *must* be cooked first.

Habitat: Shady areas with moist soil

Range: Anywhere in the United States and southern Canada. Some species of nettle can be found in temperate parts of Africa, Asia, UK, and Europe

Preparation: The plant parts must be boiled before you eat them to neutralize the stinging chemicals. It is less necessary with non-stinging nettles, though they do need some cooking to make them more edible. Cook in boiling water for at least five minutes. *Season:* Mainly spring but young leaves can be harvested any time before the plant flowers in the summer

Marsh Marigold

Foraging for marsh marigold can be risky, but because it comes out in early spring, it is one of the only plants you can find when looking for food at that time. It is poisonous unless fully cooked, so if you can manage with another food source, you might want to leave this one until you are desperate. If you are short on fire fuel, pass on this plant.

Robert H. Mohlenbrock @ USDA-NRCS PLANTS Database / USDA NRCS. 1992. Western wetland flora: Field office guide to plant species. *West Region, Sacramento.*

These plants have open yellow flowers similar to a buttercup but with a much leafier body to the plant. The leaves are round and dark green, and the plant is fairly short. They grow in wet areas and can be a good indicator of underground water if you are looking for that as well as food. Edible parts are the leaves and roots, but the leaves are the better choice simply for ease of harvest.

Habitat: Wet marshy areas
Range: Anywhere in Canada, the northeast United States, and along the U.S. Pacific coast. They are also found in the UK and Europe.

Preparation: Young leaves and unopened flower buds must be boiled for at least 30 minutes before they can be eaten.
Season: Spring for the best young plants

Plantain

In this case, plantain is a low-growing green plant rather than the banana-like fruit from the tropics. You can become accustomed to identifying this plant in your own backyard, as it is a common lawn "weed." The leaves are smooth-edged and vaguely triangular in shape with clear veins. They tend to look a little wrinkled. Some varieties have longer thinner leaves but the same overall rosette plant shape.

Young leaves are edible when cooked, but do not overdo the use of plantain because the leaves can have a laxative effect, which can be a serious problem to have in the wild.

Habitat: Open sunny areas
Range: Extensively through North America, the UK, Europe and northern Asia
Preparation: Steam or boil the leaves for a few minutes until soft
Season: Spring until mid-autumn

Lamb's Quarters

This is another plant you might know from the weeds in your own garden. It is a higher growing plant than plantain, and it can be a foot or so high. Some people know it as pigweed.

Like most other foraged leaves, you want to collect the smallest and youngest ones for eating. These are at the top of each plant. The leaves have a diamond shape with wavy edges, and the young ones usually have a white dusty look to them. If you are foraging later in the fall, you might find Lamb's Quarters that have flowered and gone to seed. The seeds can also be eaten.

Habitat: Fields and open areas with sun
Range: Across North America, Europe, Australia, and the temperate regions of Africa and Asia
Preparation: Cook for about five minutes until the leaves are soft. Small leaves and stalks can even be eaten raw.
Season: From spring until late fall

Robert H. Mohlenbrock @ USDA-NRCS PLANTS Database / USDA SCS. 1989. Midwest wetland flora: Field office illustrated guide to plant species. Midwest National Technical Center, Lincoln.

Clover

There are many types and species of clover, and they are all edible. White clover is low growing with small triplets of round leaves, and the taller red clover has more oval-shaped leaves. The plant grows to a foot or more in height. Both have the same type of spherical flowers of clustered petals that are unique to the clover.

You can eat the flowers as well as the leaves with clover, and the younger parts can be eaten raw. The blossoms are sweet and might be the most palatable of wild foods (aside from fruit of course).

Habitat: Open fields and some lightly forested areas
Range: Most of North America, the UK, and Europe and temperate regions in Africa
Preparation: Young leaves and flowers are eaten raw, but older leaves might need to be boiled briefly.
Season: Leaves from spring until autumn, flowers during the summer

Cattail

You can eat the young stalks as well as the roots, so this plant has been included in the roots section below as well. The plant is recognizable, with its brown cigar-shaped pod at the top. Before that forms, you can still identify cattails by the long, tough, grasslike leaves in swampy areas. Like milkweed, this is a plant that can provide something edible at many points of the year, depending on which parts you can harvest.

To harvest the stalks, gently pull the plant up by the base. It should come away from the buried root fairly easily. The white bottom portion is the edible area. You might want to peel away the outer leaves if they are tough right to the bottom. This part of the cattail can only be eaten before the flowers (cigar pods) develop. They will be about 2 to 3 feet high at the best point.

If the flower pods have started to form, you can collect those instead as long as they are still hard and green. You have to boil them, but they are edible. When just forming, there will be two of them (attached end to end). One is male and one is female, but they are both fine for eating.

Though not really a leafy part of the plant, the pollen of the cattail flower is also edible. The male part of the pod will produce a great deal of dusty pollen in the spring, which is high in protein and nutritious. It might not be a practical food item, but it can add some calories to your diet if you are struggling to find food to eat. Just shake the pod onto a piece of fabric to collect it. Eat as-is or add to anything else you are cooking.

While you are collecting stalks and flowers, you might want to collect some of the leaves as well. They are excellent for weaving together to create simple mats or even baskets. *There is more on this in Chapter 10.*

Habitat: Swampy areas, often with standing water but not always
Range: Across North America and most other northern hemisphere countries
Preparation: You can eat the stalks raw, but the flowers need to be boiled for about ten minutes.
Season: Stalks can be harvested in the early summer, green flower pods are found a little later in the summer.

Pine Needles

These are not truly edible as the other plants listed but they deserve to be mentioned because they are still useful. The needles can be boiled in water to make a vitamin-rich tea (mostly vitamin C and A). When food is scarce, every bit of nutrition helps even if it does not really fill your stomach.

Collect a few handfuls of white pine needles and remove any brown papery bits that stick the base of the needles. You can tell white pine by the clusters of five needles (groups of two mean it is a red pine). Red pine can be used but it does not taste as pleasant. Break up the needles and simmer them in water for five minutes. Strain the water from the needles (a piece of cloth can work for this) and drink the remaining tea once it has cooled. Do not try to eat the needles; they are far too tough for proper digestion.

Habitat: Any forested area, usually an older forest

Range: Throughout North America and most other countries in the northern hemisphere

Preparation: Simmer in water for about five minutes, strain out the needles to drink

Season: Needles can be collected for tea any time of the year

Roots

Leaves are the easiest to find and harvest, but they are not the most substantial food source unless you have a large volume. Roots are more "meaty" and can be a good addition to a survival foraging diet if you have the means to do some digging. Because you will need to wash these after you dig them up, you must have a good supply of clean water available. If you are short on water, you might want to stick to leafier food. This also applies if you are short on fuel for a fire. You will have to cook roots much longer than most leaves before they are edible.

Cattail

As mentioned above, the cattail can be used for several edible parts. Read the above section for more on the stalks and flowers and continue reading for details on the roots.

You can identify cattails by their unique flower pods or spikes or their long tapered leaves. Roots can be collected and eaten any time, but they are most useful in the early spring or winter when the other parts of the plant are not available.

When looking for cattails in the winter, look for the dead remnants of the previous summer's puffed flower pods. They are the easiest to spot when there is snow. If the ground is frozen, you are not going to be able to dig though. They are usually a few inches under the mud and can be several feet in length.

Dig and pull up a cattail plant, and wash off the thick root. Peel off the tough outer covering, which is distinctive from the inner portion. The inner core is starchy but also fibrous. Slice it up and boil until soft. It makes a filling addition to a meal, though you do have to pick the fibers out of your teeth as you eat the starchy filler.

Be warned that cattail roots have gluten in them, so anyone who has Celiac disease or a gluten-intolerance should avoid eating this. The resulting intestinal upset will be more harmful to your body than missing food.

Habitat: Wetland areas
Range: Wetlands in most northern hemisphere regions
Preparation: Cook roots until they are soft.
Season: Any time, including winter

Wild Parsnip

Wild parsnip is much like nettle in that it can be hazardous to touch, yet does provide some edible food. The danger with wild parsnip is the sap inside the stalks. It will react with the sunlight when you break open the plant and it will cause chemical burns and blistering on your skin. Only work with wild parsnip if you have a way to protect your hands and arms while you do so, and if you have found no other food sources to be more easily available.

The mature plants are several feet high, with a fine umbrella formation of small yellow flowers that look a lot like dill. The stalk of wild parsnip is heavily ridged, like a stalk of celery. This is not the version of the plant you want to dig up when looking for roots. These plants are biennial, which means they have a two-year life cycle. The tall impressive plants that you can easily recognize will not have the large taproot you can eat because they have used up the root from the year before. In alternate years, the plant is a much smaller rosette that stays close to the ground. When you find a stand of large plants, look down and you will almost always find rosettes among the others.

As mentioned, be careful around the taller plants and dig up the root of the smaller versions. Scrub the dirt of the root and cook in boiling water like you would a carrot or domesticated parsnip.

Habitat: Open fields and lightly forested areas
Range: Anywhere in Canada and the United States, except for the farther southeast states. It also grows through most of Europe and the UK.
Preparation: Cook root in boiling water

Season: Fall will produce the largest roots but only from the first-year rosette plants. The tall second-year plants will not have a taproot at all.

Burdock

We usually only notice burdock when their spiky little seed pods cling to our clothes, but watch for it when foraging for survival food. Once the burrs are dried, you will easily be able to identify the plant. Until then, look for thick ribbed stems and large leaves. It looks much like rhubarb.

The roots are the most usable portion, though the young leaves and shoots are also edible. Those can be eaten raw as well as cooked. The root can also be eaten either raw or cooked. It is one of the few roots that does not need cooking, which can be helpful when you do not want to keep a fire going or have no pots.

Habitat: Open and sunny areas
Range: It is common across North America, Europe, and Asia.
Preparation: You can eat the edible parts either raw or cooked.
Season: The young shoots are only avail-able in the spring, but you can dig roots any time.

Wild Leek (Ramps)

Wild leeks are more commonly known in some regions as ramps, so you may have heard of them in one way or another. It is also sometimes known as wild garlic. Their strong onion flavor may not be palatable to eat by the handful on their own, but you can add some of these to any of the other cooked leaves or roots to greatly improve the other foods' flavor. Unfortunately, they are not as widespread as other edible plants.

One of the key features to identify wild leek is the smell. As soon as the leaves are bruised, you can really smell the onion or garlic aroma. The leaves are elongated and smooth, and they rise at ground level from a central rosette. There are no branches or stalks. You can easily pull them up to get the small white bulb at the root. Trim off the top leaves and use the bulb.

Habitat: Fields and forests, usually on hillsides with well-drained soil
Range: In the United States, you can find them in the southeastern states as well as in California. In Canada they grow in Ontario and Quebec and the maritime provinces. Also in Europe.
Preparation: Very strongly flavored raw and can also be cooked for a milder taste
Season: Early spring before the plant flowers

Salsify
This plant is also commonly called goatsbeard or oyster plant, and it creates a large seed puff similar to a dandelion, but the rest of the plant is taller and more grass-like than dandelion.

*Jennifer Anderson @ USDA-NRCS
PLANTS Database*

The flower buds are fairly distinctive, being long and pointed. The flowers themselves are yellow or purple and have a ring of spiky leaves surrounding the blossom like a crown.

The root is the main edible part, and it tastes a little like oysters (hence the common name for the plant). You can also eat the young leaves and stalks either raw or cooked. For the roots, dig up the plant and and peel off the outer skin of the thick root. The root can be eaten raw, though it will taste better and be more digestible if you cook it first.

Habitat: Open fields
Range: Most Canada and the United States, and in Europe and Mediterranean regions
Preparation: Young leaves are edible raw and the root can also be eaten raw or cooked.
Season: Leaves can be picked in the spring or summer, and the roots can be dug anytime.

Hopniss

This edible plant is also known as the groundnut and sometimes as Indian's Potato. This is not the same as the peanut, which is also sometimes called a groundnut. The tuber it produces underground

Robert H. Mohlenbrock @ USDA-NRCS PLANTS Database / USDA SCS. 1989. Midwest wetland flora: Field office illustrated guide to plant species. *Midwest National Technical Center, Lincoln.*

makes for good eating though you can also eat the flowers and young sprouts as well. They grow somewhat like potatoes and you can find one or several under each plant. They can be varying sizes. You can sometimes find hopniss tubers that are as large as regular potatoes, if you are lucky.

The plant grows as a vine and is found climbing over other trees or along the ground. They have compound leaves, made up of five to seven smaller leaves that are smooth and come to a point. The vines of the plant are fairly thin and do not get heavy or woody with age. Because they grow long and can get tangled, it might take some effort to follow a hopniss vine back to its roots.

Habitat: Usually growing in damp, shaded areas
Range: The eastern half of the United States and some locations in Ontario and Quebec
Preparation: Tubers must be cooked until they are soft enough to eat. Flowers can be eaten raw.
Season: Tubers can be found any time of the year, even winter if you can dig the soil.

Arrowhead

The arrowhead is sometimes called wapato or Indian Potato (yes, the same common name as the hopniss).

The leaves are quite distinctive, pointed with a deep notch at the base, which makes them look like an arrowhead. The plant grows fairly low to the ground, with the leaves all rising from a central point with no side branches. The underground tubers are white with a pur-

Jennifer Anderson @ USDA-NRCS PLANTS Database

ple tinge to them. You might have to dig a bit as the roots can be up to 2 or 3 feet away from the plant before forming the tuber. This can be awkward if you have to dig underwater. Other plants might offer more accessible food, particularly in cold weather when getting wet can be a real danger.

Compared to a hopniss tuber, these are quite small, about the size of a golf ball. You will need to peel off the outer covering, which is a little tough for eating.

You can find arrowhead in swampy areas, right in the shallow standing water. They usually grow in large clusters, so if you find one, there are probably many nearby.

Habitat: Wetland areas
Range: Across North America and temperate regions around the world
Preparation: Tubers must be boiled before eating.
Season: The largest roots can be found in late fall.

Nuts

There are not a lot of nuts found in the wild that can be eaten raw or cooked over an open fire. These are not going to make up a huge part of a foraged diet, though they cannot be ignored as an emergency food source, particularly if you happen to be in an area with several wild nut trees. Knowing how to use them is important, as they are not usually as easy to eat as a simple boiled root.

Identifying wild nuts is quite easy because the nuts themselves are distinctive from one another, unlike trying to distinguish between one small green leafy plant and another small green leafy plant.

Black Walnuts

Black walnut trees can grow up to 30 feet high, and their bark is deeply grooved. The leaves are compound, and the mature walnuts grow inside a round green husk. The nuts look like green ping-pong balls when they are still on the tree, or perhaps a round lime.

Getting an edible nut out of a husk is not a quick task, and you might find your time better spent performing other foraging or survival tasks. But if you do have the time and per- haps no other food options, then go after some walnuts.

Steve Hurst @ USDA-NRCS PLANTS Database

Nuts that have fallen from the tree are ripe, but you do not want to eat any that have been sitting on the ground for too long. Pick those without any cracks or chewed holes in them. Nuts with black husks have started to go bad. With a rock or the heel of a hatchet, give them a hard smack to split open the green husk. You might be able to cut away the husk if your knife is tough enough.

Inside is a heavily ridged nutshell. This is the actual nut. This will need to be cracked open, again with a rock or hatchet heel. The nutmeat inside can be picked out with your fingers or with a sharp tool (the toothpick in a utility knife works well). The meat can be hard to get out because it is so crenelated inside the shell.

Habitat: Usually grows in heavily forested areas, though some species prefer sunnier locations
Range: Eastern United States and southern Ontario. Other species of walnut can be found through the UK, Europe, and Asia.
Season: Late summer to early autumn

Beech Nuts

Beech nuts are fairly small and much easier to get at than walnuts, though it will take a lot of them to provide any food in an emergency.

The bark of the tree is grey and smooth, and the oval-shaped leaves are dark green with wavy edges to them.

The nuts are enclosed in a spiky or hairy-looking husk that resembles a burdock seed pod. They are ripe and the most edible when the husks dry out and split open to release the nut. Some nuts might be found in the leaf litter under the tree, and some might still be trapped inside their husks. If the nuts are still in the husk, you should have no trouble picking them out with your fingers. These are one of the few nuts you can harvest without any tools.

Habitat: Typical forested areas
Range: Eastern regions of North America and the European beech can be found in the UK and Europe.
Season: Middle of autumn

Acorns

Acorns are the least palatable of this group of wild nuts, but given how widespread the oak tree is, it should not be ignored as a food source. They are also the only nut listed here that cannot be eaten straight from the tree, so you should

only use these as a source of food if you have a good source of water handy because you need to soak the nuts before you can eat them.

Acorns come from the oak tree, which is easily identified by its wavy lobed leaves. The nuts are heavy in tannins, which make them inedible if you eat them right from the tree. Collect your nuts and use a rock or other tool to crack open the outer shell to pick out the nutmeat inside. Some oaks have less tannin than others, so try one before you take the time to soak the meats. If it is edible, then go ahead and enjoy them raw. If they are bitter, you have more work ahead of you.

Soak them in clean water until you see the tannin start to leach out and darken the water. Break up the nut pieces to speed this up. Dump out the water and start again. Once the water no longer takes any tannins out, the nuts are much better for eating.

Habitat: Mature forests and some open areas
Range: There are hundreds of species of oaks, and they are found across countries in the northern hemisphere
Season: Through most of the autumn

Hickory

Ripe green husks still in the trees are similar to walnuts, but they are not so smoothly round. Each one has grooves from one end to the other marking it into quarters. The husk will split open on its own when the nut inside is ripe, though it has a shell of its own. They usually fall from the tree at this point, which makes them easier to collect.

Pull the nut out of the husk, and crack it with a rock or tool. The nutmeats should hold together a little better than a walnut, but having a small pick handy can help get every little piece out.

Hickory trees have large compound leaves, and the shagbark hickory (common in the eastern United States) has loose and "shaggy" bark.

Habitat: Typical forested areas

Range: Most species of hickory are found in the eastern parts of the United States and southeastern Canada, and there are some in Mexico and China.

Season: Nuts are ripe in the fall.

Chestnuts

Chestnuts are a little tricky because some species are edible and some are not. You will need to be able to identify them quite specifically in order to have safe food  from these trees. Sweet (or American) chestnuts are the ones you need to look for. Horse chestnuts should be avoided.

Look to the nut husks when trying to tell one from the other. A sweet chestnut has a prickly husk that looks almost feathery with a lot of fine spines. On the other hand, a horse chestnut has a lot fewer spines that are short and sharp.

Husks that are brown and dry have ripe nuts inside, and they will often split open on their own. They are pretty sharp when dry, so protect your hands when collecting. Inside the husk is the nut with its inner shell. Unlike the other nuts, the inner shell is not hard. It is more leathery, so have a sharp knife to peel it off with. The fine brown skin under the shell should be peeled off as well.

You can eat chestnuts raw from the tree, but they have tannic acid like the acorns do, though in lesser quantities. Break up the nutmeats and soak in water until the water no longer turns brown. Heating over a fire can speed this process up.

Sweet chestnut trees are quite large and grow wide in the crown with long, tapered leaves.

Habitat: Most forests, often found near bodies of water
Range: Many eastern states and some parts of southeastern Canada, and some species are found in the UK, China, and Japan.
Season: Nuts can be collected in the autumn.

Pine Nuts

These smaller nuts are often overlooked as a wild food because they are not as well known. Once they have fallen out of the pine cones, these nuts look a lot like sunflower seeds. You can collect them out of the tree if you happen to be there at the right time before they fall from the cones, but you will have to climb the tree to do so. Otherwise, you will have to forage for them on the ground. Given their small size, this will be a chore.

The shells can be broken with a rock or tool, but take care when handling them because they often have a coating of black dust on them. It is normal but it can get messy when you are in a situation where you cannot wash your hands easily. These nuts can be eaten raw without any preparation. Any nuts that have naturally cracked can usually be shelled with just your fingers. Because they are so small, you do not want to waste any nutmeat with excessive smashing.

The nuts are formed between the scales of a mature pine cone, and they can be foraged from many different types of pine trees. Pinyon pines with their short spines and stubby pinecones are the best choices (found in the southwest USA). White or red pine, with much longer needles, will have edible nuts, but they are less palatable.

Habitat: In mature forest regions
Range: Across North America, and in parts of northern Mexico and most other regions in the northern hemisphere
Season: Late summer and fall, though slow growing pine trees do not produce cones and nuts every single year.

Mushrooms

Though mushrooms can provide a great deal of edible food in the woods, there are so many deadly ones out there that it can be a risky proposition to harvest them without some experience. Try to find food from the many other plants listed in this book before resorting to mushrooms unless you have some experience identifying them in the wild.

All wild mushrooms will need to be cooked before eating, but their porous nature does not make them good candidates for boiling. They sauté or fry better, so you might have to cook them on the bottom of your cooking pot without any water to have them turn out their best. If that does not work well in your situation or you have to cook multiple foods in a single pot, you can always boil them.

Morels

Out of all the mushrooms native to North America, the morel is the easiest to identify and should cause you little difficulty even in

an emergency. Many people forage for them just because they enjoy the taste.

They have a tall, pointed cap that is wrinkled and looks almost like honeycomb or a rough sea sponge. These mushrooms are creamy white in color, though they are darker brown in depths of the cap crevices.

False morels are a somewhat similar looking mushroom that can be poisonous. The caps of these mushrooms are browner in color, are rounded, and have much smoother wrinkles than a true morel. One type of false morel, the skirt cap morel, does look quite a bit more like a true morel and is the only one to cause real confusion.

Skirt cap morels have a wrinkled cap that hangs over the stem, with the stem actually attached at the top of the cap when you look from underneath. It is sort of like how an umbrella handle is attached inside the cup of an umbrella. True morels are more solid, and their stems are attached at the bottom of the cap.

Habitat: They grow on the ground in damp, shady leaf litter.
Range: Northeastern and Pacific northwest of the United States, as well as southern Canada
Preparation: Morels must be cooked to be safe to eat.
Season: They are abundant in the spring.

Chanterelles

These mushrooms are golden yellow and have a wavy or rippled-looking cap to them. Distinctive ridges under the cap run part way down the stem. The edges of the cap often flex upward, and the whole mushroom tends to look a little like a funnel in shape.

There is more than one possible look-alike for chanterelles, so you have to be careful when collecting. You can mistake these mushrooms for either Jack o' Lantern mushrooms or false chanterelles. Both are yellow and quite similar in appearance. Both of these have a smoother cap on the top, and they have different gills underneath. True chanterelles have ridges under their caps, but the other two have much sharper and straighter gills. It is unfortunately a subtle difference, and if you are not sure, do not try to eat them. True chanterelles also have a fruity smell to them when first picked.

Range: Found widely across North America
Habitat: Moist shady areas directly under trees
Preparation: Cook your chanterelles before eating.
Season: Usually found in late summer and fall

Shaggy Mane

These mushrooms have a high, oval-shaped cap that is covered in shaggy, distinctive scales. They are mostly white with pale brown around the scales.

Older ones will start to dissolve in a black ink around the edges of the cap. Even freshly picked ones will dissolve in the same way, so make sure you have a way to cook them soon after picking. If you have to carry them back to camp for a few hours, you might have a mess on your hands. Pick only the younger fungi with no blackening visible.

Range: They are common in most areas in North America.
Habitat: Moist areas, both around trees as well as in open areas.

Preparation: You have to cook shaggy manes for about ten to 20 minutes

Season: They are one mushroom you can find in spring, summer, or fall.

Sulfur Shelf

This is a mushroom that grows directly on trees and looks like a shelf attached to the side of a trunk. They are good eating and some-times called the "chicken of

From the EJC Arboretum at www.jmu.edu.

the woods." One appealing feature is they are distinctive enough that you will not likely mistake these for any other type of mush-room, so they are safer to forage.

These are various shades of yellow, orange, and red and resemble a frilly shelf on a live or dead tree trunk. They tend to be in clus-ters. Larger ones can be woody on the inside, so you might have to break them up and only eat the tender outer margins.

Some people can have an allergic reaction to this mushroom, which can result in burning lips and even nausea and vomiting. It is not the same as being toxic, and many people are able to con-sume sulfur shelf mushrooms with no problems. Try a few small pieces before consuming more.

Range: Through most of North America, though they are more common on the west coast.

Habitat: Growing directly on trees, often oak, but not always

Preparation: These have to be cooked to be edible.

Season: The best harvesting is in summer and fall.

Desert

This is the first of the more extreme regions covered for food foraging. Many people see the desert as a barren place, but there are many options for finding food if you know how to look. Some of the cacti you can find in desert regions will provide a decent source of water as well.

These plants are found in deserts as well as other hot and arid regions.

Barrel Cacti

These stout round cacti have bright yellow or red flowers on their tops when in bloom. Their fruit is edible, and so are the flowers. The fruit looks like a small pineapple and is yellow when ripe. The pulp inside is bitter and should only be consumed when you are out of other options. The idea that you can slice them open and have a bucket of "water" inside is not accurate. There are so many conflicting accounts on the potability of the liquid

that it is better to avoid it and stick to eating the fruits unless you know one species of cacti from another.

Older cacti are actually several feet high; they lose their spherical shapes and become more cylindrical with a rounded top. They do not produce any side branches.

Range: Southwest United States
Preparation: Eat the fruit or flower blossoms raw. The fruit is dry inside, so do not be surprised by the odd texture.
Season: Usually fall, but the dry fruit can stay on the cactus for many months, so you might be able to find fruit any time of the year.

Prickly Pear

The prickly pear cactus also has edible fruit. This type of cactus grows with branches that look like adjoining flat pads and the barrel-shaped fruit is bright red or pink at the ends. The fruit has spines that will have to be removed, and you also have to peel away the outer skin to get at the edible fruit inside.

The buds and small developing pads can also be eaten. They are most edible when they are no longer than about 6 to 8 inches. Use a knife to remove the spines as well as the "eyes" where the spines join to the pad.

Range: Southwest United States as well as northern Africa, Australia, Mexico, and some parts of southern Canada
Preparation: Fruit is eaten raw and peeled, but the pads should be cooked (boiled or grilled)
Season: Most prickly pears fruit in the late summer and fall.

Agave

Agave is a great desert plant for survival because they produce large edible parts. The main plant is a rosette of stiff, pointed, upright leaves. Some species have narrow leaves, and some look much like a large artichoke with wider short leaves. The tips of the leaves usually have a hard, sharp spine.

The flower is the edible portion, and it grows on a huge stalk that grows up through the center. The large flowers and stalks can

both be roasted and eaten. If you are lucky, you can get several pounds of food this way from a single plant.

Some species of agave have sweet sap, but it can be hard to identify which species do, so it is best to stick to the flower stalks in a survival situation.

Range: Mexico, southwestern United States, and some parts of Central America
Preparation: Flower stalks should be cooked before eating.
Season: They flower only once and it can take several years to happen. This is not a typical "seasonal" plant.

Yucca

Some species of yucca looks a lot like the agave plant, but some produce a large tree-like plant (the Joshua Tree, for example). They

have flower stalks, like agave, and you can also eat the fruit from several yucca species.

The tall flowering stalks grow from the center of the plant, and the fruit is developed at the top. You can eat the flowers, flower stalks, and fruit raw, though they are not tasty. A brief cooking will make them more palatable. Ripe yucca fruits will be white inside.

Range: Central America, southwest United States, Mexico, and some parts of Alberta, Canada.
Preparation: Raw, but cooked is better. Boiling or roasting is suitable.
Season: They fruit in the late summer, and the flower stalks come out in early summer.

Wild Gourds

It might seem a little odd to find gourds in the desert, but they exist, and they make great survival food if you are stranded in Africa. The grapefruit-sized fruits grow on long vines along the ground, and the fruit's seeds and young leaves  are both edible. The fruits will be green when they are growing, and they turn yellow once they are ripe. The flesh inside is bitter, but you can pick the seeds out, though the unripe fruits can be edible if cooked.

Range: Saharan Africa and some parts of the Middle East
Preparation: Flowers can be eaten raw, unripe fruit and young leaves should be cooked first. Seeds should be roasted but could be eaten raw.
Season: They can fruit throughout the year.

Baobab Trees

These distinctive trees have wide trunks relative to the size of their stubby-branched crown, and once you know what they look like, you will not have problems identifying them.

You can eat young baobab leaves as well as their large fruits. The fruit and seeds can be eaten raw, but you will have to cut through a thick outer shell or rind. Young leaves should be boiled first.

Collecting fruit can be a challenge with some trees given their height. The large oval fruits hang down on vines from the branches, but they can still be well out of reach. Once open, the pulp will be dry. This is the normal state for baobab fruit and does not mean it cannot be eaten. You will have to pick the pieces and seeds from between the fibers.

As mentioned in Chapter 4, you can get water from a baobab tree as well as food. Use a knife or other sharp tool to dig into the trunk. The wood inside is porous and usually sodden with water.

Range: Savannah of Africa and Australia
Preparation: Fruit is fine raw, but you need to cook any of the leaves.
Season: The fruit is produced in the late winter to spring.

Tropics

For this classification, "tropics" refers to regions where it is hot and also wet (as opposed to the deserts which are hot and dry). It might seem that a tropical area would be filled with food, but you still need to know which are safe to eat. There are still many toxic plants to avoid.

Papaya

These are sometimes also called pawpaws, and they are a relatively familiar tropical fruit found in many supermarkets in more northern areas.

The papaya tree is tall with few branches along the smooth grey trunk. The leaves are deeply lobed, and it has white waxy-looking flowers.

The oblong fruits are ripe when they are mostly yellow on the outside, and the flesh inside will be bright orange with a large number of black seeds. They grow in clusters at the center of the tree canopy, and you will either have to climb or look for intact fruit that has fallen. The flesh is fine for fresh eating, and you can also eat the seeds, though they can be strongly flavored and not that tasty.

Unripe fruit should not be eaten raw but is edible if you cook the flesh first.

Range: Central and South America, Mexico, and some parts of southern United States
Preparation: Fruit and seeds can be eaten raw; unripe fruit should be cooked.
Season: They fruit any time of the year.

Coconut

The coconut palm can grow to nearly 100 feet in height and is only found along beaches and coastlines. The trunk is smooth and branchless with a cluster of feathery palm

leaves only at the top. Given the height of the tree and the smooth trunk, it is difficult to climb. Thankfully, when a coconut is ripe, it will fall from the tree so you can collect it from the ground.

The hairy brown "nut" that most are familiar with is inside another husk, so it will look different when fresh off the tree. The outside is brownish green and smooth. You will have to crack open the outer husk as well as the inner shell in order to get to the edible parts inside.

The white "meat" inside can be eaten raw, and the cavity is usually filled with a watery liquid that can also be consumed. If you are looking for a source of water, take care when cracking a coconut to not let it drain away. There is no milk inside a coconut, only the colorless coconut water.

Range: Most Caribbean islands, the Atlantic coast of Africa and most other tropical coast areas including the south Florida coast of the United States

Preparation: Eat the nutmeat raw and drink the water right from the nut.

Season: The peak is in the late fall to early winter, but some regions have them year-round.

Mango

Mango trees usually reach higher than 100 feet, so you will likely have to collect fallen fruit from the ground. The trees have wide canopies, and the fruit hangs down from short vines throughout the tree. The only edible part of a mango tree is the fruit.

The fruit is oblong and quite smooth. The flesh is sweet and edible, but the skin is bitter, so you need to peel the skin and a little of the immediately underlying flesh before you eat the rest. Mangoes are ripe when the outside is a mix of orange and red, and the flesh is also bright orange. Unripe fruit will be green.

Range: Southeast Asia, Mexico, Central and South America, and a few places in the southern United States

Preparation: Eat the fruit raw after peeling the bitter skin

Season: Through the summer and early fall, though some warmer areas might have mangoes well into the winter.

Taro

Taro offers an edible root as well as edible leaves, though neither can be eaten raw.

The leaves of the plant are large and heart-shaped with smooth edges and a slightly rippled surface. The plant has no central trunk, and the leaves grow directly from the large root underground. The root tuber looks like a cross between a turnip and a potato, and it can provide a lot of starch for your diet once cooked.

To cook the root, you can use a knife to peel off the outer skin (much easier than trying to scrub off the dirt) and chop it up into smaller pieces. Boil in water for about 15 minutes until it softens up, and then you can safely eat it. For the leaves, you can use the entire leaf as well as the stem for eating. Boil for at least 45 minutes before eating or you will have an uncomfortably itchy throat.

Range: Wetland areas in southeast Asia, West Africa, Central and South America, and some parts of southern Florida
Preparation: Well-cooked roots or leaves can be eaten.
Season: Any time of the year is fine for harvesting taro.

Cassava (Manioc)

This is another root plant that commonly goes by either the name cassava or manioc. Some regions also call it "yuca," which can be confusing with the true yucca (note the spelling differences). The starchy root is long and tapered and looks a lot like a sweet potato. The upper portions of the plant grow as a shrub, with palmate leaves and a slim woody trunk. Like taro, the leaves are also edible as long as they are cooked.

The roots can be branching, and you can find several worthwhile tubers under each plant. Once you have dug up the roots, peel off the outer skin, and leave the pieces of root to soak in clean water overnight to wash out the toxins. Then boil in fresh water until they are soft. When cooking the leaves, make sure they boil for at least 20 minutes.

Range: Central and South America, the Caribbean islands and across most of Africa due to intense cultivation
Preparation: The roots and leaves have to be cooked to be safe.
Season: There is no specific season for cassava.

Saw Palmetto Berries

The saw palmetto plant is a low-growing palm with long, sharply pointed leaves. The trunks tend to grow along the ground so it looks much more like a shrub than a tree. It also has sharp spines, so be careful when harvesting the berries. The fruit grows in tangled clusters at the base of the leaves.

Saw palmetto produces a small fruit about the size of a grape, but it is dark blue to black when ripe. Unripe fruit is green. They are safe to eat when raw, though not the tastiest of berries. Unlike most berries that are too sour to eat, these have been described as tasting like old blue cheese.

Range: Southeastern United States, particularly in Florida
Preparation: Eat the fruit fresh and raw.
Season: Late summer to early autumn

Bamboo

The edible part of bamboo is the shoot, which grows up from the base of the more familiar poles of mature bamboo. The look a little like asparagus but with a stouter bullet shape to them. Only harvest ones about 10 inches long or smaller. The outer skin has to be peeled off before eating.

Some species of bamboo will have bitter shoots, which can be made more edible by soaking the sliced pieces in clean water overnight before cooking (change the water after soaking though). You can judge the edibility by taste. If it is still bitter, it needs more cooking or soaking. Some species might be edible raw. It can be difficult to identify one species from another, so the same cooking precautions should be taken for all bamboo shoots.

Range: Southeast Asia, India, northern Australia, parts of South America, southern United States, and Africa where there are high levels of rainfall.

Preparation: You will probably have to cook it before eating.
Season: Sprouts can form any time, so you are not restricted
by season.

Sugarcane

Sugarcane looks a lot like bamboo
with tall, segmented reeds, but
these plants have long thin leaves
and are not so wooden through
their stalks. It looks much like tall
grass, though the stalks are heavier
than typical grass.

You will not get a lot of food from
sugar cane, but the sweet sugary
sap that comes out when you chew the smaller stalks can be a
great survival pick-me-up and will provide some crucial calories
even if it does not fill your stomach.

Range: Southeast Asia, many Pacific islands, and some parts of
South America
Preparation: Cut a small or tender stalk and chew on it to release
the sugar sap.
Season: Any time of the year

Far north

Now to go to the other extreme: the much colder far north regions. Northern Canada is a prime example of this environment,
and you are going to have a harder time foraging for plants in this
type of landscape. Depending on how far north you are, many of
the more typical plants mentioned in the main part of this chapter
may be found, so keep their descriptions handy. These are some

of the edible plants already discussed that can often be found in the colder north:

- Cattails
- Arrowhead
- Burdock
- Dandelion
- Clover
- Nettles
- Lamb's Quarters
- Plantain
- Salsify
- Pine nuts

And then you can add a few more options that grow specifically in the northern areas.

Cloudberries

These segmented berries have a slight resemblance to raspberries, but the plants they grow on are different and the fruit is a paler orange color. Berries that are a darker red are unripe. Cloudberry plants are low-growing, and the berries develop in thin stalks above the plant. The leaves are lobed with a frilly edge to them.

Range: Northern Canada, Scandinavia, and across northern Russia in wetland areas
Preparation: You can eat the berries raw.
Season: Summer

Salmonberries

Salmonberries look a lot like raspberries except that they can be yellow or orange as well as red when they are ripe. When the fruit pulls easily away from the stem, you know the fruit can be eaten. Because both salmonberries and raspberries are edible, there is not a huge importance on being able to distinguish one from the other.

They grow in moist and forested regions and form large clusters or thickets of salmonberry bushes.

Range: North American west coast, including north and temperate regions
Preparation: Fruit can be eaten fresh from the plant.
Season: Early to midsummer

Bearberries

Bearberries grow on a low-growing shrub with small leathery leaves, and the edible fruits are smooth (similar to a blueberry). Depending on the specific species of bearberry, the berries will be red or purple when ripe. This plant is also known as kinnickkinnick.

You can eat the fruit raw, but it will taste better after you cook it. Unlike many sour wild berries, these are bland and have little taste at all.

Range: Any Arctic regions around the world
Preparation: Ripe berries can be eaten fresh and raw.
Season: Late summer to early fall. Berries can sometimes be found well into winter.

Reindeer Lichen

It might seem a little desperate even for wilderness survival to scrape lichen off a rock, but some of these plants can grow several inches in height and can actually provide a reasonable amount of food. The branching "leaves" are usually light grey or white, and it resembles a formation of coral more than a plant.

Do not eat any lichens raw. Soak for several hours in clean water and then boil until cooked and soft.

Range: Most alpine forests where it is damp and shaded, on surfaces of rocks
Preparation: Do not eat these plants raw.
Season: You can find reindeer lichen any time of the year.

USDA-NRCS PLANTS Database

Iceland Moss

This is another rock-growing lichen you can harvest for food. It is much leafier than most lichens and will grow several inches high. It has a leafy appearance and is a pale green or even grey in color. The fronds are flattened and seem to roll in on themselves to form a tube before leafing out further.

Like reindeer lichen, you have to cook Iceland moss before you can eat it. Let it soak for a few hours or even overnight, and then cook in fresh water until it is soft.

Range: Northern Canada, northern United Kingdom, and most Scandinavian countries
Preparation: Iceland moss must be cooked before eating.
Season: It grows year-round.

Water Plants

You are not likely going to have need to forage for aquatic plants or seaweed unless you are right on the shore or trapped out on a boat. There are several good edible options in the water, and they are covered in more detail in Chapter 11.

Poisonous plants to be avoided

You might assume that anything not considered edible would fall into this category, but the reality is that the large majority of plants are neither edible nor poisonous. Some are just indigestible, and some might cause stomach upset rather than true poisoning.

Although it is always the best option to only eat foods you are *positive* are edible, you also need to know which foods must be avoided. Of course, some plants are poisonous only when consumed raw, and they are otherwise considered edible in the section above.

Just like with the list of edible plants, too many poisonous ones exist to easily list out in this book. This section does include some of the more common ones, particularly ones that you might get confused with edible plants.

These plants are going to be almost certainly fatal if consumed, and in an emergency situation, there is not going to be any reasonable treatment you could apply.

Nightshade

Known usually as deadly nightshade or Belladonna, this plant has toxic berries as well as leaves. Bittersweet nightshade is another variety that is not quite as deadly but should still be avoided.

The berries are green when unripe, and they become orange or red before darkening to a deep purple when they are ripe. They can resemble other edible berries at first glance, and they are either oblong in shape or round (depending on the species). The bittersweet variety often has several berries in each cluster at different ripening stages, so you see several colors together at once. The true deadly nightshade has berries that just go from green to black.

These plants have small purple star-shaped flowers, and the plant likes to spread out. Overall, it can get between 2 and 4 feet high.

Nightshade berries are actually sweet to the taste, so do not use that as any indicator of toxicity.

Range: (deadly nightshade) Along the Pacific coast, the northeastern United States and through southern Canada
(bittersweet nightshade) Through most of the United States except the far south

Water Hemlock

Water Hemlock is a leafy plant that could be confused with wild parsnip, though you would never eat wild parsnip leaves due to the toxic chemicals in them. It also resembles wild carrot or Queen

Robert H. Mohlenbrock @ USDA-NRCS PLANTS Database / USDA SCS. 1989. Midwest wetland flora: Field office illustrated guide to plant species. *Midwest National Technical Center, Lincoln.*

Anne's Lace, which could give the impression that it is generally harmless. Hemlock also looks a little like watercress. Unfortunately, this is one of the most poisonous plants in North America.

Hemlock grows in wet areas at the edges of marshland. The leaves branch out on either side of a central stem, and they are pointed with a toothy edge. Flowers are usually white, and they form an umbrella-shaped cluster. Unlike the cluster you see with true Queen Anne's Lace, this one is made up of smaller globular clusters on longer stems.

Most of the plants that hemlock is going to be confused with grow in open sunny areas, which is different from the wet conditions hemlock prefers.

Range: Widely found through the United States, Canada, and Europe

Virginia Creeper

This plant grows as a vine and produces clusters of fruit that can resemble wild grapes. As mentioned in the section on grapes, if the small stems holding the fruits are red, you are looking at Virginia Creeper and it should be avoided.

Robert H. Mohlenbrock @ USDA-NRCS PLANTS Database / USDA SCS. 1991. Southern wetland flora: Field office guide to plant species. South National Technical Center, Fort Worth.

The plant has five-part palmate leaves and grows as a creeping vine that can climb up other trees, posts, and through the undergrowth. In the fall, the leaves turn a vibrant red, which can make it stand out in the woods. The berries grow in grape-like clusters and will be green when unripe. They turn blue when mature.

Range: Western and central Canada and United States

Buttercups

This is not likely a plant that you will mistake for anything else, but its common and harmless appearance could lure people into trying its leaves. If you are not familiar with buttercup, it has a bright yellow flower shaped like a cup, and the plant has small deeply serrated leaves. The name alone often gives people the impression that it is an edible plant, but both the flowers and the leaves are poisonous. Thankfully, it is bitter tasting and quickly blisters your mouth, so no one is likely to eat enough of it to be fatal.

Range: Most of Canada and the United States, except the southern states. Also through Europe

On a final note, never judge a plant's toxicity level by seeing what animals eat it. The idea that any plant that is fine for an animal must be fine for humans is false. For example, rabbits eat the leaves from deadly nightshade without any ill effects. Needless to say, that is not an example you want to follow.

Foraging for Animals

Gathering wild plants for food is the more efficient way to quickly feed yourself and your group in an emergency, but longer-term survival situations might end up requiring more calories than leaves and roots can provide. Winter emergencies can also greatly reduce the amount of plant material you will be able to forage. Knowing how to get meat or fish for food will be a vital skill in these scenarios. Cleaning and preparing your catch is covered a little later in this section.

Hunting

This might seem to be the more exciting option for getting animal food, but unless you have some previous skill and experience in tracking animals in the wild, you will probably stay hungry. The next sections cover trapping and fishing, which is more likely to provide results for an outdoors novice. If you do wish to try your hand at hunting for game animal, here are a few tips.

Your first task will be to get a weapon. It is possible to fashion a bow and arrow with a little skill and a sharp knife, but the reality is that it will probably be a waste of time and resources for anyone who is not already familiar with using these tools. Instead, stick to the simpler options. A thrown rock or stout stick can daze a small animal long enough for you move in for the kill. Another stick that has a sharpened tip can be used to impale and kill the animal once you get in closer.

Finding an animal is the harder part. In the winter, tracks are more abundant to follow, but you can usually make out trails through the grass or underbrush if you are observant enough. *Chapter 10 includes more details on recognizing tracks.* If you have some food to spare, a little bait can help bring an animal to you. Sitting and waiting will be tedious, but it will save more energy than roaming through the woods for hours.

Trapping

Trapping is the better option for getting small animals, though it is far from foolproof. It will be easier to set traps or snares if you have the proper wire in your kit, but you can make do with twine or heavy string if necessary. Other types of traps can be set without any wire or string and might be a better alternative if you do not have the supplies.

There are dozens of different ways to set a trap for an animal; some will require more skill than others. To keep these instructions simple, this section will cover two basic types: the deadfall trap and the wire snare. Further research should be done to find complete diagrams of the triggering methods, and you should practice putting these together before any emergencies come up.

Deadfall Traps

A deadfall trap is built so a heavy object (a large rock or log) will fall on the animal when it is triggered, ideally killing it right away. A figure-4 trigger is the most common way of constructing one of these, with three sticks that have been cut with notches to create a precisely balanced trap. The Wildwood Survival website (**www. wildwoodsurvival.com/survival/traps/figure4/figure4.html**) has excellent photographs and diagrams on how to make the notches. Bait is either attached to the trigger stick or nearby so that the arrangement of sticks collapses, and the heavy weight falls.

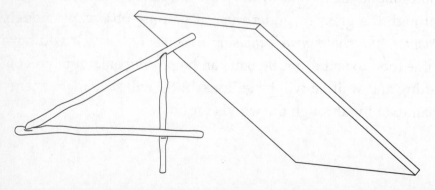

For the novice, you can prop up a heavy log with just a single stick, but then you have to securely attach the bait to that stick. When an animal pulls at the bait, it will pull the stick out to release the log above it. This is a less precise method but one that anyone can implement.

Snares

With wire, you can also trap animals with snares, which are some form of loose wire loop that will tighten around an animal when it passes through. Create a wire loop that is about the size of your fist that will tighten when 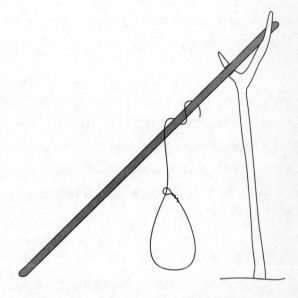 pulled, like a slip knot. Use small sticks to hold the loop up so that the opening is perpendicular to the ground, and possibly arrange other rocks or larger sticks around it so that any passing animal will have to walk through the loop as it passes. The noose then tightens up and traps the animal. The other end of the snare wire must be securely tied down or attached to a bowed branch that will pull the wire when set off.

Snares can be a hit or miss approach because animals can get free if you do not check the traps enough. But if you check them too often, you will establish your scent on the area and scare off any game. It can be a tricky situation to get just right.

The simplest trap of all is a small hole in the ground, though it will really only work with mice or small rodents. Dig a hole at least 12 inches deep, and try to slope the sides so the bottom of the hole is wider than the top. This will make it difficult for a trapped animal to climb out. Place a piece of wood or bark slightly propped over the hole, and add some bait in the bottom. A mouse can come sniffing after the food, and when it crawls under the bark it falls in the hole.

If you can establish where animals are frequently seen in your area (along a trail, or near a water source), that is the best place to set your trap. Make sure to have appealing bait, even if you have to sacrifice some of your own food. The more traps you can set, the better your chances of catching something to eat. You do need to keep track of where these traps are so you can get back to them later.

Fishing

Of these three methods for getting animals for food, fishing is the most successful even for a complete survival beginner. Of course, this will only be an option if you are able to find a body of water large enough to have a population of fish. Do not overlook the small minnows either. Every bit of potential food is important. Small fish are easy to cook and will give you some added protein.

Tiny fish that cannot be caught with a hook may be scooped out with a cup or bucket if you are quick enough, or some fabric can be used to create a rough net.

Having some fishhooks and line in your basic survival kit will make fishing a reasonably easy chore. It still might take hours before you get a bite, but you will be able to put a fishing pole together in just a few minutes. Without a branch, you can still just use the line and hook by hand; you just will not have as long a reach. Bait your hook with a worm, piece of meat, or insect and drop in your line. Snails make good bait as well once you crack off their shells.

Because fish have their own preferences for food and hiding places, you might have to make several attempts at different locations and with different baits. Keep yourself hidden while you are fishing or you might scare the fish.

When in a situation without any fishing supplies, you will have to make your own. Thread can be pulled from any type of fabric to a make a length of line, and you can make a hook from a safety pin or a carved piece of wood or bone.

Once you have a bite, give your line a quick tug to set the hook in the fish's mouth and then try to pull it in. Having a piece of clothing handy to use as a net can help you grab your fish once it is on the line. It is easy to lose a fish once caught, so you want to be careful not to lose your catch.

When near a body of water, you will have other options for food other than the elusive fish. Frogs and turtles are far easier to catch and can often be caught with just your bare hands. They can be numerous in a pond or marsh area and can provide quite a bit of food for little expended effort. Some freshwater streams may also be home to crayfish, which can be caught by a steady hand. They can be boiled in water just like a lobster.

Even though it does not take much energy for you to sit by the side of a pond and wait for fish, you might have other tasks that need attending to that makes this impractical. You can hang a baited line from a branch and leave it unattended. This does make it easier for you to manage your time, but it is not a good idea if you can avoid it. A caught fish can work its way off a hook if there is no one there to pull it in, which leaves you with lost bait and no fish. Another animal might take your bait, along with the hook and line too.

Worms, insects, and more

Although finding larger animals or fish will provide a decent meal, collecting smaller "game" is still an option in an emergency. Most insects or worms can be eaten, and they are much easier to catch. You do need to only catch insects that are edible, such as grasshoppers, crickets, beetle grubs, termites, and earthworms. You can either roast or boil them, and remove any spiny legs before you eat. For worms, keep them underwater in a cup for a few minutes

to help clean out any grit from inside of them. They will naturally expel it when in water.

Avoid spiders, as they will always have some poison in their bodies, and any insects with hairy coverings (such as caterpillars). Flies, ticks, and mosquitoes too often carry disease and should also not be eaten.

One last possibility for finding food are eggs. Bird's eggs are all considered to be edible, though they are not always easy to find. You may have to climb some trees. Holes and hollows can hold nests just as often as a tree branch, so check holes (carefully) for eggs. Wild bird eggs can be handled and cooked just like the more familiar chicken eggs. Boiling is probably the easiest method for cooking over an open fire.

Be aware that wild eggs are likely to be fertile and you may have an undeveloped bird in your egg. Of course, that is just added food for you to cook up, though it can be a bit of a shock when you crack open the shell. How to cook this will vary on the size of the "chick." A small embryo can be boiled and eaten whole because it does not have any hard bones yet (this is actually a delicacy in southern Asia). If it is more like a chick, also boil it and pick the meat off the bones as though it was a full-sized bird. Granted, the amount of meat you get will be minimal and might not be worth the effort.

Cleaning Your Catch

Being able to turn your freshly caught animal into dinner is just as vital as catching it in the first place. The following is a rough guide on how to clean your catch. You can find more detailed instructions and diagrams in any good hunter's field dressing guide.

Small animals

If your trap or snare has not killed your animal outright, you will have to do so as soon as you return to your traps. A deep cut across the neck is the quickest and easiest method. You will want to bleed out the animal anyway before cleaning it, and it will drain best through a jugular cut. Hang your animal head-down from a tree and keep the blood if you have a container for it. It has a lot of nutrition and should not be wasted if possible.

Make sure you do all of this away from your campsite area. The smell of blood can attract predators that you do not want to get too close to your living and sleeping areas.

When the blood has drained out of the carcass, you will have to remove the skin and fur.

Make a shallow slice at the base of the stomach, taking care to only cut the skin and not the muscles below yet. Cut along the belly up to the head and neck area. Work your blade under the skin to cut it loose, and then make cuts along the limbs in the same way. Peel the skin off like removing a sweater. Cut carefully around the anus and tie the end of the intestines closed with a piece of string to prevent any waste from contaminating the meat.

After the skin is removed, make another belly cut through the muscles to open up the body cavity. Do not slice the stomach or any intestines. Most of the entrails will be loose enough to pull out with just some light membrane tissue holding it all in place.

Once you have removed the entrails and skin, you can cut the muscle meat away from the bones. Do not ignore any edible parts because you do not know when you will have a meat meal again. All of the muscle meat can be cooked, as well as the lungs, heart, and kidneys.

Bury the unused parts of the animal, though small pieces can be saved to use as bait for other traps or for fishing.

Fish

Fish require different cleaning techniques, and they are usually easier to prepare than mammals. Small fish that are less than 2 inches long can just be cooked and eaten whole with no extra preparation needed. Larger fish do not need to be skinned, just gutted.

Slice the fish across the throat area just under the gills and hang upside down to drain the blood out. After that, cut from that slit down the belly to the rectal region. Just like with the small mammals, make sure you only cut the muscle layer and not the organs inside.

Remove the organs without puncturing any of them, and the rest of the fish can be eaten. You can cook it with the skin and scales on to make it easier. You then have to peel the skin off before you eat.

Cooking

Though cooking over a fire was mentioned with a few techniques in Chapter 3, here are a few more details on how to cook your freshly caught meat or fish.

Meat can be cooked in a few different ways with boiling being the easiest to manage over an open fire, providing you have a container and water to do so. Cut your meat or fish into small chunks or strips for quicker cooking, and simply boil in water until the meat is no longer pink. A few added edible plants can help improve the bland flavor if you have them, but boiled meat alone is a perfectly fine meal. Drink the water after so that no nutrients or water goes to waste.

For a change of flavor or if you are using your water boiling container, you can also cook your pieces of meat on a spit over the fire. A green branch cut fresh from a tree will work best because it will not catch on fire itself. Sharpen the end and stick a few pieces of meat on it. Hold low over hot coals but not right in the flames or you will char your food rather than cook it. Again, cook until the meat is no longer pink. Eating raw or undercooked meat can lead to stomach upset or it can give you more serious intestinal parasites or worms. If you are unable to make fire, only resort to eating raw meat if you have already gone several days without any food. Without fire, plant material is a safer bet.

Flat clean rocks can also be used as a makeshift frying pan. Let them heat up in the coals of your fire, and place your strips of meat right on the rocks. They will cook quite quickly this way.

You can roast a whole fish by wrapping it in fresh green leaves (nothing toxic) and letting it bake in the hot coals for ten to 15 minutes.

CASE STUDY: TRAINED BY MARINES

Brian Crowl
Louisville, Kentucky
www.kywildcast.com

After spending four years as a Marine, Brian still puts his training and survival skills to good use when he goes hunting or fishing. Every year he goes out for about three weeks looking for deer, rabbit, and turkey, and then there is another month spent fishing for catfish. He's definitely a regular outdoorsman.

Through the Marines, he has learned many basic survival skills including surviving off the land, producing water in the desert, basic first aid, building shelters from wood or snow, trapping small game and birds, fishing, and how to start a fire. Even with all these skills, he still carries a good kit of equipment with him whenever he is going to be out in the woods for more than two hours.

In a backpack, he carries a two-channel 17 mile walki-talkie, length of parachute cord, handkerchief, Band-Aids, antibiotic cream, roll of duct tape, a knife, and a lighter. He recently added a 9-volt battery and steel wool as a fire-starter.

All of his skills were learned during his Marine Corp training, which included a three-day and three-night survival scenario. He also learned many of his outdoor skills from his father.

If he was going to be stranded in the wild with just one tool, it would be a knife. With that, he could build a shelter, kill an animal for food, and possibly even start a fire.

Brian's advice for anyone in a survival situation is this "Make sure to be mentally tough before all else. You can possess all the survival skills in the world and master them, but if you are not tough mentally, you will break down in a hurry."

Chapter 6

Shelter

Though food and water might be the first things that come to mind when you are in a survival situation, shelter can be more important in some cases. You can go several days or even weeks without food, but you will not last long in the wild with no shelter unless you happen to be lost during stretch of dry weather in the summer. Cold nights and any rainfall will take a huge toll on your health and equipment without decent shelter.

If you have gotten lost while camping, you might already have a tent with you and you will not need to fashion your own construction. It will be an important asset until you are rescued, so treat it with care and do not set it up anywhere that would put it at risk.

Climate and Season Considerations

Not all shelters are created equal. You will want to build a shelter differently depending on what exactly you are sheltering from.

What you build in the summer might not be quite the same as what you need in the winter. This section gives you things to think about for each type of weather, but the actual construction details are later in the chapter.

Summer heat

Even in the heat of summer you will need to consider building a shelter. Thankfully, you will not have to worry much about trying to keep warm, but rather trying to stay cool. Deep forest areas will not be that much of a problem because shade is easy to come by, but if you are lost or trapped in more open countryside, you will need a way to get out of the sun.

Unlike a winter shelter, you will want to take advantage of any breezes to help keep cool. A shelter will need to be more open and somewhat moveable so you can adjust the position as the sun moves or breezes shift.

In the summer, nights will be cool but not likely cold enough to warrant a complete change in shelter construction. With a space blanket or other covering from your kit and some additional pine boughs, you should be warm enough even if the nights cool off considerably.

Winter cold

This will apply in most seasons, not just winter. If you have not spent a lot of time outdoors without shelter before, it can be shocking just how much the temperature will drop after the sun goes down even if it was a warm day to begin with. *Building a shelter out of snow is covered in Chapter 12 on winter survival.* Most of the time, though, you are dealing with cold but without all the snow.

Shelters to protect against cold will have to be closed in and not overly large, to help keep all the heat you can inside. The entrance should be out of the wind, ideally facing a natural block in case the wind direction changes (large trees, rocks).

Rainy weather

Rain can happen any time of the year, whether winter or summer, so you might have to adjust your shelter construction to suit the changing weather. Keep your eye on the sky and watch the clouds so you can improve your shelter before anything gets wet.

Shelters against the rain will mostly need to be waterproof and have no leaks above you that would let water in. Large pieces of bark, and layers of pine boughs work the best to create a roof surface that will shed the rain if you do not have a tarp to work with.

Choosing a Location

Once you keep these considerations in mind, you have to pick a spot. If you are on the move, it will only have to suit for one night, but if you are intending to stay put until rescue, you are going to have to stay in that location for a while. Take the time to scout out a spot so you do not have to waste time and resources building your shelter more than once.

Choose a place that is near other resources, like a stand of easily cut wood or a body of water. If you are going to be there for a few days (ideally not much longer), you want everything you need to be relatively handy. Scout the area for any hazards, such as any precarious rocks above you or dead trees that could blow over in a storm. Check the immediate ground for any insect activity so you can avoid building a shelter on an ant hill or something similar.

The spot should be flat, free of large rocks, and as naturally protected as possible. Valleys can be protected, but cold air can also settle in low areas during the night, so do not base your shelter at the bottom of a sloping area. It is often wetter at the bottom of a slope as well, which should be avoided. Part way up a hillside is a good compromise if the ground is not mostly flat.

Any natural shelter or possible construction aids (such as caves or fallen trees) can make your building chores much simpler. Try to build around these unless the location is otherwise unfit.

Considering all the variations in potential building sites, there is no one ideal spot for an emergency shelter. Use your best judgment and consider all the details given here. Be flexible enough to adjust your construction or move it completely if you discover a problem with the spot.

Types of Shelter

There are several different ways to build a shelter, but you do not have to stick to any one specific plan. Given your circumstances and resources, create the best shelter you can even if you have to use aspects of several different building types.

Shelter base or floor

No matter which types you are opting for, you do need to create a good solid base that will be the same in any case. You need to get up off the ground while you are sleeping to conserve heat, so the floor of your shelter is important.

If you have access to plenty of wood, create a raised "platform" for yourself by setting out a layer of branches or logs that are roughly the same thickness. Your extra tarp can go on the ground under this to prevent moisture. This should get you up off the ground by a few inches to start with. Make it long enough to accommodate you when you lay down.

On top of that, gather up a thick layer of dry or fresh leaves, pine boughs, or anything remotely soft and insulating. You want this layer to be at least 4 to 6 inches thick, so be generous. It flattens down fast when you sleep on it a few times. Once this is put together, you can get the rest of your shelter built around it.

Tarp shelter

Your survival gear should include at least one large plastic tarp, and this is where it becomes a necessary tool. With one tarp, you can create a roof over your head, and with two tarps, you can also have a dry floor.

Use rope from your kit to tie the corners of your tarp between trees to create a roof. Whether the sides of the tarp reach the ground is up to you and will depend on the immediate weather. Having just a roof can be enough to keep off the sun on a hot day or keep you dry in light rain. To keep more heat in, set your roof tarp up low enough so it will create at least one wall for you as well. During cold weather, a tarp alone will not be enough to keep you warm, and you will need a more substantial shelter built from wood and brush.

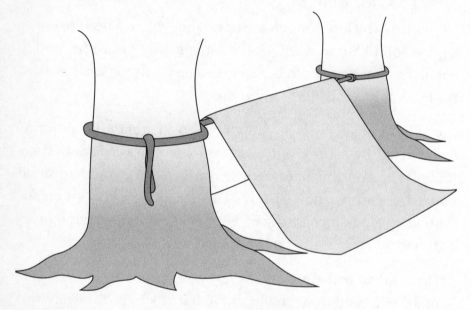

If rope is in short supply, the simplest shape is to string one length of rope between two trees to create the roof support and lay the tarp over that to create a low peaked tent. This will create a small shelter with enough space inside to lie down. Tying out the four corners will make a much wider area as long as you can spare the rope and have enough supports for it. Use rocks to weight down the sides if they reach the ground.

If your kit includes a light foil "space blanket," do not use that to create your shelter. That should be wrapped around your body to keep in your warmth while you are sleeping, and it is not sturdy enough to be used as a building material.

Lean-to

A lean-to is a sturdier option but can only be built if you have something for it to lean against. A large fallen tree or outcropping of rock is an ideal spot for a lean-to. Several long branches can be

cut or gathered and tied together with rope or even just leaned against your support without being attached to each other. You can also incorporate a tarp to make this waterproof. Brace the bottoms of the branches with rocks for more stability.

This wall is also your roof so you want to make it as water and wind proof as possible. Large, flat pieces of bark make excellent "shingles," and flexible boughs from pine or fir trees are also good for this.

Other helpful materials include long grasses, wild vines (grape vine is excellent), and cattail reeds. They can be woven together to help hold the other boughs together. This applies for lean-tos as well as a freestanding type of structure.

Cover one end of your lean-to with an extra tarp or additional branches so it is not open at both ends.

Freestanding tepee

When you are in a location with no large trees or rocks for support, you will have to work a little harder to create a more free-standing shelter. This type of shelter is more of a challenge because it needs to not only keep out the rain (or keep in the heat), but it also needs to be able to stand under its own weight. Trying to build something like this with only rudimentary tools can be hard. Any time you can start off with an existing tree or two to add support, you will be better off.

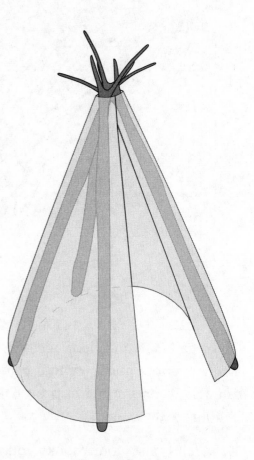

Two or three branches can be leaned toward each other to create a tepee-style structure, with each branch equally supporting the other. Forked branches are ideal for this as they create better support without any additional rope. Lash them tightly together at the top, and then start to lean additional branches around them to add to the walls. Close-growing saplings can be bent towards each other in the same way and tied to create an initial frame for your structure. The walls can be made up of more branches and layers of pine boughs, leafy branches, and other material. Rope or vines can help secure everything in place.

Sheltering in a vehicle

All of these situations pertain to a scenario in which you are lost in the wilderness. That is not always going to be the case. If you have gotten stranded in a car or boat, you are going to be much farther ahead when it comes to shelter even if the vehicle is damaged.

Use your tarp or piles of pine boughs to cover any damaged or open parts to your vehicle to make it as weather-proof as possible. If you do use branches, make sure to leave a signaling flag nearby so any passing help does not overlook your now camouflaged car.

A candle can be set up on the dash or floor to provide some heat. It does not take much of a flame to really raise the temperature inside a car as long as it is stable enough not to tip over as you move about.

Managing Fire Inside a Shelter

This is an difficult subject because how you keep your fire will depend on your own experience as an outdoors-person, the style of shelter you built, and the immediate circumstances and weather.

It might seem like a smart idea to have a fire inside your shelter if it is large enough, but an open fire will create a lot of smoke no matter what you are burning. Unless you can create a chimney or other similar opening above the fire, you will start to choke within minutes of starting a fire. It is also a great risk to setting your shelter ablaze once you are asleep. Be cautious of how you manage a fire with a makeshift shelter, or you will cause more problems than you solve.

The best option is to have your fire going just outside the entrance so you can gain some of the heat without enclosing the fire inside. Again, take care that there is enough distance so that the material in your shelter does not go up in flames. It also makes the night more comfortable if you can reach out to add more wood without having to leave your construction.

Hot rocks can be moved from the fire area to the inside of your shelter to add warmth in cold weather, though this can also be a fire risk to some degree. It is still a much safer alternative.

Another option is to light a small candle inside the shelter, just as was described in the vehicle section above. It will give off much less smoke than a burning fire and should not be a fire risk as long as you have it set in such a way that it will not get knocked during the night.

Chapter 7

Signaling

Finding your way back to safety is one important goal, but helping someone else find you is another. Depending on the situation, you will want to know some techniques on how to bring attention to yourself in the wild.

Mirrors

A small pocket mirror can be used to reflect the sunlight and create a bright flash of light. This is a good way to signal for help as long as there is a direct line-of-sight between you and the other person, such as when you are trying to signal an aircraft above you. It is not a great method to use when you are trying to get someone's attention at ground level in the woods though.

You can create a signal almost immediately when you see potential rescue in the distance, and it will take you no additional supplies to do so. Needless to say, this method only works during the day.

It can take a little practice to know how to hold the mirror with respect to the target and the sun. Try it out with the mirror in your kit to get a feel for the right angles and to see how it works before you are stuck out in the wilderness. Test it against a building or tall tree to see how the reflection falls when you handle the mirror.

Fire and Smoke

Fires can be good signals, but not in all circumstances. If you are lost in the woods, light from a fire is not going to be visible at much of a distance and probably will not attract any attention on its own during the day. On the other hand, it can be a more visible option during the night even in wooded areas.

Smoke can rise quite a distance above the tree line as a signal but only in the daytime, and usually only as a signal for anyone far enough away to see over the trees.

In open areas, you can use fire or smoke with greater success. Just remember that a larger fire is more visible, but you will put

yourself at risk if you are overzealous and start a forest fire. Make sure all signal fires are built and maintained safely.

Adding green wood or leaves can produce a lot of smoke, but it can also smother a small fire if you are not careful. Only use this method for a smoke signal if you are confident your fire is strong enough for it.

Another variation on using fire is the survival flare. These are helpful on boats when you need to be seen out on open water, but they can be helpful in other situations as well. Like with any supply item, you will only have a limited number. A flashlight might also work as a decent nighttime signal, but they produce a fairly small beam of light and might not be visible at a distance.

Trail Marking

If you are on the move, marking your trail behind, you can help rescuers who are actively looking in your area. With this approach, you are marking where you have been rather than just where you are. The purpose of these marks would be to show your trail, including which direction you have gone.

In situations where you do not expect anyone to be looking for you (which is why you are on the move in the first place) this is not going to be a helpful approach.

The trick with trail markers is that they have to be visible and also clear in their meaning. With limited supplies, this can be difficult. If you are carrying a pad of paper and a pencil, you can leave notes for potential rescuers. Pencil will not wash off even if the paper gets wet, and you can leave detailed information on where you have gone from this point.

Do not try to be too clever and hope that your rescuers will understand some obscure symbols. You may not be found by professionals, so be as obvious as you can with your marks. With a knife, you can cut a mark or "blaze" into trees as you go by and create an easily followed trail that will not be washed or blown away. Arrows work best and will be understood by anyone.

Flags of brightly colored fabric or plastic can be used to get attention to your marks if you have any material to spare.

Noise

Making noises can attract attention provided that help is within hearing range, which is a much smaller area than visual range. The positive side is that noise travels well in day or night and is not dependent on any line-of-sight. Someone can hear your noises whether they are facing your direction or not.

Whistles are good for noise signaling, and even a dime-store plastic whistle can produce a loud sound. For a little extra money, there are some whistles designed for survival use, such as the JetScream™, that are louder than most others. Metal whistles are durable, but you do run the risk of it freezing to your mouth or lips when used in cold weather.

Of course, yelling is also another option, though your voice will not last forever (especially if water is in short supply). Only yell if you feel that there is someone within range. Banging rocks or sticks together can be used, but these are not loud sounds and tend to get lost among the natural sounds of a wooded area. Create a pattern so your noises stand out. Making a sound in groups of three is a simple and effective approach.

Ground Markings

This is the type of signal you would use to get the attention of airplanes overhead. You can use rocks and logs to create an obviously manmade shape on the ground so it can be seen even from a high altitude.

In an open space, try to spell out SOS in huge letters or even just an X. An arrow pointing toward your camp would also work if you are located a distance away from the clearing. Use something bright or reflective to line the letters to make your sign more visible.

This is not the same as the trail markings mentioned above. A large construction like this is best used when you have made a permanent camp.

Cell Phones and Other Gadgets

In today's world of communication, you might be lucky enough to have a device on you that can either call for help or at least help others locate you. Even a functioning cell phone might not be a solution to your wilderness problem unless you can let someone know where you are. In other words, just because you can call someone does not make you any less lost. This is particularly true if you have been in a plane crash in a remote area or are hiking in a large wilderness region.

Some cell phones can be tracked by a GPS transmitter, and some might be trackable as long as you are able to make a connection and stay on the line. Unfortunately, with rapidly moving cell phone technology, it is not always clear what each phone is capable of.

And then there is the high-tech SPOT. This is a satellite communication device specifically designed with the outdoorsman in mind. They have various models available, including ones with GPS tracking and communication abilities. You can signal that you need help with a SPOT and then it will lead rescuers to your location. Although these can be a great assistance, they are not commonly used due to the initial cost and ongoing monthly service fees. If you spent a lot of time outdoors, you might want to look into getting one.

Chapter 8

Navigation

You have decided that waiting for rescue is not your best option, and you are getting ready to strike out for civilization. Knowing which way to go and also knowing how to stay on course are vital skills and are not as easy as they sound. Traveling through unknown territory with minimal supplies can be daunting, and the last thing you need is to make yourself "more lost."

There are two factors: knowing which way you ought to be heading and then being able to stay on that heading as you travel. Unfortunately, if you are completely unaware of your position, the first part of this can be a problem. As mentioned earlier, that is the best case for staying put and letting help come to you. If you strike out blindly, you can make the situation worse.

Choosing a Heading

You need to be honest with yourself at this point and decide whether you can accurately make a decision about which way to go. If you know you have been hiking mostly northward since you began your camping trip, reversing that to head south is a reasonable decision to help find your original starting point. If you were heading west to a certain destination, then you can continue going west rather than try to turn back. It all depends on how much you know about your location.

Look for landmarks as well, not just as a source of direction, but to help give you a heading. If your destination was near a mountain peak or hilly area, you can safely say you know the proper course to take. When you have a map with you, you can further decide which is the proper direction even when you do not know precisely where you are.

When lost in a heavily wooded area, try to find high ground so you can scope out your surroundings better.

Knowing the general lay of the land can help greatly if you are on a hiking or camping trip. The unexpected disasters like car accidents or plane crashes are more likely to leave you in an unknown area. But be as aware of your surrounding as possible in the first place, and you will find it easier to establish a location and direction when you have to.

Using a Compass

A compass is such a standard survival tool that many people add them to their kits without a second thought and without any idea on how to effectively use them. All a compass will do is point to the north. You have to know how to properly hold it and how to orient yourself so you can travel in the direction you want.

First, hold the compass steady and level. If you do not have steady enough hands, set it down on a flat rock or even just the

ground. The nee-
dle will spin freely
with one end (usu-
ally marked in red)
pointing to the
north. Once the
needle stabilizes,
turn the compass
so that the mark-
ings around the

edge match the actual north heading. Again let it stabilize and see which way is your needed direction.

It is impractical to travel on foot while staring at a compass the entire time, and you can lose your heading within a few yards without even realizing it. The best technique is to establish your direction and then choose a landmark along that line. The farther away the landmark, the less often you have to stop and check your compass. Deeply wooded areas will not allow for too much long-distance sighting, but you should be able to find a good point of reference in the distance when traveling through open areas.

When you reach your landmark, get out the compass and re-establish your direction with the new landmark.

How to make a compass

Ideally, you will not find yourself lost without this vital tool, but you can create your own if you are. You will need to have a metal needle, like you would find in a small sewing kit. You also need a way to magnetize it. A magnet will obviously do, but you can also use a small piece of silk (which admittedly is not likely to be on hand in the wilderness). A small container that can hold water is also needed.

Using either the magnet or silk, stroke the needle from the eye-end to the tip about 30 times to magnetize it. Set the needle carefully on a dry leaf floating in the container of water. The magnetism will force the needle to align with magnetic north, and it should take the leaf with it. It will spin until the point shows you north.

Using a GPS Unit

Carrying a GPS usually means you do not get lost in the first place. Being stranded is not the same as being lost. Circumstances might put you in a position of wilderness survival even when you know exactly where you are. So do not discount the possibility that you could have a GPS on hand while still being stuck in the woods.

The specific features available to you will depend on the type of GPS you have in the first place. You may have full terrain and topographical maps at your fingertips, or you just might have cross hairs on a blank screen that only shows where you have just been. No matter what type of GPS you have, they almost all have a built-in compass so you should at least be able to establish your direction that way.

You might be able to turn on or off the display of your recent route (sometimes called your track). It should be on in these circumstances so you can see where you have already been. This can be helpful in ensuring you do not get turned around and end up back-tracking. You should use this even if you are only using the GPS as a compass. Seeing your track can make it clear whether you are managing to stay in a straight line as you travel.

Some GPS units are not sensitive to movement, and it can take several yards before the cross hairs even registers that you have moved. When traveling over large distances, this will not likely have any impact on your movements, though you should be aware of it in case you are starting to panic that your GPS is not working properly. Also, it will not be of much help if you want to establish your direction on the screen by taking a few steps back and forth.

To conserve your batteries, try to run your unit as little as possible. Use the same techniques as mentioned above to sight a landmark in the direction you want to go and focus on that while the unit is off.

Map Reading

As mentioned with the GPS unit, you can still be stranded in the wilderness while carrying a map. Car, boat, or plane trouble can leave you stuck in the woods even though you have a good idea where you are. So you just need to be able to follow your map to safety.

The first step before you can start to orient yourself by map is to make sure the map is pointing the right way. If you are lucky, you will be able to see landmarks and use them to orient the map properly. If not, you have to figure out the directions on your own.

Convention has it that the top of a map is north, but check the key or legend to be positive. Once you know which way is north on the map, you have to establish which way is actu-ally north. Using a compass for this is the easiest method, which has already been discussed. In the next section, you will find out how to use the sun or the stars to establish which way is north.

Use the same techniques as explained for traveling with a compass so you do not have to continually stare at your map. Establish where you are heading based on the map and pick a landmark you can see to head toward. Use that as your guide so your map can stay safely folded in your backpack while you hike.

You also need to be aware of the scale on a map. If you are not familiar at all with map reading, this can be a little hard to visualize until you get a little more experience. Near the legend, there should be a small bar and indication as to the distance that bar represents. Hypothetically, a half-inch could represent 1 mile or 10 miles depending on the map. This is vitally important when you are striking out. What looks like a short walk to a stream may take you all day because you have misjudged the scale.

Near the scale is the rest of the legend, also worth looking at. Some of the symbols for terrain may not be that familiar (or obvious). You do not want to plan a track unnecessarily through a swamp for example.

Lastly, look for elevation lines. This is a little more complicated if you do not usually read a map but it is a crucial piece of information if your map has them. Most topographical maps do, but simpler road maps may not. They are lines marking the elevation of the ground, and they look like irregular concentric circles on your map. Each line represents a number of feet above sea level, which may not seem that important at first glance. What you do 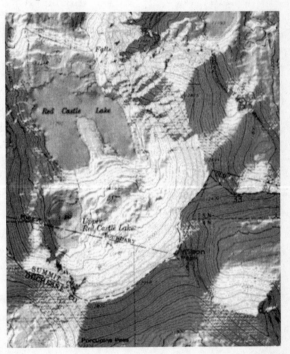 need to look for is how close the lines are to each other. When the lines are close together, it means that the terrain rapidly changes elevation. In other words, it is going to get steep. Take that into account when planning your route. A steep climb (either up or down) is not only more strenuous but also more risky.

Navigating by Nature

If you have no tools to guide you at all, then you will have to rely on other methods to get your bearings. There are a few time-honored methods for navigating by the sun and stars.

By the sun

Because you are not as likely to be traveling at night as you are in the day, this is probably going to be your main approach. Fundamentally, the sun rises in the east and sets in the west. But you can use the gradual movement of the sun through the day to establish a direction.

Find an open clearing and preferably an area of bare dirt. Cut a sturdy stick that is around 2 feet long and as straight as you can. Pound it into the earth so that it stands up freely. If the soil is too hard, you can use a pile of smaller rocks or snow to brace it up. Once it is in place, use another small stone to mark the end of its shadow on the ground.

Wait for at least half an hour, and then place another stone at the tip of the shadow. Do the same thing one more time after another half an hour. You should now have three stones in a straight line. That line runs from west to east (the newer stones are at the eastern end). Draw another line directly perpendicular and you have a pretty good northern heading.

By the stars

This is a less useful approach because you are not going to be doing much navigating at night. Nonetheless, you should at least understand how to find north by the stars. If the weather has been overcast through the day and clears after sundown, you can get a rough heading when the stars are visible rather than risk another cloudy day again.

Using the stars to guide you is a technique used by travelers for thousands of years, so it does have some merit. Of course, these were seasoned explorers, so do not expect it to be a snap to the novice. The easiest method to use is to find the North Star, which first means you have to find the Big Dipper.

The Big Dipper is one of the most easily recognized constellations in the sky, so that is the customary place to start. It looks like a large ladle with a bent handle. When you find it, the two stars that make up the edge of the cup part (opposite the handle) will line up perfectly with the North Star. In other words, let your eye follow a straight line from those two stars, known as the "pointers" until it comes to a single bright star on its own. That will be the North Star. Facing that star should point you directly north.

If the full moon is bright enough, you can use the same stick and shadow technique described in the previous section.

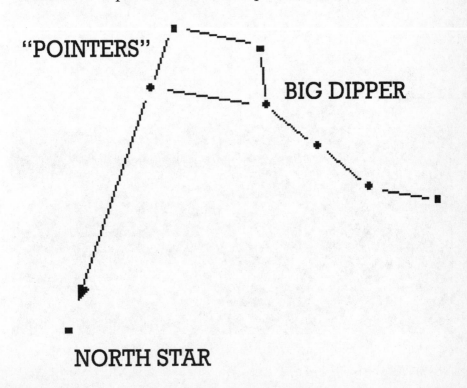

By water

Following moving water can help somewhat with navigation, though you cannot use a stream to help you locate north or any other direction. Moving water does indicate a downward slope though. If you are trying to find higher ground, follow a stream against the current (or vice versa for lower ground).

One well-known tip about getting a heading in the woods is to look for moss growing on a tree. The saying goes that moss will be lusher on the north side. Unfortunately, that is a highly unreliable method of establishing your heading. It may be true in some instances, but it is not always easy to tell and not all mosses have the same growing patterns. The other methods may take a little longer but will always give you the proper direction.

Chapter 9

First Aid

This section is a wide overview of potential first-aid situations and how to handle them, but it should not be considered a complete or thorough medical guide. When you are in an emergency situation with no medical aid and limited supplies, all first-aid issues are important and should not be ignored. A small injury that is left on its own can easily become a more serious and even life-threatening disaster in a short time.

If you are truly interested in being prepared for anything, find a local community college or St. John's Ambulance branch and take a certified first-aid course. Practical knowledge is the best approach to knowing first aid.

Burns

Trying to start and manage a fire in the wild can lead to more burns than usual. If someone does get a burn, it should be treated right away.

How to treat burns

First, immediately rinse the burned area in clean water. If your kit has burn ointment or antibiotic cream, apply them to the burn and lightly cover with clean gauze or dressing. A small burn can be left open to the air. Infection will be more likely with too much dressing so leave burns open as much as possible. When traveling through the woods, wounds like this should be covered to keep out debris.

Gauze pads or strips can be used to cover a burn, and they should be changed at least daily, more often if the burn is seeping or bleeding heavily. If you are short on bandages, you can rinse them out and boil them for at least five minutes. Once cooled and dry, you can use them again.

Sunburns

These are a unique type of burn that can easily affect anyone trapped in the outdoors for extended time. It can develop without you even realizing and can cover a large part of your body, so make sure you take care to prevent one. When walking in the sun, stay as covered as you can without putting yourself at further risk of overheating. Find a shady spot and stay put if necessary.

If you get one, there is not going to be much you can do. Covering the area lightly with gauze and keeping it wet with cool water can help.

Hypothermia

Hypothermia is a cold weather risk, and it means your body temperature has dropped below 98.6 degrees F (37 degrees C). It can quickly become fatal if not dealt with right away because your body is going to lose its ability to keep your internal organs warm enough to function.

How to recognize hypothermia

The person will have uncontrollable shivers, a lack of coordination, and mental confusion, and they will usually start to feel quite sleepy. If you are alone, you need to be careful because clouded judgment can also set in, which makes it difficult for you to realize there is a problem.

These symptoms also have to be paired with cold weather, though you can get hypothermia even if the temperature is relatively mild but you do not have sufficient clothing or shelter.

How to treat hypothermia

Needless to say, the treatment is to warm the afflicted person immediately. Wrap him or her as much as possible to prevent any further heat loss, and provide additional heat through heat packs positioned on the chest (not directly on the skin). The body heat of someone else in your group can provide extra warmth, if possible. Get them sheltered from the elements as much as you can while you warm them back up.

How to prevent hypothermia

The simple answer is that you need to keep warm at all times, but this can be a difficult task when trapped in the woods with few supplies. You have to take particular care and stay sheltered as much as possible when the temperatures are low. Built as secure a shelter as possible and stay by a fire rather than try to move even if you feel that you can reach safety. Unless you are used to traveling in cold weather, it is easy to overestimate how far you can go before succumbing to the cold.

Frostbite

This is another cold weather danger. Frostbite can be serious but it does not result in death as quickly as hypothermia will. It refers to the freezing of tissue, usually at your extremities (fingers, toes, nose, ears), and there are varying degrees of severity.

How to recognize frostbite

The first stages of frostbite usually leave the affected area itchy and quite painful, with white or red areas. It is sometimes just called frostnip at this early stage. If the tissue continues to freeze, you can develop blisters, which may fill with blood and have a black appearance. Frostbite at this point should not be ignored or allowed to get any worse.

When the skin starts to freeze, it can become numb and once the pain has passed, people often feel that they are fine. This is how frostbite can develop severely, because people who are affected choose to do nothing once the pain has gone. If you start to see red swellings, you have to stop and do your best to rewarm the tissues even if it no longer hurts.

How to treat frostbite

There are several myths about frostbite and commonly held "advice" about treating it that is no longer considered safe. Do not rub frostbitten body parts with snow or cold water. In fact, do not try to vigorously rub them at all or you could further damage the frozen surface tissues.

You need to warm these areas up with contact warmth, rather than just sitting in front of a fire. Cloth soaked in warm water, or even just contact with another part of your body will work. Do not use hot water. It should be comfortable to the touch before being used on the frostbite. If there are blisters, try not to pop them or open them up.

If you are not able to guarantee that the areas will not freeze again, you may want to wait to treat them. Any frostbitten part that is warmed, only to re-freeze again is going to be more damaged than if it had just been left alone in the first place. This can be a tricky issue in the wilderness when you do not know how long you are going to be outside. Once frostbite starts to be a concern, you might want to reconsider your plan of moving to safety and try to establish a warmer shelter to stay put.

How to prevent frostbite

As with hypothermia, the best prevention is to stay warm. Extremities are the hardest to keep warm if you are traveling in the cold, so you have to pay close attention. Keep your at-risk body parts covered as best you can, and avoid staying out of your shelter any longer than necessary. Wear two pairs of socks if you have them, or even wrap your feet with other fabric if you can to add insulation in your shoes or boots. Wrap a towel or cloth around your head to protect your ears and keep your hands tucked under your arms.

Poisoning

This is a real danger in a wilderness scenario once you start looking around to forage for food. Drinking unsafe water can also lead to poisoning, or at least illness that comes from parasites or other toxic organisms.

How to recognize poisoning

Poisoning can be harder to identify, and the symptoms might not appear right after eating or drinking the offending substance.

Not only that, there are such a wide range of potential symptoms, there is no way to list them all. You may experience any of these symptoms:

- Rapid or slowing heart rate
- Drowsiness or confusion
- Drooling
- Nausea, vomiting, diarrhea
- Dizziness or disorientation
- Changes in your breathing patterns
- Stomach or abdominal pain
- Headaches
- Hallucinations

Keep in mind that nausea and vomiting are extremely general symptoms and may not indicate that you have poisoned yourself.

How to treat poisoning

First aid is difficult enough in an emergency, but poisoning is particularly dangerous when you have no access to medical care. If you suspect you have eaten something poisonous, make yourself vomit as soon as possible. The sooner you get it out of your system, the better. When you start to get symptoms and suspect that it was something you ate or drank hours or even days ago, vomiting will not make much difference.

The ill person should rest and try to drink as much clean water as you can spare to help flush out their system. If the person is unconscious, you cannot do anything until he or she comes around. Then get him or her to drink.

How to prevent poisoning

This is a simple idea and does not require much explanation: Do not eat or drink anything that is suspect or that may not be safe.

Water is the biggest risk because you cannot go long without drink. On the other hand, starvation can take weeks, so keep the risks in perspective when trying to eat or drink anything in the wild. Suffering the effects of poisoning may not be worth it if you can avoid eating something questionable.

Always boil or otherwise purify your drinking water, and keep your hands clean when handling anything you eat. Never try to eat anything unless you are extremely sure of its safety. Any meats should be cooked extremely thoroughly even if you do not like the texture.

Cuts and Abrasions

These types of simple wounds are the most common problem in a wilderness situation, and they are easy to see and understand. Any time that you have an open wound, with a cut, tear, or puncture, treat it seriously even if it is not bleeding excessively.

Treating the wounds

For a bleeding wound, your first goal is to stop the bleeding as much as possible. A deep cut might need stitches in order to do this (see next section on that) but you can get bleeding to cease with the application of pressure. Use clean cloth or bandages to cover the wound, and hold tightly until the blood stops flowing. A tourniquet is only necessary if the bleeding is really heavy and regular pressure to the wound is not enough.

To make a tourniquet, use a length of cloth, rope, a belt, or anything similar. Tie it around the arm or leg above the wound to stop the blood flow (this method will only work on an arm or leg that can be tied off). Leave it in place until you are able to staunch the blood with more bandages or stitches. Remove it as soon as you are able to prevent any further tissue damage to the limb due to the stopped blood.

Antibiotic ointment can be applied to the wound once the blood stops. Then you want to cover it with dressing to keep it clean.

Bandages and dressings

Small cuts can be covered easily with an adhesive bandage strip (a Band-Aid), and these come in many shapes and sizes for various wound types. These are great for convenience and to keep a small wound clean, but they are not good at absorbing much blood. If the wound is still bleeding, then you will want a larger kind of dressing.

A more versatile approach is a pad (or two) of gauze, held in place by a larger wrapping of gauze strips or adhesive medical tape. This can absorb more fluid and is a more sturdy way of wrapping a wound.

Change the bandages regularly, at least daily, to keep the wound clean. Twice a day would be better. When supplies are limited, clean used dressings by boiling them for about five minutes in water. Let them dry thoroughly and reuse. Apply additional ointment as long as your supply lasts.

Stitches and sutures

If the tear in the skin is wide or deep enough, the wound might not stop bleeding on its own. You will have to close it with either stitching or adhesive sutures. It might seem like a daunting task, but it is not that difficult.

Small but deep cuts can be closed with adhesive butterfly sutures. *These were mentioned in Chapter 2 as supplies for a first-aid kit.* These small bandages are roughly H shaped, with two small adhesive pads on either end and a thin strip of non-stick material in the middle. Their purpose is to pull to sides of a cut together and hold them. You do not use these to stop blood flow or to protect a wound.

Attach one half of the strip to one side of the wound, and then pull the cut closed as best you can and then attach the other half of the strip on the other side. Use several of them along the length of the cut to keep it even. Use a loose bandage over top to keep the cut clean and to absorb any blood.

If you do not have any suture strips, or the cut is too large, you will have to resort to emergency stitches. You can use a regular needle and thread that would come in a small sewing kit as long as you sterilize your tools in boiling water. In an emergency, how you work the stitches is not that important as long as you are able to bring both sides of the cut together. Proper techniques can be learned through a first-aid course if you want to master the art a little better.

Super glue is one other alternative to help close up a cut in an emergency, though it can be a little dangerous to use. If you use in improperly, you can do further damage to the skin (or to the fingers of the person applying it). It is not as simple as it sounds either. The glue should be applied on the skin just beyond the cut where the skin is intact, and then the raw edges need to be rolled under. You need to glue intact skin together and not let any glue get right in the wound itself.

Doing any of these procedures improperly can result in a nasty scar, but compared to the alternatives — bleeding to death or getting a massive infection out in the woods — it is not that important a detail.

Broken Bone

A broken bone is a serious injury and can be difficult to properly deal with without the right equipment. There are some techniques you can use to treat the injury until a proper cast can be applied.

How to recognize a broken bone

Surprisingly, you can break a bone in a seemingly minor fall and might not realize you have done so. It is painful and you might not be able to move the limb properly. The person who is injured might hear a distinctive snap, and he or she might be able to feel the edges of the bone grinding when moving.

Swelling at the point of the break is common, either from inflamed tissue or the actual displaced bone itself. Small hairline breaks can be harder to determine because they will not necessarily feel like a break.

How to treat a broken bone

Only try to treat an arm or a leg break. Any bones that might be broken in the torso (ribs, collar bones, pelvis, etc.) should be left alone, and the injured person should not be moved.

The basic premise is to immobilize the broken bone. You will further injure the limb if the raw edges of the bone move against each other because it will make the break worse and damage the surrounding tissue. The severe pain can also be debilitating and can lead to the person going into shock.

You immobilize the break with a splint, which is actually quite easy to fashion out of simple on-hand materials. One or two heavy sticks and a means to tie them to the broken limb are all you need. Rope, strips of fabric, or duct tape can all be used. The sticks or branches should be straight and free from sharp protruding twigs. Tie one on either side of the break, and make sure there is some cloth or padding between the skin and the splints.

A broken arm can be further protected by making a cloth sling, but you cannot do the same with a leg. A crutch can be used if you are traveling over easy terrain, though it may be wiser to stay in one place when someone in your group has a broken leg.

Blisters

If you have made camp and are not traveling too much, then you might be able to avoid getting blisters in the first place. But hiking all day will quickly take its toll on your feet, and that usually means blisters. A blister is a fluid-filled bubble that forms under your skin in response to friction against a part of your foot over time. You can also get them on your hands if you are doing heavy work in gloves.

How to avoid blisters

Well-fitting shoes and socks are your best bets to preventing a blister in the first place. If you feel your shoes are starting to rub and creating a sore spot, treat it right away before the blister forms. Cover the rubbed area with a Band-Aid or piece of moleskin to prevent any more chafing. Take a break from walking if you have to. It is better to lose a little time now than be completely unable to walk later due to blistered feet. When your socks are damp, remove them and either air them out or change to dry ones.

How to treat blisters

If the skin has already come away from the blister, treat it like any other open wound with antiseptic and a bandage. The skin over a blister can protect the flesh underneath from infection, so you do not want to pull it off on your own. That includes popping a blister that is intact.

Covering a small blister with a bandage is fine, but if it is too large, you will have to carefully drain it so that the skin does not burst on its own. Use a flame to sterilize a needle and gently puncture the blister. Let it seep as much as possible and then cover with a bandage.

Sprains

A sprain is much less serious than a broken bone, but it can be a serious enough injury to keep you from traveling or doing any heavy work.

How to recognize a sprain

A sprain is the twisting or pulling of the ligaments surrounding a joint and can sometimes be as painful as a break at first. There will be pain, swelling and, difficulty moving the injured joint. It typically happens when you get your ankle twisted when walking over uneven terrain, but any joint can be sprained.

A person with a sprained elbow or wrist can still travel, but a sprained ankle will mean you have to make camp and stay put for a day.

How to treat a sprain

There is little you can do but rest the injured joint. Keep it elevated while you rest, and try to keep it as cool as possible. Soaking in a stream can help with this. If your first-aid kit has any elastic bandages, you can wrap the joint to keep it immobile and to help keep the swelling down. Do not wrap so tightly as to cut off the natural flow of blood. After about 24 hours, you should be able to walk again as long as you are careful.

Rashes

A rash is a skin irritation that is less serious than the injuries so far described but that should still be taken seriously. It is usually itchy and can be painful as well. Left untended, even a simple rash can become severe and get infected.

How to identify a rash

Because there are dozens of potential causes for a rash, it can be difficult to determine what exactly you have. In the wilderness, most rashes are either going to be causes by an allergic reaction with a plant or some sort of chafing due to the rough conditions.

A rash caused by poison ivy is common. *There will be more on identifying poison ivy plants is in Chapter 10.* This is going to be an itchy rash that looks like small fluid-filled blisters. Though you should not scratch such a rash, doing so will not cause it to spread. The plant oil already on your fingers is what spreads it.

How to treat rashes

This can be difficult without supplies. Unless you have calamine lotion or cortisone creams in your kit, you can do little other than keep the rash area clean. If your skin is chafing against your clothes or the gear you are carrying, cover the sore area with bandage so nothing rubs against it, or change how you are carrying your equipment. Damp clothing can also cause a chafing-type of rash, so do not let your clothes stay wet for any longer than necessary.

Wash your hands as often as possible to keep any possibly toxic plant residues that you have touched from spreading.

Bites

Bites can come in many shapes and sizes, and they are all going to be a problem. Some will be mostly a nuisance, but some can create significant injury.

Animal bites

These types of bites can cause a sizeable injury just in tissue damage, but then can be a greater risk by causing illness or infection if the animal was sick. An illness like tetanus or rabies is a serious problem that cannot be treated unless you happen to be carrying the proper medication with you (which is highly unlikely). So the only aspect of a serious animal bite you can deal with is the injury itself, just like any other cut or abrasion.

Insect bites

Most insect bites are going to be an annoyance rather than a serious threat. Mosquito and fly bites are the most common and bee stings are another possibility (though technically not a bite, a sting injury is similar). If you have an allergy to bee stings, make sure you are carrying an EpiPen® (Epinephrine Auto-Injector) or similar treatment with you. Without one, a sting can be fatal and there is little you can do in the wilderness should this happen. For anyone not allergic to bee stings, carefully pull out the stinger before you put on any kind of bandage.

Other insect bites will hurt and are often quite itchy. Do not scratch; cover the bite with a bandage if you cannot seem to stop yourself. A cloth with cool water can help with the itch temporarily.

A spider bite is going to be more serious and possibly fatal. To avoid these types of bites, do not stick your hands into any confined areas you cannot examine for spiders first. Use a stick to clear out an area before any hands are used unless you have heavy gloves.

All spider bites are going to be poisonous to some degree. Most will only cause a swelling at the bite area and a painful sore. Keep these bites clean and bandaged as they can develop into larger lesions. If further symptoms of poisoning develop, let the person who was bitten rest and try to provide them with as much water as possible.

Snake bites

Snake bites are a bigger potential danger in southern or tropical areas, compared to farther north, so you might not have to contend with this. Many snakes are not poisonous enough to seriously harm a person, so do not assume a snake bite is automatically a death sentence. Knowing how to identify the snakes in your area can help you know what has bitten you, though you will not be able to do much about it in any case.

As with other bites, first wash the wound thoroughly. If the snake is a poisonous one, the person should stop traveling. Make camp to let him or her rest. Too much exertion will speed up the poison's effects.

Common survival myths about snake bites are well known, such as cutting around the bite to release the venom or trying to suck it out by mouth. These are not effective and usually cause more harm than good.

You are best to avoid any snakes you do see, and keep your eye open when traveling in high grassy areas to spot them before a bite is a risk. Listen for the sound of a rattlesnake if they are common in your area, and take every precaution to avoid them.

Leeches

Getting bitten by a leech is a little different than the previously mentioned scenarios, and you will only have this happen if you are wading around in stagnant or swampy water. Tropical regions (such as a true rainforest) will also have some leeches that live outside of water, so you might get a bite just walking through the forest.

These black slug-like creatures are not going to be particularly harmful, though it can be disconcerting to see one attached to your arm or leg. The bite will not hurt, and you probably will not even feel that you have been bitten. The danger is any subsequent infection from having a cut.

The standard technique of sprinkling salt on a leech will work but is not a safe way to remove it. They have a habit of reacting when stressed this way and will regurgitate their blood meal back into your wound. Infection will be much more likely if you let this happen, so you will have to be more gentle. Theoretically, you could just leave it alone and it will safely drop off on its own once it has finished its meal. Otherwise, use your fingers to gently push the leech from the side where it is attached to you. Just make sure it does not bite you again once you pry it free.

Once the leech is gone, you can cover the bite with a bandage; there is little else that needs to be done. It will probably bleed more than you would expect because the leech secretes an anticoagulant when it bites you. Keep it clean, and you should have no further problems.

Heart Attack

This is a serious health risk, and it is most likely going to happen during the incident that puts you in your survival situation (car accident or plane crash). It can also hit during periods of high exertion or stress.

How to recognize a heart attack

The main symptom is pain and extreme tightness or pressure across the chest. The pain might radiate down the left arm, though not in all cases. Some heart attack victims do not get any chest pain at all.

Other possible symptoms include:

- Lightheadedness or dizziness
- Confusion
- Nausea
- Vision problems
- Shortness of breath
- Excessive sweating
- Rapid or otherwise irregular heartbeat

A small episode might seem more like heartburn or acid reflux than a true heart attack, so pay attention to even minor symptoms.

How to treat a heart attack

There is no real treatment you can provide in the wilderness for a heart attack, unless you happen to be packing nitroglycerin pills. In that case, follow the instructions you were given when they were prescribed.

If someone in your group has what you think is a heart attack, let them rest and try to recover. Travel is not a good idea at this point, so make permanent camp and wait for rescue.

How to prevent a heart attack

Even with high exertion, a heart attack is unlikely unless a person already has a heart condition or is older. The best prevention is to try to reduce your stress levels, which is admittedly difficult in an emergency situation, and to also keep your physical activity to a reasonable level. If you are out of shape, trying to hike up a mountain can be too much for you to handle. Be realistic in your attempts to travel or do other building chores.

Choking

Choking is easy to recognize as long as you do not overreact to a coughing fit. True choking means the person cannot breathe at all, so if they are talking while coughing then they are not actually choking.

How to treat someone who is choking

Treatment will need to be provided immediately, as choking can lead to death in a matter of minutes. A hard whack on the back is a common attempt at assistance, though it usually does not do all that much good.

The Heimlich maneuver is your best approach to dislodge whatever is obstructing the other person's airway. This is something to learn in practice rather than just by reading the instructions if possible. Watching first-aid videos or taking a course will help you. The basic steps are:

- Stand behind the choking person
- Put both arms around them and join your hands in a fist
- Position your fists right below their ribcage
- Give four or five sharp pulls inward with your arms

This will force the abdomen and diaphragm upward, which will create a hard push of air outward from the lungs. Ideally, that will dislodge what is caught in the throat.

Dehydration

Dehydration will start to affect your body when you have not had enough water to drink. This is a common problem in any survival situation and should be a constant concern. *Chapter 4 covers all the details on acquiring water and how much you need to be drinking.* You will need to have at least a gallon of water per day for drinking to stave off symptoms of dehydration.

How to recognize dehydration

The obvious first symptom is that you feel thirsty. Once it gets past that early stage, you will start to get headaches, confusion, nausea, and fatigue and you will start to have impaired judgment. If you have not had much to drink after a day or two, you will already know that dehydration is a risk regardless of what symptoms you may or may not have.

How to treat dehydration

Drinking water is clearly the best treatment, though adding a little salt can help your body balance its electrolytes quicker if you have gone without water for too long. About half a teaspoon of salt in a quart of water is enough. Without this, it will just take longer to recover, so it is not crucial. Having a few packets of salt in your supply pack would be handy for this purpose.

If you do not have any drinking water at all, you can do little other than try to rest and avoid losing any more water from your body than necessary. Even potentially contaminated water is better than nothing because thirst will kill you in a few days guaranteed. Bad water may give you parasites, but you can deal with that after you have gotten back home.

Do not resort to drinking your own urine, an idea that has become popular in survivalist circles lately. Your body has disposed of all those chemicals for a reason, and you will do your body more harm by trying to reclaim the water this way. On the other hand, you can collect your urine in a container and use a solar still (*described in Chapter 4*) to pull some much cleaner water from it.

Heat Stroke

This often goes along with dehydration when traveling or working in hot weather. In many ways, it is the direct opposite of hypothermia and happens when your body can no longer maintain the proper internal temperature.

How to recognize heat stroke

A person with heat stroke will obviously have a high body temperature, but also difficulty breathing and a rapid heartbeat. A thermometer (you likely will not have one) will register at least 104 degrees F or higher, and the skin will be red and flushed.

How to treat heat stroke

You need to cool the person down immediately. Get a rough shelter in place and get him or her out of the sun right away if you have no natural shade nearby. Fabric soaked in cool water can be placed on the head and neck (even if the water is not drinkable) to help speed the cooling process. Drinking extra water is helpful even if he or she has no immediate signs of dehydration.

How to prevent heat stroke

Staying cool when you are struggling to survive in hot weather is just as difficult as staying warm in cold weather. Without proper shelter and water supply, this can be a real challenge. No difficult work or strenuous travel should be undertaken during the hotter parts of the day. Try to rest during these times and make use of the cooler periods of early morning and evening for anything really active. Covering your head with a hat or even leaves can help keep you cool while you walk or work.

Because you cannot control the weather, you have to plan your activities so you are not at risk in the heat.

Diarrhea and Vomiting

These are not illnesses or conditions themselves, but rather symptoms of some other problems. They are fairly common symptoms for many different things, and on their own they can be a serious health risk, so they are being included for their own treatment.

Of the two, diarrhea is the more common and is also more likely to be the result of something otherwise harmless. In other words, you can get diarrhea simply due to the change in diet even though all of the food you have eaten is safe and healthy. Vomiting is much more likely to be the result of an underlying health problem.

If you can, establish the cause of the problem and treat the person for that. In situations when you cannot tell exactly why the symptoms are occurring, you need to treat each person on his or her own. The loss of water is the biggest problem, so the person suffering must have additional clean water to drink as long as the symptoms persist.

Over-the-counter medications can go a long way in treating either of these problems, particularly diarrhea. Having several doses in your kit is a smart idea. However, even if you have this on hand, do not rush to medicate someone. Vomiting and diarrhea are your body's way to getting rid of something unhealthy or toxic, so allow the symptoms to persist for at least six hours before you try to provide medication.

Though they can be symptoms of poisoning, heat stroke, or other illnesses, most cases of diarrhea and vomiting are from unclean eating and drinking conditions. Try to improve your water treatment and hygiene if possible if you find this is becoming a problem over several days.

CPR

Cardio-pulmonary resuscitation (CPR) is a technique to stimulate breathing and heart rate in an unconscious person who has stopped breathing. Like the Heimlich maneuver, this is something best learned through practice, so you might want to take a first-aid course to learn how to do this properly.

Knowing when to perform CPR

This can be as important as knowing how to do it correctly, as you can cause a person more harm if you are trying CPR when it is not necessary. You can interrupt a healthy heart rhythm this way.

CPR is the correct course of action when someone is not breathing and has no pulse that you can find. If you do detect a pulse but no breathing, then you can perform just the respiration portion of the technique to keep the air flowing into their lungs. You should do full CRP when the person has no pulse. Someone who is conscious should never get CPR.

Situations when someone is most likely to correctly need CPR are after a near drowning or after the heart has stopped in a small heart attack.

Proper CPR technique

As mentioned, this is something that should be learned from professionals. Most people do have a general idea of the procedure after having seen it done countless times in movies or on TV, but that is not sufficient "training" to say you know how to do CPR.

The basic idea is that you put pressure over the heart with both hands and give a solid push downward (a compression) to replicate a heartbeat. After 15 compressions, you pause and give the victim a deep breath through the mouth. Provide another breath, then go back to chest for 15 more compressions. When the person starts to breathe on his or her own, stop working.

This is a simplistic view of CPR and should not be considered a full or complete tutorial on how to perform it.

Medicinal Plants

Plants are not only an important source of emergency food, they can also supply some basic medicine when you are in the wild. Although this information can be helpful, use any proper first-aid supplies first and only rely on these suggestions when you are running out of options.

Plantain

A description of this common "weed" plant can be found in the foraging chapter on page 109. Not only is it edible, but you can also take advantage of the anti-bacterial compounds  in the leaves to make a wound treatment. Heat torn leaves up in hot water, not to cook them, but enough so the leaves are soft and releasing their juices. Pack the leaves onto a wound to help keep it clean and to stop the bleeding.

Blackberry Leaves

Blackberries are a common edible fruit found in many regions of the world, but this plant has more uses than just a food source. A tea made from the plant's leaves can be consumed as a treatment for general stomach upset and diarrhea. Remember that you are boiling the leaves, not the fruit, so it will not taste sweet.

Mint Leaves

This is one medicinal plant that was not mentioned as a food source because it does not offer any nutrition.

The plants grow in shady areas but can

also thrive in the full sun. The leaves have a distinct textured appearance and often have a gray shading of fuzz to the undersides.

You can rub a leaf between your fingers and inhale the familiar scent to know if it is mint. You can drink tea made from the leaves for the fresh minty taste, but it also can help with nausea. Chewing the leaves can also freshen your breath.

Red Clover

Red clover is easily identifiable with its triples of oval leaves and purplish-red round flowers. You can use clover to help relieve cold symptoms, which are more likely

Robert H. Mohlenbrock @ USDA-NRCS PLANTS Database / USDA NRCS. 1992. Western wetland flora: Field office guide to plant species. West Region, Sacramento

to crop up when your body is under stress in an emergency situation. Simmer the flowers in water to make a tea, and drink it daily if possible to reduce symptoms, particularly a cough.

Feverfew

This last plant is known as a potent anti-inflammatory that can help bring down swelling and reduce pain. Feverfew has flowers like a small daisy (white petals with a yellow center), though it grows in clusters instead. If you can stand the bitter taste, chew on a few leaves to help lessen inflammation or headaches. Tea with a small handful of leaves will also work.

Chapter 10

Survival Skills

s just mentioned in the CPR section, some things are better to learn before you find yourself in a survival situation. These skills are "carried" with you regardless of where you are and can be more valuable than the physical gear you have on hand.

Being able to put a shelter together, build a fire, and identify edible plants are all crucial and fundamental survival skills that have already been covered in their respective sections of this book. But beyond this collection of core skills, you might want to learn some additional things to ensure you are well prepared for any scenario.

Knots

The rope in your kit can be used for a multitude of purposes, and knowing how to make the right knots is part of that. You might be surprised at the difference the right knot can make.

Different purposes will require different knots. Attaching a rope to a tree or a branch will need a different knot than trying to lash several smaller items together, such as a load of firewood or branches for a shelter.

Square Knot

This is a good basic knot, which some people call a reef knot. It is used to tie down a load when you need to fasten two ends of a rope together. The square knot is not strong enough to attach two separate pieces of rope together if there is going to be a lot of pull or a heavy load on it.

Hold one end of each piece of rope in either hand. Tie an over-hand knot by looping the right hand piece under the left one (like the first step in tying a shoe). Then you do the same action again, but now the left is looped under the right.

Square Knot

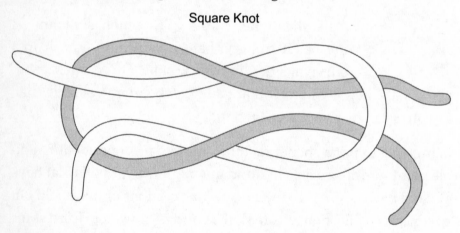

Clove Hitch

You use a clove hitch when you are attaching one end of rope to a secure object, such as a tree branch or a pole. This comes in handy if you are trying to string up a tarp when making a shelter, for example.

Take the end of the rope and wrap it once around the branch. Wrap it again, but tuck the end under the wrap you just made. Pull the loose end to tighten up the knot.

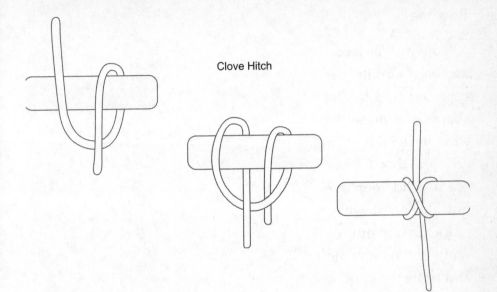

Clove Hitch

Slip Knot

This was mentioned as one of the knots used when making a wire snare, and it can be helpful in many other ways as well. Any time you need a knot with an adjustable loop, you can use this.

Hold the rope in two hands, and twist it to make a loop. Pull the rest of the rope (not the loose end) back through the loop so that you have created a loop that slides through a simple knot.

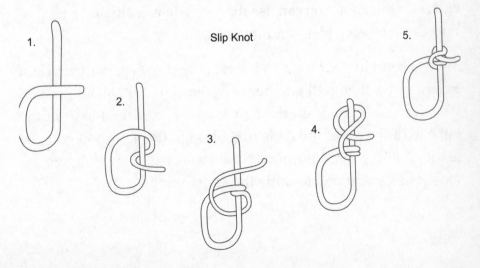

Slip Knot

1.

2.

3.

4.

5.

Bowline

A bowline also cre-
.ates a loop in the
rope but it holds its
shape and does not
slip or tighten. You
can use this to cre-
ate a solid loop for
quickly hooking over
branches or stumps
without having to tie
and untie the knot.

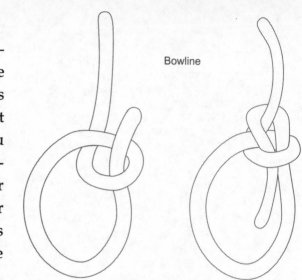

Bowline

About a foot or so from the end, make a loop in your rope. Bring
the loose end down through the loop, wrap it once around the
main length of rope just below the loop. Then pull the end back
through the loop. Give it a solid tug to tighten, and you have a
loop in your rope that will not slip.

Highwayman's Hitch

This is a secure knot that will untie quickly if you pull the trailing
end from the knot. You can use this one when setting up a temporary camp or even just bundling up gear.

Make a bend in your rope on the far side of the anchor (such as a
tree branch), then pull another bent portion of the main rope on
the nearer side, through the first loop. Make a final loop in the
tail end of the rope, and slide that through the new loop you just
made. Pull the main portion of the rope to tighten and give the
loose tail a sharp pull to untie the entire thing.

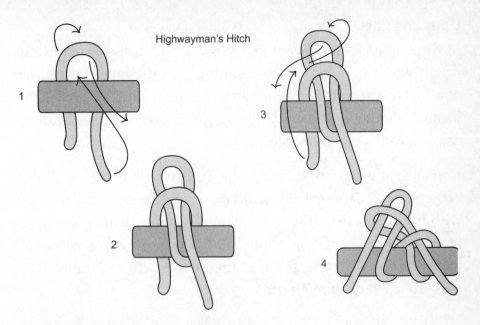

Highwayman's Hitch

Animal Tracks and Signs

You can use animal tracks for many reasons. Hunting down game to eat, following animals to water sources, or avoiding larger predators are a few examples. Muddy ground or snow will make it easier to recognize tracks, and you might have difficulty making out prints on dry grass or other less impressionable terrains. In that case, you might need to rely on other signs, such as scat (animal feces) to locate animals.

Some of these are animals you might want to find for food, and some might be animals you want to avoid. In either case, you will be more aware of the area around you if you can get a look at the wildlife population.

One other reason to look for animal scat is to help locate food. It is not an ideal method, but it can be helpful. If you find a lot of animal droppings with seeds in them, fruit is in season and within a reasonable distance.

Dogs and Cats

Most people are somewhat familiar with domestic dog and cat prints, and you *might* see these animals in the wild. If you see many of their prints, it might mean you are getting closer to civilization, though that is certainly not guaranteed, as feral animals can live well away from people.

Dog and cat prints are similar to each other, with most dog prints being slightly larger. They will both have a round central pad with four toe pads in the print that are separate from each other and the central pad. Dog prints have claw impressions while cat prints do not. The other prints in this section will be compared to these for a frame of reference.

Dog

Cat

Rabbit

Unlike most other animals on this list, a rabbit has a hopping motion to its gait. That means its hind legs tend to stay together rather than leave prints that alternate with the front legs. You will see two hind prints side by side and then front prints ahead of them. A rabbit's back feet leave long prints compared to the front feet, so you will have little difficulty recognizing these tracks.

Their scat is made up of small hard pellets that are quite round and a little smaller than a marble.

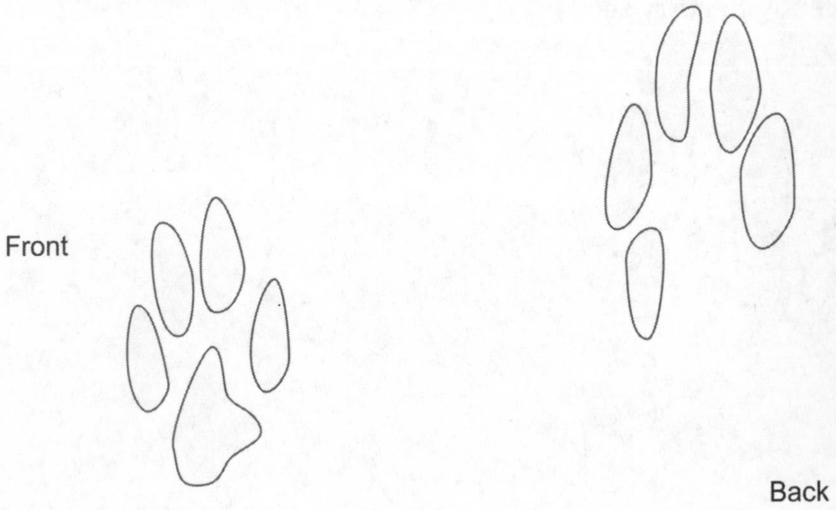

Front

Back

Raccoon

Raccoons make decent eating, but you might want to avoid camping in an area where there is a large population of them. They are curious and will wreak quite a bit of destruction in your camp overnight, which might cause you to lose valuable supplies you cannot replace.

The most distinctive feature of raccoon tracks are the finger-like toes. With cats and dogs, the pads of the toes create a print where you see four round toes that are separate from the rest of the footprint. With a raccoon, the print is more in one piece. It is narrow and looks like a small and elongated human handprint.

Muskrat tracks are similar but smaller, and you will not see any claw imprints with a muskrat. Raccoon prints usually have small marks from the claws.

The scat left by a raccoon will be tubular in shape and often is filled with berry seeds.

Front

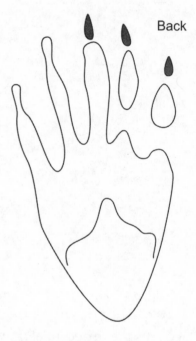

Back

Wild Turkey

You will get a lot of meat from these large birds if you are lucky enough to catch one. They do not fly long distances but are quite quick on their feet.

Their prints are hard to mistake for anything else. They have three large toes and no back toe, unlike many other birds. A turkey print will be between 3 and 4 inches long, much larger than any other land-walking bird in most regions. Pheasant and grouse make similar prints, though they are much smaller.

Droppings left by a wild turkey are similar to other birds, with a darker portion and white portion in one piece.

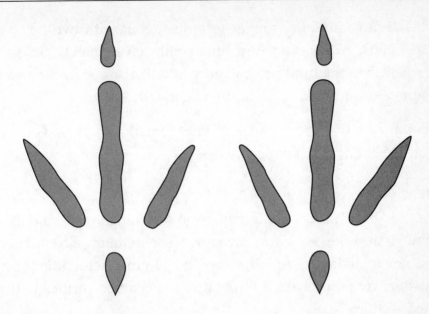

Skunk

The main reason you would want to identify a skunk would be to avoid it. Its strong defensive spray is not only unpleasant but also a little dangerous. It will sting badly if you are unlucky enough to get sprayed in the face. Also, if you were to be sprayed, you would have no luck whatsoever afterward in setting traps or sneaking up on any other animals.

Back

Front

Their prints are quite similar to a dog's, but with two notable exceptions. With a skunk, the hind prints have much larger center pad than the front prints, and you will also see five toe pad impressions instead of the four you get with a dog.

As for their scat, it is tubular and not remarkable. It tends to be pointed at one end, but not always.

Bear

Finding bear tracks should only mean one thing to you, and that is to go the other way. You have no reason to follow a bear. They are fierce predators and can easily kill a human with little provocation. Avoiding bear confrontations is covered further in the next section.

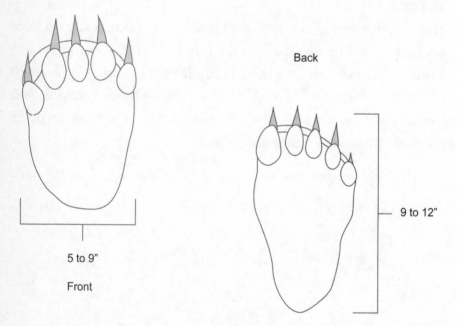

Back

9 to 12"

5 to 9"

Front

Bear prints are some of the largest you will find in the woods and are easy to identify. The hind paws are easily 8 inches long and the front ones are about 4. For the hind prints, the central pad is longer and slightly curved.

For droppings, bear scat is round and lumpish and often not particularly well formed. You can usually recognize it by the size rather than the shape. A pile of droppings is several inches across and can be seedy if fruit is in season.

Deer

It is unlikely you can hunt a deer with only your bare hands, but tracking one can lead you to a water source. The hoof prints of a deer are unmistakable. Each print is one solid imprint with a cleft in the front, and they will be about 2 to 3 inches long. Anything longer, closer to 4 inches or more is likely to belong to a moose. Although a moose trail can also lead you to water, a grown moose is a large animal, and they will attack humans.

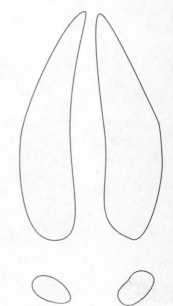

Deer scat is similar to rabbit, only larger. They produce piles of round pellets that are around the size of a grape.

Squirrel

Squirrels are common in the woods and are excellent targets for catching with wire snares. Their prints are smaller than the ones listed so far, though they do take the same pattern as the rabbit prints. That is, the hind feet are together rather than alternating with the front prints.

The back prints are narrow and about 2 inches long. The central pad usually only leaves a partial print, making it seem quite fine with a hollow space in the middle. The front prints have longish toes that are separate from the print of the central pad.

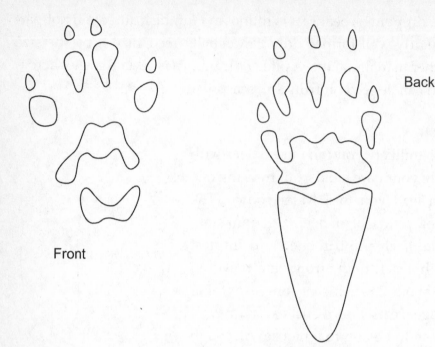

Back

Front

Beaver

If you find beaver tracks, you are almost certainly near a body of water. They also make a fine game animal, though they do not spend a lot of time on dry land and can be hard to trap.

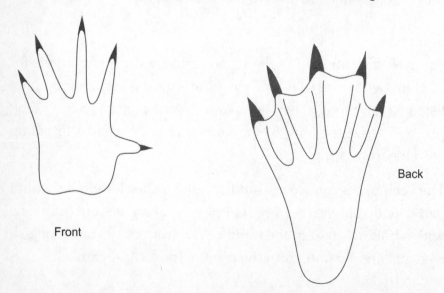

Front

Back

A beaver's tracks do not have distinct toes due to their webbed feet. Their hind prints look somewhat like a large duck, and their front paws give a hand-shaped impression. You can often see the trail from their large tail being dragged behind them as well.

Beaver scat is round, pale brown, and made up of woody material.

Mountain Lion

Like the bear, this is another large predator that you should not pursue or try to follow. As a big cat, their prints are virtually identical to smaller cats or even house cats. The only difference is the size. A mountain lion print is about 4 inches long. Their scat is also just like a house cat's: long and tube-like.

Opossum

An opossum has hand-shaped tracks similar to a raccoon's, though you will not see any claw impressions. The fingers are more spread out as well. The hind paws leave a more distinctive impression, with the "thumb" being bent almost backward. These animals can be snared and eaten and are considerably larger than a rabbit.

If you are tracking an opossum, they will have a "play dead" behavior that can work to your advantage. When you find one, give it a good scare and hope it drops "dead." That will give you a much better chance at catching it. Just take care when you pick it up. They can wake back up quickly and will put up a fight when they do.

Their droppings are tubular and will look quite a bit like a domestic house cat's.

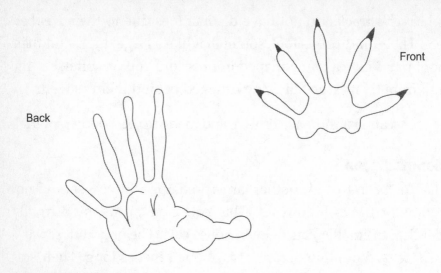

Front

Back

Other Wild Animals

Other wild animals that can have prints similar to a dog or cat are the weasel, mink, fox, coyote, and bobcat. Unless you are an experienced tracker, you probably will not be able to tell these prints apart. There are slight variations in size, shape, and claw length that you can use to tell one from the other as long as you have a really clear print to work with. If you are able to see claws, then it is related to the dog (fox, coyote); if there are no claws, then it is a cat track (bobcat or lynx).

This section has included the most common small game animals you are going to come across through most of North America. If you are going to be traveling in another part of the world, find a field guide to local animal tracks before you go out in order to be further prepared.

Avoiding Dangerous Animals

As if the lack of food, water, and shelter was not enough of a problem, you also have to contend with large predators and other dangerous animals when out in the wilderness. This would include animals such as bears, wolves, and mountain lions but also smaller ones such as snakes and spiders. Even normally docile animals such as raccoons can be dangerous if you corner them and they have to fight.

Large animals such as a moose can also be dangerous if you surprise them, and they will charge a human if they feel cornered (or if it happens to be mating season and they are feeling territorial). Moose attacks are not as uncommon as you might think because people make the assumption that they are harmless.

Obviously, the main tactic is to avoid them. For the most part, these animals will only attack if they feel threatened. They are unlikely to track you and deliberately hunt you down. The biggest threat is when you come across one unaware, so you are best to make your presence known as you travel. Humming, singing, or even making loud noises as you walk can help.

Watch out for tracks and scat belonging to potentially threatening animals, and change course if you are entering what looks like bear or lion territory. Also watch for any dead prey animals that have been torn or partially eaten. The predator might still be close by.

Never deliberately confront an animal or attempt to take it on. If you have come across one, the first thing to do is back away. Do not turn your back to it but also do not look it directly in the eye. Most animals will take this behavior as a challenge and will be more likely to attack if you do. Slowly back away while waving your arms and making some noise. You want to look bigger than you are while not directly challenging the animal. Once you are out of sight, make sure to adjust your route to stay out of the way or stay in one spot until the animal has moved on.

Carrying a stout stick with you can be helpful should you have to fend off an attack of any kind. On the off chance that an animal does attack you, drop to the ground and protect your head and neck with your arms or backpack.

Hiking Techniques and Safety

Experience hikers or campers might be familiar with the outdoors and will know the best way to travel safely. Walking through the woods can have its risks. Plan the easiest route if you can to keep yourself and your group safe. Even if it seems quicker to go over a rocky outcropping or through a steep valley, you are putting yourself at unnecessary risk by doing so.

Trying to travel at night is also dangerous. Not only can you not see, but many animals are more active at night. Stick to daytime travel and use your nights for sleeping. One exception would be during the hot summer weather. Taking advantage of cooler nights for some limited travel might be a smarter approach.

Do not plow through the woods without paying attention to where your feet are going. A misstep can lead to a badly twisted ankle or scraped up hands and knees if you trip. Cutting yourself a long and sturdy walking stick can be a great help to help keep you balanced and to add a little reach if you need to push brush aside or poke something suspicious.

When traveling in a group, watch out for the person behind you. Do not push a branch aside and let it smack him or her in the face as you let it go. Announce if you are about to travel through a thistle or burdock patch. This is just common courtesy, but you are trying harder than usual to avoid any small injury and keep morale up.

Also, when in the wilderness with a group, make an effort to stay together. Having one or two people head off on their own can lead to more trouble should there be an accident or they get further lost. Children should never be out of sight.

Climbing

The landscape might not be that easy to travel through. Forests and fields mean a lot of walking, but steeper or rocky areas can make things more difficult. Even a seemingly level forest can suddenly drop off into a ravine.

Plan your route to follow the safest route possible even if it seems to be a much longer path. Trying to climb up a rocky face is difficult in the best of times, but it can put your life in danger when trying to do it under strenuous circumstances. Loose rocks can come tumbling down at any time, adding further risk to you and anyone else climbing below you.

Should you fall down a steep slope, you might be unable to safely get out on your own. Examine the situation carefully before trying to climb up. If you are currently uninjured, consider yourself lucky and do not take on further risk. Either make camp where you are, or travel further along the base of the slope to find a more easily accessible spot to get out.

When you are traveling with others, you can get someone to help you out as long as you have some rope. Handmade cordage should not be used to pull a person because it will not likely be strong enough. Only try climbing up a slope with proper rope. If the person who has fallen is injured and cannot climb well on his or her own, use a bowline knot to create a non-slipping loop around his or her body and pull him or her out.

Crossing water

If your trail crosses water, do so carefully. Even a small stream can be a hazard with slippery rocks or a quick current. Only use rocks as stepping stones if they are fully above the waterline and dry. Submerged rocks will be risky to step on even if they seem flat or stable. Though it might seem prudent to keep your shoes dry, do not try to cross water in your bare feet. A sharp rock or piece of glass can easily be hiding under the surface and can leave you seriously injured. It is best to take off your socks and wear your shoes to protect your feet. Plan on resting on the other side while they dry, though, because walking in wet shoes is not good for your feet.

Choose a narrow and slow-moving area to cross, even if it means you have to travel a distance up or downstream from where you initially started. If there are no rocks to step on, you will have to walk along the stream bottom. Take small steps and always face toward the current. You can get knocked off your feet in 6 inches of water, so do not take it lightly.

Avoiding poison ivy

Though many dangers exist in the wild, poison ivy has a special place because it is so easy to come across and it will cause you serious discomfort just by brushing across it.

The old saying, "leaves of three, leave it be" is a sound piece of advice. Of course, many plants have triple leaves, but it gives you a place to start. Poison ivy is a low-growing plant with finely serrated leaves in groups of three. The leaves are glossy green for most of the year but can be reddish in the early spring as well as in the fall. Examine some photos before you head outdoors and get familiar with what it looks like.

Because it is low-growing (seldom taller than 12 inches high), your feet and legs are most at risk for contact. As long as you have your legs covered by high boots or pants, you do not have much to worry about unless you are rummaging in the undergrowth with your hands for something. But when just walking, you should be fine.

If you do come in contact with poison ivy, wash the area immediately. The oils from the plant will easily spread and make the oncoming rash worse.

Watching the Weather

Even modern science cannot predict the weather with pinpoint accuracy, but a watchful eye can help you figure out when rain is about to strike. When trying to survive with minimal shelter, knowing when rain or other inclement weather is coming can be important.

Gathering clouds will let you know rain is coming, particularly if they are dark and low. High clouds are not as likely going to lead to precipitation, so they should not be much of a concern. Take note of which direction the wind tends to come from. When it changes direction, it means a change in weather (not necessarily a storm, but a change of some sort).

Take a look at the sky at sunrise and sunset. The old saying "Red skies at night, sailor's delight. Red skies in the morning, sailors take warning" is an apt one that can help determine some short-term weather changes. The sky itself will be red for this to mean anything, not just the sun. When it is red at night, the next day or two will be clear and fair. If you see red at sunrise, you can expect a storm soon.

To avoid lightning, stay away from high exposed areas. If you are going to have to climb a rocky ridge, wait for the storm to pass before doing so. When in the woods, take shelter under shorter trees and avoid getting close to the tallest ones. Those will be struck first.

Lightning off in the distance will pose no threat to you or your camp, so listen for the thunder to establish how far away the storm is. The old tales we tell children about the time between a thunder roll and a lightning strike are pretty accurate. Count the seconds from when you hear thunder to when you see lightning. Divide by five to get the number of miles away the storm is. So if you hear ten seconds between thunder and lightning, you know that the storm is 2 miles away.

Getting struck by lightning is not a common occurrence, and these simple precautions are usually enough to stay safe.

Hygiene

Staying clean and as germ-free as possible is not easy even on a planned camping trip. But you will be healthier and in better shape to survive if you are able to manage at least some rudimentary personal hygiene until you are rescued.

Cleaning yourself

If you are lucky enough to have a campsite near a good source of water, you will have a much easier time keeping yourself clean. However, when water is in short supply, your cleanliness has to take a backseat to being hydrated.

Hand sanitizing gel is a good item to have on hand, but it will not last forever. Use it only to keep your hands clean before handling food and water to make it last. A simple bar of hand soap is another option for your kit, though it will not be much use if you have no water. With soap and water, you can keep your hands and face clean fairly easily. Beyond that, focus on your arm pits, feet, crotch area and genitals, and your hair. If your hair is long, you might want to cut it shorter with a knife or scissors to avoid additional cleaning difficulties.

Without soap, keeping your clothes clean will not be easy. With water, give your clothes a rinse and scrub with your hands every day or so and let them dry completely before re-wearing. If you

do not have any change of clothes with you, you may have to go without while they dry. Leaving the same clothing on for too long can lead to skin irritations and infections, not to mention emotional and morale problems. Even without water, take off worn clothing and let it air in the sun for a few hours to "clean" it.

Clean sand can be used in place of soap to help scrub away dirt, though it can be quite abrasive on delicate skin.

Teeth can be a difficult area to keep clean as well. If you have a thorough kit, you may have a travel toothbrush and toothpaste with you, but most people do not carry items like this with them. A small piece of cloth wrapped around your finger can be used to scrub your teeth each day. You can also cut a small twig from a birch tree and chew up one end to free up the fiber. This will make a decent temporary toothbrush. If there are no birch trees around, most others will do as long as they are not too heavy with oils or resins such as pine.

Waste disposal

This has yet to be addressed, and it is an important part of keeping a safe and clean camp area. If you are on the move and not staying in one place for more than a night, then it becomes less of a problem. Regardless of your moving plans, however, you will have to establish a proper latrine.

In either case, you will want to use the latrine at least 200 feet from your camp and just as far from any water source. For a temporary or one-time use spot, dig a hole about 8 to 10 inches deep and cover back over with dirt and rocks when you are done. When using the same spot for a longer period, dig a deeper hole. A small shovel will help here, but you might have to use your hands or a branch to help. Try to go 2 feet deep if possible.

Arranging a branch or log over the hole can help with seating or comfort but it is not necessary.

Each time you use the latrine, cover your deposit with a few inches of loose soil or ashes from your campfire. When the hole is full, cover it with another good layer of soil and rocks, then choose another location for the next latrine.

Needless to say, toilet paper may be unavailable or in short supply. Use it sparingly. When it runs out, you will have to make do with leaves. Either green or dry leaves will work as long as you make sure they are not poison ivy. Used leaves should be added to the hole and covered up.

Covering your waste is important to minimize the spread of germs and also to keep animals from coming to your camp area to investigate the smell. A proper area for this is vital for feces, but urination can be handled in a more casual basis as long as you are still 100 feet from camp or your water supply.

Fashioning Tools

When trapped in the outdoors with no supplies or only minimal items, you will need all the additional tools you can get. With a little ingenuity, you can create a number of helpful items from the materials you find in the outdoors.

Besides the obvious practical benefits to having additional tools to use, the act of making something can be a good way to pass the time and avoid boredom.

Containers

It might not seem obvious at first, but having enough containers is important. When gathering water or food, you will need to have someplace to put everything in order that nothing is lost or dirtied. Bowls, pots, bags, and boxes will all be quite valuable while you try and get by with only your existing set of supplies.

If you have access to birch trees, the bark is extremely useful for many things including some makeshift containers. Peel off a wide strip of bark (not just the fine papery layer on top, but the thicker layer underneath as well). To make an envelope-type pouch, gently fold the bark across the middle and then attach the two open sides together. Folding the bark with the inner surface inside will create a more cup-shaped pouch due to the natural curve of the bark.

How you attach the sides will depend on your supplies. You can stitch up the sides of the pouch with heavy thread or string, using the tip of your knife to puncture holes in the bark. A Swiss Army knife or other multi-tool may have a proper sharp awl you can use for the holes. Lace the string through the holes and tie a tight knot.

You can use split reeds or braided grass instead of string if necessary, which is covered more in the next section. To use less cordage, cut a half-circle piece of bark and twist it into a cone shape. Then you only have one seam to seal up.

Wooden bowls can be made from a large enough piece of wood. Using a knife or sharp-edged rock, dig away the wood from the center of the log. You can even light a small fire to burn away the center. Just make sure you have water nearby to put it out before it burns right through the log.

Cattail reeds or leaves are also good raw materials for making tools. Being able to weave them into a rough basket is simple, but you do need to know the right pattern and technique. An easy form would be to weave a flat mat by laying out a number of leaves and then adding a second layer going over and under the first leaves. Roll the mat into a tube and tie the end shut with rope or homemade cordage. It will not be as strong as bark, but it could hold collected berries, nuts, or other plant material.

Rope and lashing

Ideally, your survival equipment includes a good supply of rope. If not, you can use some natural materials to improvise some simple rope, string, or other lashing material.

The best source for lashing would be a naturally sturdy yet flexible vine. Wild grape is excellent for this and can be used to tie gear down or tie logs together for a shelter.

Many long fibrous plants can be used to make rope, though some are better than others. If you can locate milkweed, that is a good one to make cordage from. Nettle will also work, but it can be a little riskier to handle. The chapter on foraging for plants has a description for identifying milkweed as well as nettle. Neither is a quick process, so only bother with this if you have the time to spend on it.

Find milkweed stalks that are dead, and break them off at the base to get as long a piece as possible. Soak in water and leave them wet for a day or two so the fleshy material will rot away and leave you with easily handled fiber from inside the stalks. Once they are nice and soft, crush the stems lengthwise to break up the outer husk. Do not snap it across the stalk, or you might break the fibers. When the tougher pieces break away, you are left with thin fibers. This is what you want to work with.

It will not be as simple as spooling up some thread, but the fibers can be twisted and braided together to make a reasonably strong length of fine rope. Braiding is a simple technique that most people are already familiar with. You will need three lengths of fiber, knotted together at the ends. Lay them out straight, and then take the one on the right in your hand. Twist it over the middle piece so it is now in the middle of the three. Then take the left hand piece and put it in the middle of the other two. Continue this process all the way down to make a three-ply cord.

Long grasses can also make decent cord, and they can be used more easily than milkweed fiber. Twist several stalks together, and use three of these to braid into a heavier piece of rope. Overlap the next stalks as you get to the ends so the new pieces are braided in with the original pieces for a secure join.

Some tree barks can provide fiber for braided cords as well. Cedar is good for this if you can find it, but so is oak, cottonwood, or maple. Peel back the outer bark to get at the more fibrous material at the next layer. Take care to leave the pieces as long as possible to make a stronger final cord.

If you have any animals killed for food, you can use tendons or thin slices of hide to create more options for cordage. Any cord made from animal material like this can be quite strong but also less flexible than plant material once it dries. You will have to have killed several animals to have a decent amount of cord, so you would probably do better to rely on plant materials instead.

Bone tools

You do not necessarily have to have killed your own game in order to have a supply of bones. Any dead animal can provide you with good bones to use if you need to fashion certain items. Birds or mice will have fine bones that may not be sturdy enough, though that will depend on your intended purpose. Bones from larger animals will have more use.

Sharpening the tip of a bone can provide you with a reasonable awl, which is just a tool to punch small holes in things. The tip of your knife is not always the best tool for this because it tends to make a slit rather than a hole. A small bone awl can come in handy. You can create a bone awl by sharpening the end of a bone, but be careful not to make the tip needle-sharp or it will just break off.

Fish hooks can also be made from bone. Use your knife to create a sharp notch in the end of the bone and make sure the lower tip is quite sharp and that it points upward. Wood will also work, but it is usually not as hard or as sharp as a bone hook.

Bone is a versatile material, so if you have some bones on hand, use your imagination and see what you can make.

Making tools from stone, particularly chipping a stone to make a blade edge, is not something a novice will have much success with. It takes a practiced hand to crack stones together at the precise angle to knock chips off correctly. As long as you always carry a knife with you, you should not need to create any new blades anyway.

Chapter 11

Survival on the Water

his chapter is going to cover some of the unique aspects of wilderness survival should you be trapped on a boat or otherwise out on the open water. If you are stranded on a boat, many things so far discussed are not going to apply. You will not be able to do much for fire, and your options for food foraging are going to be quite limited. However, that does not mean you do not have a good chance at survival.

Signaling

In some ways, signaling can be more effective on the water than on land because there is nothing to obscure a potential rescuer's view. Your signals can be seen for a long way. You can use the same techniques as in Chapter 7, though there may be some adjustments for your circumstances that may make them more effective on the water.

Mirrors

With a lack of obstructing vegetation, a flash from a signal mirror can go a long way. Be diligent using it though, and try to establish a pattern if you see a plane or boat. The sunlight can shine brightly off the water, which can make your flash unnoticeable.

Flares

If you want to use light as a signal, chemical signal flares will work better, as they create a much brighter light that will stand out against the glare of the water. For a more noticeable signal, use flares that are shot out of a gun. They do not work in the woods but are ideal for signaling off a boat. Your supply will be limited, so only use them when another boat or plane is within view.

Smoke

Smoke can be a good signal because it is visible for such a distance and is unmistakable. Unfortunately, making smoke can be a problem on a boat, especially if you are on a small boat. You can purchase chemical smoke signals similar to the flares that can produce a large amount of smoke (usually orange). Orion makes good marine signals that produce orange smoke in a huge plume. It does not last long, so wait until a potential rescuer is within sight.

Flags

Although there is an official and internationally recognized set of flag signals, they are not commonly used among small-scale boaters. They involve a set of 26 specific flag designs and understanding the codes that go along with them. For example, the F flag means you are disabled, and NC means you need immediate assistance. Larger commercial vessels or rescue personal are more likely to know what they mean. You will have to have the set of flags on board though, and they are not cheap. Otherwise, a simple flag made out of red material should provide a universal signal of distress should someone be near enough to see it.

Flotation and Swimming

If your boat has completely sunk, you are going to be in a difficult position, and your first priority will be to stay afloat. Your boat should be equipped with proper safety equipment, including emergency flotation devices of some kind. Ideally, you will have a life vest on you to begin with.

If you spend time on a boat, you will also know how to swim to some degree. If you can see land, or know which direction land is in, then you will want to get out of the water as quickly as you can instead of just floating in one place and hoping for rescue. Simple skills such as treading water and the dog paddle are sufficient as long as you do not have to travel too far to get to land. A few basic swimming lessons at your local pool are all it takes to pick up these skills.

The human body is naturally quite buoyant, so you can stay afloat on your own without that much effort as long as you do not panic and flail around. You also cannot be loaded down with equipment in order to stay floating. If you must, let go of your gear. It is better to get to land unequipped than to drown with a loaded backpack of supplies. That said, you might want to have a flotation device of some kind already attached to a bag of supplies for this reason.

Repairing a Boat

A small boat such as a canoe or kayak can tip over and put you in the water without any damage to the boat. You just have to get it tipped back upright again and get back in (without tipping again). As soon as you tip over, make sure to grab your paddles and try to

get your bag of gear as well. Ideally, your equipment will be strapped to a floatation device or to the boat itself so nothing will be lost.

Other than a tip-over, you can get all kinds of leaks or other damage to your boat that may be repairable before you find yourself floating out in open water. A quick patch kit should be kept on your boat; read the instructions on using it before you head out. You may only have a few minutes to get the patch in place once your boat springs a leak. In a pinch, duct tape can do wonders.

A bucket to bail water or even a small pump should be on hand as well. Even if you cannot get the boat fixed or patched, you may be able to clear out the incoming water quickly enough to still navigate the boat to shore.

Engine difficulties will also strand you, but they are not that simple to repair on your own unless you are already familiar with boat motors and mechanics. To be on the safe side, always have extra gas and spare parts in case something needs a quick repair.

Navigating to Find Land

If your boat is still sound and even still running fine, you can still be in trouble if you get yourself lost. With no landmarks around, this is a significant possibility when boating. Knowing how to navigate can help you locate the nearest land. Once landed, you are in a better position to survive and get rescued.

With a map or a chart, you may be able to establish roughly where you are in relation to the coast. The techniques in Chapter 8 will all apply, except using a stick in the ground to follow the path of the sun. Because your boat is not stationary, this approach will not work. You will have to rely on the stars, the position of the sunrise/sunset, or a working compass. And because you may not have any solid landmarks to use to create a bearing, it will be much harder to maintain a steady course.

The other solution is to look around for signs of land that you can more easily see and plot a course toward. Cumulus clouds (the large puffy kind) usually form over land, so if you see clouds like this on the horizon, that would be a good direction. Also, many common sea birds (such as gulls) will fly over the water to feed but never stray too far from land. Seeing birds is another good sign that you are going in the right direction.

Just as in a land scenario, you do need to use your judgment in terms of staying or going. If you are guessing on a direction, it may lead you farther from civilization and rescue. Only try to find land if you genuinely have a good sense of where you are going and where you have ended up. Otherwise, you could make your situation worse.

Food and Fishing

Being stranded on a boat will mean you have a limited range of options for getting food beyond your packed supplies. Fishing will come to mind immediately, but you have a few other choices for getting additional food while out on the water.

Fishing

A small fishing kit should be part of your survival gear. With a hook and some line, fishing from a boat is probably one of the easier ways of getting fish, though you should not expect an instant result. You might have to wait for hours before anything bites. Unlike fishing on land, you are not going to have much bait handy. Sacrificing a bit of your existing food supply may be necessary. Many fish will also come to a hook without bait if you can add some other type of non-food lure to the line. A slip of red fabric or a piece of shiny metal attached to the line right near the hook can make a big difference when you have no food bait to offer.

The more important problem is not only getting food, but preparing it once it has been caught. Depending on the size of your boat and the equipment you have on board, you might not be able to cook any fish you get. Eating raw fish can be quite risky, and you should not resort to doing it unless you have been without food for more than a week (or two). A small fire could be started in a coffee can or other metal container for a short time, which would be sufficient to cook most small fish.

Aquatic plants

Other than fish, you can get food in other ways. Seaweed is a nutritious source, though not all waters will have a decent supply of it. These aquatic plants will be more difficult to find in open water, but if you are lost and traveling by boat along the shore, you can get added food without having to try and moor your boat. Small islands can also harbor a lot of seaweed along their shores, which might be the only edible thing available.

Kelp

Kelp is an easily identifiable plant that is common in Pacific waters, though not in any smaller freshwater bodies. It has long, broad leaves and is often found floating in patches on the surface. You can eat kelp raw or boil it for a few minutes in water for a more appealing taste. Kelp can be an important foraging food because it is found in open water rather than just along the shorelines.

Dulse

Dulse is another broad and leafy seaweed that has a dark reddish color. It usually grows near the northern shores of either the Pacific or Atlantic. If you are stranded far from shore, you will not likely find any. But if you are foraging near shore or are trapped on a small island, you will have better luck. You can eat dulse raw, boiled, or dried out in the sun.

Irish Moss

You can find this along the Atlantic shores of Canada, the UK, and some other parts of Europe. It is red in color similar to dulse, but the form is much more branching. Also like dulse, you can eat it raw or dried. It can be a little slimy if you eat it fresh out of the water, so you could dry it out in the sun until it is a little crisper.

Bladderwrack

Another northern ocean seaweed, found on both Atlantic and Pacific coasts, bladderwrack is dark green and more branching than kelp, and the leaves have little air sacs on them (hence the "bladder" in the name). Again, you can eat this food either raw or cooked. It will store nicely for later if you let it dry.

Duckweed

This is a lake or pond plant, so it will be more helpful if you are trapped on a large lake rather than out in the ocean. At a distance, it might look like a uniform layer of green "pond scum," but on closer inspection, it is a large number of tiny

Robert H. Mohlenbrock @ USDA-NRCS PLANTS Database / USDA NRCS. 1995. Northeast wetland flora: Field office guide to plant species. *Northeast National Technical Center, Chester.*

round leaves with small fine roots attached. Though small, the leaves are tough to eat raw, so you should boil it along with the water for a few minutes before eating/drinking.

Drinking Water

If you are trapped on a body of fresh water, getting drinking water will be less of a problem than if you are on a body of salt water. Fresh water will need to be dealt with in much the same way as any other water you would find in the woods. *That is covered in Chapter 4.* The only difference is that most larger bodies of water (assuming you are unable to see land on all sides) are going to be relatively cleaner than a smaller stream or lake. If you have the means to purify the water, then certainly do so. But if you do not, the water is less likely to be contaminated, so do not risk serious dehydration by avoiding drinking it.

With salt water, you will have less of an option. You can do little to make salt water safe to drink other than running a small solar still. *This was outlined in Chapter 4.* Solar stills are a reasonable approach even on a small boat as long as you have some plastic you can use to catch the evaporating water from a container.

Other than using the water you are floating on, you will have to capture rain in whatever containers you can find. Spread out a tarp or sheet of plastic to increase the amount you can funnel.

CASE STUDY: ALWAYS BE PREPARED

Mike Wilson
Kingston, Ontario
www.mikeoutdoors.com

Mike enjoys all the usual outdoor activities you would expect in Canada. He hikes, camps, and boats and spends time bow-hunting and fishing. Over the years, he has learned many important survival skills just through his own trial-and-error experiences.

When it comes to a survival kit, he has a good pack of basic supplies, and it goes with him anytime he leaves the house. He has a good quality multi-tool, GPS, compass, binoculars, small hatchet, wool hat and gloves, bottle of water, lighter, and a compact first-aid kit.

Aside from the gear he carries, he also has several good skills at hand to be used in any emergency situation. Mike can build a shelter from nearly any material, find edible plants, navigate by compass or just the sun, and set simple snares. He can also get a fire started by more than one method. To keep his skills sharp, he spends time outdoors nearly every week practicing at least one of these skills. Given the opportunity, he would love to travel north to learn more about survival in the high Arctic areas.

If Mike had to be trapped in the wilderness with only one thing, he would probably choose either his multi-tool or a flint/steel fire starter. He really couldn't decide on just one.

Thankfully, he hasn't been in any serious emergency situations yet to test his gear or skills, though he has had a few close calls out on the boat. He found himself lost on more than one occasion but was able, with some navigation skills along with the GPS, to establish his position and set a path to get back to where he intended to be.

For anyone else wishing to learn about survival skills, he recommends taking a good first-aid course. He also had this to say, "A human is much tougher than people think. Be prepared for anything and stay confident that you will get through."

Chapter 12

Winter and Snow Survival

Many aspects of survival in the cold have been mentioned in the sections on shelters and fire, but more challenges come with winter survival that should be addressed specifically.

Building a Snow Shelter

Ironically, building a shelter in the winter can be easier than in other seasons because snow is such a handy and abundant building material. When you have lots of snow to work with, and it is wet enough to "pack" nicely for building, you can put a quick shelter together with only snow. If the snow is drier, use branches and boughs like in a non-snow shelter to give it additional support.

With just snow, pile your snow and pack it down in a U shape. You do not need to leave a huge hole for the door, just space for you to wiggle through. Less heat will escape with a smaller door.

If the snow packs well, you can taper the walls in at the top to make a roof. Otherwise, pile branches and pine boughs across the tops of the walls for better roof support. Make your shelter large enough to hold yourself comfortably but not much larger. A smaller building holds the heat in better and will keep you warmer. If you have a group of people, it would be a good idea to build several smaller shelters that can hold two or three people. You can benefit from shared body heat. Much larger than that and the structure will be difficult to build and might not be sound enough to support a wide roof.

As with standard shelters, if you can find a place to build that is sheltered naturally against a rock face or fallen tree, do so to save time and energy in your building.

Another common way of building a shelter is called a quinzee, and it is not really the best idea when you are in a survival situation. With this method, you pile up a huge mound of snow and then dig out the center. It takes a lot more effort to move that snow just to dig it back out again. With food and heat in short supply, you do not want to exert yourself to that extent.

These mounds do not have as good a roof support; the top is not packed down properly, and they tend to collapse.

Staying Warm

This will be your first and foremost concern when stranded in the wintertime. The cold will kill you faster than hunger or thirst, so think about getting a heat source arranged before anything else. This means starting a good fire. *Chapter 3 covered all the details on this.* It may be harder to find a dry area to build your fire, though. A layer of branches or small logs can be used as a platform to get your fire up off the ground for easier starting.

Build your fire close to the entrance of your shelter but obviously not close enough to melt it if it is made with snow.

You can add additional insulation to your clothing with dried leaves. Just give them a shake to get rid of any bugs that may be hibernating and stay away from poison ivy leaves. Stuff handfuls of them in any space you can, particularly around your torso, arms, and legs.

Unlike a shelter built only with branches and boughs, a snow shelter is more airtight and will hold the heat in well. Even without an outside heat source, your own body heat will help raise the temperature inside more than you might expect. With additional insulation (leaves, pine boughs, emergency space blanket), you can find yourself relatively comfortable even in cold weather.

Getting Water

Finding an unfrozen source of water can be hard, maybe even impossible, in the dead of winter. Your only option will be to melt the snow, which is not as easy as it sounds. Snow is mostly air, and even a large bucket of snow will melt down into a small volume of water.

Once you have a fire going, keep the snow in a container near the fire to let it melt. It can take longer than you might think, so get it started as soon as your fire is roaring.

If you have a sealable plastic bag (such as Ziploc®), you can put a little bit of snow in it and tuck it inside your clothing as long as you are confident it will not leak. Only do this if you are not struggling to stay warm. This is a good way to melt snow overnight so you will have drinking water when you first wake up.

Never eat snow as a way of getting water. It will drain the heat out of your body and do you more harm than good. Also, wait for melted water to warm up before you consume it for the same reason. Drinking warm water is a good way to heat your body from the inside.

Safe Traveling

Traveling in the winter is rough and dangerous even in the best of times. Hiking through the woods in the cold or snow should only be attempted if you are certain you are able to get to safety in a short period of time. You stay warm and safe with a well-built shelter, so build a good, solid base camp and wait for rescue if you can.

Otherwise, take particular precautions when traveling in the winter. The deep snow can be treacherous to hike through; it might hide unexpected rocks or roots to trip you up. Gullies can fill up with snow and lead you to think you are about to walk on level ground. You can literally be buried alive in snow if you step into an unexpected valley and sink. Frozen bodies of water can also be hidden under the snow, and they might not be safe to cross. There are many potential dangers to winter travel.

Hiking in deep snow

Your biggest risk in deep snow is not knowing what dangers (and obstacles) can lie beneath. Take a long and sturdy stick with you, and test the path before you at each step.

Walking through snow that is more than a couple inches deep is tiring and will deplete your energy reserves quickly, not to mention the additional cold and wet you have to deal with when you are up to your knees in snow. If you can stay on top of the drifts, you will be much better off, and that means making a pair of snowshoes.

You will need to be creative with any materials you have on hand for this. Their purpose is to keep you on top of the snow, so they need to be wide, flat, and light. If you have been in a vehicle accident, the seat cushions are good to work with. Tear out a large piece of foam to tie to each of your feet to create a much larger footprint for yourself. Extra foam can be tied around your lower legs for added insulation and weather-protection against the snow.

If you have no other materials to use, then pine or fir boughs will work decently. Bundle enough to fit under your boot and tie them in place.

Traveling over ice

Traveling over any frozen body of water is risky, as falling through the ice into the water can be a death sentence when you are alone in the wilderness. The best option is to find another way around or to make camp rather than cross. If you must cross, take all possible precautions.

To be safe when walking over frozen water, the layer of ice needs to be at least 4 inches thick to support an adult man. Six inches is better. Unfortunately, the only way to know the thickness is to break up the ice and actually measure it.

Take a look at the water you are crossing, and see if you can see any obvious signs of thin areas. Dark patches in the ice mean you can see through to the water below, which means it is almost certainly too thin. If you can see branches, rocks, or tree stumps sticking up through the ice, those areas are prone to breaking as well. Furthermore, you need to look at the shape of the body of water.

For a lake, stay away from the places where streams enter or exit. When crossing streams, the center of the river can be thinner in straight stretches. Maneuver closer to the bends once you get to the middle of the ice.

If you are traveling in a group, do not stay clustered together. Spread your weights out even though it might mean putting unwanted distance between you. It can be a tricky judgment call because you also do not want to be alone should the ice start to crack.

Avalanche

A literal avalanche is only going to be a risk in mountainous areas, but even lower altitude areas can be at risk for sliding snow. Huge slabs of snow can come loose and start to slide, or you can get avalanches of loose powdery snow that roll down the mountain like a tidal wave.

Do not cross any open areas that are below a snow-covered slope. Stay on the tops of ridges and in heavily wooded areas as much as possible. Before you cross an open area below a potential avalanche site, test the snow. Dig down through the snow and look at the cross-section. If the snow is the same texture for the entire depth, you are less likely to have an avalanche farther up the slope. But if you can clearly see different layers of harder snow between softer snow, that is a dangerous situation that should be avoided. These layers are what cause an avalanche as one slides against another.

As you are moving through the risky area, avoid doing anything that might trigger an avalanche. Keep noise to a minimum, though loud sounds are not as dangerous as movies lead us to believe. Use some sort of snowshoes on your feet to keep from disturbing the snow any more than necessary. You can make a pair with handy materials, as described in the above section on hiking in the snow. If possible, one person should cross the slope at a time so an avalanche does not take your entire party if it were to happen.

If an avalanche strikes, you cannot do much. Climb onto any rocky outcroppings nearby (plan your route close to any you see), and try to avoid the oncoming snow. When caught in the flowing snow, keep yourself close to the surface with swimming motions as though you were in the water.

When under the surface of the snow, create an air pocket for yourself before it settles. Use your hands and arms to push the snow away from your face immediately, and take a deep breath to expand your chest. When the snow settles, it can be hard to take a breath if the snow is solid around your body because you might not have enough room for your chest to expand naturally. Then you have the challenge of digging yourself out.

Winter-Specific Health Risks

The two main health risks associated with cold-weather survival are hypothermia and frostbite. *Both of these were covered in their own sections of Chapter 9.*

Snow blindness

The sunlight will reflect off stretches of clean white snow and create a serious glare. Too much of this can harm your eyes and cause snow blindness. The brightness will eventually cause pain, watering, and the feeling of grit in your eyes.

Sunglasses can go a long way toward protecting your eyes if you happen to have a pair with you. You can make a temporary pair of eye shades with a thin piece of bark (birch works best for this). Use a piece of bark large enough to cover your eyes, and make a thin slit across the sides of the bark in front of each of your eyes. You need to be able to see through it, though it should still block out most of the light. Tie it in place over your face and wear it as you walk.

The symptoms of snow blindness may not show up until you have been exposed to the glare for several hours, so take care as soon as you are out in the snow rather than when the pain begins. By then, it is too late.

Snow Sunburn

Few people even consider the threat of snow sunburn, which is related to the blindness mentioned above. The sunlight reflecting off pure snow can create a sunburn on exposed skin no matter what the temperature is. Keep any exposed skin covered when you are walking in the snow, even if it does not seem necessary because of the cold temperature.

Metal Frozen to Lips

This might seem like an unlikely risk, but you can get an awkward injury if this happens. When you are struggling on your own to get things done in difficult circumstances, you easily resort to old habits without thinking. And that can include putting something in your mouth to hold it while your hands are occupied. In cold temperatures, exposed metal will freeze and bond to your tongue or lips instantly. The metal will not easily pull loose without taking your skin with it.

A small object (like a key) will warm up due to the contact with your skin and should come off on its own in a few minutes. If not, you will have to warm it yourself. Warm water is the best way if you can manage it. It is best to be careful not to let the freezing happen in the first place.

Depression

Depression is always a risk when trying to survive outdoors in a bad situation, but the shorter days of winter can make it worse. When the sun sets at 5 p.m. and does not come up again until 9 a.m., your emotional state of mind can be affected. This even happens to people living their normal lives in the safety of their homes, so you can imagine what it can do when you are sitting in the cold dark forest under a pile of branches with nothing to eat.

Do everything you can to keep your spirits up, and spend time in the daylight when you can. A snow shelter can be quite warm, and you might be tempted to stay holed up as much as possible, but you do need to move around and spend time in the sunshine in order to stay both physically and mentally healthy.

Chapter 13

Disaster Survival at Home

I f you are willing to learn how to survive in the wild, then take the time to learn some skills about surviving a disaster right at home. Many of the skills and scenarios covered so far can be applied to a home-based disaster, but there are other ways to be prepared for anything.

Unlike a wilderness disaster that leaves you stranded with only the gear on your back, a disaster at home can mean a sizeable amount of supplies if you are ready for it. However, it also means more pre-planning.

Potential Disasters at Home

An almost endless number of possible disasters exist that can strike right at home, some that come with warning and some that will strike you unaware. It can be something as simple as a prolonged power outage to the destruction caused by a tornado.

Some possible events that could put you in a survival situation include:

- Flooding
- Earthquake
- Lighting storm
- Severe snow or ice storm
- Local disease quarantine
- Job or income loss
- Tornado
- Hurricane
- Fire

Any major weather event can take its toll on your home, but many other situations can cause a survival-type outlook as well. This is only a snapshot list of things that could happen. Some may be so severe that you lose your home and would then be relying on the wilderness information already provided, but you will usually be able to get by with staying in your house in most of these cases.

The underlying problem with many of these disasters (but not all) is the lack of electrical power. Being able to handle everyday activities without power will put you ahead of the game in many emergency situations.

Storing Food

Assuming you are able to weather the event in your home, shelter should not be a concern. So having something to eat will be the next thing to prepare for. Families used to have a sizeable pantry of stored food at all times, but modern life has changed that tradition, and many people only have enough food on hand for two or three days. With that mindset, you are vulnerable to even a minor interruption in local services.

Some situations might only take a few days to resolve. Some can take weeks (possibly even months). In order to take care of yourself and your family, you will need a way to stay fed.

Depending on what food you are storing, also plan a way to cook it. Without power, your stove might not work. A small camp stove that takes bottles of fuel can be stored with your food and will let you cook in any situation. Make sure to store a few extra fuel canisters as well.

If you are in a situation with no power, use up the food in your fridge or freezer as quickly as possible before going to your store of canned or dried goods. Perishable food will go bad quickly, and it might be the last fresh food you eat for a while.

Storing regular supermarket food

You can have a good stash of food at home without resorting to buying anything out of the ordinary. Most canned goods will last at least a year, so they can be your main food storage items.

Keep a mix of fruit, vegetables, meat, and beans to maintain a healthy diet and have more than one can opener stored nearby. Many foods that have been canned are pre-cooked (such as stews or pastas), so you can even eat them cold from the can if you are unable to produce heat to cook.

Other foods are shelf-stable as long as you keep them in the proper containers. A 5-gallon bucket can be used to store a lot of dried rice or beans, and that bucket can last quite a long time even though it will be a boring diet if that is all you have. Bags of dry pasta will also last for months as long as the packaging is not torn; make sure to store cans of sauce to go with them.

If you have space and want to be prepared for more than a few days of meals, here are other basic food items to always have on hand:

- Cans of juice
- Dried milk powder or cans of evaporated milk
- Ground coffee
- Sugar
- Salt
- Vegetable oil
- Multi-vitamin capsules

Storing specialty survival food

Canned foods are good for storage but they are heavy and can take up a lot of space due to the water inside. If you want to save on space, or want food supplies that will last for a decade or more, you can do some shopping for true survival food.

You can purchase cans of dehydrated or freeze-dried food from specialty retailers such as Mountain House, and they usually have a wide range of foods available. They are much lighter than a can of standard wet-packed food and contain more servings per can. When it comes to storage, it is more efficient. The costs are considerably higher, so consider it an investment. These foods will last ten years or more.

To use them, you normally have to measure out a certain amount and simmer in water until reconstituted. Again, have a mix of fruit, vegetables, meat, and starches to maintain a healthy diet when relying on this food. You will also need a steady supply of water, which you would not need with most canned goods.

A more sophisticated version of survival food comes in a ready-to-eat format; they are known as MREs (meals ready to eat), and the original ones are from the military. Survival stores can sell original military surplus or those made by other manufacturers. They are going to cost more than other types of food, but they usually produce the tastiest meals and are easier to use.

Each MRE has a full meal, including entrée, dessert, and snacks. Many come with a chemical hot pack to heat up the meal pouches so you can eat a hot meal even with no other way of cooking or any other source of water. The food is vacuum packed in specially designed mylar pouches but not dried. They are handy to have but are usually too expensive to have a large stash of them on hand.

Fresh Water

When the power is out, most homes will also be without water because the pumps that run the water system will not be functioning. This includes homes on private wells as well as anyone on a town or city water system.

Many of the tips given in Chapter 4 apply here, though city-dwellers will have more difficulty finding natural sources of water. Collecting rain can be a good source if the weather is agreeable. Any natural water will have to be purified as per any of the techniques in Chapter 4.

If you know a particular storm or other event is forthcoming, fill up any clean containers you have with tap water. Your tub is a good choice, but it can be awkward after a while, especially if you need to use it.

One option you have at home that you would not in the wild is purifying water with bleach. Bleach is a good way to purify water, and a standard jug of supermarket bleach will last you a long time for this purpose. One quart of water will need between three and five drops of bleach (go with five if the water is cloudy or looks dirty). Add the drops and give your container of water a vigorous shake. It should *slightly* taste and smell of bleach when you are done. Let it sit for at least 30 minutes before drinking.

If you have the space, you can also store commercially bottled water. It will last for years if kept in a dark cool area and will provide the quickest source of drinking water in an emergency. It does take up a lot of space though, so you might want to consider having bleach on hand as well.

Surprise emergency water sources in your home

If an emergency situation arises and you either do not have water stored or you begin to run out of stored water, you can find some surprising places in your house to get the necessary water. If you think any sewer or water lines were damaged in the emergency, close off the main water valve to your house to protect the water you already have inside. Do this before attempting to use any of the water sources listed below.

- **The hot water heater:** There should be a spigot or valve at the bottom of the hot water heater, which can be used to drain the tank. Make sure the electricity is off at the main breaker (even if there is a power outage) or the pilot light is off if you are going to drain the tank. Once you have turned off the power source, drain the tank into some buckets. A typical water heater tank holds about 40 gallons when full, and the water cycles through whenever a hot water faucet is turned on. This water will probably be stale or flat, but it is still drinkable. *The next section offers ideas on improving the taste of flat water.* Older water heaters might have a little built-up sediment at the bottom — make sure you do not drain this into your buckets.

  o   Note: You will need to refill the heater before reconnecting it to the power or gas.

- **The water pipes:** You can pull any water from your cold water pipes by placing a bucket under the lowest cold-water faucet in your home and turning it on. Then go to the highest cold-water faucet in your home and open it to allow air into the system. This method should send the water in the cold-water pipes within the house out of the lowest faucet. Depending on the size of your house, you could gain several gallons of water this way. If you live in a single story home, make sure all faucets are turned off and place a bucket under the lowest faucet you can find, such as the bathtub tap or where the water comes into your washing machine.

- **Waterbed:** If you have a waterbed in your home, the bed can be a source of water in an emergency. Some waterbeds contain toxic chemicals, so if you plan to use a waterbed as an emergency water source, fill it once a year with water treated with bleach. If you do use the water in an emergency, drain the mattress and boil or treat the water with chlorine for drinking or save the water for toilet flushing, shower bags, or washing clothes.

- **Ice:** If you have any ice in your freezer, pull the ice out and let it melt into drinking water. Do this early on, especially if you lose power, as the ice will melt anyway.

- **Canned foods:** Many canned vegetables and some fruits are packed in water. Save that water when you cook the vegetables. Drinking green bean water might not be tasty, but in a true emergency, staying hydrated is more important than loving the taste of things.

- **Bathtubs, sinks, and baby swimming pools.** If you have time and know a water emergency is coming, fill your tubs, sinks, and baby wading pools with water and let it sit. You can always dip into these stores with a bucket for a little extra water.

Improving the taste of boiled and treated water

Boiled water or chemically treated water will not taste like the water you are used to drinking right out of the tap. Your treated water might have a lingering odor of chlorine, and freshly boiled water might taste stale, but this water is still perfectly safe to drink. It is just not palatable.

Using a mechanical or additional purification method such as those mentioned in the previous chapters will alleviate some of this problem, but there also a few quick fixes for emergencies that can help fix the taste issue. Of course, in an emergency situation and if you are thirsty enough, you will not care what your water tastes like. Keeping a couple of these handy supplies with your stored water, though, will help you through longer emergencies and provide just a little bit of creature comfort in a difficult situation.

After boiling, add oxygen by stirring the water with a sterilized spoon or pour it from one sanitized container to another a few times; both these methods will improve the flat taste. While the water is still hot from boiling, use it for herbal or decaffeinated tea, hot lemon water, or gelatin. For chemically treated water, the best remedy to poor taste is to also incorporate air. If chlorine has been used to treat the water, let it sit in an open air container (protected from debris) for 30 minutes. This will allow the fumes to dissipate, which will improve the taste. Be careful, though, as FEMA guidelines say properly disinfected water should have a slight bleach scent.

Flavored drink mixes are another way to mask the taste of flat or funny-tasting water. Many brands are now available on the market that mix right into water without the addition of sugar. Some even offer extra electrolytes, which are nice to have on hand in case of dehydration. Avoid using high-sugar content or caffeinated drink mixes, as these can affect how your body absorbs water. The most recognizable brands here are Gatorade® and Propel®, and you can purchased them in small and large quantities at any grocery store. They will keep indefinitely in a dry environment. Store these flavor packets and other drink mixes in a sealed plastic container with your emergency water supplies.

If you are trying to get children to drink the water, adding a small amount of fruit juice might make the water more appealing. You can also try adding fruit slices — lemon, lime, or orange — to add variety. Do not let citrus slices sit in water overnight though; the pith (the white spongy material on the rind) will make the water taste bitter.

Preparing meals with reduced water

Feeding your family during an emergency will require some creativity, not only in acquiring supplies but when the choosing foods to cook. As part of an overall emergency plan, make sure to stock your pantry with food that can be cooked with little or no water. Most canned foods such as vegetables, fruits, and soups already contain a lot of liquid, so you will not have to add more water, and you will gain a little hydration benefit from that food. For example, canned vegetables can be cooked in their own juice, and the juice from cans of fruit can be added to water for extra flavor. Cans of chicken or beef broth will also come in handy for cooking rice and other grains. Beware of the sodium content in these products, however, and choose no-salt or low-sodium for your emergency supplies. As mentioned previously, salt intake can lead to dehydration. Also, when washing fresh produce or cooking with water, be sure to save this the water and reuse it for dishwashing or toilet flushing.

First-Aid Supplies

Most of the supplies and equipment listed in Chapter 2 are suitable for a home kit as well as an outdoor kit. With the additional space for storage, you can add more of the same items. Having more gauze pads and surgical tape would be the most practical to have in larger quantities, rather than more boxes of little Band-Aids.

On top of first-aid supplies, you can also have a small stockpile of over-the-counter medications that might be in short supply during an emergency. If they are stored in a cool, dry, dark place, they can last for many months if not a full year without losing any potency. These can include treatments for diarrhea, nausea, allergies, heartburn, and any type of pain reliever you prefer to use. Also keep cold mediations on hand. Sleeping pills can be helpful, as getting rest in stressful circumstances can be difficult. Do be careful about dosage, and do not let anyone in your home become dependent on them for sleeping.

Some additional items to have include:

- Tweezers
- Blunt-tipped scissors
- Latex gloves (several pairs)
- Bottle of hydrogen peroxide for sterilizing wounds and tools
- Triangular bandage for slings
- Elastic tension bandages for sprains
- Large bottle of alcohol hand sanitizer
- Antiseptic ointment
- Burn ointment
- A proper suture kit (as opposed to the makeshift sewing kit)
- Chemical cold packs
- A comprehensive first-aid guide

Heat and Light

A summer disaster or a southern location will leave the heating chores out of the equation, but if you are in an emergency situation in cooler climates, your nights can be uncomfortable without any heat. But if you can survive in the outdoors, you can stay warm enough inside your home even without a typical heat source.

A power outage can knock out many different types of heat, even if you are relying on natural gas or oil in your home. Most furnaces rely on electricity for ignition and fans, so you might not have heat in a power outage even if your heater runs on something other than electricity.

Portable heaters that take tanks of propane can be used for heating, as long as you are able to vent the room when you use them. Some are made for use indoors and require less venting. You can also have a woodstove installed in your home. This does mean a bit of an investment cost-wise, but you will always have a source of heat once you have it.

If you are unable to create a source of heat in your home, you will have to resort to more primitive methods. Wear several layers of clothing, including hats and gloves if necessary. Keep everyone together in one room if possible for sleeping to make the most of your body heat, and get out the sleeping bags if you have them.

For lighting, you have several options. Flashlights are great for handheld light, but if you want something that sits on a table to light up a room, make sure you have at least one battery-powered lamp designed to sit upright as well as flashlights. Do not forget to have batteries on hand as well.

There are also flashlights on the market that operate by turning a crank rather than by typical batteries. Though they are a little less convenient to use, having one means you never have to worry about having fresh batteries. NOMA™ and Energizer® have their own makes of crank flashlights. You crank for a few minutes to get a charge for half an hour of light. Garrison makes a good version you shake rather than crank.

Or you could forgo the battery need altogether and have several boxes of candles stored away. They can be a fire risk if not handled properly, but they offer a good source of light as well as a bit of heat.

You can purchase survival candles designed to last a long time, but save some money with less expensive candles that work nearly as well. Along with your candles, store matches and appropriately sized candleholders.

Having a generator

One way around having to supply light and possibly heat during a power outage is with a portable gas-powered generator. Although these can be handy in an emergency, you should not blindly make assumptions about their capabilities.

You can spend a few hundred to a few thousand dollars on a good generator, so compare makes and brands to see what they offer. Rather than trying to get a generator large enough to power your entire home, keep the size to something more reasonable so you can keep some lights going and some appliances. It could run the accessories for an oil or gas furnace (fans, igniters) but would not likely have enough power to keep an electric heat system running.

The power capabilities for a generator are measured in watts, so add up the wattage requirements for everything you hope to run and use that as a guide before buying a machine.

The easiest way to run a generator is to have a heavy-duty extension cord that runs from the machine into the house. From there, you can plug in what you need powered. This does limit the number of items you can run, but it saves you from having to do any serious or complicated wiring. A more thorough method is to have the generator hooked up to your home's electrical system so it powers the entire house.

Have a store of gasoline on hand to keep your generator running. How much to have will depend on your machine and how often you intend to keep it running. Also, some generators will require a pull-start.

Remember that a generator is quite loud and should be kept outdoors. Besides the personal annoyance of listening to it, you are also letting everyone in your neighborhood know you have power. During a serious disaster, this might not be a smart idea. You will have to judge for yourself if it is worth the risk to have some lights on.

Securing Your Home

Life can be stressful during a disaster, and if the rest of your neighborhood is affected, you might have to deal with desperate people who are unable to take care of themselves. Looting, vandalism, and theft are unfortunately common occurrences during an emergency, so be prepared to keep your home and family safe.

This can be a tricky situation, as you do not want to add further danger to your household with excessive precautions. Having a firearm or two is the most common way and can be a great deterrent against criminals as long as you handle them safely and learn the proper way to shoot. People have been killed in their own homes because someone was careless with a gun in countless cases. Tensions will be high in an emergency, so guns will have to be treated with even more respect than usual.

Large sheets of plywood are perfect for covering windows if they are broken or to prevent them from being broken in the first place. Although covering the windows immediately might be safest, wait to do so until you have a pressing need. Boarded windows can have a large and negative impact on morale because of the dark atmosphere, and you will need to have a light source. Instead, have the wood on hand and cover the windows only if the situation warrants it.

Make sure you have good locks on all your doors and windows, and keep them locked at all times even if you usually do not.

Take steps to make your home look like a poor target to potential thieves or looters. When the power is out, do not have all the lights burning brightly if you have a generator. Keep the blinds or curtains drawn, and be discrete with your power usage. Before any disasters, keep your preparations to yourself. Discussing your stash of food and supplies with anyone can let others know you have things worth stealing. Keep your readiness to yourself, and only let immediate family members know about your supplies.

Additional Supplies

The basics have been covered so far, but weathering an emergency at home can take weeks and can involve a lot of additional supplies in order to stay reasonably comfortable until things are back to normal. Along with storing food, first-aid supplies and candles, you should have many other items on hand. Check your pantry or basement and make sure you have extras of:

- Toilet paper
- Matches
- Reading material
- Deck of cards or other entertainment items
- Fuel for any camp stoves or a wood stove
- Batteries in several sizes
- A spare can opener (or two)
- Portable radio (powered by crank or battery)
- Empty containers for storing any rainwater you collect
- Soap, deodorant, toothpaste, and shampoo

How much you store of any of these items will depend on how many people are in your family and how long you want to be self-sufficient. All these things might seem like a daunting amount to purchase and store. If you are careful to look for sales or used goods, you can save some money that way. A few sturdy shelves in a basement or spare bedroom will hold most of your supplies without taking over your house.

Getting it Organized

Having extras of everything can lead to clutter, and you might lose track of important items when time is of the essence. Knowing what you need and what you have is vital.

Your first step is to decide how long you want to stockpile supplies for in the first place, and gauge your supplies to that. There is no sense having six months of toilet paper, two weeks of food and four hours of candle supplies. At the minimum, be ready for at least three days on your own. But to be more properly prepared, try to aim for two weeks to a month. You should be able to weather most disasters in that time.

Keep all of your supplies in one place if possible, in well-marked containers. Mark food items with a date so you know how old everything is (use the food before it expires, and replace it next time you shop for groceries). Always keep your supplies rotating so nothing is too old when you finally need it.

Take a few minutes once a month to make sure everything is in place and undamaged. Water or rodents might have gotten into something without your knowledge.

A Bug-Out Bag

Sometimes disaster strikes at home but you cannot stay there safely. Floods or other natural disasters can drive you from your house — and all your carefully maintained supplies — but that scenario does not have to be a disaster in itself.

If you are leaving home in a hurry, pack a handy bag you can grab on your way out the door. This would typically contain the same gear as a complete survival kit for outdoors as laid out in detail in Chapter 2. This type of bag can be used as a basic set of supplies to help you during transit from home to a secondary location (relative's home, town shelter) and does not necessarily need all the wilderness gear intended for outdoor survival.

Extras that might be handy for a bug-out bag are:

- An extra change of clothes (or at least socks and underwear)
- Copies of important personal documents such as birth records and passports
- Some cash, $20 to $50 in small bills
- Phone numbers of family or friends you would need to contact
- Entertainment items such as a deck of cards, crossword books, or a novel
- Toothbrush, soap, deodorant, shampoo (travel sizes work best)

Store your bag somewhere convenient and easy to access in an emergency. If your house starts to flood or a tornado is on its way, you will only have moments to grab your supplies before leaving.

Conclusion

Y ou now have a clear idea about what is required to survive in the wilderness should an emergency or disaster occur. Getting shelter, making a fire, finding water, locating edible food, and navigating yourself back to safety are all part of a good survival approach.

Though this book should provide a good framework and basic knowledge for survival, nothing beats hands-on practice. If you truly want to be prepared, take the time to try many of these techniques and learn how to do them before an emergency comes up. Use your fire starting tools and make a fire in your backyard, practice tying various knots, see if you can identify edible plants around your home, and practice using a compass or finding north without one.

Once you are armed with the right skills and are carrying the right equipment, you should be prepared for anything. Not only can this save your life someday, it will also give you a greater confidence when outdoors. It is much easier to relax and enjoy a camping or hunting trip if you know you are going to be safe even in an emergency.

Bibliography

About First Aid, **http://firstaid.about.com**

Editors of Stackpole Books, *Survival Wisdom & Know How: Everything You Need to Know to Subsist in the Wilderness*, Black Dog & Leventhal Publishers Inc., New York USA, 2007

John and Geri McPherson, *Ultimate Guide to Wilderness Living*, Ulysses Press, California USA, 2008

John Lofty Wiseman, *SAS Survival Handbook*, Collins, London UK, 2006

"How to remove a leech," Wild Madagascar.org, **www.wildmadagascar.org/overview/leeches.html**

Les Stroud, *Survive!*, HarperCollins Publishers, Toronto Ontario Canada, 2008

Mike Outdoors, **www.mikeoutdoors.com**

"Outdoor Action Guide to Winter Camping," Outdoor Action, **www.princeton.edu/~oa/winter/wintcamp.shtml**

Paul S. Auerbach, M.D., *Medicine for the Outdoors: Essential Guide to First Aid*, Mosby Books, Philadelphia USA, 2009

Roy Bernendsohn, "How to Buy the Right Backup Generator for Your Disaster & Budget," Popular Mechanics, **www.popularmechanics.com/science/4281042**, 2009

Samuel Thayer, *Forager's Harvest: A Guide to Identifying, Harvesting and Preparing Edible Wild Plants*, Forager's Harvest, Wisconsin USA, 2006

Tom Brown Jr., *Tom Brown's Field Guide to Wild Edible and Medicinal Plants*, Berkley Books, New York, USA, 1985

Wilderness Survival, **www.wilderness-survival.net**

Author Biography

Terri is living on 5 rural acres and slowly building it into a thriving farm. Though she grew up in the city, today she prefers a natural country life with her significant other and young daughter. By managing a freelance writing career from home, she can spend most of her time outdoors both on the farm and off in the woods. She knows that emergencies can come at any time and prefers to be prepared for anything when she is away from home.

Her skills are constantly growing and she hopes to master the art of foraging for wild food this year. She also wants to start learning archery this coming summer. When not in the garden, she heads farther from home to camp or go geocaching.

Index